The Law and Politics of Intervention in Federal Systems

ELGAR STUDIES IN LAW AND POLITICS

This series examines the infrastructure of collective governance: the legal regulation of the political realm and political catalysts for legal change. Its depth of focus expands and contracts with the subject of each volume, from the micromechanics of local electoral struggles to the rise and fall of constitutional democracy. With expert and interdisciplinary analysis drawing on law, political science, history, and social psychology, the series aims to interrogate the actors, institutions, and structures of political engagement. The series highlights new modes of mobilization and contestation as well as new perspectives on familiar but enduring controversies. Both monographs and edited collections are welcomed.

For a full list of Edward Elgar published titles, including the titles in this series, visit our website at www.e-elgar.com.

The Law and Politics of Intervention in Federal Systems

Corrective or Coercive?

Edited by

Yonatan T. Fessha

University of the Western Cape, South Africa

Karl Kössler

Institute for Comparative Federalism of Eurac Research Bolzano/Bozen, Italy

ELGAR STUDIES IN LAW AND POLITICS

Edward Elgar PUBLISHING

Cheltenham, UK • Northampton, MA, USA

Published by

Edward Elgar Publishing Limited
The Lypiatts
15 Lansdown Road
Cheltenham
Glos GL50 2JA
UK

Edward Elgar Publishing, Inc.
William Pratt House
9 Dewey Court
Northampton
Massachusetts 01060
USA

Authorised representative in the EU for GPSR queries only: Easy Access System Europe – Mustamäe tee 50, 10621 Tallinn, Estonia, gpsr.requests@easproject.com

A catalogue record for this book is available from the British Library

Library of Congress Control Number: 2026934134

This book is available electronically in the **Elgar**online
Law subject collection
https://doi.org/10.4337/9781035348268

MIX
Paper | Supporting responsible forestry
FSC® C013604

ISBN 978 1 0353 4825 1 (cased)
ISBN 978 1 0353 4826 8 (eBook)
ISBN 978 1 0353 9979 6 (ePub)
Printed and bound by CPI Group (UK) Ltd, Croydon, CR0 4YY

Contents

List of contributors

Zemelak Ayele is Associate Professor at Addis Ababa University, Ethiopia. He is also Extraordinary Professor at the University of the Western Cape, South Africa.

Gosaye Berhanu is Doctoral Candidate at the Faculty of Law, University of the Western Cape.

Jaap De Visser is Professor of Law and National Research Foundation Chair in Multilevel Governance, Law and Development at the University of the Western Cape, South Africa.

Lisa Draga is Lecturer at the University of the Western Cape, South Africa.

Yonatan T. Fessha is Professor of Law and Research Chair in constitutional design and divided societies at the University of the Western Cape in South Africa.

Henry Gichana is Lecturer and Head of the African Centre for Governance, Leadership and Ethics (ACGLE) at Kabarak University School of Law in Kenya.

Lara Goyburu lectures and conducts research at the University of Buenos Aires (UBA) and, more recently, at Torcuato Di Tella University (UTDT).

Andrew Harding is Professor of Law at the University of Reading Malaysia.

Karl Kössler is Senior Researcher and Group Leader at the Institute for Comparative Federalism of Eurac Research Bolzano/Bozen in Italy. He is also Extraordinary Professor at the University of the Western Cape, South Africa.

Marcelo Labanca Corrêa de Araújo is Full Professor of Constitutional Law at the Catholic University of Pernambuco in Brazil.

Ignacio Molina is Associate Professor of Political Science and Public Administration at the Department of Politics and International Relations (Universidad Autónoma de Madrid) and Senior Analyst at the Elcano Royal Institute.

Mayte Salvador Crespo is Professor of Constitutional Law and Deputy Director of Research at the Centre for Political and Constitutional Studies, Madrid.

Nico Steytler is Emeritus Professor of Law at the University of the Western Cape, South Africa.

Rotimi Suberu teaches politics and international relations at Bennington College, Vermont, USA.

Louise Tillin is Professor of Politics at the King's India Institute.

Alice Valdesalici is Research Group Leader and Senior Researcher at the Institute for Comparative Federalism of Eurac Research.

1. The law and politics of intervention in federal systems: framing the debate

Yonatan T. Fessha and Karl Kössler

1. THE RELEVANCE OF THIS BOOK: POWERS OF INTERVENTION AS A TREND IN FEDERAL SYSTEMS

When one thinks about 'federalism' and 'intervention', certain historical episodes probably come to mind in which multilevel government was imposed by an external power. One recent example was in 1995 when Bosnia and Herzegovina was turned into a 'loose multinational federation'.[1] After a NATO military intervention ended the armed conflict in the country, its constitutional future was determined at a US military base in Dayton, Ohio. The purpose of the 'Dayton Agreement' was, in the words of a leading negotiator, 'to end a war',[2] but it also ushered in a federal constitution with a blatant lack of local ownership. Two facts illustrate this point.[3] First, the Dayton Agreement, negotiated in just a few weeks, includes in Annex IV the text of the constitution; second, the country's Constitutional Court treats the English version of the text as authentic and the standard for correcting misleading translations in the other three versions (Bosnian, Croatian and Serbian). In this light, it is hardly surprising that several publications about Bosnia and Herzegovina after 1995 have 'international intervention' in their titles.[4]

---

1 Bieber F *Post-war Bosnia: Ethnicity, inequality and public sector governance* London: Palgrave Macmillan (2006) 60–2.

2 Holbrooke R *To end a war* New York: The Modern Library (1999).

3 See Kössler K 'Who are "We, the people"? Pluralist constitutional identity after democratic transitions in African and European countries' in Fombad CM & Steytler N (eds) *Constitutional identity and constitutionalism in Africa* Oxford: Oxford University Press (2023) 110–36 at 117.

4 See, for example, Bose S *Bosnia after Dayton: Nationalist partition and international intervention* Oxford: Oxford University Press (2002).

An even more recent example of intervention is Iraq. Even if important aspects of the country's post-war federalism were negotiated between major stakeholders in 2005, doubt has been cast on local ownership of these negotiations, as they were compromised by the logic of external imposition and political exclusion. To put it succinctly, a 'coalition of the willing outsiders' imposed ideas and an agenda and ignored the 'unwilling insiders',[5] resulting in the obvious lack of a federal compact.

These two countries, along with several others, are standard cases that have been explored at length in the literature about 'imposed federalism',[6] a strand of scholarship examining the coercive nature of the formation processes of federal systems that involved interference by outside powers. Such external intervention is *not* what this book is about, as this is an already well-researched issue.

Instead, our focus is on federalism and internal intervention carried out by one level of government at the expense of another one. It is obvious that such meddling runs contrary to the promise of self-rule which is central to federalism. In fact, it represents an exception to the principles of democracy and federalism. Such intervention harms democracy, as it takes away decision-making power from the body duly elected to make decisions at the subnational or local level. It harms federalism by undermining the self-governance rights of a territory. Indeed, this has been emphasised (perhaps over-emphasised) by early theorists, as epitomised by Wheare's definition of federalism as a method of separating government levels such that each is 'able to act independently within its own watertight sphere of responsibility'.[7]

However, powers of intervention appear to be one of three major trends in federalism that run contrary to the traditional vision of separating governments, the other two being concurrent powers and enhanced intergovernmental cooperation. While the latter two have been well researched, not least over the past decade,[8] the topic of interventions within federal systems remains under-studied. It is this research gap which this book aims to fill.

5 Belser EM 'A failure of state transformation rather than a failure of federalism? The case of Iraq' (2020) 19(4) *Ethnopolitics* 383–401 at 385–9.

6 Kössler K 'Aggregative and devolutionary federalism revisited: The impact of founding processes on federal systems' in Bußjäger P, Eller M & Oberdanner J (eds) *The making and ending of federalism* Leiden & Boston: Brill-Martinus Nijhoff (2024) 65–91 at 71.

7 Wheare KC *Federal government* New York: Oxford University Press (1947) 11 at 14.

8 On intergovernmental cooperation, see, for instance, Poirier J et al. (eds) *Intergovernmental relations in federal systems: Comparative structures and dynamics* Oxford: Oxford University Press (2015) and Fessha YT, Kössler K

The crucial relevance of the topic of this volume results from the inherent dilemma that intervention powers entail in federal systems. On the one hand, such powers may be justifiable or indeed necessary. Two main reasons have been identified for their entrenchment: the failure of a subnational entity to maintain basic democratic standards, and the need for the central government to safeguard the fundamental rights of the citizens of such an entity.[9] There are further reasons as well, such as public security, effective governance and administrative performance. On the other hand, intervention powers are inconsistent with federalism's basic tenet of protecting self-government of own affairs against central government interference.[10]

It has been argued that the concept of autonomy in its modern form was initially very much focused on such protection, which did not mean complete freedom from any central directives but at least erected 'political, economic, and legal barriers to arbitrary central intervention'.[11] Only subsequently was this negative understanding of self-government complemented with a positive one as it (self-government) became increasingly regarded as 'an instrument for the realization of communal interests'.[12] It is important to bear in mind that these two conceptualisations of autonomy are closely interconnected, as the freedom to realise own preferences can thrive only if and when the (near) freedom from intervention is ensured.

In view of this, it is clear that an innate tension exists between interventionism and federalism, more precisely autonomy as one of its cornerstones. What is at stake, therefore, when it comes to powers of intervention is nothing less than federalism itself, which we understand as something going beyond the classical national–subnational dualism to include the local level of government.[13] In our view, such an understanding is justifiable not only more generally but also

---

& Palermo F (eds) *Intergovernmental relations in divided societies* London: Palgrave Macmillan (2022); on concurrent powers, see, for instance, Steytler N (ed.) *Concurrent powers in federal systems: Meaning, making, and managing* Leiden: Brill–Nijhoff (2017).

[9] See Bulmer E *Federalism* International IDEA Constitution-Building Primer 12 available at https://www.idea.int/sites/default/files/publications/federalism-primer.pdf (accessed 1 May 2025) 37–38.

[10] See Saunders C 'Comparative conclusions' in Le Roy K & Saunders C (eds) *Legislative, executive and judicial governance in federal countries* Montreal: McGill–Queen's University Press (2006) 371.

[11] Agranoff R 'Autonomy, devolution and intergovernmental relations' *Regional & Federal Studies* (2004) 14(1) 26–65 at 28.

[12] Kjellberg F 'The changing values of local government' *Annals* (1995) 540(3) 40–50 at 43.

[13] Palermo F & Kössler K *Comparative federalism: Constitutional arrangements and case law* Oxford: Hart Publishing (2017) at 281–315.

for the purpose of this book in particular, even though we acknowledge that interventionism in some respects impacts differently on the autonomy of local governments than it does on the autonomy of subnational entities conceived, in a narrow sense, as intermediary government levels (provinces, regions, states, cantons, *Länder*, and so on).

First, with a few exceptions such as South Africa, subnational entities typically have a clearly wider range of legislative, executive and fiscal powers than local governments. In short, there is more autonomy that central intrusion can take away. Second, the distribution of powers between the central and subnational governments is usually entrenched to a larger extent in constitutional law, even if significant parts of it are de-constitutionalised in some countries (for example, Belgium and Spain). This ensures greater legal protection of autonomous powers, even while local governments are increasingly overburdened by powers that are simply delegated to them by other levels of government.[14] Third, certain federal loyalty principles guiding the constitutional interpretation of the distribution of powers only apply to national–subnational relations, a case in point being the legal duty, confirmed by Germany's Constitutional Court, to adopt 'federal-friendly behaviour'.[15] This duty, which prohibits undue intervention even in the exercise of own powers, merely concerns the federal government and *Länder* in their relations with each other but not with local governments.

Despite these differences, it seems possible, indeed important, to examine, within the scope of one book, interventions in both subnational as well as local governments, as the autonomy of each is likewise at risk of falling victim to interference from a higher level of government. This is because the three differences above, which privilege subnational governments, concern the distribution of powers only in ordinary times. However, the nature of provisions enabling central intervention is precisely that they suspend this distribution in extraordinary times.

2. RESEARCH DESIGN: DEFINITIONS, GUIDING QUESTIONS AND CASE STUDY SELECTION

For the purpose of the comparative analysis undertaken in this book, it is essential to define with the utmost clarity which actions we see as interventions in federal systems and which ones not. It is also important to distinguish intervention from other, related concepts in order to ensure uniformity throughout

---

[14] See Steytler N 'Comparative conclusions' in Steytler N (ed) *The Forum of Federations handbook on local government in federal systems* Cham: Palgrave Macmillan (2024) 533–86 at 556–7.

[15] 1 BVerfGE 299, 315.

the book. In brief, our focus in this book is on interference driven by (1) the executive of a higher level of government, which (2) targets a lower government level (subnational and/or local), (3) on grounds related to the preservation of national interests (for example, security and economic unity), financial mismanagement and legal obligations of subnational and local authorities. This definition has several implications.

First, with 'the executive of a higher level of government' as the intervening power, our definition encompasses interference by both central and subnational governments; it therefore treats the latter not only as victims of intervention but also as potential perpetrators. Secondly, as entities at 'a lower government level' are singled out as targets of such action, our book does not focus on interventions based on country-wide emergencies that have no specific link to one or several subnational or local governments. This narrower focus is important because the broader literature on federalism and national (or even international) emergencies has flourished over the past few years, not least due to research related to the fight against terrorism, for example, or the Covid-19 pandemic, with the result that there is not much of a gap to fill. Third, limiting our focus, as emphasised above, to instruments related to the grounds of national interests, financial mismanagement and legal obligations entails that several other powers sometimes called 'interventionist' are excluded. Such a characterisation has been used, for example, for the use of a general financial spending power (typically of the central government) beyond an entity's own legislative and administrative competences,[16] or for the adoption of extra-jurisdictional legislation based on various justifications (for instance, based on some implied powers doctrine[17]). Powers of intervention which are included by our definition (because they are invoked on above-mentioned grounds) are, for instance, the right to issue instructions to officials at lower levels of government, to take over their functions and to remove and replace them.

On the basis of this definition, our book aims to explore powers of intervention from a comparative perspective and, importantly, in regard to both their legal entrenchment and their political implementation (or not) in practice. In the light of this approach combining law and political science, as well as to ensure the coherence of the book and facilitate our comparative conclusions, all chapters provide answers to the same set of guiding questions:

1) Underlying rationales: What are the rationales in terms of the historical, political, social or cultural context for the introduction of powers of intervention in the respective countries?

---

16 See Palermo & Kössler (2017) at 228–35.
17 See Palermo & Kössler (2017) at 149–56.

2) Legal bases: How are the constitutional and legislative provisions granting intervention powers designed? This includes several sub-questions. What are the grounds for intervention and at what level (constitution, ordinary legislation, and so on) are they entrenched? What more or less intrusive forms of intervention are used and how are these forms interrelated?
3) Procedures: What mechanisms ensure checks and balances regarding the use of intervention powers by the executive (for example, the involvement of other political institutions, such as the national parliament or subnational institutions, in the approval of this use or judicial control *ex post*), and are these procedures effective?
4) Politics: Is the use of intervention powers a rampant phenomenon or limited to exceptional cases, and are there differences in terms of the frequency of interference concerning local governments, on the one hand, and subnational entities, on the other? What factors account for differences concerning the prevalence of intervention both between countries and within countries over time? Are intervention powers used for their envisaged purpose or misused, and what factors facilitate political abuse? Are such powers, even if they are not misused, in the end really effective instruments, or does their use sometimes end up as a cure which is no better than the disease? Do intervention powers have a 'chilling effect' by hanging over the heads of potential targets like a sword of Damocles and thus making an impact even if they eventually remain unused?

This edited book explores the four topics above with regard to a set of federal systems which naturally requires us to clarify what we take such systems to mean. As is well known in our field of study, there is the apparent paradox that federalism has attracted in recent decades significant political and scientific interest, whereas 'our conceptual knowledge of federalism has remained more confused than refined'.[18] It is, as one scholar put it, 'one of those protean concepts … that has a claim to great breadth and scope but is often contested, with little clarity or focus'.[19]

Quite recently, an attempt has been made at conceptual clarification which postulates that three criteria are necessary and sufficient for identifying a political system as federal: (1) the existence of two orders of government with

---

18 Hueglin TO 'Comparing federalism: Variations or distinct models?' in Benz A & Broschek J (eds) *Federal Dynamics: Continuity, Change, and the Varieties of Federalism* OUP Oxford, (2013) 27–48 at 27.

19 Simeon R 'Is Federalism like Snow, and Is It Exportable?: Some Cautionary Notes on the Study of Federalism' in Basta K, McGarry J & Simeon R (eds) *Territorial Pluralism: Managing Difference in Multinational States* University of British Columbia Press (2015) 99–120 at 99.

constitutional status; (2) each of them enjoying a direct relationship to the people and exercising meaningful powers; (3) each of them having their status and powers constitutionally protected.[20] As the authors emphasise, their definition focuses on 'autonomy' and opposes the view that also 'co-determination' by constituent units through bicameralism and/or intergovernmental relations is an essential criterion.[21] In other words, this understanding concentrates on self-rule without shared rule, at least in the sense in which the latter notion is commonly understood.[22]

We agree with critics of this definition[23] that a more inclusive understanding of federalism and federal systems is in order. Indeed, as has been argued, it might be that 'the primary virtue' of federalism (and democracy for that matter) is 'its capaciousness and openness to multiple definitions and interpretations'.[24] This thought goes back as far as Daniel Elazar, the founding father of modern federalism studies, who viewed as the great strength of 'the federal idea and the structures and processes that follow from it' precisely its flexibility. According to him, this flexibility 'makes federalism difficult to discuss on a theoretical level' but 'has great operational advantages'.[25]

In this light, we follow in this volume a rather capacious approach to identifying federal systems which also includes some 'borderline cases' that are not always counted among such systems. Concretely, we rely on three criteria as 'a minimum of institutional and procedural elements':[26] (1) a plural allocation of powers (unlike in unitary systems) by either the division or sharing of powers between different levels of government; (2) existential guarantees against an involuntary transfer of powers through their entrenchment (unlike in decentralised systems) in treaty-like agreements or in a constitution with a – compared

---

[20] Fenna A & Schnabel J 'What is Federalism? Some Definitional Clarification' *Publius: The Journal of Federalism* (2024) 54(2) 179–200 at 191.

[21] Fenna A & Schnabel J (2024) at 186–8.

[22] The authors contend that the 'shared rule' has been widely *mis*understood, diverging significantly from Daniel Elazar's original intent when he coined the term (Elazar D *Exploring Federalism* Tuscaloosa: University of Alabama Press (1987) at 12). Elazar, they claim, would have taken it to mean only 'the existence of a central government, a government the whole country shared in' (Fenna A & Schnabel J (2024) at 185). Even if this were true, one might argue, however, that 'shared rule' has meanwhile taken on in federalism studies another, different meaning.

[23] Hueglin T & Mueller S 'A Reply to Fenna and Schnabel's (2024) "What is Federalism?"' *Publius: The Journal of Federalism* (2025) 55(2) 399–407 at 404.

[24] Simeon R (2015) 104–5.

[25] Elazar D *Republicanism. Representation and Consent: Views of the Founding Era* New Brunswick: Transaction Books (1979) 16.

[26] Hueglin TO (2013) at 29; Hueglin T & Mueller S (2025) at 404–5.

to ordinary legislation – qualified amendment procedure; (3) mechanisms for negotiating compromise between the government levels through formal bicameralism and/or mostly informal intergovernmental relations.

In this light, three factors informed our selection of case study countries: (1) the aforementioned understanding of federal systems; (2) the presence of intervention powers, defined above as instruments of a higher-level executive to target subnational and/or local governments on the basis of certain, specified grounds; (3) geographical diversity to enable a global comparative perspective. On this basis, case studies on the following countries are represented in our volume: Argentina, Brazil, Ethiopia, India, Italy, Kenya, Nigeria, Malaysia, South Africa and Spain.

3. STRUCTURE OF THE BOOK

The book consists of ten case-study chapters. Each chapter provides a brief overview of the federal system of the country on which it focuses. This includes an introduction to the historical, political and social context that explains the adoption of a federal system of government. The section includes a discussion of the major federalism-related features of the country under consideration. This is followed by a section that considers the historical, political, social or cultural situation of the country in question and relates this to its underlying rationale for the legal entrenchment of powers of intervention.

Each chapter then shifts to the main business of the book and discusses the constitutional and legislative basis for intervention. More importantly, it examines the legal requirements for using these powers of intervention in terms of who may use them against whom and under what substantive conditions (security, failure to comply with legal obligations, or others). At what level (constitution, ordinary legislation, and so on) are they enshrined?

Each chapter focuses too on the procedures of intervention and examines whether they ensure checks and balances on the use of these powers by the executive (for example, the involvement of other political institutions such as the legislative branch in the approval of this use or *ex post* judicial control) and whether those mechanisms are effective. Each chapter also examines the politics of intervention. The question here is: How and to what extent are powers of intervention used (or misused) in political practice?

Chapter 2 commences the case studies by focusing on Argentina, a country with a long history of federal intervention. This chapter explores the legal and political dimensions of executive-based intervention by tracing its historical development. It reviews the justifications for such interventions and the procedural protections offered by the constitution, which are designed to prevent the federal government from interfering at lower levels of government without proper authorisation. The chapter argues that federal interventions have become less significant in the 21st century and seeks to explain this shift, highlighting the emphasis on strengthening the democratic system and improving intergovernmental relations.

Chapter 3 examines whether federal intervention in Brazil, intended to serve as a tool for defending democracy, actually leads to improvements in democratic processes. The Brazilian Constitution of 1988 permits federal government intervention in state and local governments under specific circumstances. These include the need to repel the invasion of one subnational entity by another, financial crises or serious threats to public order. This chapter analyses instances where the Brazilian central government has intervened in states and where states have intervened in municipalities. It explores the justifications for these interventions and the procedural protections which the Constitution offers to safeguard subnational entities from unwarranted interference.

Chapter 4 discusses the Constitution of Ethiopia and elucidates the substantive grounds and procedures it provides for federal intervention, all of which are elaborated in legislation enacted by the federal parliament. Upon scrutinising both the Constitution and the intervention law, the chapter argues that the grounds for intervention are vague and ambiguous. This ambiguity can be demonstrated by a careful reading of both the Constitution and the provisions of the legislation. Furthermore, political practice shows that the federal government frequently intervenes in state affairs without adhering to the parameters specified in the Constitution. The two chambers of parliament, which are responsible for preventing unlawful federal interference, have not always been successful in their efforts.

Chapter 5 focuses on India. Indian federalism grants the central government significant authority to intervene in the affairs of the states. The central government has the power to impose President's Rule in a state upon receiving a report from a centrally appointed governor indicating that, as per article 356 of the Constitution, a 'situation has arisen in which the government of the State cannot be conducted in accordance with the provisions of [the] Constitution'. The chapter examines the procedures for intervention in two key areas: first, the role of the legislature and the courts in reviewing attempts to apply President's Rule; second, the role of the governor's office in facilitating communication between the central executive and the elected state government. The chapter analyses the political dynamics surrounding intervention, highlighting how shifts in the party system – from dominance by a single party to a period of multiparty regionalisation, and then back to single-party dominance – have influenced the application (and potential misuse) of President's Rule.

Chapter 6 explores the law and politics surrounding federal intervention in Italy. It begins by defining federal intervention as outlined in the Italian Constitution and examining the various methods through which this intervention occurs. The Constitution establishes three distinct forms of intervention: the power of legislative substitution, which is invoked when a region fails to comply with the implementation of European Union law (article 117(5)); the extraordinary power of substitution (article 120); and the authority to dismiss or remove the political bodies of territorial entities (article 126). These interventions differ in how they are executed.

Chapter 7 focuses on Kenya, where the 2010 Constitution established a system of government that includes empowered subnational governments known as counties. However, the autonomy granted to them is not absolute, as the national government is authorised to intervene in county affairs. The Constitution does provide procedural and substantive safeguards to minimise the risk of abuse and to ensure that such intervention does not lead to undue interference in subnational matters. Over the past ten years of implementing devolution, there has been minimal national intervention in the counties. This is notable despite the fact that both the Constitution and legislation allow for national intervention as a secondary mechanism to promote subnational accountability, particularly in cases where thresholds for intervention are met. This chapter investigates the reasons for the national government's lack of action. It seeks to determine whether this inaction is driven by political factors or by the federal mandate that supports subnational independence. Furthermore, the chapter explores the implications of this situation for the future of the devolution initiative and the achievement of its intended goals.

Chapter 8 examines Malaysia's federal government's power to intervene in state governments. The Federal Constitution (1957), drafted when the federation of Malaya became independent and amended in 1963 to deal with adding new states under the Malaysia Agreement, does not explicitly provide for such intervention. As a result, the federal government's sole means of influencing the activities of state governments is to declare an emergency under article 150 of the Constitution. Accordingly, the only way the federal government can control the actions of state governments is by a proclamation of emergency under article 150 of the Constitution. This, the chapter argues, necessarily means that federal powers of intervention are untransparent and liable to undermine democratic institutions at the state level. The situation is particularly concerning for the states of Sabah and Sarawak, which joined the federation under the Malaysia Agreement and now seek greater autonomy in response to ongoing interference.

Chapter 9 focuses on Nigeria, a country with a long history of selective and politicised federal interventions. This chapter examines the continuity and change in the politics surrounding these federal interventions. It includes specific sections that analyse the legacy of the historic 1962 declaration of a state of emergency in the Western region, the nature of federal interventions during military rule and the uses and abuses of emergency powers by post-military civilian governments since 1999 within the framework of multi-state federalism. The chapter also discusses issues related to subnational state interventions in local administrations, the judicial arbitration of intergovernmental interventions and the future of federal interventions in the light of ongoing calls for a restructuring or constitutional decentralisation of the Nigerian federation.

Chapter 10 deals with South Africa, where the Constitution gives senior levels of government the authority to intervene in the powers and functioning of lower levels of government. Unlike other federations, South Africa does not require the consent of the government subjected to intervention: in other words, the national or provincial government may declare an intervention unilaterally. This sets the South African approach apart from that of other countries where intervention, at least with respect to certain grounds and conditions, requires the consent or request of the level of government that is subject to intervention. Again, unlike the case in other federations, where the intervention is allowed to deal with national security or human rights-related situations, intervention in South Africa is aimed largely at enabling senior levels of government to address dysfunctionality and poor performance in lower levels of governments, including in regard to finance-related concerns at the municipal level.

Although there has been an alarming rate of intervention, the chapter argues that this is not surprising given the level of dysfunctionality that has plagued lower levels of governments. Nevertheless, the troubling truth about interventions in South Africa (so the chapter concludes) is that in many cases the governments that have been subjected to intervention come out of it in a worse shape than they were to begin with.

Chapter 11 focuses on article 155 of the Spanish Constitution, which grants the central government of Spain a coercive mechanism to force a region (that is, an autonomous community) to comply with the law when the regional government seriously contravenes the Constitution and threatens the state's general interest. A similar mechanism exists for local governments. Over the nearly fifty years that the Spanish Constitution has been in force, there has been only one intervention by the central government at the regional level – Catalonia, for seven months between Autumn 2017 and Spring 2018 – and only one other intervention at the local level, in Marbella, between 2006 and 2007. The chapter explores the potentials and limitations of this instrument, as well as its consequences for the territorial structure of the state.

The book then shifts from specific country case studies to broader comparative observations. In *Chapter 12*, Nico Steytler shares insights on intervention gained from his 25 years of consulting on constitutional reform processes. Drawing on his field notes from South Africa, Kenya, Yemen, and the Solomon Islands in the South Pacific, he reflects on the struggle to find the right balance between autonomy and intervention.

Chapter 13 presents a comparative analysis of the rules governing interventions across the ten jurisdictions discussed in the book. It explores the reasons behind governmental interventions, highlighting similarities and differences across different jurisdictions. It offers a comparative analysis of the constitutional and legal frameworks that guide these interventions, focusing on the grounds that allow higher levels of government to intervene in subnational or local governance. The chapter also examines the various forms that such interventions can take, as well as the procedures involved. Additionally, it discusses how political dynamics affect the use, misuse and frequency of federal interventions.

2. Argentina: federal interventions as a constitutional way of doing politics

Lara Goyburu

1. INTRODUCTION

The political science literature on federalism – and federal interventions – has been scant. Apart from the attempt by Gibson and Falleti[1] to construct ideal types of federalism and apply them to the Argentine historical reality, the detailed analysis of Serrafero[2] and the work of Zepeda,[3] where he examines recent federal interventions in Tierra Caliente (Mexico) due to increases in homicides and organised crime in the area, there are no other comparable works in the discipline. Intervention has been addressed mainly by studies in constitutional law, yet due to their legal approach, these works fail to engage with relevant contextual factors (socio-historical, economic, cultural, political, and so on) and compare what is described 'by the letter of the Constitution' with the real interactions of the political actors who apply these rules.

Proceeding from a political science perspective, this chapter attempts a classification of interventions as a legal tool for conducting national and local politics. It delves into the dynamics of federal intervention in Argentina, a pivotal mechanism in the constitutional framework and one designed to resolve conflicts within the federal system. The discussion explores the historical context for this, tracing the use of interventions from Argentina's early post-independence period to the present day. The analysis underscores the dual nature

---

[1] Gibson EL & Falleti TG 'La unidad a palos: Conflicto regional y los orígenes del federalismo Argentino' (2007) 12 *Revista POSTData: Revista de Reflexión y Análisis Político* 171.

[2] Serrafero M *La Intervención Federal En Argentina: Experiencia y Jurisprudencia* (draft, n.d.) *Forum of Federations* available at https://www.forumfed.org/libdocs/Misc/Arg8_Serrafero%20paper%20Esp.pdf (accessed 1 March 2025).

[3] Zepeda G *Violencia en Tierra Caliente: Guerra Criminal e Intervenciones Federales de 2000 a 2014* (Unpublished Master's thesis, College of Mexico, 2016).

of interventions as instruments for ensuring national cohesion and as mechanisms potentially susceptible to political exploitation.

Through an examination of key episodes, the chapter illuminates the constitutional underpinnings that legitimise federal interventions, highlighting their intended purpose of safeguarding the republican form of government and upholding the principle of federalism. It critically evaluates the evolution of these interventions over time, noting shifts in their application and the legal and political discourse surrounding them. Special attention is given to the 1994 constitutional reform, which aimed to refine the process and criteria for federal interventions, thereby seeking to balance the central government's authority with the autonomy of provinces.

The chapter provides an overview of factors that historically have precipitated federal interventions, such as political instability, social unrest and economic crises within provinces, and discusses the outcomes of these interventions, assessing their effectiveness in resolving the underlying issues and their impact on the political landscape and intergovernmental relations in Argentina.

The chapter also contemplates the future trajectory of federal interventions in the Argentine political system. It speculates on their continued role as a tool for managing provincial crises and maintaining national unity, while also considering the challenges and criticisms associated with their use. Through this analysis, the chapter contributes to a deeper understanding of the complexities of federal interventions, offering insights into their significance for Argentine federalism and democratic governance.

In short, this comprehensive exploration sheds light on the multifaceted role of federal interventions in Argentina, providing a nuanced perspective on their historical development, constitutional basis and implications for the country's federal structure and political stability.

2. BRIEF HISTORY OF INTERVENTION

Ever since Argentina gained independence in 1816 and consolidated itself as a state under a federal constitution in 1853, disputes over the form of government to be adopted, over the role of the province of Buenos Aires and over the control of the resources generated by the port and the customs offices located in that province have been a constant source of political and economic conflict. After several early disputes and insurrections in this regard, the country adopted a federal framework and became what Riker would call a 'decentralized' federal system.[4] However, the advent of the National Constitution in 1853

4 Gibson & Falleti (2007).

did not mean an end to confrontation between the central power and the provinces, nor to confrontations between the provinces themselves. Thus, federal interventions became an important tool to control and enforce discipline on subnational governments and subnational political actors.

During the second half of the 19th century and the first half of the 20th, these interventions functioned as a political instrument to control subnational governments and political actors and discipline provincial opposition groups. Federal interventions increased after the introduction of the Electoral Law of 1912, which gave rise to an expanded democracy, but did not leave behind the recourse to intervention by the central government. From 1916 to 1930, there were 33 federal interventions, and between 1946 and 1976 14 interventions. At that time, interventions were used as an instrument of control against opposition forces of various kinds, as a device to resolve territorialised conflicts within a group or a dominant party and to reinforce the hegemonic presence of the national executive branch.

A change began in 1983 with the recovery of democracy and the seal that President Raúl Alfonsín gave it. His government did not undertake any federal interventions, a departure that marked the beginning of a path towards 40 years of democratic stability. Since then, there have been only six federal interventions, most of them in response to controversial elections (and the uncertainty to which those controversies gave rise), serious irregularities in the provincial executive branch and lack of efficient provincial public policies to resolve serious economic problems (which caused social instability at the provincial level) and serious allegations of corruption and political persecution by the provincial executive branches. Therefore, federal interventions have been less important in the 21st century, and the focus has been on strengthening the democratic system and intergovernmental relations.

In all of these interventions we observe a difference in performance by the central government, a performance executed in accordance with the principles and conditions provided for in the National Constitution to determine federal interventions. This is precisely the object of study in this chapter, which examines interventions within the framework of the federal design to understand their impact on both the political-party system and intergovernmental relations, on the one hand, and the creation of a strong central government with the ability to confront the provinces, on the other.

3. THE RATIONALE FOR FEDERAL INTERVENTION

Argentina's federal system emerged from historical, political and social dynamics aimed at balancing regional autonomy with national unity. After independence in 1816, integrating a vast and diverse territory was a key challenge. The 1853 Constitution, influenced by US federalism, institutionalised this model, granting provinces autonomy while establishing a strong national government.

Tensions between Buenos Aires and the provinces shaped federalism, as the capital controlled trade and revenue. The 1831 Federal Pact advanced decentralisation, but Buenos Aires resisted full integration until constitutional amendments were effected in 1860. Argentina's federal structure allocates powers between national and provincial governments, with article 121 defining their scope. The Senate ensures provincial representation, while judicial federalism balances national and local legal authority. Over time, political and legal developments have shaped this evolving system.

The reforms discussed in 1860 related, inter alia, to federal intervention, since the province of Buenos Aires regarded federal intervention as a device that an arbitrary central government could use to usurp its autonomy and threaten the political and economic resources under its control. Although the text of article 6 was amended to address the province's concerns, the interpretation of the new article presented the same ambiguities raised by the 1853 version. The new formulation of article 6 left ample room for interpretation and presidential manipulation. It was unclear who constituted the 'federal government'. Was it the President, Congress, or both who had the right to declare intervention in the provinces? Furthermore, according to the text, the 'federal government' could intervene without local requirement, in order to 'guarantee the republican form of government'. A request by a province was necessary if the causes of the intervention were sedition or invasion by another province, but nothing was said about which branch of provincial power – the executive, the legislative, or both – should request the intervention.

Bartolomé Mitre, the former governor of Buenos Aires and first President of the Nation in 1860 under a constitution inclusive of all provinces, governed in a context of growth in agricultural exports, which galvanised the union. However, he had to apply different mechanisms to suppress provincial conflicts, including federal interventions, which also made him the first President of the unified national territory to use this mechanism. The Mitre government's centralist approach led to numerous federal interventions in the provinces, except for Buenos Aires and Entre Ríos, which maintained significant autonomy. Between 1853 and 1860, a period before Buenos Aires was fully integrated in the nation, the central government intervened in all provinces except Entre Ríos and San Luis, with all of the interventions having been ordered by presidential decree.

During Mitre's presidency, central authority was imposed and the national state built, making his federalism hegemonic and centralised. All federal interventions under his government targeted the provinces of the interior, while the dominant province, Buenos Aires, along with the second most politically and economically powerful one, Entre Ríos, retained considerable autonomy from the central government. However, hegemonic federalism was eventually weakened due to its institutional fragility.[5]

After 1880, Argentina adopted a republican, representative and federal system, one led by the Partido Autonomista Nacional (PAN). This party managed the relationship between the central government and the provinces, ensuring political stability. Power was concentrated in a government of notables – members of the economic and social elite with political influence. The system's main advantage lay in the continuity of successive administrations, including presidents, provincial governors and municipal authorities. This ruling class shared a unified vision rooted in common interests, values, ideas and beliefs. But the representative façade hid a different reality. In effect, the non-universality of the suffrage led to majorities that were absent from the Argentine political landscape. Furthermore, a policy of centralisation that did not respect the provincial autonomies guaranteed in the Constitution entailed the constant exercise of federal intervention, as a result of which there were 39 such interventions between 1880 and 1916.

In 1912, Argentina, under the presidency of Roque Sáenz Peña, enacted the law of secret, universal, male voting. This new electoral law introduced mandatory voting to reduce abstention, ensured vote secrecy to combat electoral fraud, and implemented an incomplete list system to guarantee minority representation. However, due to Argentina's federal structure, which granted significant political autonomy to the provinces, the law effectively secured only the electoral integrity of the Federal Capital. In the provinces, ensuring fair elections depended on the goodwill of local authorities – failing that, the federal government could resort to intervention, a powerful political-constitutional mechanism.[6]

The Electoral Law of 1912 gave rise to an expanded democracy, but did not spell the end of the central government's practice of constantly, and often abusively, resorting to the use of federal intervention. In fact, it was accentuated after the application of the Sáenz Peña Law, which in 1916 allowed the accession of Hipólito Yrigoyen (Radical Civic Union, or UCR) to the Presidency of the Nation. From 1916 to 1930, there were 33 federal interventions. Although the use of federal intervention decreased in the 1930s (13 interventions), it did not stop either during the period of Peronist governments between 1946 and

---

[5] Gibson & Falletti (2007).

[6] In fact, the first provincial elections, held in Santa Fe on 31 March 1912, were preceded by a federal intervention that facilitated the victory of the UCR candidate, Manuel Menchaca. This was the first governor elected through the Sáenz Peña Law, while the first minority guaranteed by the incomplete list corresponded to the Southern League. The strengths conservative was left relegated to a third place.

1955 (14 interventions) or during subsequent presidencies between 1958 and 1976, a period of pendulum-like oscillation between governments both de facto and constitutional. All national governments, for different reasons, intervened in the provinces and replaced their authorities.

According to Botana,[7] federal intervention was an instrument of control against provincial oppositions; it acted as a device to resolve conflicts within a group or a dominant party, and reinforced the hegemonic presence of the national executive. Ever since the consolidation of the national state via the Constitution of 1853, the incorporation of the province of Buenos Aires in 1860 and the federalisation of the Federal Capital in 1880, and over the course of much of the 20th century, federal intervention functioned as a mechanism that guaranteed the incumbents the necessary political resources to forge electoral and parliamentary coalitions.

In 1916, with the first presidency that emerged from the electoral reform of 1912, a new period of interventions began in which they were somewhat different from previous ones. That difference lay in the intention of those interventions. It could be argued that interventions from that year onward occurred largely within the framework of deliberate disciplining and were effected through what O'Donnell calls 'brown zones', which are characterised by the construction of a 'traditional' local power, in Weberian terms, and function 'on the basis of phenomena such as personalism, familism, prebendalism, clientelism, and others of the kind'.[8] While these local power schemes are supported by, among other things, links with the national executive, the need to maintain a sphere of autonomy and 'sustain the system of privatised domination that has elected them and channel the greatest amount into that system possible of state resources'[9] is likely to generate vertical conflicts at both the state and intra-party levels.

Although O'Donnell points out what could happen if the national executive is weak – namely, that the 'brown leaders' have greater opportunities to take control of the state agencies that provide them with resources – he does not contemplate the reverse case: a strong national executive power. A clear example of this reverse situation, as will be seen later, is provided by the governments of Juan Domingo Perón in the 1940s. However, it is necessary to briefly

---

7 Botana N 'Prólogo' in Calvo E & Abal Medina JM (eds) *El federalismo electoral argentino. Sobrerrepresentación, reforma política y gobierno dividido en la Argentina* Buenos Aires: Editorial Universitaria de Buenos Aires-Instituto Nacional de la Administración Pública (2001).

8 O'Donnell G 'Acerca del estado, la democratización y algunos problemas conceptuales: Una perspectiva Latinoamericana con referencias a países poscomunistas' (1993) 33(13) *Desarrollo Económico* 163 at 170.

9 O'Donnell (1993) at 171.

mention the interventionist practices of what would be the two leading parties in the national electoral and political arena for much of the 20th century: the UCR and the Justicialist Party (PJ).

The first radical governments took office in 1916, with the majority of the governorships occupied by the conservative party – a framework that helped make Yrigoyen (UCR) the democratic president who undertook the most interventions during his administration. He relied on the argument that there was a need to control electoral fraud at the provincial level as well as curb reactionary practices against the central power in opposition-held provinces.

During his first term (1946–1952), Juan Domingo Perón for his part used the federal intervention mechanism as an internal disciplinary tool, that is, as a means to quell dissent in his party and, consequently, promote unity.[10] Similarly, during his third term – which was set to extend from 1973 to 1976, but was truncated by his death in 1974 and definitively interrupted by the 1976 coup d'état against his successor, María Estela Martínez de Perón – federal intervention was used for 'purifying' the party of the increasingly influential 'Peronist left'.[11] After a period of democratic instability that lasted from the first coup d'état in 1930 until the democratisation of 1983 (interspersed as it was with intervals of democracy followed by periods of military dictatorship, party bans and crimes against humanity), a change occurred in the form and grounds for federal interventions.

Starting in 1983, with the recovery of democracy in a context of severe economic crisis and a regime transition focused on civil trials for crimes against humanity during the dictatorship, President Raúl Alfonsín (1983–1989) did not undertake any federal interventions. His successor, Carlos Menem (1989–1999), ordered an intervention in the province of Tucumán in 1991, one which was formally justified in the presidential intervention decree by the inefficiency of the provincial government in resolving the province's financial problems; the particular situation of the then governor, who was undergoing impeachment; and the lack of enforcement of the provincial constitution which had been enacted recently.

Then, in 1991, the province of Catamarca was placed under intervention after the murder of a teenager from that province and the evident connections between the crime and political power. In 1992, Presidente Menem did the same with the province of Corrientes due to political uncertainty arising from

[10] Marcilese JB 'La intervención del sistema judicial bonaerense durante el primer peronismo: la subordinación de la justicia al poder político' (2010) 11 *Historia Constitucional* 275.

[11] Servetto A (2009) 'El sentido político de las intervenciones federales en el tercer gobierno peronista: desplazar' a los' infiltrados' y' depurar' al peronismo' 8(2) *Revista Escuela de Historia*.

the 1991 gubernatorial elections, which led to local unrest. Santiago del Estero met the same fate in 1999, when an intervention in it was prompted by atrocities committed during socio-political protests known as 'El Santiagueñazo'. Likewise, in 1999, President Fernando de la Rúa (1999–2001) ordered an intervention in the province of Corrientes due to poor provincial administration that had led to a violent protest known as the 'Massacre at the General Belgrano Bridge'. Finally, in 2004, when Néstor Kirchner was president (2003–2007), an intervention in the province of Santiago del Estero was approved on the grounds of serious allegations of corruption and political persecution made against the provincial governor, Nina Juárez, and her husband Carlos Juárez, one of the most influential leaders of the province.

In all of these interventions we observe a difference in performance by the central government, a performance executed in accordance with the principles and conditions provided for in the National Constitution to determine federal interventions. Although this was long the case in federal interventions in the period 1853–1983, since the return of democracy a different pattern has emerged, one characterised by the national executive's greater restraint in invoking the tool and its tendency to use it only as a last resort in the face of public scandals or major protests involving provincial authorities. That is to say, the nationalisation of local political conflicts has occurred in the face of protests, massive mobilisation and intra-elite crises.[12] In addition, some literature[13] refers to interventions that sought to prevent provincial economic crises from impacting the national economy. This suggests that, in the future, there may be consensus among political actors on instituting legal regulation of the mechanism.

4. LEGAL AND CONSTITUTIONAL GROUNDS AND PROCEDURES FOR INTERVENTION

As described in the historical overview above, federal intervention was established in the National Constitution of 1853, having as immediate antecedents the Federal Pact of 1831 and the San Nicolás de los Arroyos Agreement of 1852. Originally, it had been intended as a resource for defending the provinces against possible attack from an external or internal powers in their territory. Federal intervention sought to restore peace in case of internal commotion and

---

12 Behrend J & Whitehead L *Illiberal practices: Territorial variance within large federal democracies* Baltimore: Johns Hopkins University Press (2016).

13 See Pratto J *Determinantes de intervenciones aplicado al caso argentino: Intervenciones federales a partir de 1983* San Andrés, Colombia: Universidad de San Andrés, Departamento de Ciencias Sociales (2015).

support the legally constituted provincial and national authorities. Specifically, article 6 of the Constitution enshrined this principle:

> The federal government intervenes with a request from the provincial legislatures or governors, or without it, in the territory of any of the provinces, for the sole purpose of restoring public order disturbed by sedition, or to attend to national security threatened by an external attack or danger.

However, the ambiguity of the constitutional text – and Buenos Aires's notable opposition to the tool (given the potential threat to its autonomy) – led to the text's modification by the Convention Constituent Assembly of 1860.[14] This is how article 6 was revised in an attempt to correct the previous ambiguities:

> The Federal Government intervenes in the territory of the provinces to guarantee the republican form of government, or repel foreign invasions, and at the request of its constituted authorities to support and restore them, if they have been deposed by sedition or by invasion of another province.

Furthermore, the constitutional text of 1860 allowed interventions with or without the request of local governments, and without clearly establishing a role for Congress in this mechanism, leaving the executive branch with the power to make discretionary use of federal intervention. Between 1860 and 1880, 29 federal interventions took place; of these, only five were approved by an Act of Congress, while the rest were the result of presidential decrees. Thus, despite changes in wording, the breadth and ambiguity of the modified text continued to pose the danger of excesses by the national political powers,[15] a danger which, as we saw above, indeed came to pass. Later constitutional reforms, in 1866, 1898, 1949, 1957 and 1972, neither modified the article on federal intervention nor added new specifications to its regulation, meaning that the situation continued to prevail until the constitutional reform of 1994.

As for the figure of the federal auditor or controller, this was historically an official, or group of officials, appointed by the national executive branch. This figure, a delegate or commissioner, temporarily replaces the local authorities until provincial powers are reorganised and/or the reason for the intervention is stabilised. At the same time, he or she has the power to take over the powers of the three local powers, without the province losing its status as its own legal personality.

---

[14] Badeni G 'Intervención federal en las provincias' (1992) 56 *Lecciones y Ensayos* 11.

[15] Ferrer GB 'Intervención federal en las provincias en el derecho constitucional Argentino' (1965) 144 *Revista de Estudios Políticos* 153.

Although federal intervention has varied significantly over the decades in terms of use, motivations and procedures (as shown in the previous section), its employment is inseparable from its historical and current context. The constitutional reform of 1994 was the first that attempted to regulate the intervention mechanism more precisely, specifying – in articles 75(31) and 99(20), dealing with, respectively, the powers of the legislative branch and executive branch – the scope and limits of the invocation of the procedure by both powers:

> Article 75. It is up to Congress:
> Subsection 31. Provide federal intervention to a province or the city of Buenos Aires. Approve or revoke the intervention decreed, during its recess, by the executive branch …
>
> Article 99. The President of the Nation has the following powers:
> Subsection 20. Decrees federal intervention to a province or the city of Buenos Aires in the event of a recess of Congress and must simultaneously convene it for its treatment.

This reform makes it possible to better delimit the functions of federal bodies with the power to intervene in a province, thereby to some extent filling a gap in previous texts. These sections explicitly establish the authority of the legislative branch to invoke the mechanism, indicating that the executive may use it only in the event of a recess of the legislative branch (as long as it orders the latter's convocation for consideration of the bill). Furthermore, the enacted laws began to include tentative terms for the duration of interventions (180 days extendable for an additional 180 days). Thus, the new specifications sought to address a historical problem in relation to federal intervention, namely that the mechanism has been repeatedly invoked unilaterally by the national executive without consulting Congress. In effect, the 1994 conventions were aligned with the interpretations of the Supreme Court of Justice, as derived from the rulings in the cases of *Cullen v Llerena* (1893) and *Orfila* (1929), where it is made clear that the power of federal intervention is attributed to the National Congress.[16]

[16] See Badeni (1992). In *Cullen v Llerena* (1893), the Argentine Supreme Court ruled that decisions regarding federal intervention in provinces are political acts under the exclusive jurisdiction of the legislative and executive branches and not subject to judicial review. This case established a key precedent affirming the constitutional authority of the National Congress in such matters. Similarly, in *Orfila* (1929), the Court upheld this principle while addressing a *habeas corpus* petition filed by Alejandro Orfila, who challenged the legality of a judge appointed by a federal intervener in Mendoza. The Court ruled that such appointments were constitutional, as they fell within the political powers granted to the National Congress

Yet despite the improvements contemplated in the 1994 constitutional reform, many issues remain in a state of constitutional uncertainty. Historical practice shows the need to regulate federal intervention through a law that specifies the procedure in more detail in order to prevent it from becoming an instrument of the ruler in power, something which is alien to the principles informing the constitutional provision.

Throughout Argentine history, there have been attempts to implement regulations in this regard. Among them, that of 1868 stands out. Two major positions clashed: on the one hand, Mitre defended the exclusive power of Congress to sanction the intervention in cases in which the republican form of government was endangered;[17] on the other, a group of national ministers insisted on the power of the executive branch to intervene in all cases provided for by the Constitution. However, all efforts have been unsuccessful so far. Some authors refer to the practical impossibility of implementing a regulatory law: they argue that, in view of history, political powers do not want to tie their hands with a regulatory text, and seek instead to enjoy freedom of movement when it comes to a political instrument that has proven so fundamental in important periods of Argentine history.[18]

In other words, and to summarise, each provincial intervention is carried out through a specific law enacted by Congress. For example, the most recent intervention, conducted in 2004, was implemented through the enactment of Law 25.881. Its first article states: 'The province of Santiago del Estero is hereby placed under federal intervention in all its constituted powers to guarantee the republican form of government.' This occurs within the framework of article 6 of the Constitution, the sole legal provision authorising federal intervention. That is to say, apart from this constitutional article, no overarching law or similar regulation provides further detail on the procedure or limitations of the intervention.

5. THE POLITICS OF INTERVENTION

The attempt to consolidate the federal government's power over the provinces in the 19th century involved using a range of institutional tools, including federal intervention, to subordinate them individually or to form alliances with

---

and the executive branch during federal interventions. These rulings clarified that federal intervention in Argentina is primarily a political mechanism and served to reinforce Congress's constitutional prerogative in such cases.

17 Cucchi R 'El modelo norteamericano en la reglamentación de las intervenciones federales en la Argentina decimonónica: Debates en el Congreso Nacional (1869 y 1894)' (2017) 74(2) *Anuario de Estudios Americanos.*

18 Ferrer (1965).

Table 2.1 Federal interventions, by province and legal origin (1854–2004)

Province	Decree	Law	Total
Chaco	1	0	1
Formosa	0	1	1
La Pampa	0	1	1
Misiones	1	0	1
Río Negro	1	0	1
Santa Cruz	1	0	1
Entre Ríos	2	2	4
Salta	6	1	7
San Luis	3	4	7
Córdoba	6	4	10
Mendoza	6	4	10
Jujuy	10	1	11
Buenos Aires	8	4	12
Santa Fe	11	1	12
Tucumán	7	5	12
La Rioja	8	5	13
San Juan	10	4	14
Santiago del Estero	9	7	16
Catamarca	10	8	18
Corrientes	16	3	19
TOTAL	116	55	171

Source: Author's analysis of Mario Serrafero (draft, n.d.) and information in the database of the Comparative Politics Workshop (Goyburu chair) of the Political Science Department of the Universidad de Buenos Aires.

the most relevant provincial figures or those closest to national political power. The paradigmatic example was the fact of trying to counteract the fortress of Buenos Aires to subject it to central power, but throughout the 20th century this tool was used throughout the national territory in many diverse cases.

As time went by, a practice was consolidated that would last until the democratisation of 1983: federal government interference in provincial governments aimed at controlling local politics. As Ramirez Braschi notes, 'The weakness of local political frameworks, which often ended in local rebellions or seditions, became an excuse and argument to apply the measure, sometimes becoming a factor for manipulating national political power, thus controlling the provincial political opposition'.[19]

Throughout the more than 200 years of Argentine history, there have been more than 150 interventions, of course focusing on the democratically elected presidencies, where the National Constitution prevailed, and not on the periods of military governments.

As can be seen in Tables 2.1 and 2.2 and Figures 2.1 and 2.2, while certain provinces have been intervened in more than ten times, others have seen few interventions. One of the likely reasons for this has to do with the fact that, until the mid-20th century, they were national territories without autonomy. It is also evident in the tables that interventions dictated by decree have been more frequent than those dictated by law, which means Congress has been less relevant than the President in deciding on interventions.[20]

Likewise, analysis of the data shows that presidents in certain historical periods have been more prone to intervention than others (see Table 2.2).

On the basis of the data presented above, one may analyse the history of federal interventions in Argentina by dividing them into six stages; in turn, each of the periods can be classified in three dimensions according to the direction the interventions took:

1) Against opposition leaders: Periods characterised by interventions in provinces governed by parties opposed to the party in national government.
2) Intra-party conflicts: Periods where interventions took place within the context of an intra-party conflict, meaning they were directed against governors with the same political affiliation as the President.
3) Political normalisation: Periods where interventions sought to normalise extraordinary situations, armed conflicts, social crises and the like.

First, the period 1880–1916, identified as conservative and fraudulent, is marked by interventions initially aimed at imposing and consolidating the nation-state, relating to the conflicts inherent to this process and thus being classified in the third proposed category. Later, these interventions evolved towards supporting the conservative order in reaction to democratising pressures and the rise of radicalism.

The second period (1912–1930), that of radical presidencies after the Saenz Peña Law, shows interventions with the purpose of normalising conflicts

[19] Ramírez Braschi D 'Doctrina e interpretación jurisprudencial sobre la intervención federal a las provincias argentinas en el siglo XIX' (2012) 6(10) *Revista de la Facultad de Derecho y Ciencias Sociales* at 166.

[20] Serrafero (draft, n.d.).

Table 2.2 *Federal interventions, by president and legal origin (1862–2004)*

Presidents	Period	Total federal interventions	Executive branch	Congress
Mitre	1862–1868	7	6	1
Sarmiento	1868–1874	5	4	1
Avellaneda	1874–1880	6	5	1
Roca	1880–1886	2	0	2
Juárez Celman	1886–1890	2	1	1
Pellegrini	1890–1892	3	2	1
Luis Sáenz Peña	1892–1895	8	1	7
Uriburu	1895–1898	6	1	5
Roca	1898–1904	6	3	3
Quintana	1904–1906	1	0	1
Figueroa Alcorta	1906–1910	7	4	3
Roque Sáenz Peña	1910–1914	2	2	0
De la Plaza	1914–1916	3	1	2
Yrigoyen	1916–1922	19	15	4
Alvear	1922–1928	12	8	4
Yrigoyen	1928–1930	2	2	0
Justo	1932–1938	6	4	2
Ortiz	1938–1942	4	3	1
Castillo	1942–1943	3	3	0
Perón	1946–1952	10	7	3
Perón	1952–1955	5	4	1
Frondizi	1958–1962	9	6	3
Illia	1963–1966	1	0	1
Perón	1973–1974	2	0	2
Martinez de Perón	1974–1976	4	3	1
Alfonsín	1983–1989	0	0	0
Menem	1989–1999	7	6	1
De la Rúa	1999–2001	1	0	1
Kirchner	2003–2007	1	0	1

Source: Author's analysis of Mario Serrafero (draft, n.d.) and information in the database of the Comparative Politics Workshop (Goyburu chair) of the Political Science Department of the Universidad de Buenos Aires.

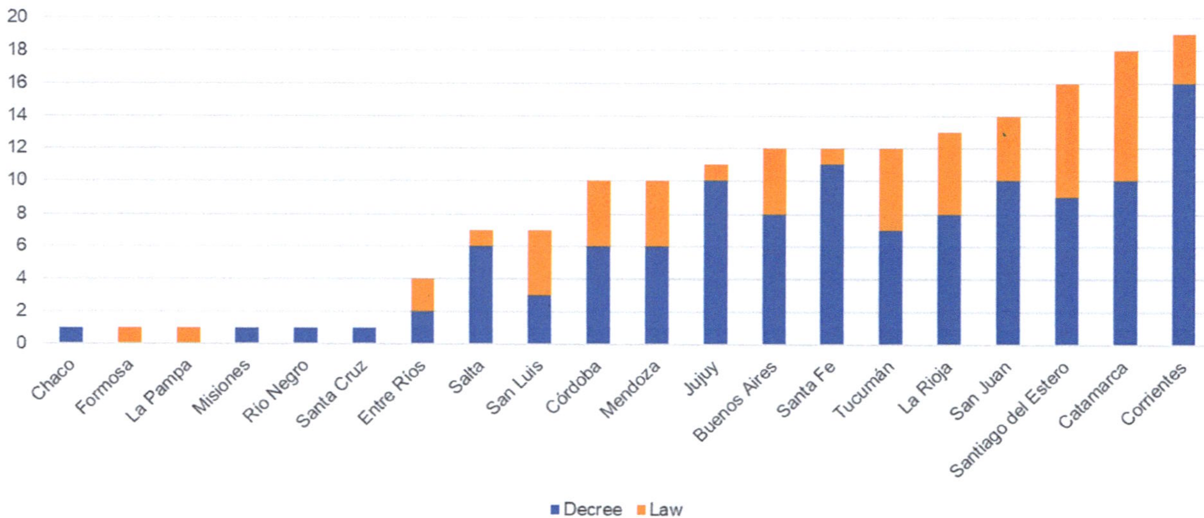

Source: Author's analysis of Mario Serrafero (draft, n.d.) and information in the database of the Comparative Politics Workshop (Goyburu chair) of the Political Science Department of the Universidad de Buenos Aires.

Figure 2.1 *Federal interventions, by province and legal origin (1854–2004) – a bar chart*

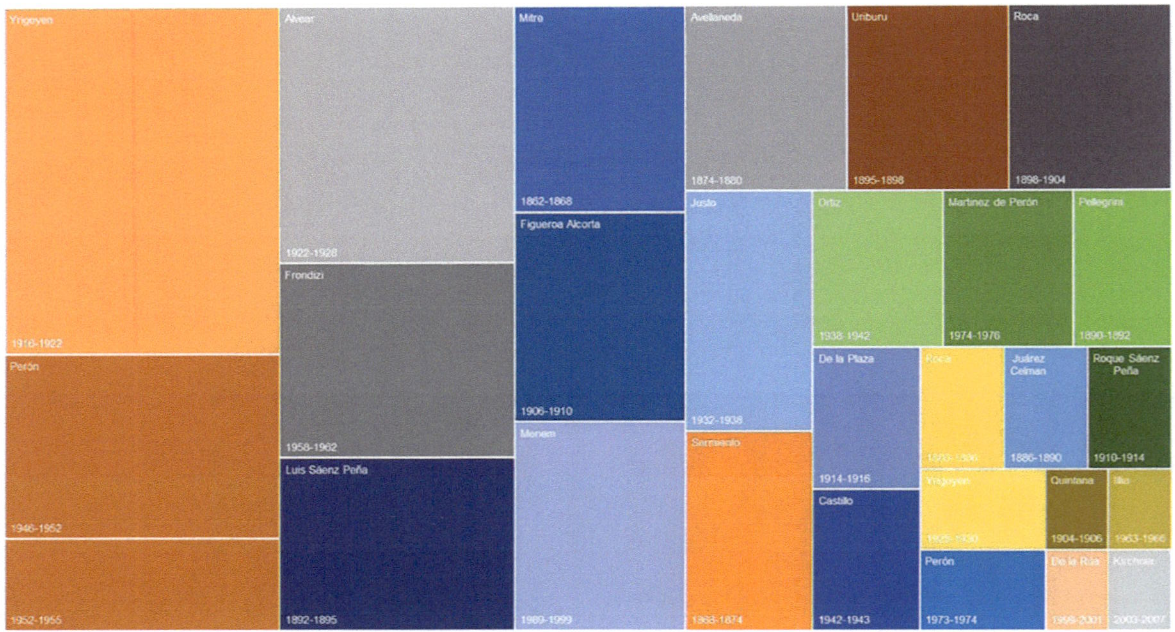

Source: Author's analysis of Mario Serrafero (draft, n.d.) and information in the database of the Comparative Politics Workshop (Goyburu chair) of the Political Science Department of the Universidad de Buenos Aires.

Figure 2.2 Federal interventions, by president and legal origin (1862–2004) – a treemap

derived from recent democratisation and intervening in opposition provinces. The coexistence of the first and third categories is observed.

In the third period (1946–1955), that of the Peronist presidencies, interventions sought mostly to impose Peronism's top-down rule on governors of the Justicialist Party in conflict with the national government; such interventions are hence classifiable in the second category of intra-party conflicts.

The fourth period (1958–1966) includes the presidencies of Arturo Illia and Arturo Frondizi. Here, interventions had a clear focus 'against opponents', related to the proscription of Peronism and its maintenance. Most of the interventions occurred within the framework of the first category, because they took place in provinces where Justicialist leaders were successful in midterm elections.

The fifth period (1973–1976), that of the third government of Perón and his successor, María Estela Martínez, shows interventions classifiable in the second category of 'intra-party conflict' and directed at provinces with governors linked to revolutionary or left-wing Peronism.

Finally, interventions since the return of democracy in 1983 constitute the sixth period. Although they are not generalisable, they became a tool of last resort for cases that impact public opinion, such as corruption, drug trafficking and crimes against humanity. In general terms, they fall into the third category: normalisation. Logically, the fact that federal intervention during this period has been a measure of last resort has to do with the constitutional reform of 1994, which better delimited the functions of federal bodies with the power to intervene in a province.The only two interventions during this period occurred as a result of homicides that shook public opinion and put traditional families of provincial power in check.

6. CONCLUSION

As Serrafero points out,[21] through federal intervention in the provinces, the presidents enjoyed a powerful tool to control the provinces and/or their extra- or inter-partisan opponents, as well as to circumvent Congress through the management of the parliamentary agenda. On occasion, they even issued decrees while the legislature was in session (two-thirds of federal interventions were by presidential decree and without involvement by Congress).

The most important current limitation on the use and abuse of the power of federal intervention is the constitutional reform of 1994, which enshrines the obligation on the national executive to simultaneously convene Congress when decreeing the measure during a recess of the legislature. In the light of

21 Serrafero (draft, n.d.).

Table 2.3 *Classification of federal interventions*

Period	Characteristics	Category of intervention	Comments
1880–1916	Consolidation of national state Order: Oligarchic-Conservative	Political normalisation Against opposition leaders	During the consolidation of the national state, political normalisation in terms of 'unity by the sticks' During the Oligarchic-Conservative Order a goal is to maintain the results of electoral fraud and avoid democratisation.
1916–1930	Law Saenz Peña Presidencies UCR Democratisation	Political normalisation	Tool used for own conflicts of the recent democratisation and civil and political rights.
1946–1955	Justicialist Party (Peronism)	Intra-party conflicts	Tool used to impose verticalism of the Justicialist Party National on the provincial PJs.
1958–1966	Justicialist Party Presidents Illia, Guido and Frondizi	Against opposition leaders	During this period, interventions were used to support the banning of the PJ. Those provinces intervened where candidates linked to Peron triumphed in mid-term elections.

Period	Characteristics	Category of intervention	Comments
1973–1976	Third Peronism Peronist left–right conflicts Triple A and armed organisations	Intra-party conflicts	During this period, the interventions were used in the frame of the conflicts between the revolutionary left wing of the PJ and the traditional wing. Provinces governed by leaders of the Peronist left were intervened in.
1983–present	Democratisation	Political normalisation	After the return to democracy, the tool of federal intervention becomes of exceptional use: generally, to normalise the political and social situation in the provinces in the face of media and police cases or human rights violations, among others.

Source: Author's analysis of Mario Serrafero (draft, n.d.) and information in the database of the Comparative Politics Workshop (Goyburu chair) of the Political Science Department of the Universidad de Buenos Aires.

this reform, it is the case that even where the national executive branch has the incentive to intervene in a province (and would thus be inclined to act unilaterally), the requirement of congressional approval implies the need for political coordination between the President and governors.

In Argentina, fiscal federalism and the equitable development of the provinces are the issues that are currently at the centre of the federal debate. The central government collects taxes and distributes a share of them to the provinces, creating a dependence on the central government which is a source of constant complaint from the provinces. But political federalism is not a resolved issue either. The possibility that the federal government will intervene in provinces in a way that involves abuse of its powers is an ever-present risk, especially during economic crises. To reduce this risk, on numerous occasions there have been proposals for the issuance of or improvement in the sanction of a law that unequivocally and precisely regulates federal interventions to avoid abuses.

However, at the moment, this legal and political issue is not on the agenda. It remains to be seen whether the country's continuing economic crises, which usually lead to social crises, will again require the use of this tool and therefore raise the need for the political regime to provide for its regulation within a framework of respect for federalism and democracy. Although the power of intervention may have had its uses in the past, Argentina today faces challenges that call for its reform. Clear and unambiguous regulation is of paramount importance in preventing abuse and ensuring the mechanism's alignment with democratic principles and fiscal federalism. Moreover, the risk of federal overreach, especially during economic crises, highlights the delicate balance between national authority and provincial autonomy.

The future of federal intervention in Argentina thus hinges on the existence of the legal and political will to regulate this mechanism much more clearly. While the potential for consensus among political actors exists, it remains to be seen how such regulations will be enacted, if at all. Respect for federalism and the democratic process is essential in shaping the regulation of federal interventions so as to ensure that they serve their intended purpose without compromising the autonomy of provinces or tearing apart the democratic fabric of the nation.

In summary, federal interventions in Argentina represent a complex interplay of constitutional principles, historical practices and contemporary challenges. As the country moves forward, the evolution of this mechanism will be a key indicator of its commitment to federalism and democracy.

ACKNOWLEDGEMENT

This work had the research assistance of Professor Maria de los Angeles Iglesias as well as the students and coordinator of the Comparative Politics Workshop of the Department of Political Science in the Faculty of Social Sciences at the University of Buenos Aires – Guido Tamer (coord.), Rolando Jaime-Malhue, Juan Manuel Conde Cárcamo, Melisa Procopio and Tadeo Flores – who collaborated in the collection of data and the development of the typology.

BIBLIOGRAPHY

Books

Alberdi JB *Bases y puntos de partida para la organización política de la República Argentina* Ciudad Autónoma de Buenos Aires, Argentina: Vi-Da Global (2010)

Behrend J & Whitehead L *Illiberal practices: Territorial variance within large federal democracies* Baltimore: Johns Hopkins University Press (2016)

Botana N *El federalismo liberal en la Argentina: 1852–1930* Mexico: Fondo de Cultura Económica (1993)

Calvo E & Escolar M *La nueva política de partidos en Argentina: Crisis política, realineamientos partidarios y reforma electoral* Buenos Aires: Editorial Prometeo (2005)

Halperín Donghi T *Una nación para el desierto argentino* Buenos Aires: Centro Editor de América Latina (1982)

Lazzari E *Federales y unitarios: el origen de las guerras civiles argentinas* Argentina: Revista Nuevos Papeles (2020)

Oszlak O *La Formación Del Estado Argentino* 2nd ed Buenos Aires: Editorial Belgrano (1985)

Pratto J *Determinantes de intervenciones aplicado al caso argentino: Intervenciones federales a partir de 1983* San Andrés, Colombia: Universidad de San Andrés, Departamento de Ciencias Sociales (2015)

Chapters in Books

Botana N 'Prólogo' in Calvo E & Abal Medina JM (eds) *El federalismo electoral argentino. Sobrerrepresentación, reforma política y gobierno dividido en la Argentina* Buenos Aires: Editorial Universitaria de Buenos Aires-Instituto Nacional de la Administración Pública (2001)

Carnota WF 'Intergovernmental relations in Argentina: Systemic confusion and predominance of the centre' in Poirier J, Saunders C, & Kincaid J (eds) *Intergovernmental relations in federal systems (comparative structures and dynamics)* Ontario: Oxford University Press (2015)

Journal Articles

Badeni G 'Intervención federal en las provincias' (1992) 56 *Lecciones y Ensayos* 11–19

Cucchi R 'El modelo norteamericano en la reglamentación de las intervenciones federales en la Argentina decimonónica: Debates en el Congreso Nacional (1869 y 1894)' (2017) 74(2) *Anuario de Estudios Americanos*

Ferrer GB 'Intervención federal en las provincias en el derecho constitucional Argentino' (1965) 144 *Revista de Estudios Políticos* 153–66

Gibson EL & Falleti TG 'La unidad a palos: Conflicto regional y los orígenes del federalismo Argentino' (2007) 12 *Revista POSTData: Revista de Reflexión y Análisis Político* 171–204

Marcilese JB 'La intervención del sistema judicial bonaerense durante el primer peronismo: la subordinación de la justicia al poder político' (2010) 11 *Historia Constitucional* 275–96

O'Donnell G 'Acerca del estado, la democratización y algunos problemas conceptuales: Una perspectiva Latinoamericana con referencias a países poscomunistas' (1993) 33(13) *Desarrollo Económico* 163–84

Ramírez Braschi D 'Doctrina e interpretación jurisprudencial sobre la intervención federal a las provincias argentinas en el siglo XIX' (2012) 6(10) *Revista de la Facultad de Derecho y Ciencias Sociales*

Sabsay DA 'Situación del federalismo luego de la reforma constitucional' (1998) 4 *Anuario de Derecho*, Universidad Austral, Buenos Aires

Servetto A (2009) 'El sentido político de las intervenciones federales en el tercer gobierno peronista: desplazar' a los' infiltrados' y' depurar' al peronismo' 8(2) *Revista Escuela de Historia*

Legislation

Constitution of the Argentine Nation, 1853

Case Law

Cullen v Llerena (1893)

Orfila (1929)

Internet Sources

Serrafero M *La Intervención Federal En Argentina: Experiencia y Jurisprudencia* (draft, n.d.) *Forum of Federations* available at https://www.forumfed.org/libdocs/Misc/Arg8_Serrafero%20paper%20Esp.pdf (accessed 1 March 2025)

Theses

Zepeda G *Violencia en Tierra Caliente: Guerra Criminal e Intervenciones Federales de 2000 a 2014* (Unpublished Master's thesis, College of Mexico, 2016)

3. Brazil: federal intervention as a paradox of unity and autonomy

Marcelo Labanca Corrêa de Araújo

1. A BRIEF INTRODUCTION TO THE BRAZILIAN FEDERAL SYSTEM

A broader understanding of Brazilian federalism is helped by an analysis of its state-level origins. Much is owed to the colonisation process carried out by Portugal at the beginning of the 16th century. This played a significant role, as Portugal sought to maintain territorial unity by adopting a centralising approach so as to prevent fragmentation, an approach that consistently attempted to monitor any potential development of subnational autonomy that might threaten territorial unity.[1]

[1] An example was the Portuguese crown's creation of a General Government in 1548 to maintain control of the colony and prevent fragmentation. Granting a degree of subnational autonomy to the captaincies was itself, too, a strategy to ensure the unity of the country. For further discussion, see Calmon P, *História do Brasil: As origens (1500–1600)* São Paulo: Companhia Editora Nacional (1951). Taking the colonial period as a temporal landmark in the historical and social foundations of Brazilian federalism does not aim to disregard a decolonial perspective, as the existence of indigenous groups prior to Portuguese colonisation is recognised. However, political-administrative decentralisation in Brazilian territory was shaped not by the demarcation of indigenous peoples' territories but by the divisions imposed by the Portuguese crown during colonialism. Thus, debates about federalism, centralisation–decentralisation or diversity–unity are only comprehensible within the framework of European occupation in the context of colonialism. For a discussion of Brazilian federalism since the colonial era, see Corrêa de Araújo ML 'Subnational constitutionalism in Brazil: The space of state constitutions for improving Brazilian federalism' in Popelier P, Delledonne G, & Aroney N (eds) *Routledge handbook of subnational constitutions and constitutionalism* London: Routledge (2022).

The European colonists' main purposes in Latin American territory were extractive rather than developmental, resulting in many disputes over land and borders.[2] The Portuguese colony which later became Brazil was marked by these disputes, as were the Spanish colonies that later became Spanish-speaking states in Latin America. During the navigation period, territorial boundaries were imposed to prevent the loss of land to other European invaders. Moreover, the institution of 'hereditary captaincies' allowed the King of Portugal the discretion to concede extensive lands to specific persons, who were then responsible for occupying and economically exploiting the region. The current 26 Brazilian states (such as Pernambuco, Rio de Janeiro, São Paulo, and others) were forged from the historical experiences of territorial subdivision in the colonial era.

At the end of the colonial period, the captaincies were transformed into provinces and general elections were held for local leaders to assume legislative functions. Positions of executive authority were appointed by the central government, with these lacking in political autonomy.[3] In fact, the first Brazilian Constitution (adopted in 1824) maintained the provinces' arrangement with explicit rules until 1834. Only then did a degree of partial political autonomy emerge, following an amendment which established a constitutional division of legislative powers. Political autonomy emerged gradually, and mainly through the creation of provincial assemblies that were established by the Additional Act of 1834. These replaced the General Councils of the Provinces. The assemblies were elected directly by the population and given defined legislative powers (a system of distribution of competence). Although the President of the Province (who held executive authority) continued to be appointed by the central government, the establishment of the legislative assemblies marked a significant step towards decentralisation. The

---

[2] Portuguese colonisation in Brazil was based on an extractive economic model in which natural resources were exploited without any promotion of sustainable economic development in the colony. This pattern of exploitation began with the extraction of *pau-brasil* wood and continued with the implementation of a sugarcane monoculture. For a comprehensive account, see the collection edited by the Brazilian Federal Senate on the history of Portuguese colonisation in Brazil, available at https://www2.senado.gov.br/bdsf/handle/id/600025 (accessed 1 March 2025).

[3] In fact, the members of the General Councils of the Province were elected in accordance with article 90 of the Constitution of 1824. However, the President of the Province was appointed by the Emperor (article 165).

constitutional division of legislative powers signalled the beginning of a more autonomous regional governance structure.[4]

A federal state was formally adopted in Brazil only with the passing of Decree No. 01 of 15 November 1889. This was not merely an infra-legal act but clearly constitutional in nature.[5] A broad range of factors, including dissatisfaction with the abolition of slavery,[6] tax issues and demands for greater provincial autonomy led to the fall of the monarchy and the beginning of the Federative Republic. The constitutional documents of this period were strongly influenced by the constitutionalism of the United States (US). This is evident in the adoption of both the republican system and of federalism (key features of the American model). After two years, the Constitution of 1891 was promulgated, in the process converting the subnational entities from provinces to states with political autonomy, as is characteristic of subnational entities in a federal system.

Despite the strong influence of the American example on Brazilian constitutionalism, Brazil's federal history is closely linked to territorial subdivision. This was established over the years through the tension between centralisation-decentralisation in the colonial, imperial and, later, federal phases. Although there are significant economic and population differences between the different states, the creation of subnational entities in Brazil is not related to identity, language or cultural issues. States exist as elements of political

---

4 For this reason, it is common to say that during the Brazilian monarchical period there was federalism but without a federation. See Liziero L 'Was there federalism in the Brazilian Empire? A case of contrast between federal state and federalism in 19th century' (2019) 2(2) *International Journal of Law and Public Administration* 41.

5 Normally, decrees are classified as infra-legal acts. However, despite its title, Decree No. 1 of November 1889 was clearly constitutional in nature, as it transformed the form of government from a monarchy to a republic and the form of state from a unitary to federal one. Indeed, the fall of the Brazilian monarchy occurred through an institutional rupture, with the military seizing power and proclaiming the new regime by decree. The 15th of November remains a national holiday in Brazil, where it is commemorated as the day of the Proclamation of the Republic. See Decree No. 1 of November 15, 1889 available at https://www.planalto.gov.br/ccivil_03/decreto/1851-1899/d0001.htm#:~:text=DECRETO%20N%C2%BA%201%2C%20DE%2015,devem%20reger%20os%20Estados%20Federais (accessed 15 January 2024).

6 This change of policy had the support of the elites; many landowners, however, felt betrayed by the abolition of slavery. Consequently, 'the planters allegedly turned in bitterness against their erstwhile ally – or creature – and worked to overthrow Pedro II'. See Graham R 'Landowners and the overthrow of the empire' (1970) 7(2) *Luso-Brazilian Review* 44.

decentralisation for self-governance within a territory rather than as elements that bring together people with different cultural or linguistic characteristics. Because of this, the tension between centralisation and decentralisation in Brazilian federalism is largely fuelled by the interpretation of central constitutional legal norms, as well as by the dynamics of intergovernmental relations between the central government and the subnational entities.

The basic constituents of Brazil's federal structure at the beginning of its federal era were a central government, the states and the Federal District. Although the 1891 Constitution nominally recognised the autonomy of municipalities concerning matters of their 'peculiar interest (article 68), it was only with the 1988 Constitution that municipalities were explicitly recognised as federative entities and members of the federation with political autonomy (articles 1 and 18). The Brazilian federation involves three levels of government, with the municipalities comprising the federal system only coming into play after 1988.

In regard to the origins of the Brazilian federation, it should be remembered that the creation of states as subnational entities after the monarchical period broadly followed the existing territorial division of the former provinces. It is also important to note that the demand for greater autonomy and decentralisation had already existed during the monarchy (as witnessed by the several separatist revolutions which were suppressed by the Brazilian Empire).[7] In the end, the Brazilian federal structure creates a constant interplay between decentralisation and centralisation, one shaped by constitutional interpretation and specific political dynamics.

2. THE HISTORICAL-POLITICAL CONTEXT OF FEDERAL INTERVENTION IN BRAZIL

In a federation, no subnational entity is entirely unregulated. There are minimum standards of political, institutional and legal behaviour that have to be respected. Several federal constitutional norms work to limit the 'freedom' of subnational entities, establishing different consequences in case of violations. The minimum standards set the limits of state autonomy and consequences follow any breach of these. The aim is to balance unity and diversity and to ensure that diversity in the exercise of power does not become so extensive as to undermine the overall unity of the federal system. Federal intervention arises if and when federal parameters and behavioural standards are challenged by subnational entities.

7 See Machado RP *Brazilian history: Culture, society, politics 1500–2010* Cambridge: Cambridge Scholars Publishing (2017).

Federal intervention allows the central entity to override subnational autonomy in order to protect the integrity of the federal system (that is, when the minimum standards accepted by the federation are violated by a subnational entity). In this sense, federal intervention represents something of a contradiction. The central entity withdraws the autonomy of the subnational entity in order to protect the federal pact which requires and enables subnational entities to be autonomous and free from central government interference. It seems, therefore, to be a remedy that uses poison to cure the disease.

In Brazil, the provision for federal intervention in the first 1891 federative constitution was strongly influenced by the so-called guarantee clause of the US Constitution.[8] The 'guarantee' reference was there to ensure that the Union was obliged to provide the application of the republican form of government in the member states, as well as to guarantee protection against external or internal violence. The purpose of maintaining the republican form of government has a historical explanation: it sought to prevent the reestablishment of monarchy, the system of government used by the British colonisers.[9] The republican form of government requires a clause of homogeneity, an unsurpassable minimum standard that must be adopted by subnational entities. The states are not allowed to have a monarchical system of governance. Since the colonising nations of Britain (in the US) and Portugal (in Brazil) had monarchical forms of government, preserving the Republic would be tantamount to preventing the return of colonial rule and maintaining a system of governance untroubled by the traumatic memories of the past. Thus the 'guarantee clause' was reproduced by other Latin American constitutions that adopted the federal system.[10]

The text of Brazil's first federative constitution was in some ways similar to the US Constitution. Article 6 of the 1891 Constitution stated that 'the Federal Government may not intervene in affairs peculiar to the States, except to repel foreign invasion or one State into another' and 'to maintain the federative

---

8 Article 4, section IV. The similarities between article 6 of the 1891 Brazilian Constitution and article IV, section 4, of the US Constitution – particularly in allowing federal intervention to guarantee a republican form of government, as well as to repel foreign invasions or invasions between states to preserve national integrity – point to the clear influence of the American model on Brazil's first federative constitution.

9 See Cornell Law School 'ArtIV.S4.1: Historical background on guarantee of republican form of government' (n.d.) *Legal Information Institute* available at https://www.law.cornell.edu/constitution-conan/article-4/section-4/historical-background-on-guarantee-of-republican-form-of-government (accessed 3 January 2025).

10 Corzo Sosa E 'Consideraciones en torno al origen y evolución de la intervención federal en Argentina, Brasil y México' (2020) 120 (September–December) *Revista Española de Derecho Constitucional* 139.

republican form'.[11] There was also a provision for federal intervention upon the request of the states to restore order and tranquillity, as well as intervention to ensure the execution of federal laws and judgments.[12] Similar wording can be found in article 6 of the Argentine Constitution, in its 1860 version,[13] which also incorporated the guarantee clause. Authorisation for central government action in the states was allowed in order to ensure the republican form. Considering the presence of the republican clause in countries that were colonised by monarchies (such as Brazil, Argentina and the US), the provision for this type of intervention serves as protection against the re-establishment of monarchical systems in the territories of former colonies. This holds for countries that were colonised by monarchies.[14]

---

11 Constitution of Brazil, 1891.

12 Given the political instability of the transition from an empire to a federative republic, the issue of federal intervention was discussed in the 1981 Constituent Assembly. The creation of the possibility of intervention at the request of the states, with the aim of restoring public order, stemmed from recognition that the state governments alone might not be capable of dealing with internal disturbances; thus, the states were assured of the central government's support in restoring public order. In addition, intervention to guarantee the execution of federal laws and sentences ensured that the Union's authority prevailed throughout the national territory, preventing some states from adopting obstructive actions or neglecting the application of federal legislation, and thereby seeking to balance state autonomy with national cohesion. See the constitutional debates in the 'Anais da República', available on the official website of the Brazilian Federal Senate at https://www25.senado.leg.br/web/atividade/anais/anais-da-republica (accessed 8 January 2025).

13 Although provision for intervention upon request by the states was already made in the 1853 Argentine Constitution, the republican clause was introduced only in the 1860 constitutional reform, when it explicitly established the preservation of republicanism as a reason for federal intervention. See Dirección Nacional del Sistema Argentino de Información Jurídica *Constituciones Argentinas: Compilación histórica y análisis doctrinario* 1st ed (November 2015) available at https://www.saij.gob.ar/docs-f/ediciones/libros/Constituciones_argentinas.pdf (accessed 11 January 2025).

14 This evidence comes from Brazil's emulation of the American model and is highlighted in the following discussion of the reasons for adopting the 'guarantee clause' in the US: '[T]he Guarantee Clause was intended to be more than an authorisation for the federal government to protect states against foreign invasion or internal insurrection, a power already conferred elsewhere in the Constitution. While the precise contours of what constitutes a "republican form of government" are debatable, an additional object of the Guarantee Clause was to prevent states from establishing monarchical or despotic governments.' See Cornell Law School (n.d.).

The system of federal intervention did not stop there. The 1926 constitutional reform in Brazil expanded the guarantee clause by including several authorising grounds for intervention, many of these displaying a normative content which was open to various interpretations.[15] Additionally, this reform authorised the federal government to intervene in the states to ensure respect for constitutional principles such as the independence and harmony of powers, the autonomy of municipalities, presidentialism, representative government, an electoral system that allows the representation of minorities, the immovability of judges and the political and individual rights guaranteed by the Constitution. In addition, if states prove unable to pay their debts for two years, intervention is allowed to ensure the possibility of constitutional reform, as well as the reorganisation of state finances.

The need to address political crises explains this expansion of federal intervention. The Constitution allowed for a series of exceptional measures: namely, a state of war; a state of emergency; a state of defence; and federal intervention.[16] Moreover, in the early years of the First Republic (1889–1930) challenges to federal balance emerged, particularly when Marshal Deodoro da Fonseca (the first President of the Republic in the post-imperial period) was succeeded by Marshal Floriano Peixoto in 1891. Peixoto faced a number of

---

[15] The 1926 reform was part of the federal government's attempt to strengthen centralisation in opposition to state powers during the '*Café com Leite Republic*' (the period of the First Brazilian republic, 1889–1930, when political power was dominated alternately by the states of São Paulo, a coffee producer, and Minas Gerais, a milk producer). This reflected a broad trend towards greater centralisation of power, the aim of which was to counterbalance the influence of states. The reform paved the way for authoritarianism in Brazil: it restricted the guarantee of *habeas corpus* solely to the right to come and go (article 72, section 22), allowed for the expulsion of foreigners considered 'dangerous to public order or harmful to the interests of the Republic', introduced vague concepts (article 72, section 33), and prohibited judicial review of federal intervention and states of siege (article 60, section 5). This centralising tendency continued under the government of Getúlio Vargas in the 1930s, one which was essentially centralised. See De Gaspari FN Narrativas autoritárias: Reforma constitucional de 1926 (5 January 2021) *Consultor Juridico* available at https://www.conjur.com.br/2021-jan-05/gaspari-narrativas-autoritarias-reforma-constitucional-1926/ (accessed 13 January 2025).

[16] Although federal intervention differs from other exceptional measures, it is clearly designed for extreme circumstances. Its very nature entails a temporary suspension of state autonomy to allow, under the constitutional framework, federal interference aimed at addressing crises that threaten the federal pact.

revolts and orchestrated the removal of state governments that had supported Fonseca.[17]

One such revolt was the 'federalist revolution' of 1893.[18] This sought more power for the states. However, the 'iron fist' government of Floriano Peixoto exerted force and managed to contain political fragmentation, including that promoted by monarchist movements which wanted the return of the royal family. In this context, creating rules to authorise the Union to intervene in the states was one of the features necessary for preserving the unity of the territory. Notably, the institution of intervention was foreseen at an early stage of the Brazilian Federal State, a period of territorial crisis, and, hence, during this initial phase of the first Republic several interventions were decreed, which is why jurists considered the intervention '[a] mechanism for resolving intra-oligarchic disputes in the states. Due to its broad interpretation, article 6 allowed government jurists to impose or prevent federal intervention, depending on the specific case.'[19]

The 1891 Constitution proved to be one of the most durable in the history of Brazil's developing constitutional framework. However, it was alone in addressing the institution of intervention. Article 12 of the 1934 Brazilian Constitution[20] provided for the classic grounds of intervention: the need to repel foreign invasion or the invasion of one state by another. However, it also maintained the logic of underlining the constitutional principles that must be respected by all states lest they incur intervention. These concepts are positioned as minimum standards and limits to state autonomy and cover both

---

17 Marques de Saes GA *A República e A Espada: A primeira década republicana e o florianismo* (unpublished Master's thesis, Universidade de São Paulo, 2005) 80 available at https://www.teses.usp.br/teses/disponiveis/8/8138/tde-28042006-181955/publico/Tese_-_Saes-Guillaume_Azevedo_Marques.pdf (accessed 6 July 2023).

18 A civil conflict in southern Brazil, primarily in Rio Grande do Sul. It stemmed from tensions between the federalists (*maragatos*), who wanted greater state autonomy, and the republicans (*pica-paus*), who supported the centralised government of President Peixoto. The conflict was marked by intense violence, including mass executions, and ended with the victory of the republican forces. It was one of the first major challenges to the newly established regime in Brazil, highlighting tensions between centralisation and state autonomy. See Vieira AN *Lenço vermelho de sangue: Um olhar sobre a Revolução Federalista de 1893* Curitiba: Editora Appris (2023).

19 De Moraes MR *A Reforma Constitucional de 1926: Análise das emendas ao artigo 6° da Constituição de 1891* (unpublished PhD thesis, Universidade de Brasília, 2018) 32 available at https://bdm.unb.br/bitstream/10483/23781/1/2018_MatheusRochaDeMoraes_tcc.pdf (accessed 2 December 2023).

20 Constitution of Brazil, 1934.

political and administrative issues. For instance, the accountability of the administration becomes a principle whose failure constitutes the possibility of decreeing intervention. The 1934 Constitution which authorised states to intervene in municipalities in Brazil is also applied to financial issues. Article 13(4) of the 1934 Constitution allowed the states 'to intervene in the Municipalities in order to regularise their finances (as arising from the late servicing of loans guaranteed by the states, or from lack of payment of debt for two consecutive years)'.

Although the 1937 Constitution never truly entered into force,[21] it provided for federal intervention in article 9, expanding the grounds for intervention to cover administrative issues as well. The Constitution authorised the Union to intervene to 'administer the State when, for any reason, one of its Powers is unable to function'. Similarly, the 1946 Constitution,[22] in article 7, maintained an extensive list of hypotheses authorising intervention. These included cases of disrespect for the temporary nature of elective functions, the separation of powers, municipal autonomy, the guarantees of the judiciary and the provision of public administration accounts. The same constitution allowed the intervention of states in municipalities, but only regarding the organisation of their finances.[23]

The 1967 Constitution[24] broadened the interpretive flexibility of the constitutional norm (although it essentially provided, in article 10, the same hypotheses).[25] For instance, it authorised federal intervention to reorganise

---

[21] In November 1937, Getúlio Vargas staged a coup and began ruling as a dictator. The 1937 Constitution, once enacted, should have been submitted to a plebiscite, but this never took place; as a result, Brazil did not have a constitution in the sense of a document that limits state power. Article 178 ordered the dissolution of the legislative branch until a popular plebiscite approved the Constitution. Indeed, article 180 granted the President the power to govern by issuing decrees with the force of law, while the legislature remained inactive. Article 187 stipulated that the Constitution would come into effect and should be submitted to a plebiscite (it is worth noting that a plebiscite is a prerequisite for approval, whereas a referendum serves to validate an existing norm). Since the plebiscite was never held, it may then be argued (as above) that the Constitution of Brazil of 1937 was never truly in force. As such, the reality is that, despite the latter's formal existence, the Vargas regime was a dictatorship that ruled by decree and without limitation on its power.

[22] Constitution of Brazil, 1946.

[23] Article 23.

[24] Constitution of Brazil, 1967.

[25] In legal theory, certain norms contain 'indeterminate legal concepts' characterised by a high degree of interpretative openness. Some of these concepts can be found among the grounds for intervention. To give but one example, the 1946 Constitution listed 'civil war' as one of the grounds for intervention. This

state finances in states that 'adopt measures or execute economic or financial plans that contradict the guidelines established by the Union'. The same logic was followed in the 1969 Constitutional Amendment. Finally, the current 1988 Constitution also addresses the issue of federal intervention in the states and state intervention in municipalities (see below).

3. CONSTITUTIONAL GROUNDS FOR INTERVENTION

In Brazil, the ability to update the constitutional text to the socio-political reality that has emerged from phases of institutional instability is intrinsically related to the establishment of new constitutions. For instance, following the transition from a monarchical to a republican system of government, the 1891 Constitution was adopted. President Washington Luis was overthrown by a military coup, and the 1934 Constitution was drafted as a result, while the 1946 Constitution reflected another period of re-democratisation following the dictatorship of Getúlio Vargas. The 1988 Constitution was no exception: it was created following two decades of military dictatorship (1964–1985). As in previous constitutions, the current Constitution (adopted in 1988) established the institution of federal intervention, best understood in relation to the federalism which implies a tension between unity and diversity. All in all, there are minimum standards which the states must respect on pain of losing their autonomy.

Initially, it should be highlighted that the Brazilian Constitution phrased the intervention in a prohibitive form. It states that "the Union *will not* intervene in the States or the Federal District, except for ..." This wording indicates that intervention is an exception rather than a rule. The Union is authorised to intervene only in exceptional circumstances such as when there is a need: (a) to maintain national integrity; (b) to repel foreign invasion or the invasion by one unit of the federation of another; (c) to put an end to any serious failure in public order; (d) to guarantee the free exercise of any of the powers in the federation units; (e) to reorganise the finances of the federation unit that suspends payment of the debt for more than two consecutive years or fails to deliver tax revenues established in the Constitution to the municipalities, within the deadlines established by law; (f) to ensure the execution of any federal law, court order or decision; (g) and to ensure compliance with the following constitutional principles: republican form, representative system and democratic regime, human rights, municipal autonomy, accountability of public administration and application of the minimum required of revenue resulting from

provision was changed in 1967 to include 'serious disturbance of order' (article 10, III), an expression open to broad interpretation.

state taxes – the latter includes transfers, the maintenance and development of education, and public health and services.

There is also an extensive list of the grounds that authorise the Union's intervention in the states. Some of these are objective, such as the need to repel foreign armed aggression. Either there is such aggression or there is not. If there is, then intervention is allowed (but not mandatory). Similarly, it is easy to see whether there has been any debt repayment over a period of two years: if not, intervention is possible. However, there are other grounds mentioned in the text that lack interpretation and have the potential to undermine the autonomy of the states, which often are dependent on the interpretation of these grounds by central bodies. This is the case, for example, with intervention allowed to ensure constitutional principles, such as the concept of a 'democratic regime' or the maintenance of public order (which applies for security reasons).

I argue that some grounds for federal intervention operate as homogeneity clauses that serve to ensure a minimum level of constitutional uniformity across the federation. This is the case, for instance, with the possibility of intervention to safeguard the republican form of government, the democratic regime and the representative system (principles that define the core identity of the federal pact and must be upheld by all subnational entities). If it is true that subnational entities in Brazil have political autonomy, it is also true that this autonomy cannot be unlimited to the point of disrupting the country's unity. Undemocratic political autonomies must be inconceivable, meaning that no state has the competence to adopt policies that undermine democracy.

However, not all the grounds for intervention can be understood as homogeneity clauses. Some provisions are designed not to enforce constitutional uniformity but rather to preserve security and territorial integrity. For example, an intervention to repel a foreign invasion (or prevent an attack by one state against another) does not impose a standardised constitutional framework on subnational entities but instead seeks to protect the federation from external or internal threats. Federal intervention seems to have two distinct roles: first, as an instrument of homogeneity, ensuring that subnational entities adhere to essential constitutional principles; second, as a mechanism for crisis response, addressing threats that do not necessarily impact the constitutional uniformity of the federation.

Since some of the grounds for federal intervention can be understood as homogeneity clauses, this naturally interferes with the state's autonomy, including its ability to exercise its subnational constitutional space. However, this issue becomes more problematic when a uniformity clause is both a ground for federal intervention and an indeterminate legal concept, requiring broader interpretation due to its conceptual scope. This is the case with the democratic clause. Here, the use of subnational constitutional space may vary depending on exactly how the homogeneity clause is interpreted by the courts.[26]

A recent example involving the interpretation of the republican clause for the states concerns provisions in subnational constitutions regarding the re-election of presidents of state legislative assemblies. Here, the Brazilian Supreme Court changed its jurisprudence. Previously, it held that the decision on the number of possible re-elections of the president of a legislative assembly fell within the bounds of the state's autonomy to regulate. However, in 2021 the Court reversed its position, ruling that allowing more than one re-election would violate the republican principle. As a result, state constitutions had to be amended to permit only a single re-election. This issue was addressed through a direct action of unconstitutionality (ADI). However, if a state had refused to adopt the new interpretation, it could have served as grounds for federal intervention for violating the republican principle, according to the Court's understanding.[27]

The discussion of subnational constitutional space becomes relevant due to the federal Constitution's imposition of a restriction on the autonomy of the states. This can be understood either as a normative duty of the state or as a factual obligation. National constitutions would, therefore, introduce two mechanisms to dictate the subnational constitutional space: either explicit provisions that impose or prohibit certain institutional arrangements for subnational entities (such as constitutional provisions that determine that the state legislature must be unicameral or bicameral), or homogeneity clauses. These constitutional clauses do not explicitly impose institutional arrangements on subnational entities. Instead, they impose on subnational constitutions only the duty to stand in accordance with the 'fundamental principles and the general spirit of the national constitution' (as is the case in article 25 of the Brazilian Constitution, which provides that states are organised through their constitutions, respecting the principles of the federal Constitution). Where these principles are violated, federal interventions in the state may follow.

The purpose of the homogeneity clause is to ensure a certain level of uniformity among subnational units. However, unlike the first mechanism (explicit

---

26 Robert Williams compares subnational constitutional space to an accordion expanding and shrinking over time as a result of the homogeneity clauses. In other words, this space sometimes contracts and sometimes expands, all depending on the performance of the central norms of homogeneity as regards the space available for state action. See Williams RF 'Teaching and researching comparative subnational constitutional law' (2011) 115(4) *Penn State Law Review* 1109.

27 Direct Action of Unconstitutionality ADI 6706-PA. See the official website of the Brazilian Supreme Court, available at https://portal.stf.jus.br/processos/detalhe.asp?incidente=6120455 (accessed 5 January 2025).

provisions), these clauses are inherently vague and subject to broad interpretation. Their flexibility allows them to be invoked to expand or restrict the subnational constitutional space, depending on how they are construed. In this context, some federal intervention norms work to establish minimum federal parameters that states must respect. However, the open-ended nature of certain intervention grounds (such as ensuring compliance with constitutional principles) creates room for interpretative variation, thus allowing federal authorities and courts to shape the scope of state autonomy based on evolving legal and political understandings.

The doctrine of the 'homogeneity clause' allows for open and generic norms (such as the concept of the democratic regime) to be used by courts or central bodies to scrutinise the performance of the state.[28] Hence, the control of states is carried out based on open-parameter norms and the extent of the subnational constitutional space is determined by the desired interpretation (more or less restricted) that one wants to give the homogeneity clauses. A parallel may be drawn between the use of the democratic principle as an open homogeneity clause by the Brazilian Federal Supreme Court with other constitutional courts.[29]

---

[28] Viotti-Schlobach R *Homogeneity clauses in federal countries: A comparative analysis* (2019) available at https://www.mcgill.ca/law/files/law/2019-baxter_homogeneity-clauses_rafael-viotti-schlobach.pdf (accessed 22 October 2024).

[29] A few decades ago in Austria, a country with a complete and uniform national constitution that leaves little constitutional space for the constitutions of the *Länder*, the Austrian court used the democratic clause to hold unconstitutional a provision of the Vorarlberg constitution that expanded direct democracy in that subnational unit, establishing popular initiatives and referendums that were non-existent in other subnational units. According to the court, there was a discrepancy between the direct democracy and other components established at the Vorarlberg subnational level and the representative democracy of the federal level; as such, there was a violation of the idea of homogeneity related to the idea of democracy. To that end, the court judged Vorarlberg's subnational constitutional provisions unconstitutional. Note the parallel between the Austrian case (relating to the control by the court of the subnational initiative in expanding democratic practice based on the provision of popular initiatives and referendums in the subnational legislative process of Vorarlberg) and the Brazilian case (concerning the control of the autonomy of the member state in regulating the date of election and re-election of a deputy member of Parliament's governing body). Both the Austrian and Brazilian courts interpreted the democracy clause in such a way as to impose national homogeneity based on a particular understanding of what democracy is, thus contracting subnational constitutional space. For that reason, Anna Gamper has criticised the Austrian court's decision, asserting that the concept of democratic homogeneity was interpreted narrowly and ignored the federalist

The role of the judiciary in ensuring uniformity and national federative cohesion should not be disregarded. A federation is, after all, a union of diversities, and higher courts play a crucial role in maintaining their cohesion. However, for a federation to continue enabling the practice of diversity and creating subnational spaces conducive to innovation, the interpretation of homogeneity clauses must always be restrictive rather than expansive, lest it violate the political autonomy of subnational entities.

The existence of open constitutional norms for authorising federal intervention (such as the protection of the democratic regime) could lead to the conclusion that the central government might surreptitiously use intervention to impose political control over subnational governments, placing them under a constant sword of Damocles. While this remains a theoretical possibility, it has never yet materialised in practice under the current constitutional framework. In fact, violations of homogeneity clauses (which also serve as grounds for federal intervention) have been addressed through judicial mechanisms rather than direct intervention. The Supreme Court has consistently denied multiple intervention requests, emphasising that alternative procedural remedies are available for the resolution of such disputes.[30]

It is worth pointing out that the state's non-observance of these homogeneity standards may have consequences other than federal intervention. In many cases, issues of subnational indiscipline can be addressed through ordinary legal mechanisms (such as judicial rulings) without resorting to intervention (for example, in the case of the re-election of presidents of state legislative assemblies). Federal intervention should be understood as an exceptional measure justifiable only when other institutional responses prove insufficient to restore compliance with constitutional principles.

Next, we will examine the formal procedure for triggering intervention.

4. PROCEDURE FOR DECREEING INTERVENTION

Article 34 of the Brazilian Constitution establishes several different procedures for activating federal intervention. Federal intervention has enjoyed full constitutional treatment in Brazil. There are no laws regulating intervention, since the constitutional text is already quite detailed on this subject. Article

ideal. See Gamper A 'Homogeneity and democracy in Austrian federalism: The Constitutional Court's ruling on direct democracy in Vorarlberg' (2003) 33(1) *Publius* 45.

30 See the recent cases, IF 5.226 and IF 5.227, both from São Paulo, available at https://portal.stf.jus.br/processos/downloadPeca.asp?id=15366348105&ext=.pdf and https://portal.stf.jus.br/processos/downloadPeca.asp?id=15369597141&ext=.pdf (accessed 15 January 2025).

34 provides seven grounds for allowing the federal government to intervene in state governments.[31] In every case it is the President who decrees the intervention, either on his own initiative (spontaneous or *ex officio* intervention) or as provoked intervention, that is, when someone calls on the President to make the decree.

In the case of spontaneous or *ex officio* intervention, the Brazilian Constitution states that the President is free to issue a decree of intervention when presented with the grounds mentioned in article 34 – namely, when there is a need to maintain national integrity (clause I); to repel foreign invasion or invasion from one state into another (clause II); to put an end to the instability of public order (clause III); and to reorganise the finances of a state that has not paid its debts for two consecutive years or that has not transferred tax revenue to the municipalities (clause V). In such cases, the President issues an intervention decree and has broad political discretion to implement it.

While the question whether the constitutional grounds exist for intervention depends on the President's understanding, the President needs to hear the Council of the Republic and the National Defense Council (articles 90 and 91) before such intervention; he or she also needs the approval of the national legislative power[32] (article 49, IV) before the intervention can take effect. No intervention may be made without the approval of the legislative branch.

The provoked intervention applies, according to article 34 of the Constitution, when intervention is necessary (IV) to guarantee the free exercise of the executive, legislative or judicial power of the member states; (VI) to provide for the application of federal law or judicial order that is being disrespected by the member state; and, ultimately, (VII) to ensure the observance of constitutional principles such as the republican form, the democratic regime and the representative system, the rights of the human person, municipal autonomy, the duty of transparency with public accountability and, finally, the application of the minimum percentage of revenue obtained from state taxes for education and health.

Much depends on whether the President of the Republic is the recipient of a mere '*solicitação*' (request) or a formal '*requisição*' (requisition). In Portuguese legal terminology, these terms carry very different implications. While a '*solicitação*' can be refused by the President, a '*requisição*' constitutes a legal obligation to act.

When the executive or legislative branch of a state believes its freedom is at risk, it may make a 'request' for intervention and ask the President of the Republic to issue an intervention decree. However, the decision remains with

31 Constitution of Brazil, 1988.
32 Meaning deputies and senators.

the President: he may either accept or deny the request. If he agrees, the decree is issued and must be approved by the National Congress.[33] By contrast, intervention triggered by a '*requisição*' takes place in specific situations outlined in items VI and VII of article 34 of the Brazilian Constitution – namely, when a federal law, court order or constitutional principle is being disrespected. In such cases, judicial authorities can compel the President to declare intervention.[34] When the violation concerns a court order, the judiciary directly forces the President to issue the decree. However, if the violation involves a constitutional principle, the Attorney-General of the Republic has to initiate a case before the Federal Supreme Court, which ultimately decides whether intervention is warranted.[35]

If the Federal Supreme Court rules in favour of intervention, the President is legally required to issue the decree, specifying its scope, term and execution conditions. Legal interventions do not require the approval of the National Congress, as the decision relies solely on legal assessment and (unlike political interventions) not political discretion.

In the case of state intervention in municipalities facing financial problems, the state chief executive decrees and the state legislature must give its approval. In contrast, the only scenario in which the legislature is not called upon to approve is when the intervention is requested by the Attorney-General directly to the court in order to ensure compliance with principles foreseen in the state constitution, or to provide for the execution of a law, order or judicial decision. In this case, if the suspension of the act is sufficient to resume normality, the intervention is not carried out, but rather the act that violates the constitutional principle is annulled.

Despite the broad grounds that exist for intervention, they are tied to strict constitutional controls and procedural conditions. These are there to prevent the arbitrary or trivialised use of this mechanism. Such controls include the requirement of prior consultation with the Council of the Republic and the National Defense Council; parliamentary approval (in certain cases); and in other cases judicial authorisation from the Federal Supreme Court or a formal request.

5. THE POLITICS OF INTERVENTION

Despite the wide range of constitutional grounds for federal intervention in the states, this rarely happens in Brazil. Over the 35 years in which the current

33 Article 36, I.
34 Article 36, II.
35 Article 36, III.

constitution has been in force, only three federal interventions have ever been enacted. Two of these took place in 2018 under President Michel Temer. The third happened at the beginning of 2023 during the Lula government. The three are linked to the constitutional ground for decreeing federal intervention for reasons of public order and security, and due to failure to comply with legal obligations related to the preservation of democracy and the rule of law.

The first intervention occurred in the public security sector of Rio de Janeiro.[36] It was not enacted throughout the state. Given the lack of control of violence in Rio's *favelas*, security was the only domain transferred from the state administration to the federal administration. The second intervention,[37] also carried out in 2018 and decreed by the same president, Michel Temer, took place in the State of Roraima when a military police strike led to riots in the prisons. In response, President Temer issued a general rather than sector-specific decree. This was done for a specific reason: the decree appointed as intervenor, in December, the governor who was elected in October to take office in January. The governor-elect's term was merely advanced by a month due to the incapacity and leadership failure of the outgoing governor during a security crisis. Clearly, this anticipation of the new term functioned as a de facto intervention, granting both the appointed intervener and the incoming governor full access to public resources and the federal government's structure to address the chaos that had overtaken the prison system.

The third case of federal intervention also related to the public security sector and took place in the Federal District at the beginning of 2023.[38] It is a particularly intriguing case, as it relates to an attempted coup by supporters of former President Bolsonaro. These invaded and vandalised the Supreme Court and the Federal Senate on 8 January. Because these actions were aligned with the former President, the subnational government of the Federal District did not act to contain the coup plotters.[39] A few days later, the governor of the

[36] Decree No 9.288 of 16 February 2018.

[37] Decree No. 9.602 of 8 December 2018.

[38] Decree No. 11.377 of 8 January 2023.

[39] The subnational government of the Federal District failed to act to contain the coup plotters, a fact that led the Supreme Court to describe Governor Ibaneis Rocha's conduct as 'wilfully omissive' in the face of an 'organisation that had been committing crimes for months, including in the Federal District'. In his decision to remove the governor from office, Justice Alexandre de Moraes highlighted that Rocha publicly defended so-called free political demonstrations in Brasília despite being fully aware that attacks had been planned on institutions and their members. The ruling pointed out, furthermore, that both the omission and connivance of the governor and the Secretary of Public Security with criminals who openly announced their violent acts against the constituted powers provided

Federal District was removed from office, but as the result of a court decision rather than federal intervention.

At the state level, there is no rule that blocks state constitutional reform on the occasion of state intervention in a municipality. As a result, a broader range of cases may be at issue, the majority of which are connected to generally poor financial management by municipalities. It is common to use state intervention in municipalities through a request from the state attorney-general to the state judiciary, always in cases of problems of non-payment and possible disrespect for the execution of a court decision.[40]

Why are there so few federal interventions in Brazil? One important factor is that the federal Constitution contains a clause that forbids the processing of amendments to the constitution in the National Congress while a federal intervention is taking place.[41] This creates a strong disincentive for the federal government to resort to this measure, especially when constitutional reforms are under discussion (as frequently happens in Brazil). This is not, however, the only reason for the low frequency of interventions. The exceptional nature of the institution, the strict procedural requirements imposed by the Constitution and the availability of alternative judicial and administrative mechanisms to address subnational issues all contribute to making federal intervention a rare occurrence. Interestingly, the most significant barrier is not a rule directly related to the need to safeguard the federal pact, but rather a restriction from another sector of the Constitution. This is the provision which blocks the constitutional reform process whenever an intervention is in place.

---

strong indication of public authorities' acquiescence with the crimes committed. These factors demonstrated that Rocha was sympathetic to the demonstrations by Bolsonaro's supporters, the very group responsible for the coup attempt and the acts of vandalism that destroyed public buildings. See 'Minister Alexandre de Moraes removes Ibaneis Rocha from the government of the DF' (9 January 2023) *STF Supremo Tribunal Federal* available at https://portal.stf.jus.br/noticias/verNoticiaDetalhe.asp?idConteudo=500254&ori=1 (accessed 20 January 1995).

40 A search in the São Paulo Court of Justice's case database for the procedural class 'municipal intervention' returned 108 cases. The vast majority were related to the non-payment of court-ordered debts and non-compliance with judicial decisions. Notably, only one case involved intervention due to a public health emergency in the municipality of Casa Branca, São Paulo. To verify this data, visit the court's official website and search for the term 'intervention in municipality' under the 'class' category. Available at https://esaj.tjsp.jus.br/cjsg/resultadoCompleta.do (accessed 20 January 2025).

41 Article 60, Brazilian 1988 Constitution.

I conducted a search on the Brazilian legislation portal[42] using the terms 'decree' and 'federal intervention' and retrieved 50 cases of federal intervention prior to 1988. Most of these decrees were issued primarily to preserve public order, with the majority enacted under the constitution immediately preceding the 1988 Constitution. Many of them involved direct federal intervention in municipalities, especially after the 1967 Constitution.

The 1988 Constitution brought two major innovations in federal intervention. First, it prohibited the federal government from directly intervening in municipalities and allotted this power to the states instead.[43] Second, it established that, while federal intervention is in effect, constitutional amendments can neither be discussed nor approved.[44] In my view, this latter restriction is the main reason why only 3 federal interventions have taken place under the 1988 Constitution, compared to the 50 interventions that took place in previous years. These figures provide strong evidence that the constitutional amendment restriction acts as a significant constraint on the use of federal intervention.

A number of other factors contribute significantly to this. The period of Brazilian re-democratisation following the 1988 Constitution came after the military dictatorship (1964–1984), marking a prolonged phase of constitutional and institutional stability under the same constitutional framework.[45] This enduring stability, combined with alternative legal mechanisms to address public order issues (such as the Guarantee of Law and Order, GLO),[46] helps to explain why federal intervention remains rare in Brazil and is employed almost exclusively in cases related to public order.

It is worth noting that the primary constraint on the use of federal intervention in Brazil is not a provision aimed at safeguarding the federal system, but rather a constitutional rule that suspends the amendment process whenever

---

42 See Câmara dos Deputados 'Legislation' available at https://www.camara.leg.br/legislacao and 'Search for legislation' available at https://www.camara.leg.br/legislacao/busca?tipo=Decreto&origem=Poder%20Executivo&geral=Decreto%20e%20Interven%C3%A7%C3%A3o%20Federal (accessed 30 January 2025).

43 Articles 34 and 35.

44 Article 60, section 1.

45 Notable exceptions include the 2016 parliamentary coup that removed President Dilma Rousseff through impeachment and the attempted coup on 8 January 2023 (events highly publicised in the world press).

46 Complementary Law No. 94 of 1999 establishes that the armed forces may be deployed to guarantee law and order within states at the request of any of the constitutional powers, in accordance with directives issued by the President of the Republic. However, this mechanism may be activated only once all other instruments for preserving public order and ensuring the safety of individuals and property, as outlined in article 144 of the Federal Constitution, have been exhausted.

a federal intervention is in effect in any state. Brazil has an analytical constitution, with hundreds of articles. As a result, it is common for politicians to promote the idea of constitutional reform as a kind of election campaign platform, and many are elected on the promise of constitutional reform. Decreeing intervention would make constitutional reforms unfeasible. The figures speak for themselves: in the 35 years since the 1988 Constitution, there have been only three federal interventions, whereas there have been more than 130 constitutional amendments (almost 4 per year).[47]

6. CONCLUSION

Federal intervention is an institution normally provided for federal countries with the purpose of protecting the federation itself. It is generally understood to be an extreme resource to suspend part of the autonomy of the subnational entity if and only if there is some dysfunction in the federative balance. This institution should never be used to undermine the autonomy of the subnational entity; it should not be used as an instrument of federal government policy regarding state governments. One of the key ideas in Brazil's federal system is the rejection of any hierarchical relationship between the federal government and subnational governments (their autonomy is recognised by article 18 of the 1988 Constitution). Because of this emphasis on autonomy, federal government can only override state governments in cases as expressly determined in the federal Constitution. The same caution applies to state governments in relation to municipal governments.

Brazil is a mononational federation, one which provides considerable autonomy for its subnational entities (whether states or municipalities). In the Brazilian case, the federation is well outlined in the 1988 Constitution, with the competences of the Union, states and municipalities clearly defined and detailed. The Constitution, including the Act of General and Transitional Provisions, contains more than 300 articles. This autonomy, in turn, cannot be used to exceed the limits imposed by the Constitution. As a traditional federation, Brazil in its Constitution provided for the institution of intervention in article 34, delimiting the grounds on which it could be used.

[47] The Brazilian political system places the Constitution at the centre of disputes between political parties. Since its promulgation in 1988, the Constitution has undergone 132 constitutional amendments, plus six revision amendments, totalling 138 amendments in 37 years. None of these amendments modifies just a single article (some alter entire chapters). It is a fact that presidential campaigns often use constitutional reforms (such as tax, pension and administrative reforms) as part of their campaign platforms, given that these matters are all addressed within the Brazilian Constitution.

While there are several grounds for intervention, each involve a set of norms for authorising federal intervention that seek to create a minimum standard of unity between the component parts of the federative pact. To that end, the minimum standard can be established from constitutional rules mentioned in this chapter (clear rules such as the one that determines intervention when states are not doing well financially or go more than two years without paying off debts). But we also have rules that are less precise. These rely on open concepts as grounds for federal intervention, linked to norms that define the need to protect democracy or public order through federal intervention. The fact that the only three interventions since the 1990s were based on public security demonstrates how the broader interpretative scope of such grounds facilitates their application.

There have been just three cases of federal intervention decreed in Brazil since the 1988 Constitution has been in force. All three cases concerned the need to preserve public order and security and involved issues related to non-violence as a value to be promoted and protected. The major reason why federal intervention is not used in a trivial way is the fact that the 1988 Constitution created a rule stating that the Constitution itself cannot be amended during federal intervention. Evidence of this is the fact that, before 1988, there were dozens of cases of federal intervention, and only in 1988 was there a rule prohibiting the passing of amendments when federal intervention is in force. In this way, the decree of federal intervention has the effect of freezing any constitutional amendment process. It turns out that the Brazilian Constitution is analytical and very extensive. It has been constantly subject to reform and amendment (more than 130 amendments in 37 years!). Decreeing an intervention means making it impossible for the federal government to change the constitutional text through coordination with its parliamentarians who form the basis of the government in the National Congress.

The reduced use of federal intervention in the post-1988 era can be attributed to the availability of the Guarantee of Law and Order (GLO). Under this mechanism the Armed Forces can support state military police forces in maintaining public order, as provided by Complementary Law No. 94 (1999). Finally, the prolonged period of institutional stability under the 1988 Constitution also contributes to the infrequent use of federal intervention.

Thus, all problems relating to states, whether non-compliance with laws or lack of security, have been resolved through means other than federal intervention in a natural and political process of dialogue and negotiation between central power and subnational entities.

Finally, it is important to note that, while the President of the Republic has the power to decree federal intervention in Brazil, significant checks are imposed on that power by other branches of government. When intervention is initiated at the President's discretion, it must be approved by the National

Congress. Additionally, intervention may be mandated by a decision of the Supreme Court. In such cases the President has no discretionary power, as he is bound to comply with the Court's ruling. These oversight mechanisms function as checks and balances, ensuring that federal intervention is not used to undermine the autonomy of subnational entities.

BIBLIOGRAPHY

Books

Calmon P *História do Brasil: As origens* (1500–1600) São Paulo: Companhia Editora Nacional (1951)
Machado RP *Brazilian History: Culture, society, politics 1500–2010* Cambridge: Cambridge Scholars Publishing (2017)
Vieira AN *Lenço vermelho de sangue: Um olhar sobre a Revolução Federalista de 1893* Curitiba: Editora Appris (2023)

Chapters in Books

Corrêa de Araújo ML 'Subnational constitutionalism in Brazil: The space of state constitutions for improving Brazilian federalism' in Popelier P, Delledonne G & Aroney N (eds) *Routledge handbook of subnational constitutions and constitutionalism* London: Routledge (2022)

Journal Articles

Corzo Sosa E, 'Consideraciones en torno al origen y evolución de la intervención federal en Argentina, Brasil y México' (2020) 120 (September–December) *Revista Española de Derecho Constitucional* 139–168
Gamper A 'Homogeneity and democracy in Austrian federalism: The Constitutional Court's ruling on direct democracy in Vorarlberg' (2003) 33(1) *Publius* 45–57
Graham R 'Landowners and the overthrow of the empire' (1970) 7(2) *Luso-Brazilian Review* 44–56
Liziero L 'Was there federalism in the Brazilian Empire? A case of contrast between federal state and federalism in 19th century' (2019) 2(2) *International Journal of Law and Public Administration* 41–7
Williams RF 'Teaching and Researching Comparative Subnational Constitutional Law' (2011) 115(4) *Penn State Law Review* 1109–31

Legislation

Complementary Law 97 of 9 June 1999
Constitution of Brazil, 1824
Constitution of Brazil, 1891
Constitution of Brazil, 1934
Constitution of Brazil, 1937

Constitution of Brazil, 1946
Constitution of Brazil, 1967
Constitution of Brazil, 1988
Decree No. 1 of 15 November 1889
Decree No. 11.377 of 8 January 2023
Decree No. 9.288 of 16 February 2018
Decree No. 9.602 of 8 December 2018

Internet Sources

'Minister Alexandre de Moraes removes Ibaneis Rocha from the government of the DF' (9 January 2023) *Supremo Tribunal Federal* available at https://portal.stf.jus.br/noticias/verNoticiaDetalhe.asp?idConteudo=500254&ori=1 (accessed 20 January 1995)

Brazilian Federal Senate (ed) *The Federal Senate and the 200 years of the independence of Brazil* Brazil: Federal Senate Special Curatorial Committee (2022) available at https://www2.senado.gov.br/bdsf/handle/id/600025 (accessed 1 March 2025)

Brazilian Federal Senate 'Anais da República' available at https://www25.senado.leg.br/web/atividade/anais/anais-da-republica (accessed 8 January 2025)

Câmara dos Deputados 'Legislation' available at https://www.camara.leg.br/legislacao (accessed 30 January 2025)

Câmara dos Deputados 'Search for legislation' available at https://www.camara.leg.br/legislacao/busca?tipo=Decreto&origem=Poder%20Executivo&geral=Decreto%20e%20Interven%C3%A7%C3%A3o%20Federal (accessed 30 January 2025)

Cornell Law School 'ArtIV.S4.1: Historical background on guarantee of Republican form of government' (n.d.) *Legal Information Institute* available at https://www.law.cornell.edu/constitution-conan/article-4/section-4/historical-background-on-guarantee-of-republican-form-of-government (accessed 3 January 2025)

De Gaspari FN 'Narrativas autoritárias: Reforma constitucional de 1926' (5 January 2021) *Consultor Juridico* available at https://www.conjur.com.br/2021-jan-05/gaspari-narrativas-autoritarias-reforma-constitucional-1926/ (accessed 13 January 2025)

Dirección Nacional del Sistema Argentino de Información Jurídica *Constituciones Argentinas: Compilación histórica y análisis doctrinario* 1st ed (November 2015) available at https://www.saij.gob.ar/docs-f/ediciones/libros/Constituciones_argentinas.pdf (accessed 11 January 2025)

Direct Action of Unconstitutionality ADI 6706-PA (2021) *Supremo Tribunal Federal Brazilian* available at https://portal.stf.jus.br/processos/detalhe.asp?incidente=6120455 (accessed 5 January 2025)

Viotti-Schlobach R *Homogeneity clauses in federal countries: A comparative analysis* (2019) available at https://www.mcgill.ca/law/files/law/2019-baxter_homogeneity-clauses_rafael-viotti-schlobach.pdf (accessed 22 October 2024)

Theses

De Moraes MR *A Reforma Constitucional de 1926: Análise das emendas ao artigo 6° da Constituição de 1891* (unpublished PhD thesis, Universidade de Brasília, 2018) 32 available at https://bdm.unb.br/bitstream/10483/23781/1/2018_MatheusRochaDeMoraes_tcc.pdf (accessed 2 December 2023)

Marques de Saes GA *A República e A Espada: A primeira década republicana e o florianismo* (unpublished Master's thesis, Universidade de São Paulo, 2005) 80 available at https://www.teses.usp.br/teses/disponiveis/8/8138/tde-28042006-181955/publico/Tese_-_Saes-Guillaume_Azevedo_Marques.pdf (accessed 6 July 2023)

4. Ethiopia: the use and abuse of intervention powers

Zemelak Ayele and Gosaye Berhanu

1. INTRODUCTION

On 3 August 2023, Yilkal Kefale, then president of the Amhara state, one of the constituent units of the Ethiopian federation, sent a letter to the country's Prime Minister Office requesting federal intervention in his state. In the letter, Kefale said that the deteriorating security situation in Amhara was causing a grave economic and humanitarian crisis that the state's regular law enforcement apparatus could not control. He asked the Prime Minister to take 'the necessary measure based on the appropriate constitutional and legal framework'.[1] The security situation to which Kefale referred had to do with the conflict that had broken out between, on the one hand, a militia group called the Fanno and, on the other, the state security forces and federal army.[2] The Council of

[1] 'Amhara regional state president calls for federal gov't intervention' (3 August 2023) *Borkena* available at https://borkena.com/2023/08/03/amhara-regional-state-president-calls-for-federal-govt-intervention/ (accessed 1 March 2025).

[2] The Fanno had fought on the side of the federal government in the two-year war between the latter and the Tigray state. After the Pretoria Peace Agreement was signed between the Tigray People's Liberation Front (TPLF) and the federal government in 2022, the Amhara state government, supposedly at the behest of the federal government, moved to disarm and disband the Fanno. This led to an armed confrontation between the Amhara Special Forces (ASF) and the Fanno. Matters worsened when the federal government decided that all state special forces should be disbanded and integrated into the federal army, the federal police or other federal or state security apparatuses. Some members of the ASF refused to disarm and joined the Fanno, which began attacking the military posts of the Ethiopian National Defence Force (ENDF). This militia even controlled, albeit briefly, major towns in the state, including Gonder, Debre Markos and Lalibela – hence the request for federal intervention.

Ministers (CoM) declared a state of emergency in Amhara soon after Kefale's request, which the House of Peoples' Representatives (HPR), the lower house of the federal parliament, in turn approved a few days later.[3]

This is perhaps the most publicised and debated federal intervention in an Ethiopian state in recent years, but it is only one of many. The federal government has intervened in all of the country's original nine states, mostly without their request or consent, in the process removing their heads of government and/or deploying the national army in the name of maintaining law and order. This raises several questions. Does the federal government have a constitutional power to intervene in a state? What are the substantive and procedural requirements that have to be fulfilled before a federal intervention in a state may take place? Can there be federal intervention in local government? Is state intervention in local government properly regulated? More widely, is the political practice in sync with the constitutional framework?

This chapter attempts to provide answers to these questions. It begins with a description of the Ethiopian federal system, followed by a discussion of the political rationale and constitutional and legislative framework for federal intervention in the states as well as state intervention in local government. It then discusses federal and state interventions as practised in Ethiopia.

2. ETHIOPIA'S DUAL FEDERAL SYSTEM

Two levels of government, the federal and the state, make up the Ethiopian federation.[4] In this dual federal system, each of the two levels of government has its own political and judicial organs, constitutionally enumerated functional competencies and sources of revenue.[5] The federal government has a bicameral parliament comprising the HPR and House of Federation (HoF). The HPR has 550 seats, the members of which are directly elected by the people,[6] and enjoys exclusive legislative power over federal matters. The upper house, the HoF, comprises representatives of the country's ethnic communities.[7] It has non-legislative functions, such as constitutional interpretation and determining the formula for the division of federal financial transfers among the states.[8]

---

[3] Endale A 'Clashes in the region puts the constitution at risk, says gov't' (5 August 2023) *The Reporter* available at https://www.thereporterethiopia.com/35816/ (accessed 1 March 2025).

[4] Article 50(1), Constitution of the Federal Democratic Republic of Ethiopia (FDRE), adopted in 1994.

[5] Article 50(2), FDRE Constitution.

[6] Article 54(1)–(3), FDRE Constitution.

[7] Article 61(1), FDRE Constitution.

[8] Article 62, FDRE Constitution.

The CoM is the highest executive organ of the federal government, while the federal Supreme Court is its highest judicial organ.[9] The Constitution created 9 states as the original constituent units of the federation, but the number of states increased to 12 after the division of the Southern Nations, Nationalities, and Peoples' Region (SNNPR) into four states.[10] Local government does not have explicit constitutional recognition, even though the Constitution implies that the states could establish a local government to manage intra-state ethnic diversity and/or to ensure the provision of basic services to citizens.[11] States have established a multitiered local government at zonal, *woreda* (city) and *kebele* (ward) levels. The *woreda* (in rural areas) and city administration (in urban areas), which have elected councils, form the most important tier of local government. Some multi-ethnic states have established ethnic-based local governments at the zonal level as ethnic zones and special *woredas* (*liyu woredas*).[12]

3. CONSTITUTIONAL RATIONALE FOR FEDERAL INTERVENTION

The Ethiopian federal system is a response to one of two major issues that dominated the country's past political discourse for almost six decades: the nationalities question. The demand for the redistribution of land, the other major issue – which the Ethiopian Student Movement of the 1960s propounded under the motto 'land to the tiller' – was more or less settled in the 1970s.[13] The Derg, the military junta that ruled the country from 1974 to 1991, nationalised and redistributed rural and urban lands. The question of nationalities had to wait for the Derg's ousting from power in the early 1990s before it found a constitutional response. At the heart of the question of nationalities was the

---

[9] Article 72, FDRE Constitution.

[10] The Constitution, in articles 50(3) and 78(3), allows sub-state ethnic minorities to form their own states if they wish to do so; three new states have been created based on the constitutional principle that allows internal secession for sub-state ethnic minorities. Each of the 12 states has a state council, an executive council (headed by a chief administrator or state president), and a judiciary with a state supreme court as the highest judicial organ at the state level. For a detailed discussion, see Ayele Z, Fuller B & Raleigh C 'Ethno-federalism and subnational conflicts in Ethiopia' (2023) *Civil Wars* 1.

[11] Ayele Z & Fessha Y 'The place and status of local government in federal states: The case of Ethiopia' (2012) 58(4) *African Today* 89.

[12] Ayele & Fessha (2012).

[13] Balsvik RR *Haile Selassie's students: The intellectual and social background to revolution, 1952–1974* East Lansing: Michigan State University (1985).

claim that Ethiopia was not a nation-state, as it portrayed itself, but a country of 'nations', many of which had enjoyed political and cultural independence before being coercively incorporated into it.[14] Advocates of the nationalities question insisted that Ethiopia acknowledge its diverse population and undergo territorial and institutional restructuring to enable its ethnic communities to exercise maximum self-governance at the subnational level. The Derg was not ready to respond fully to the nationality question despite ungrudgingly having responded to the land question. Ethnic armed groups, organised under the umbrella of the Ethiopian Peoples' Revolutionary Democratic Party (EPRDF), fought against the Derg in the name of the right to self-determination of the Ethiopian nationalities and emerged victorious in May 1991. Four years later, the EPRDF saw the constitutional entrenchment of a federal system which was designed primarily to respond to the age-old nationality question.

The federal system uses mainly territorial methods to manage ethnic diversity at the subnational level.[15] Initially, it had nine states, with boundaries demarcated along ethnic lines. This does not mean each state has an ethnically homogeneous population. Given that Ethiopia has more than 80 ethnic communities, doing so would not have been practical. Boundary demarcation ensured instead that, with a few exceptions, an ethnic community did not fall into more than one state. Five of the original nine states thus had an ethnic majority, while the rest of them did not. The Constitution allows each ethnic community to establish self-government either at the sub-state level or by means of its own state, regardless of the community's population size or economic context.[16] Hence, demands by certain ethnic communities for their own states resulted in three additional states.

Ethnic representation primarily determines the composition of federal political institutions. By design, the country's electoral system and constituency demarcation ensure equitable ethnic representation in the HPR.[17] The constitutional framers structured the HoF as a house of ethnic communities. It comprises representatives of such communities, and has powers to defend and promote their federal-level interests, including approving federal intervention and engaging in constitutional interpretation.[18] There is also a general constitutional principle that requires the CoM, the federal bureaucracy, the army and the like to have equitable ethnic representation.[19]

---

14 Fessha Y *Ethnic diversity and federalism: Constitution making in South Africa and Ethiopia* Farnham: Ashgate (2010).
15 Article 39(3), FDRE Constitution.
16 Article 39(3), FDRE Constitution.
17 Fessha (2010).
18 Articles 61 and 62, FDRE Constitution.
19 Article 39(3) and 87(1), FDRE Constitution.

During the drafting of the Constitution, there was heated debate on how to regulate federal intervention. As the Minutes of the Constituent Assembly show, the constitutional drafters sought to protect the subnational units from undue federal interferences.[20] They were, however, equally wary of the possibility of overzealous state politicians and ethnic nationalists using their subnational autonomy to undermine the federal equilibrium that the former sought to create.[21] The framers of the Constitution thus attempted to introduce a system of federal intervention that balances the need to protect the ethnically organised subnational units from federal overreach with the need to safeguard the federal equilibrium from radical state political actors. This raises the questions: What is the constitutional framework for federal intervention? How does the Constitution envisage the use of federal intervention to safeguard the federal system without unduly undermining the states' autonomy? The following sections provide answers to these and related questions.

4. INTERGOVERNMENTAL INTERVENTION: THE CONSTITUTIONAL FRAMEWORK

4.1 Federal Intervention in the States

The Constitution enjoins each level of government to respect the autonomy of the other. It provides that 'the states [shall] respect the powers of the federal government [and that] the federal government [shall] likewise respect the powers of the states'.[22] Intervention by one level of government in another is thus, as a rule, proscribed. Indeed, the rule requiring states to respect the autonomy of the federal government does not have any exceptions, whereas the principle preventing the federal government from intervening in states does. The Constitution provides substantive grounds for federal intervention, which are elaborated in Proclamation 359/2003, enacted by the HPR.[23]

The Constitution contains three grounds for federal intervention in states, even if it mentions the word 'intervention' only once in the context of defining the powers of the HoF.[24] It authorises the HoF to order a federal intervention

---

20 የኢትዮጵያ ሕገ መንግስት ጉባኤ ቃለ ጉባኤ ጥራዝ 5 (ኅዳር 21–24/1987), 12–13 (The Minutes of the Ethiopian Constitutional Assembly, Vol. 5 (30 November–3 December 1994; hereafter, 'The Minutes').

21 ኢትዮጵያ ሕገ መንግስት ጉባኤ ቃለ ጉባኤ ጥራዝ 5 (ኅዳር 21–24/1987), 12–13.

22 Article 50(8), FDRE Constitution.

23 System for the Intervention of the Federal Government in the Regions, Proclamation No. 359/2003, Federal Negarit Gazette of the FDRE.

24 Article 62(9), FDRE Constitution.

in a state when the latter endangers the constitutional order.[25] It does not define what constitutes 'endangering the constitutional order'. Proclamation 359/2003, which regulates federal intervention in a state in detail, lists acts that could endanger the constitution, albeit (again) without providing a precise definition of what endangering the constitutional order means. According to the proclamation, acts that endanger the constitutional order include 'armed uprising', resorting to violence to deal with disputes with another state or an ethnic community of another state and disturbing the peace and security of the federal government.[26] These become threats to the constitutional order when committed by, or with the participation or consent of, a state government.[27]

A state's failure to comply with a directive by the HPR enjoining it to take measures to cease violations of human rights also constitutes an act that endangers the constitutional order.[28] The proclamation seems to suggest that federal intervention is unwarranted if a state seeks to resolve disputes violently between endogenous ethnic communities, which makes no sense. Besides, it is unclear what counts as 'disturbing the peace and security of the federal government'. This is so vague a ground for federal intervention that it is open to abuse by the federal government.

As noted, the Constitution and Proclamation 359/2003 provide that human rights violations are a ground for federal intervention.[29] The Constitution implies that the human rights violations should involve violence and be so widespread that 'state authorities [cannot] arrest' in order to warrant a federal intervention'. It is unclear whether private individuals or state officials should be the culprit of the human right abuses for such abuses to warrant federal intervention. It is also unclear whether human rights violations that do not involve violence can be a ground of federal intervention. For instance, a failure of a state to provide basic services would have human rights implications, but it is unclear if the federal government could invoke this failure as a ground for intervening in the state. Proclamation 359/2003 provides that the violation of any constitutionally and legally protected rights may lead to federal intervention, implying that the violation of civil, political and socio-economic rights could give rise to such intervention.

The other ground for federal intervention is a breakdown of law and order which is beyond the control of a state's regular law enforcement agencies.[30] A request for a federal intervention must come from the authorities of a state

25 Article 62(9), FDRE Constitution.
26 Article 12, FDRE Constitution.
27 Article 12, FDRE Constitution.
28 Article 12(4), FDRE Constitution.
29 Article 55(16), FDRE Constitution.
30 Article 51(14), FDRE Constitution.

affected by breakdown of law and order.[31] The federal government cannot intervene without the state's request in the name of restoring law and order, unless (as discussed below) the breakdown in law and order becomes an emergency.

The last ground of intervention is the existence of an emergency situation, such as a foreign invasion, a breakdown of law and order, a natural disaster or an epidemic. Indeed, federal intervention in a state does not automatically follow a declaration of an emergency by the federal government unless there is a breakdown of law and order in the relevant state. Emergencies such as natural disasters or pandemics might not necessarily disrupt public order or national security. For instance, the federal government did not need to intervene in any state due to Covid-19, despite its declaring a national state of emergency in the name of controlling the spread of the pandemic. However, a breakdown of law and order leading to an emergency declaration could prompt a federal intervention if the severity of the problem is such that it endangers the constitutional order and cannot be 'controlled by the regular law enforcement agencies and personnel'.[32]

As discussed, the Constitution and the federal law on intervention provide that federal intervention may take place only in a context of violence, large-scale human rights abuse or a breakdown of law and order. It does not explicitly allow federal intervention in a state in a peaceful context, even if the state government is violating the Constitution and federal laws by commission or omission. This is also clear from the minutes of the constitutional drafting. To illustrate the situations that justify federal intervention, a member of the drafting committee mentioned the rise of a group called Al-Itihaad al-Islamiya, an armed group in what was then called Region 5 (now Somali state), and the ensuing military intervention by the transitional government of the time.[33]

It is easy to imagine circumstances where a state could violate its legal obligations despite there being no breakdown of peace and order. It may fail to administer properly because, for instance, the state council does not meet regularly or adopt budgets timeously, or because the state executive is dysfunctional for various reasons, leading to a total breakdown of public services. There could also be gross violations of fiscal rules and misappropriation of funds in a state. It seems the federal government cannot invoke these to intervene in a state. This appears to be the understanding of federal authorities. When the Federal Auditor-General reported gross misappropriation of funds in the Afar state, Meles Zenawi, the late prime minister, said the federal

31 Article 51(14), FDRE Constitution; article 4, Proclamation 359/2003.
32 Article 51(14), FDRE Constitution; article 4, Proclamation 359/2003.
33 The Minutes at 13.

government could not intervene in the states by invoking financial misconduct even if the latter 'burn their money'.[34] In other jurisdictions, such as South Africa and Kenya, these are explicitly stated grounds for federal (national) intervention in subnational governments. This is not the case in Ethiopia. Indeed, first on the list of the federal government's powers is its power (and obligation) to protect and defend the Constitution – and, as clearly stated in the preamble of Proclamation 359/2003, this underpins all federal interventions. The federal government's duty to defend and protect the Constitution extends beyond times of disorder.

One may hence argue that the federal government can, indeed must, intervene in a state if the latter acts in gross violation of the Constitution or cannot discharge its constitutional duty. However, a federal intervention should not be based on such abstract notions, and the grounds for intervention should be stated clearly and explicitly. At any rate, as the next section shows, the Constitution and the proclamation do not explain how the federal government would intervene unless the constitutional violation involves violence, a breakdown of law and order or large-scale human rights violations.

To recap, the 1995 Constitution recognises the need to balance state autonomy with federal intervention and seeks to regulate when and how the federal government can intervene in states. It provides three grounds for intervention – endangering the constitutional order, a deteriorating security situation and human rights violations – albeit without clearly and strictly defining what each phrase means. This allows the federal government to justify federal intervention in the states by characterising every state action and decision of which it disapproves as an action that endangers the constitutional order. The Constitution allows the states not to request or even to refuse federal intervention. It also gives the HoF the responsibility of preventing undue federal intervention and protecting the autonomy of the states.[35] Yet it contains provisions, such as those that allow it to declare a state of emergency, to eschew the need to secure the approval of the HoF before intervening in a state.

Moreover, having implied that responding to violence is the sole purpose of a federal intervention, the Constitution omits to consider legitimate grounds for intervention that may arise in a peaceful context, such as malfunctionality in a state government, breakdowns in service delivery or gross financial misconduct by state authorities. Put differently, the federal constitution does a poor job of regulating the grounds of federal intervention.

---

[34] *Ethiopian Reporter* (Amharic) (2022) 28(2356) at 58.

[35] Tewfik H *Transition to federalism: The Ethiopian experience* Ottawa: Forum of Federations (2010) at 21.

4.2 State Intervention in Local Government

Ethiopia's dual federal system places local government under the exclusive jurisdiction of the states. According to the country's constitutional design, there cannot be direct interaction between local government and the federal government. As such, there cannot be federal intervention in local government: only the states have the authority to intervene in local government.[36] However, other than Tigray, Oromia, and Benishangul-Gumuz, the states have not properly regulated state intervention in local government in their constitutions.

The Tigray state found itself in a constitutional impasse when its state government needed to intervene in some *woredas* and cities following political divisions in the TPLF, the regional ruling party, in the early 2000s.[37] It was to fill this constitutional gap that the state amended its constitution in 2006 and inserted grounds and procedures of state intervention in local government.[38] It also issued Proclamation 99 (2006) which, among other things, elaborated upon state intervention in local government.[39] For its part, the Benishangul-Gumuz state used a proclamation to regulate state intervention in *woredas*. In addition, state proclamations that establish urban local government (that is, city administrations) contain provisions allowing state intervention in cities within the states.

Grounds for state intervention in local government, as indicated in the state laws mentioned above, include acts endangering the constitutional order, failure to maintain peace and security and a local government's failure to exercise its legal and constitutional functions effectively.[40] A state may also intervene in a *woreda* or city in the event of misappropriation of funds or properties. The

---

36 For further discussion, see Ayele Z *Local government in Ethiopia: Advancing development and accommodating ethnic minorities* Baden-Baden: Nomos Verlagsgesellschaft (2014).

37 The divisions that pitted Meles Zenawi, the leader of the TPLF and then Prime Minister of the federal government, against various heavyweight politicians in the TPLF ended with the latter's expulsion from the party. Certain local authorities were supporters of those expelled, and the TPLF sought to remove them from power. However, the state constitution provided no clearly defined substantive ground and procedure for doing so.

38 Fiseha A (2019) 'Local level decentralisation in Ethiopia: Case study of Tigray Regional State' 13(1) *The Law and Development Review* 95 at 114.

39 The Tigray Regional State Proclamation to Strengthen Self-administration and to Determine the Functions and Powers of *Woreda* Administration, Proclamation No. 99/2006, Federal Negarit Gazette of the FDRE.

40 Articles 73(4) and 58(1), Tigray Regional State Constitution (2001); article 58(1), Tigray Regional State Proclamation 99 ('TRS Proclamation 99'); article 103(1), Benishangul-Gumuz Regional State Proclamation to Strengthen a

failure of a *woreda* executive council to convene a meeting for more than six months could also be a ground for state intervention in local government. A state may also take the violation by local authorities of its laws as a ground for intervention.[41] As was the case in Oromia, a state may intervene in a city if it believes that 'the operation of the city council poses a threat to the federal and regional state's constitution or [to the public interest], or where serious security problems or human right violations [occur]'.[42]

The grounds for state intervention in local government are numerous and not clearly defined, and thus local governments lack proper constitutional protection from undue state intervention. For instance, a failure to exercise a 'constitutional function', or the infringement of a law by a *woreda*, is overbroad and too ambiguously formulated as a ground of intervention: one could then invoke almost anything as an infringement of the law. This lack of specificity is likely to endanger a *woreda*'s autonomy.

5. PROCEDURES FOR INTERVENTION

5.1 Procedure for Federal Intervention in a State

The procedures that the federal government has to follow in order to intervene in states vary depending on the ground of intervention. Where it receives a report of human rights violations in a state, the HPR must first send an investigative team to inspect whether there is indeed large-scale human rights abuse in the state.[43] The report of the investigating team has to show whether there is concrete evidence of widespread human rights abuse within the state, identify those who are responsible for the problem, enumerate efforts that the state made and measures it took to control the problem and assess whether the state could deal with the problem on its own. If such investigations reveal there is a widespread human rights abuse that the state cannot control, the HPR calls a joint meeting of the HoF and HPR to deliberate on the matter.[44] The HPR then gives a directive to the state authorities on the measures they must take to address the problem. Such directives constitute a federal intervention, even though perhaps the least intrusive method of intervention. The Prime Minister bears the responsibility to 'follow up and ensure the implementation [of the

Decentralised Woreda Level Administration, Proclamation No. 86/2010, Lissane High Gazeta ('BGRS Proclamation 86').

41 Article 58(1), TRS Proclamation 99; article 103(1), BGRS Proclamation 86.

42 Article 50, A Proclamation to Revise Oromia Regional State Cities Establishment, Proclamation No. 195/2015.

43 Article 55(16), FDRE Constitution.

44 Article 55(16), FDRE Constitution.

measure the HPR adopts]'.[45] As mentioned, failure by the state to comply with such directives would constitute an act or omission that endangers the constitutional order, hence warranting a more intrusive form of federal intervention.

In case of a breakdown of law and order, the state council or state executive council could request that the Prime Minister initiate a federal intervention.[46] The Prime Minister may then deploy the federal military and other security forces to enforce law and order in the state.[47] The Amhara state president (to refer to the episode recounted at the start of this chapter) made the request for federal intervention on the basis of this substantive ground. The proclamation does not explicitly authorise the Prime Minister to initiate a federal intervention in the name of restoring law and order in a state in the absence of a request from the state. Besides, it specifies that the Prime Minister must terminate federal intervention in the state if the security situation improves or if the state requests termination.[48] This means that the state can request an end to federal intervention to restore law and order even if the underlying issue remains unresolved. This in turn suggests that the intervention could occur in the first place only if the state, having declared that the problem is beyond its capacity, requests federal intervention.

The federal government can, however, circumvent the need to receive a request for a federal intervention by declaring a state of emergency. This was precisely what Gedion Timotewos, the Minister of Justice, said in Parliament when defending the declaration of a state of emergency in the Amhara state.[49] Asked whether the Amhara state president could request federal intervention without securing the consent of the Amhara state council or the state's executive council, the Minister replied that the federal government has the power to declare a state of emergency and intervene in the state even without the state president's request.[50]

The other issue is whether the HoF has any role, in terms of authorising federal intervention, when a state requests federal intervention. The law is silent on this issue. It simply allows the Prime Minister to order or end federal intervention when a state so requests. The involvement of the HoF in authorising a

---

45 Article 74(3), FDRE Constitution.

46 Article 4, Proclamation 359/2003.

47 Article 5, Proclamation 359/2003.

48 Article 5(5), Proclamation 359/2003.

49 'በሕዝብ ተወካዮች ምክር ቤት አባላት ሰፊ ውይይት የተካሄደበት የአስቸኳይ ጊዜ አዋጅ ጸደቀ (The state of emergency was approved by members of the HPR after discussion)' available at https://www.youtube.com/watch?v=MkgpPjq_bA0&ab_channel=EBC (accessed 1 March 2025).

50 'በሕዝብ ተወካዮች ምክር ቤት አባላት ሰፊ ውይይት የተካሄደበት የአስቸኳይ ጊዜ አዋጅ ጸደቀ (The state of emergency was approved by members of the HPR after discussion)'.

federal intervention is meant to protect the states from undue federal intervention. The logic seems to be that, as a rule, the federal intervention is initiated by a request from a state, making the involvement of the HoF less than relevant.

The HoF plays a key role when an accusation against a state of acts endangering the constitutional order prompts federal intervention. The HoF can order an investigation when informed by the HPR, the CoM or another interested organ of an act or omission endangering the constitutional order.[51] The investigation report must show whether concrete evidence exists proving the alleged act and present various options for addressing it. The HoF may order a federal intervention if it deems this appropriate.[52] The method of intervention may include deploying federal forces and/or dissolving the state government and establishing an interim administration.[53] The interim administration, which would have a life-span of two and a half years, would be responsible for bringing to justice the state officials and others who are involved in the act endangering the constitutional order and restoring the constitutional order.[54] It should be noted that intervention due to human rights violations and breakdown of law and order does not always lead to the dissolution of a government since the state authorities might not have direct involvement in the acts. 'Endangering the constitutional order' assumes active involvement on the part of state authorities in the acts that threaten the constitutional order, and hence leads to the state government's dissolution.

A further issue is whether there are mechanisms for preventing or aborting undue or unconstitutional federal interventions. The HoF presumably plays an important role before and after ordering a federal intervention where that intervention addresses an act endangering the constitutional order. It has the responsibility of preventing the federal executive from intervening in a state in the absence of a ground warranting an intervention; it also has the authority to receive periodic reports from the Prime Minister on the process and effect of the federal intervention. Furthermore, the HoF can order the federal government to cease its intervention if the grounds for the intervention are no longer extant. To defend its autonomy, a state can request the termination of a federal intervention that the HoF has initiated.

5.2 Procedure for State Intervention in Local Government

Existing state laws that regulate state intervention in local government provide the suspension or dissolution of a *woreda* or city council as the only method

---

51 Article 62(9), FDRE Constitution; article 13, Proclamation 359/2003.

52 Article 13(3), Proclamation 359/2003.

53 Article 14.

54 Article 14(3).

of intervention, regardless of the grounds of intervention.[55] The state council may suspend a *woreda* or city council and order an investigation into whether the alleged grounds of intervention exist. If the investigation shows that there is a ground for intervention, the state council may order the dissolution of the *woreda* or city council and authorise the state executive to appoint an interim administrator to be in charge of the *woreda* for a maximum of one year. The interim administrator would not exercise any legislative function and would serve only to enforce existing laws.[56]

It is not justifiable to dissolve a *woreda* or city council for every alleged failure to exercise a constitutional function. State authorities could well interpret any minor legal infraction by local authorities as a 'failure to exercise a constitutional function' and order the dissolution of a local council. This not only undermines local autonomy but also wastes time and resources in holding new elections. Before resorting to dissolving a *woreda* council, the state could employ other, less intrusive methods of intervention, such as assuming the function of a *woreda* or city. Here, the state takes over the responsibility of providing the services that a *woreda* or city fails to provide without the need to dissolve the *woreda* council. As a comparative example, a method of intervention in South Africa is for a senior level of government to assume some of the local government's executive powers. This does not require the dissolution of municipal councils, and yet ensures uninterrupted service delivery in ailing municipalities.[57]

6. MEASURES TAKEN IN FEDERAL INTERVENTIONS

The measures the federal government may take during an intervention depend on the nature of the grounds of intervention. Where the ground for intervention is a deteriorating security situation, the federal government deploys its security forces.[58] These forces thus undertake measures to restore peace and order. This includes bringing to justice those responsible for the deteriorating security situation.[59] Where the ground for intervention is an act of a state that endangers the constitutional order, there are two measures the federal

---

55 Article 50(2), A Proclamation to Revise Oromia Regional State Cities Establishment Proclamation No. 195/2015; article 74(4), Tigray Regional State Constitution; article 103, BGRS Proclamation 86.

56 See Ayele (2014).

57 Steytler N & De Visser J *Local government law of South Africa* South Africa: LexisNexis (2007).

58 Articles 5 and 51(14), Proclamation 359/2003.

59 Article 5(4), Proclamation 359/2003.

government applies. The first is to avert the danger by deploying its security forces;[60] the second is dismissing the highest executive body and the state council, and establishing a provisional administration.[61] This is, arguably, constitutionally suspect, as the latter is not explicitly provided in the Constitution.

The measures that the federal government applies when the ground for intervention is violation of human rights differ from those in the case of the two previous grounds. The HPR and HoF, as the organs vested with the power to intervene when there is violation of human rights, have the power only to issue a directive to the state in which the alleged human rights violation is occurring.[62] The directive sets out, inter alia, what measures the state is supposed to take or refrain from in order to arrest the human rights violation in the state, as well as the measures it has to bring those involved in the violation to justice.[63]

7. POLITICAL AND LEGAL SAFEGUARDS

The FDRE Constitution is silent on the political review mechanism for federal intervention. It is instead the proclamation that specifies some of the political checks and controls on federal intervention.[64] The power to authorise the federal executive to intervene when a state engages in an act that endangers the constitutional order is vested in the HoF; in turn, the federal executive has the duty to submit a report in this regard to the HoF every three months.[65] Moreover, the HoF retains the power to send its team to oversee the implementation of the intervention, as well as the power to give directive corrective measures to be taken by the federal executive.[66] Thus, the HoF oversees the implementation of the intervention it authorised. As one of the highest bodies within the federal government, however, the HoF's decision to authorise intervention is not subject to checks by any other organ, leaving the framework for intervention in Ethiopia without any political mechanism for reviewing the proper use of federal intervention.

As intervention on the ground of a deteriorating security situation is based on the consent of the state concerned, the decision to intervene is made by the federal executive. Neither the HPR nor the HoF is involved in approving or terminating the intervention. The federal executive, however, has the duty to

60 Article 14(2)(a), Proclamation 359/2003.
61 Article 14(2)(b), Proclamation 359/2003.
62 Articles 11 and 55(16), Proclamation 359/2003.
63 Article 11, Proclamation 359/2003.
64 Meaning Proclamation 359/2003.
65 Article 16, Proclamation 359/2003.
66 Article 16(3) Proclamation 359/2003.

submit reports to the HPR.[67] As it is the least intrusive of all the grounds of intervention and the consequence is only giving a directive to the state, there are no mechanisms for political review when the ground for intervention is violation of human rights.

The framework for intervention is also deficient from the perspective of providing a robust constitutional check on intervention. This is largely because it is the HoF, rather than the courts, which has the final responsibility for constitutional review. The HoF – which plays a major role in two of the three grounds of intervention, authorising the intervention either exclusively (where the ground for intervention is an act that endangers the constitutional order) or jointly with the HPR (where the ground for intervention is violation of human rights) – is responsible for entertaining constitutional challenges to federal intervention. Since this means that any constitutional challenge to federal intervention will have to be submitted to the HoF, it puts the House in the position of being in charge of determining the constitutionality of its own decision. While the courts may have a role to play in checking federal intervention, their exclusion from constitutional review and their duty to refer a matter that involves a constitutional issue to the Council of Constitutional Inquiry (within the HoF) appears to have crippled them from taking an active role in providing a judicial check on federal intervention.

8. THE POLITICS OF FEDERAL INTERVENTION

Nearly three decades have passed since Ethiopia adopted the 1995 Constitution establishing a federal system. In that time, there have been too many state interventions in local government to describe here. States' authorities routinely pass instructions, redraw *woreda* boundaries, remove elected *woreda* officials and take other interventionist measures, often for political reasons.[68] This section will thus focus instead on federal interventions in states.

The federal government has intervened at least once in all of Ethiopia's original nine states, with the Somali, Gambella, Benishangul, Oromia and Amhara states in particular having been subjected to numerous federal interventions. However, the August 2023 intervention in the Amhara state was perhaps the only federal intervention that came close to adhering to the constitutional procedure for such intervention: as mentioned in the introduction to this chapter, the state president asked for a federal intervention and the federal government responded in the affirmative. All the other federal interventions fall into three categories: those that followed a declaration of a state of emergency; those

67 Article 6, Proclamation 359/2003.
68 Fiseha (2019).

based on constitutional grounds but involving a constitutionally skewed procedure; and those based on grounds that are provided neither in the Constitution nor Proclamation 359/2003.

8.1 Federal Intervention by Declaring a State of Emergency

The federal government has declared a state of emergency seven times since the adoption of the Constitution in 1995, with six of them having involved federal intervention in a subnational unit. At the time of writing, the most recent state of emergency is the one which it declared in the Amhara state in September 2023; as for the first emergency declaration, it was meant to contain post-election violence in 2005, but was not declared according to the constitutional procedure. Prime Minister Meles Zenawi simply appeared on state television and declared a one-month state of emergency, announcing that, to restore law and order, he had placed all security forces, police and local militias under a single command accountable to him.[69] The HPR did not approve, and nor was it asked to approve, the state of emergency.

The states of emergency in 2016 (lasting from October 2016 to August 2017) and 2018 (coming barely six months after the expiry of the 2016 emergency) were declared so as to contain the breakdown of law and order stemming from anti-regime protests in the states of Oromia and, later, Amhara.[70] It should be noted that the federal government had already deployed the army in Oromia, given that the protests began a year prior to the declaration of the emergency, and that during this time the army reportedly killed dozens of civilians in attempting to contain the protests.[71] The Oromia state did not officially request a federal intervention, and nor was it sanctioned by the HoF. It was after the Irrecha incident[72] that the federal government formally declared a state of

---

69 Degiffie Z *The architecture and use of emergency powers: The case of Ethiopia from 1995 to 2020* Addis Ababa: Konrad-Adenauer-Stiftung (2022).

70 Shaban ARA 'Ethiopia declares 6 months state of emergency over Oromia protests' (9 December 2019) *Africa News* available at https://www.africanews.com/2016/10/09/ethiopia-declares-6-months-state-of-emergency-over-oromia-protests// (accessed 1 March 2025).

71 Shaban ARA 'Ethiopia activists activate shutdown in Oromia to protest emergency rule' (5 March 2018) *Africa News* available at https://www.africanews.com/2018/03/05/ethiopia-activists-activate-shutdown-in-oromia-to-protest-emergency-rule// (accessed 1 March 2025).

72 This refers to the confrontation between security forces and youth attending the 2016 Irrecha celebration – a traditional Oromo holiday – which resulted, as admitted by the government, in the death of 55 people. See Human Rights Watch '"Fuel on the fire": Security forces response to the 2016 Irrecha cultural festival'

emergency; according to Haile Mariam Dessalegn, then Prime Minister, this was necessary 'to reverse the danger posed by destabilising forces undermining the safety of the people and security and stability of the country'.[73] A so-called Command Post was established: composed of the Prime Minister, the Minister of Defence, the federal police commissioner and state police commissioners, this body effectively put the state police under federal command.[74]

The CoM declared another state of emergency in February 2018, just six months after the expiry of the 2016 state of emergency, following Haile Mariam's resignation as Prime Minister. The proclamation was entitled '[a] state of emergency proclamation issued to defend the constitution and the constitutional order from threat', which implies that there was a threat to the constitutional order.[75] The preamble also states that the state of emergency was necessary since ethnic-based attacks had been committed, private property looted and destroyed and the public peace disturbed, all of which endangered the constitutional order.

As defined in the proclamation, the constitutional order is endangered when there is state-sponsored violence. However, it was not mentioned in the proclamation if any particular state supported the violence. Besides, when the ground of intervention is the existence of a threat to the constitutional order, the HoF is expected to play a central role in authorising federal intervention without even the need to declare a state of emergency. However, the HoF played no role here, and it was only the HPR that approved the state of emergency. Further, many argued that the motion to approve the state of emergency declared by the CoM did not receive the required two-thirds majority vote in the HPR.[76]

(20 September 2017) available at https://www.hrw.org/report/2017/09/20/fuel-fire/security-force-response-2016-irreecha-cultural-festival (accessed 1 March 2025).

73 Embassy of Ethiopia 'Press Release: State of Emergency declared in Ethiopia' (10 October 2016) *Ethiopian Embassy* available at https://ethiopianembassy.be/press-release-state-of-emergency-declared-in-ethiopia/ (accessed 1 March 2025).

74 Article 6, State of Emergency Proclamation for the Maintenance of Public Peace and Security Implementation Council of Ministers Regulation No. 391/2016, Federal Negarit Gazette of the FDRE.

75 State of Emergency for the Maintenance of Public Peace and Security Council of Ministers Proclamation No.1/2016 Ratification Proclamation No. 984/2016, Federal Negarit Gazette of the FDRE.

76 *Addis Standard*, a private news website, posted footage which showed Abadula Gemeda, then speaker of the HPR, stating that 'at the end of the session … 346 parliamentarians had voted in favour'. This did not amount to a two-thirds majority. However, state media reported that the motion was supported by 395 members of HPR and that the speaker made a minor arithmetical error when calculating the votes. In an interview on Ethiopian television, the speaker also apologised for the error. However, this sparked major controversy, with many political

In any case, the federal government deployed federal police and army in different states, in particular Oromia and Amhara. It also put state security organs under the command of the Command Post, which was made up exclusively of federal authorities, including the deputy prime minister, the Minister of Defence, the Chief of Staff of the Ethiopian National Defense Force (ENDF), the head of the intelligence agency and the federal police commissioner.

The federal government declared two emergencies in relation to the war in Tigray. The first was imposed in November 2020, immediately after the 2020 civil war broke out, while the second was declared a year later. The Prime Minister appeared on television on the night of 3 November 2020 and, having accused the TPLF of attacking the ENDF, ordered the army to take what were then dubbed 'law enforcement' measures. On 4 November 2020, the CoM declared a six-month state of emergency in Tigray, which Parliament immediately approved.[77] A State of Emergency Task Force was established under the chair of the Chief of Staff of the ENDF, while 'all military and law enforcement forces that are deployed to implement the state of emergency' were brought together under a single 'command structure'. The task force was authorised to disarm the Tigray armed forces, impose curfews and detain those it 'suspects [of] taking part in illegal activities that endanger the constitutional order'.

After taking control of Mekelle, the capital of Tigray state, the federal government issued a regulation (479(2020)) establishing an interim administration in Tigray state.[78] The regulation referred to the intervention clause in the Constitution.[79] The implication was that the federal government acted as if it

---

actors claiming that the state of emergency, along with all measures taken on the basis of it, were unconstitutional. See Maasho A 'Dispute over Ethiopia emergency rule vote after footage posted online' (4 March 2018) *Reuters* available at https://www.reuters.com/article/us-ethiopia-politics/dispute-over-ethiopia-emergency-rule-vote-after-footage-posted-online-idUSKCN1GE1XJ/ (accessed 1 March 2025); Abera E 'House speaker Abadula Gemeda apologizes for erring vote counting on state of emergency as decision sparks fresh protests' (4 March 2018) *Addis Standard* available at https://addisstandard.com/news-house-speaker-abadula-gemeda-apologizes-erring-vote-counting-state-emergency-decision-sparks-fresh-protests/ (accessed 1 March 2025).

[77] Voice of America 'Ethiopia declares emergency after attack on federal military base' (4 November 2020) https://web.archive.org/web/20250308054929/https://www.voanews.com/a/africa_ethiopia-declares-emergency-after-attack-federal-military-base/6197965.html (accessed 1 March 2025).

[78] A Regulation Concerning the Established Provisional Administration in Tigray National Region Regulation No. 479/2020, Federal Negarit Gazette of the FDRE.

[79] Articles 62(9) and 14(2)(b) of Proclamation 359/2003.

intervened in Tigray on the grounds that the latter 'threatened the constitutional order' and on the HoF's order.

The federal government announced the second emergency in November 2021 after the TPLF offensive dislodged the federal army from Mekelle and marched southward. The federal government declared the emergency in the name of averting 'the threat against national existence and sovereignty', even though this is not on the list of grounds for intervention or for declaring a state of emergency. The war in Tigray was in any case concluded after the TPLF and the federal government signed a peace deal (the Pretoria Agreement) in November 2022. The two parties agreed to the establishment of an interim administration in which the TPLF and other political actors in the Tigray state would be represented.[80] This implied an agreement to dissolve the state council that had been established following the election Tigray unilaterally held in September 2020. Regulation 533(2023), which the CoM issued to establish the Tigray Interim Administration, explicitly states that the interim administration was established pursuant to the peace deal as well to the intervention clause in the Constitution and the HoF's decision and order to the same effect.[81]

As is clear from the above, the federal government routinely declares emergencies to intervene in states; it does so even when it could intervene on other grounds. For instance, the federal government did not need to declare an emergency in the Amhara state to intervene there since its president had already invited it to intervene. The federal government seems to choose to use a declaration of emergency to intervene in states because this allows it wide authority to restrict personal freedoms. It also picks mixes and matches different grounds for and methods of intervention upon declaring an emergency. For instance (as happened in the case of Tigray), after declaring an emergency, it will invoke the existence of a threat against the constitutional order so as to clear the way to dissolution of the state government.

8.2 Interventions based on Constitutionally Undefined Grounds

As mentioned, the Constitution envisages federal intervention only in times of violence and disorder that threaten the constitutional order or stand to result in the widespread violation of human rights. However, the federal government

80 Article 10(1), Agreement for Lasting Peace through a Permanent Cessation of Hostilities between the Government of the Federal Democratic Republic of Ethiopia and the Tigray People Liberation Front (TPLF) (Pretoria, 2 November 2022) available at https://igad.int/wp-content/uploads/2022/11/Download-the-signed-agreement-here.pdf (accessed 1 March 2025).

81 A Regulation Establishing an Inclusive Interim Administration in the Tigray Regional State Regulation No. 533/2023, Federal Negarit Gazette of the FDRE.

is seen intervening in states' daily activities through actions such as issuing instructions to state authorities as to what they must or must not do, sending federal agents to the states to 'advise' them or appointing or removing the heads of state governments in the absence of violence or disorder.[82] Interventions like these have been the hallmark of the Ethiopian federal experience for the past 30 years. For instance, the federal government enforced leadership change in the Somali state (without officially dissolving the state government).[83] The Somali state has thus had 13 presidents, including the current one. All of them, barring the current president and his predecessor, remained in office for at most three years; one president had a tenure of just 14 days. These changes were not a result of democratic alternation in leadership but ones enforced by the federal government.[84]

In May 2020, due to Covid-19, the federal government decided to postpone the sixth general election to Parliament and state councils, which was supposed to have been held before 5 October 2020. The TPLF maintained that the postponement was unconstitutional and declared that it would establish a state election commission and unilaterally hold elections within the Tigray state. This was before the war between the Tigray state and the federal government began. The speaker of the HoF first issued a warning to the Tigray state government to refrain from holding an election while the latter was making preparations for the elections (which itself is a form of intervention). He maintained that only the National Election Board of Ethiopia (NEBE) had the power to administer elections and that the decision of the Tigray state to establish a state election commission and hold elections would be tantamount to 'endangering the constitutional order' and hence courting federal intervention.[85] The Tigray state went ahead with the election, which was held on 9 September 2020 and saw the TPLF declared victorious.

---

[82] Fessha Y 'A federation without federal credentials: When politics trumps law' in *Between failure and redemption, the future of the Ethiopian social contract*: *Proceedings of a convening of scholars on Ethiopia's constitutional future* Evanston, IL, USA: Northwestern Roberta Buffett Institute for Global Affairs and Northwestern University Libraries (2022) 143 at 145–149 available at https://hrp.law.harvard.edu/wp-content/uploads/2023/02/pp.-143-156.pdf (accessed 1 March 2025).

[83] Samatar AI 'Ethiopian federalism: Autonomy versus control in the Somali region' (2004) 25(6) *Third World Quarterly* 1131.

[84] Hagmann T & Khalif MH 'State and politics in Ethiopia's Somali region since 1991' (2008) 6 *Bildhaan* 26.

[85] 'የፌዴሬሽን ምክር ቤት የትግራይ ክልል መንግስትን አስጠነቀቀ (The House of Federation warns the Tigray state government)' (30 July 2020) *Ethiopia Insider* available at https://ethiopiainsider.com/2020/1452/ (accessed 1 March 2025).

The HoF, however, held that the Tigray election had no legal effect.[86] Adem Farah, then speaker of the HoF, said that by conducting what he called an illegal election, the Tigray state had 'violated the constitution and there were enough grounds to take constitutional measures', including ordering federal intervention in the form of deploying the ENDF, dissolving the state government, and establishing an interim administration in the state.[87] In any case, the Tigray state rejected this, arguing that it was not bound by the 'laws, directives, and regulations [of] the federal government after its current term in office came to an end on 05 October 2020'.[88] The HoF finally ordered the federal government to sever relations with the Tigray state government and suspend fiscal transfers. It also stated that, for the purpose of ensuring the continued provision of basic public services, the federal government should commence direct interaction with local authorities in Tigray.[89]

The HoF's order to the federal government to sever relations with Tigray and halt financial transfers to the latter indeed constitutes federal intervention. However, these measures were constitutionally suspect, not to mention ineffective in convincing the TPLF to change its course of action.[90] 'Holding illegal elections' is not on the list of acts that threaten the constitutional order. Indeed, it entails the involvement of a state in an illegal or unconstitutional conduct, but it does not necessarily involve violence as required by the constitution and the law on federal intervention. Severing ties with an offending state is not a method of intervention envisaged in the Constitution. Moreover, it is not an

---

86 'House of Federation votes Tigray regional election contravenes the federal constitution, non-binding & non-applicable' (5 October 2020) *Addis Standard* available at https://addisstandard.com/news-house-of-federation-votes-tigray-regional-election-contravenes-federal-constitution-non-binding-non-applicable/ (accessed 1 March 2025).

87 Ekubamichael M 'HoF speaker says establishing transitional gov't, dispatching fed. security forces in Tigray among constitutional options' (2 October 2020) *Addis Standard* available at https://addisstandard.com/news-hof-speaker-says-establishing-transitional-govt-dispatching-fed-security-forces-in-tigray-among-constitutional-options/ (accessed 1 March 2025).

88 Ekubamichael (2 October 2020).

89 'Federal government severs relationships with the Tigray state government' (7 October 2020) *Fana Broadcasting Corporate* available at https://www.fanabc.com/english/federal-govt-severs-relationship-with-tigray-regional-state/ (accessed 1 March 2025).

90 Ayele Z 'Far-sighted federal solidarity, not power politics and legalism, is needed to solve Tigray dispute' (9 October 2020) *Ethiopia Insight* available at https://www.ethiopia-insight.com/2020/10/09/far-sighted-federal-solidarity-not-power-politics-and-legalism-is-needed-to-solve-tigray-dispute/ (accessed 1 March 2025).

effective method to deal with an act of a state that endangers the constitutional order.

As mentioned, the above interventions (warning state authorities, removing state presidents, suspending fiscal transfers) did not involve the deployment of federal troops or police and are thus not the kind of federal intervention which the Constitution envisages. They are federal interventions, nevertheless, since they have the effect of constraining states' autonomy.

8.3 Interventions that Skewed Constitutional Procedures

The federal government has intervened in all states (except Tigray) in the name of maintaining law and order, to this end deploying the federal army or federal police, yet without following the intervention procedure or declaring a state of emergency. It deployed its military in the Somali state several times in the name of restoring peace and order. Most recently, federal troops were deployed in Jigjiga, the capital of the Somali state, briefly controlling the state government offices (including the state council and the presidential office) and arresting Adi Illey, the then president of the state. What triggered the federal intervention were riots, looting and attacks on non-Somali residents of Jigjiga. However, the state government did not declare that it was unable to control the problem, and nor did it invite federal intervention. Indeed, it was claimed that the then state president, who was unhappy with the oil-revenue division scheme, was behind the riots and even attempting to have the state secede from Ethiopia.[91] If this were the cause for the federal intervention, the federal government must have sought an authorisation from the HoF that never took place.

There is an ongoing war in parts of the Oromia state between the federal government and a rebel group called the Oromo Liberation Army (OLA). The war began in 2019 when the military wing of the Oromo Liberation Front (OLF) refused to disarm, while the political wing agreed to take part in a peaceful political process.[92] The ENDF has been conducting military operations in Oromia, with the Oromia special police also involved in them. Here, the federal government did not invoke any of the grounds of interventions mentioned above when conducting these military operations; it did not declare a state of emergency in the Oromia state, or parts of the state, in the name of dealing with the threat the OLA poses to the constitutional order; and the HoF did not provide express consent for the intervention.

---

91 'Violence as troops deploy in Ethiopia's Somali region' (4 August 2018) *BBC* available at https://www.bbc.com/news/world-africa-45070213 (accessed 1 March 2025).

92 Endeshaw D 'OLF politics, military splits' (6 April 2019) *The Reporter* available at https://www.thereporterethiopia.com/7750/ (accessed 1 March 2025).

In a similar vein, there have been several federal interventions in inter-state boundary areas aimed at thwarting inter-state conflict. The federal government has on several occasions deployed federal troops in the border areas of the Somali and Oromia states when the two states have used their special forces to attack each other.[93] The army was also deployed in the Afar and Somali border areas to control an armed conflict between the two states.[94] It is unclear on what constitutional basis these interventions were ordered, since none of the constitutional procedures for federal interventions were followed.

The federal government also deployed its forces in Oromia after a riot erupted in the state in October 2019 when Jawar Mohammed, an Oromo activist and politician, announced on social media that his house was surrounded by federal security forces and that his security detail had been removed. This led to a riot in the Oromia state in which non-Oromos were targeted for violent attack. In reaction, the federal government deployed the army in some parts of the state. According to a statement by the ENDF, 'the Oromia state government had asked them to intervene and … army units had thus been deployed in the region to maintain law and order'.[95] It appears that the request for intervention was informal and directed at the army rather than the Prime Minister, as required by the intervention law.

It should be noted, though, that at the moment Mohammed posted his statement on Facebook on the night of 23 October 2019, Oromo youth known as Qerro began wreaking havoc in different towns in Oromia, including the capital, Addis Ababa, and that dozens of people were reportedly killed.[96] The state police were either unable or unwilling to stop the violence; this seems to be why, in the interests of swift action, the state request went to the army rather than the Prime Minister, who was out of the country at the time.

9. CONCLUSION

The constitutional framework governing federal intervention in states lacks clarity and opens the door for undue federal intervention. Besides, the institutions that are supposed to avert illegal intervention (especially the HoF) are too weak to prevent the federal government from engaging in illegal interventions

---

93 Endeshaw (6 April 2019).

94 'Ethiopia intervenes in the Somali-Afar conflict' *Mustaqbal Media* available at https://mustaqbalmedia.net/en/ethiopia-intervenes-in-somali-afar-conflict/amp/ (accessed 1 March 2025).

95 Tadesse G 'Ethiopia: In troubled Oromia areas' (25 October 2019) *AA* available at https://www.aa.com.tr/en/africa/ethiopia-army-deployed-in-troubled-oromia-areas/1626278 (accessed 1 March 2025).

96 Tadesse (2019).

in the states or to enforce the termination of illegal federal intervention. Potential grounds for federal intervention exist, such as financial misconduct and a state government's failure to govern properly; however, these do not have clearly defined methods of intervention. Instead, the political practice shows that the federal government often conducts interventions without heeding the constitutional rules governing federal intervention.

This is so partly because the framers of the Constitution borrowed rules of federal intervention that were designed for functioning federal systems, where it is assumed that incidents requiring intervention would be exceptionally rare. Federal interventions in functioning countries usually address less intense problems; high-intensity incidents are not typical. As such, there is a mismatch in Ethiopia between the legal framework governing federal interventions and the incidents that give rise to federal intervention.

Certain federal interventions, even though constitutionally suspect, were not totally unjustified when seen in the overall context in which the federal system operates. First, this is a context where the federal government does not have a monopoly on the means of violence. Every state has a paramilitary force, called the special police, which is highly armed, notwithstanding that there is no constitutional authorisation for this. The states use their special forces not only to suppress internal opposition but also to resolve, by force, boundary and other disputes with neighbouring states. A case in point is the fighting between the Afar and Somali special forces, which has been going on for several years. The Tigray state also relied, at least initially, on its special forces when it went to war against the federal government.

Second, the federal system operates in a context where ethnic polarisation has widened and violent conflicts have become routine. These require swift action from the federal government lest lives are lost and property destroyed. A single night saw the killing of almost one hundred people after Jawar Mohammed's social media post; similarly, rioters killed more than one hundred people in various Oromia towns after the assassination of Hachalu Hundessa, an Oromo singer.[97] In both cases, the rioters chose their victims based on ethnic considerations. The military had to intervene swiftly; following the existing legal procedure for federal intervention would have resulted in many more deaths. Events such as these highlight the need for the intervention clauses to be revised in the light of the challenges the country faces.

---

97 Gardner T 'How a musician's death unleashed violence and death in Ethiopia' (3 August 2020) *The Guardian* available at https://www.theguardian.com/global-development/2020/aug/03/how-a-musicians-death-unleashed-violence-and-death-in-ethiopia (accessed 1 March 2025).

BIBLIOGRAPHY

Books

Ayele Z *Local government in Ethiopia: Advancing development and accommodating ethnic minorities* Baden-Baden: Nomos Verlagsgesellschaft (2014)
Balsvik RR *Haile Selassie's students: The intellectual and social background to revolution, 1952–1974* East Lansing: Michigan State University (1985)
Degiffie Z *The architecture and use of emergency powers: The case of Ethiopia from 1995 to 2020* Addis Ababa: Konrad-Adenauer-Stiftung (2022)
Fessha Y *Ethnic diversity and federalism: Constitution making in South Africa and Ethiopia* Farnham: Ashgate (2010)
Steytler N & De Visser J *Local government law of South Africa* South Africa: LexisNexis (2007)
Tewfik H *Transition to federalism: The Ethiopian experience* Ottawa: Forum of Federations (2010)

Journal Articles

Ayele Z & Fessha Y 'The place and status of local government in federal states: The case of Ethiopia' (2012) 58(4) *African Today* 89–109
Ayele Z, Fuller B & Raleigh C 'Ethno-federalism and subnational conflicts in Ethiopia' (2023) *Civil Wars* 1–28
Fiseha A 'Local level decentralisation in Ethiopia: Case study of Tigray Regional State' (2019) 13(1) *The Law and Development Review* 95–126
Hagmann T & Khalif MH 'State and politics in Ethiopia's Somali region since 1991' (2008) 6 *Bildhaan* 26–49
Samatar AI 'Ethiopian federalism: Autonomy versus control in the Somali region' (2004) 25(6) *Third World Quarterly* 1131–54

Legislation

A Proclamation to Revise Oromia Regional State Cities Establishment Proclamation No. 195/2015 (4 January 2016)
A Regulation Concerning the established Provisional Administration in Tigray National Region Regulation No. 479/2020, Federal Negarit Gazette of the Federal Democratic Republic of Ethiopia 27th Year No. 5 (Addis Ababa, 30 November 2020)
Agreement for Lasting Peace through a Permanent Cessation of Hostilities Between the Government of the Federal Democratic Republic of Ethiopia and the Tigray People Liberation Front (TPLF) (Pretoria, 2 November 2022)
Benishangul-Gumuz State Proclamation to Strengthen a Decentralised Woreda Level Administration Proclamation No. 86/2010, Lissane High Gazeta
Constitution of the Federal Democratic Republic of Ethiopia Proclamation No. 1/1995, Federal Negarit Gazette of the Federal Democratic Republic of Ethiopia 1st Year No. 1 (Addis Ababa, 21 August 1995)
Council of Ministers A Regulation Establishing an Inclusive Interim Administration in the Tigray Regional State Regulation No. 533/2023, Federal Negarit Gazette of the

Federal Democratic Republic of Ethiopia 29th Year No. 18 (Addis Ababa, 22 June 2023)
State of Emergency for the Maintenance of Public Peace and Security Council of Ministers Proclamation No.1/2016 Ratification Proclamation No. 984/2016, Federal Negarit Gazette of the Federal Democratic Republic of Ethiopia 23rd Year No. 1 (Addis Ababa, 1 November 2016)
State of Emergency Proclamation for the Maintenance of Public Peace and Security Implementation Council of Ministers Regulation No. 391/2016, Federal Negarit Gazette of the Federal Democratic Republic of Ethiopia 23rd Year No. 2 (Addis Ababa, 27 October 2016)
System for the Intervention of the Federal Government in the Regions Proclamation No. 359/2003, Federal Negarit Gazette of the Federal Democratic Republic of Ethiopia 9th Year No. 80 (Addis Ababa, 10 July 2003)
Tigray Regional State Proclamation to Strengthen Self-administration and to Determine the Functions and Powers of *Woreda* Administration Proclamation No. 99/2006, Federal Negarit Gazette of the Federal Democratic Republic of Ethiopia
Tigray State Constitution, 2001

Internet Sources and Others

'Amhara regional state president calls for federal gov't intervention' (3 August 2023) *Borkena* available at https://borkena.com/2023/08/03/amhara-regional-state-president-calls-for-federal-govt-intervention/ (accessed 1 March 2025)
'Ethiopia intervenes in the Somali-Afar conflict' *Mustaqbal Media* available at https://mustaqbalmedia.net/en/ethiopia-intervenes-in-somali-afar-conflict/amp/ (accessed 1 March 2025)
'Federal government severs relationships with the Tigray state government' (7 October 2020) *Fana Broadcasting Corporate* available at https://www.fanabc.com/english/federal-govt-severs-relationship-with-tigray-regional-state/ (accessed 1 March 2025)
'House of Federation votes Tigray regional election contravenes the federal constitution, non-binding & non-applicable' (5 October 2020) *Addis Standard* available at https://addisstandard.com/news-house-of-federation-votes-tigray-regional-election-contravenes-federal-constitution-non-binding-non-applicable/ (accessed 1 March 2025)
'Violence as troops deploy in Ethiopia's Somali region' (4 August 2018) *BBC* available at https://www.bbc.com/news/world-africa-45070213 (accessed 1 March 2025)
'በሕዝብ ተወካዮች ምክር ቤት አባላት ሰፊ ውይይት የተካሄደበት የአስቸኳይ ጊዜ አዋጅ ጸደቀ (The state of emergency was approved by members of the HPR after discussion)' available at https://www.youtube.com/watch?v=MkgpPjq_bA0&ab_channel=EBC (accessed 1 March 2025)
'የፌዴሬሽን ምክር ቤት የትግራይ ክልል መንግስትን አስጠነቀቀ (The House of Federation warns the Tigray state government)' (30 July 2020) *Ethiopia Insider* available at https://ethiopiainsider.com/2020/1452/ (accessed 1 March 2025)
Abera E 'House speaker Abadula Gemeda apologizes for erring vote counting on state of emergency as decision sparks fresh protests' (4 March 2018) *Addis Standard* available at https://addisstandard.com/news-house-speaker-abadula-gemeda-apologizes-erring-vote-counting-state-emergency-decision-sparks-fresh-protests/ (accessed 1 March 2025)

Ayele Z 'Far-sighted federal solidarity, not power politics and legalism, is needed to solve Tigray dispute' (9 October 2020) *Ethiopia Insight* available at https://www.ethiopia-insight.com/2020/10/09/far-sighted-federal-solidarity-not-power-politics-and-legalism-is-needed-to-solve-tigray-dispute/ (accessed 1 March 2025)

Ekubamichael M 'HoF speaker says establishing transitional gov't, dispatching fed. security forces in Tigray among constitutional options' (2 October 2020) *Addis Standard* available at https://addisstandard.com/news-hof-speaker-says-establishing-transitional-govt-dispatching-fed-security-forces-in-tigray-among-constitutional-options/ (accessed 1 March 2025)

Embassy of Ethiopia 'Press Release: State of Emergency declared in Ethiopia' (10 October 2016) *Ethiopian Embassy* available at https://ethiopianembassy.be/press-release-state-of-emergency-declared-in-ethiopia/ (accessed 1 March 2025)

Endale A 'Clashes in the region puts the constitution at risk, says gov't' (5 August 2023) *The Reporter* available at https://www.thereporterethiopia.com/35816/ (accessed 1 March 2025)

Endeshaw D 'OLF politics, military splits' (6 April 2019) *The Reporter* available at https://www.thereporterethiopia.com/7750/ (accessed 1 March 2025)

Ethiopian Reporter (Amharic) (2022) 28(2356)

Fessha Y 'A federation without federal credentials: When politics trumps law' in *Between failure and redemption, the future of the Ethiopian social contract: Proceedings of a convening of scholars on Ethiopia's constitutional future* Evanston, IL, USA: Northwestern Roberta Buffett Institute for Global Affairs and Northwestern University Libraries (2022) 143–156 available at https://hrp.law.harvard.edu/wp-content/uploads/2023/02/pp.-143-156.pdf (accessed 1 March 2025)

Gardner T 'How a musician's death unleashed violence and death in Ethiopia' (3 August 2020) *The Guardian* available at https://www.theguardian.com/global-development/2020/aug/03/how-a-musicians-death-unleashed-violence-and-death-in-ethiopia (accessed 1 March 2025)

Human Rights Watch '"Fuel on the fire": Security forces response to the 2016 Irrecha cultural festival' (20 September 2017) available at https://www.hrw.org/report/2017/09/20/fuel-fire/security-force-response-2016-irreecha-cultural-festival (accessed 1 March 2025)

Maasho A 'Dispute over Ethiopia emergency rule vote after footage posted online' (4 March 2018) *Reuters* available at https://www.reuters.com/article/us-ethiopia-politics/dispute-over-ethiopia-emergency-rule-vote-after-footage-posted-online-idUSKCN1GE1XJ/ (accessed 1 March 2025)

Shaban ARA 'Ethiopia activists activate shutdown in Oromia to protest emergency rule' (5 March 2018) Africa News available at https://www.africanews.com/2018/03/05/ethiopia-activists-activate-shutdown-in-oromia-to-protest-emergency-rule// (accessed 1 March 2025)

Shaban ARA 'Ethiopia declares 6 months state of emergency over Oromia protests' (9 December 2019) *Africa News* available at https://www.africanews.com/2016/10/09/ethiopia-declares-6-months-state-of-emergency-over-oromia-protests// (accessed 1 March 2025)

Tadesse G 'Ethiopia: In troubled Oromia areas' (25 October 2019) *AA* available at https://www.aa.com.tr/en/africa/ethiopia-army-deployed-in-troubled-oromia-areas/1626278 (accessed 1 March 2025)

Voice of America 'Ethiopia declares emergency after attack on federal military base' (4 November 2020) https://web.archive.org/web/20250308054929/https://www

.voanews.com/a/africa_ethiopia-declares-emergency-after-attack-federal-military-base/6197965.html (accessed 1 March 2025)
የኢትዮጵያ ሕገ መንግስት ጉባኤ ቃለ ጉባኤ ጥራዝ 5 (ኅዳር 21-24/1987) 12 at 12–13 (The Minutes of the Ethiopian Constitutional Assembly, Vol. 5 (30 November–3 December 1994)

5. India: President's Rule and permissive interventionism

Louise Tillin

1. INTRODUCTION

By design, Indian federalism accords the central government considerable scope to intervene in the affairs of the states. India's central government can alter the boundaries of the constituent states of the Indian Union (article 3) or declare President's Rule in a state. This is possible on receipt of a report from a centrally appointed governor that a 'situation has arisen in which the government of the state cannot be carried on in accordance with the provisions of [the] Constitution' (article 356). The central government also has wide powers to legislate on matters in the state list in various circumstances. For these reasons, India was described by KC Wheare as only 'quasi-federal', a description which continues to be regularly used in judicial and political discourse in India.[1]

In this chapter I focus on the main form of intervention that meets the definition provided by the editors, namely the use of President's Rule. I will examine the procedures for intervention in two domains: first, the role of the legislature and the courts in sanctioning attempted applications of President's Rule; second, the role of the governor's office in serving as a conduit between the executive at the centre and the elected state government. Finally, in examining the politics of intervention, I will show how changes in the party system (from one-party dominance to multiparty regionalisation, then back again to one-party dominance) have been associated with changes in the use and abuse of President's Rule. This will include consideration of a historic Supreme Court judgement in the mid-1990s, a period of political regionalisation in which state governments were relatively empowered, enforcing stronger safeguards against the declaration of President's Rule.

[1] Wheare KC *Federal government* London; New York: Oxford University Press (1963).

Even with these safeguards, it is possible for a central government to make a major change to the constitutional status of a constituent unit while it is under President's Rule (as in the case of Kashmir). The chapter will thus also consider how the office of the governor (and, in recent years, in union territories, the lieutenant governor) has been politicised in certain periods to enhance the centre's powers of intervention.

2. BRIEF INTRODUCTION TO FEDERALISM IN INDIA

India adopted a unique form of federalism in its post-independence constitution, drafted between 1946 and 1949 and promulgated in 1950. The form of federalism adopted in the Constitution was original, and deviated from what had previously been considered a cardinal principle of federal constitutions: the idea that federal and subnational governments should each have independence in their own sphere of authority. In contrast, the Indian Constitution was designed to expressly permit federal intervention in the affairs of states. It enshrined a strong centre, extensive forms of inter-dependence between the Union government and states, and emergency powers to dismiss elected state governments on the basis of a concern that government cannot be carried out 'in accordance with the constitution'.

Furthermore, the Constitution itself did not use the words 'federal' or 'federalism': this signalled the conscious departure that its architects were making from 'classic' models of federalism. As the chair of the Constitution's drafting committee, Dr BR Ambedkar, said (introducing the draft constitution to the Constituent Assembly), the Constitution was federal to the extent that it introduced a 'dual polity' in which the centre and states each have sovereign powers in the fields enumerated in the Constitution.

But the Constitution was also designed to be flexible, and it was this 'flexibility' that distinguished the proposed Indian model of federalism from all others:

> All federal systems including the American are placed in a tight mould of federalism. No matter what the circumstances, it cannot change its form and shape. It can never be unitary. On the other hand ... [India's] Draft Constitution can be both unitary as well as federal according to the requirements of time and circumstances. In normal times, it is framed to work as a federal system. But in times of war it is so designed as to make it work as though it was a unitary system ... Such a power of converting itself into a unitary state no federation possesses. This is one point of

difference between the Federation proposed in the Draft Constitution, and all other Federations we know of.[2]

The centralised and flexible design of Indian federalism was informed by the circumstances of its birth – notably by the effects of India's traumatic partition, as well as by the challenge of embedding democracy and a universal franchise in a deeply unequal society.[3] The Constitution, in its intergovernmental distribution of powers, also demonstrated continuity with the experiments with decentralisation and federation of late colonial constitutionalism as enshrined in successive, partially implemented Government of India Acts.[4] In addition, India's federal design was influenced by broader global concerns. By the mid-twentieth century, there was an increasing recognition of the limitations of older models of federalism, such as those of the United States or Canada, in responding to the challenges of post-war reconstruction and the building of welfare states.[5] The mid-twentieth century, in general, saw a move towards centralisation in federal systems across the world.[6] India was one of the first new federations to be created after the Second World War.

Federalism in India includes an intergovernmental distribution of powers between the Union and state governments that is protected by a written constitution. The Constitution introduced direct elections to two tiers of government – to the lower chamber of the central parliament (the Lok Sabha, or 'House of the People') and state legislative assemblies. Direct elections to a third tier (Panchayats and municipal corporations) were introduced via constitutional amendment in 1992. The upper house of the central parliament, the Rajya Sabha ('Council of the States'), is indirectly elected by an electoral college comprising members of the state legislative assemblies. States are represented in the Rajya Sabha according to the size of their populations rather than on an equal basis.

2 Ambedkar BR 'Constituent Assembly of India Debates (Proceedings)', Vol VIII, 4 November 1948.

3 Khosla M *India's founding moment: The constitution of a most surprising democracy* Cambridge: Harvard University Press (2020).

4 See Elangovan A 'Provincial autonomy, Sir Benegal Narsing Rau, and an improbable imagination of constitutionalism in India, 1935–38' (2016) 36 (1) *Comparative Studies of South Asia, Africa and the Middle East* 66; Sengupta A *The colonial constitution* New Delhi: Juggernaut Books (2023); Thiruvengadam AK *The Constitution of India: A contextual analysis* Oxford; Portland, Oregon: Hart Publishing (2017) at 75.

5 Birch AH *Federalism, finance and social legislation in Canada, Australia and the United States* Oxford: Clarendon Press (1955).

6 Dardanelli P, Kincaid J, Fenna A, et al. 'Conceptualising, measuring, and theorising dynamic de/centralisation in federations' (2019) 49(1) *Publius* 1.

While the upper house is an important revising chamber, its character as a territorial chamber in which states' interests are protected is relatively weak. Its role as a territorial chamber was further eroded by the Supreme Court ruling in *Kuldip Nayar v Union of India* (2006).[7] This established that candidates for election to the Rajya Sabha did not need to be registered as voters in the state or territory they sought to represent. Here, the chief justice made a distinction between Indian federalism and other federal constitutions with bicameral legislatures. He emphasised – following Ambedkar – that the essential feature of federalism in India was the partition of executive authority between the Union and state governments, and did not reside in its territorial character. The weak protection of territorial interests in the Constitution is also reflected in article 3. This allows the Union government to alter the boundaries of states by dividing them, amalgamating or removing areas from their jurisdiction.

Like a great deal more in India's federal design, political change and the strengthening of regional political parties has imparted a stronger territorial character to the practice of federalism. But it is precisely on account of these deviations from a separate spheres model of federalism (as well as the provision of President's Rule outlined below) that the constitutional scholar KC Wheare described India as only 'quasi-federal'.[8] This designation has become widely accepted in Indian political and judicial discourse.[9] In this regard at least, India exhibits similarities with South Africa's situation.

The Seventh Schedule of the Constitution enumerates the distribution of legislative responsibilities between the Union and state, as well as containing a fairly extensive concurrent list. Many critical nation-building tasks (including in regard to economic and social planning, trade unions, industrial and labour disputes, social security and social insurance and labour welfare) were seen to need central leadership even when state governments would be key implementation partners and so were placed on the concurrent list.

Beyond the enumerated shared domain on the concurrent list, the Constitution also empowered the Union government to intervene in, or even

---

7 Supreme Court of India *Kuldip Nayar v Union of India* (2006), AIR 2006 SC 3127, Appeal (civil) 217 of 2004, 22 August 2006.

8 Wheare (1963).

9 James K & Arora B 'The judicial journey of Indian federalism' in Madhava M (ed) *Continuities and discontinuities: Politics and society in contemporary India* Hyderabad: Orient Blackswan (forthcoming); Arora B & Kailash KK 'Beyond quasi federalism: Change and continuity in Indian Federalism' (2018) 6(2) *Studies in Indian Politics* 297.

to take over, policy execution in the domain of the states not only in situations of emergency but also in routine matters, under certain specified conditions.[10]

Under article 253, the central government can legislate on matters in the state list where these relate to the implementation of international treaties or agreements. Under article 250, the central government can legislate on state matters when a national emergency is declared. And under article 249, the centre can legislate on matters in the state list if this is deemed to be in the national interest and if a resolution is passed by two-thirds of those present in the upper house of parliament (or under article 252 if two or more state legislatures request Parliament to do so). The Union parliament also supersedes state legislatures if a subject can be read in the Union list, even if it also appears in the state or concurrent list. Finally, residual powers lie with the Union government. The Supreme Court has usually upheld the dominance of the Union parliament in cases where there has been a dispute over the interpretation of the overlap between the lists or residuary powers.[11]

The most controversial – and most abused - provision relating to the central government's powers of intervention is article 356, found in Part XVIII of the Constitution ('Emergency Provisions'). This chapter focuses on the power of intervention which it allows.

Article 356 ('Provisions in case of failure of constitutional machinery in States') provides the central government with the right to declare President's Rule in a state if, on the basis of a report received from the (centrally appointed) governor, it is deemed that the government is unable to govern 'in accordance with the provisions of the Constitution'. This provision allows the President to suspend a directly elected state legislative assembly and 'assume to himself all or any of the functions of the Government of the State', with 'the powers of the Legislature of the State [to] be exercisable by or under the authority of Parliament'. Alongside this, article 357 enables Parliament to delegate the legislative power of the state to the President or another specified authority.[12] In essence, this constitutional provision provides for the Union government to rule the state directly from the centre.

This power of intervention was visibly abused for political reasons by Union governments between the late 1960s and the mid 1990s, when it was used

---

[10] See Tillin L *Indian federalism* New Delhi: Oxford University Press (2019) Chapter 1.

[11] Singh MP 'The federal scheme' in Choudhry S, Khosla M, & Mehta PB (eds) *The Oxford handbook of the Indian Constitution* Oxford: Oxford University Press (2016).

[12] Sagar R 'Emergency powers' in Choudhry S, Khosla M, & Mehta PB (eds) *The Oxford handbook of the Indian Constitution* Oxford: Oxford University Press (2016) 213.

to dismiss or destabilise opposition-ruled state governments. Article 356 has been more closely regulated since the landmark Supreme Court judgment of 1994, but it remains a potent threat in the hands of the Union executive. As the use of President's Rule has decreased, the office of the governor has become increasingly politicised, and particularly so since the consolidation of a new dominant-party system in 2014. The many interventions that have occurred may fall short of the suspension of elected governments, but they still constitute interference by the Union government in the affairs of the states.

While the focus of this chapter is on federal powers of intervention under article 356, it is important to note that many Indian states have a parallel mechanism that enables state governments to intervene in the third tier of local government. State-level legislation regulating municipal government often empowers state governments to dissolve municipal corporations on grounds such as that they are not considered competent to perform their duties or that they fail to comply with state government directions. In such instances, the state government can appoint officers to carry out the functions of the municipal corporation.[13] Municipal legislation in many states also gives the state government the power to direct the municipal corporation to perform a duty if it is of the view that this is not being performed in a satisfactory manner.[14] These powers are frequently used. In 2023, for instance, a majority of municipal corporations in the state of Maharasthra were run by state-appointed administrators rather than the actually elected officials.[15] In some states, there are active efforts to restrict the powers of state governments to dissolve municipal governments.[16]

---

13 See, for instance, section 520D of the Mumbai Municipal Corporation Act, 1888; section 452 of the Maharashtra Municipal Corporations Act, 1949; section 99 of the Karnataka Municipal Corporations Act, 1976; section 62 of the Andhra Pradesh Municipalities Act, 1965; and section 64 of the Kerala Municipalities Act, 1994. I am grateful to Mathew Idiculla and an anonymous reviewer of this chapter for providing insight into the operation of these provisions.

14 Idiculla M 'Unpacking local self-government: The uncertain power of cities in the Indian Constitution' (2020) 53(1) *Law and Politics in Africa, Asia and Latin America* 30 at 46.

15 Acahrya P & Bose N 'BMC completes 18 months without corporators; no elected reps in 24 municipal bodies in state' *The Indian Express* (20 September 2023) available at https://indianexpress.com/article/cities/mumbai/bmc-completes-18-months-without-corporators-no-elected-reps-in-24-municipal-bodies-in-state-8932683/ (accessed 27 January 2025).

16 For example, in the state of Karnataka, a proposed draft for a new Greater Bengaluru Governance Bill, produced by the Brand Bengaluru Committee, contained a proposal to introduce an independent committee to advise on dissolution. Available at https://bbmprestructuring.wordpress.com/wp-content/uploads

3. RATIONALE FOR LEGAL ENTRENCHMENT OF INTERVENTION POWERS

To understand the factors shaping decisions about the shape of Indian federalism taken by its Constituent Assembly, it is first necessary to examine the impact of Partition. When the Constituent Assembly met in December 1946, India's future Prime Minister, Jawaharlal Nehru, had introduced an Objectives Resolution that outlined the shape of a future constitution that would have looked quite different to the one eventually promulgated in 1950. In December 1946, the Partition of the subcontinent had not yet been announced. The Objectives Resolution set out the vision of the Cabinet Mission Plan for a thoroughly decentralised federation, one in which the centre's powers would be limited to foreign affairs, defence and communications, and with all other powers remaining under the provinces. This was designed to encourage the Muslim League to join the Constituent Assembly.

However, immediately after the announcement of Partition in June 1947 (just two months before independence), the Union Constitution Committee of the Constituent Assembly moved a new motion to adopt a much more centralised model of federalism. This reversion to a more centralised model was made possible by the fact there was no longer any need to accommodate the Muslim League, but it also reflected concerns that communal violence unleashed by Partition itself would require a strong central government. This would be critically necessary to subdue the likely communal violence and enable the successful transfer of power and the resettlement of millions of Partition refugees.[17]

Recent work has drawn attention to additional factors which have a bearing on the choice of a strong centre. Key figures in the Constituent Assembly, especially Jawaharlal Nehru and BR Ambedkar, believed a strong centre necessary to securing the embedding of democracy in a deeply hierarchical local society.[18] They also sought to empower the Union to consolidate a national economy and lay the foundations for building an Indian welfare state while overcoming the deleterious impact of inter-provincial industrial competition for industrial relations and labour conditions.[19] Centralisation may also have reflected pressures arising from the approximately 560 princely states and 17 former British Indian provinces. The princely states had radically different systems governance. Indeed, most lacked effective governance structures, though some (such

/2024/07/gbg-final-submission_with-bill__july-2024-1.pdf (accessed 5 December 2024).

[17] Austin G *The Indian Constitution: Cornerstone of a nation* Oxford: Oxford University Press (1966) at 236.

[18] Khosla (2020).

[19] Tillin (2021).

as Hyderabad) enjoyed well-developed administrative architectures and had claims to sovereign status in their own right.[20] A strong central government would serve as a vehicle for integration and be well placed to face the particular challenges posed by the princely states.[21]

Our concern in this chapter is specifically with the rationale for the powers of intervention granted to this strong centre. We focus on two elements of intervention: President's Rule, and the powers of the office of the governor in serving as a conduit between the executive at the centre and elected state governments.

President's Rule, under articles 356 and 357, was placed in Part XVIII of the Constitution dealing with emergency provisions. The other articles under Part XVIII deal with the proclamation of a nationwide state of emergency on national security grounds, and with financial emergencies. President's Rule was included in the Constitution in order to provide the Union government with powers of intervention in circumstances in which there was a failure of constitutional machinery. This has been interpreted as a measure included in the Constitution to provide safeguards for India's fledgling experiment with democracy. As the Sarkaria Commission on centre-state relations, appointed in the early 1980s in a period of dissension in centre–state relations (especially because of the abuse of President's Rule), explained:

> The Constitution-makers were alive to the fact that several regions or areas of the country had no past experience or deep-rooted tradition of Parliamentary form of Government, and a failure or break-down of the constitutional machinery in a State could not be ruled out as an impossibility. A further duty [beyond the security of the nation as a whole] was, therefore, laid on the Union to ensure that the government of every State is carried on in accordance with the provisions of the Constitution.[22]

At least in its language, the provision mirrored the emergency powers enumerated in the colonial Government of India Act of 1935. Here, under section 93, it was provided that the governor of a province could issue a proclamation to assume to himself the powers of provincial administrative or legislative bodies if a situation had arisen in which 'the government of the Province cannot be carried on in accordance with the provisions of this Act'.[23] However, the Constitution of India differed from the 1935 Act: it introduced a vertical dimension to federal intervention. Rather than conferring the power of

---

[20] Purushotham S *From Raj to republic: Sovereignty, violence, and democracy in India* Stanford: Stanford University Press (2021).

[21] Thiruvengadam (2017).

[22] Government of India 1988, section 6.1.02.

[23] Government of India 1988, section 6.1.02.

intervention on the unelected governor of a province (as the 1935 Act did), the Constitution conferred this power on the central government.[24]

The Sarkaria Commission offered a loose interpretation of the circumstances that the founders had in mind when they included article 356 in the 1950 Constitution. They pointed to the concerns among Constituent Assembly members that Partition might provoke violent disturbances and consequently raise the need for special provisions to 'effectively and swiftly' deal with grave law-and-order situations.[25] Above all, the Sarkaria Commission interpreted President's Rule as a measure intended to serve as a 'bulwark of the Constitution, an ultimate assurance of maintaining or restoring representative government in States responsible to the people'.[26] Looking back on the debates in the Constituent Assembly, Rahul Sagar has gone further to argue that the Drafting Committee had a more specific rationale for including article 356: this was to defend against the possibility that *militant* methods, especially communism, might be used to subvert Indian democracy.[27]

Nevertheless, it was also clear that the Constitution's founders envisaged that article 356 would be used only rarely. It would not be the first recourse in the context of concerns about governance in a particular state. Dr BR Ambedkar stated:

> I do not altogether deny that there is a possibility of these articles being abused or employed for political purposes. But that objection applies to every part of the Constitution which gives power to the Centre to override the Provinces. In fact I share the sentiments ... that such articles will never be called into operation and that they would remain a dead letter. If at all they are brought into operation, I hope the President, who is endowed with these powers, will take proper precautions before actually suspending the administration of the provinces. I hope the first

---

24 The persistence, and adaptation of, this colonial power of intervention speaks to a crucial ambivalence in the project of democracy and popular sovereignty enshrined in the Indian Constitution. As Nazmul Sultan notes, the question of whether Indians constituted a people ready for 'popular sovereignty' was a central dilemma of anti-colonial thought. The idea that central powers of intervention might be necessary in India's postcolonial constitution to rescue or safeguard democracy is arguably consistent with this ambivalence. See Sultan N *Waiting for the people: The idea of democracy in Indian anticolonial thought* Cambridge: Harvard University Press (1994).

25 Government of India 1988, section 6.2.02.

26 During the Constituent Assembly debates, it was stated that article 356 was based on the same principle as article IV, section 4 of the United States Constitution – the 'guarantee clause' ('The United States shall guarantee to every State in this Union a Republican Form of Government, and shall protect each of them against invasion').

27 Sagar (2016).

> thing he will do would be to issue a mere warning to a province that has erred, that things were not happening in the way in which they were intended to happen in the Constitution. If that warning fails, the second thing for him to do will be to order an election allowing the people of the province to settle matters by themselves. It is only when these two remedies fail that he would resort to this article.[28]

Contrary to Ambedkar's hopes, article 356 has been invoked more than 130 times since 1950.

Article 360 also provided the Union with executive powers of intervention in the affairs of state governments in situations when their financial performance was in question. Under article 360, the President can proclaim an emergency when 'satisfied that a situation has arisen whereby the financial stability or credit of India or of any part of the territory thereof is threatened'. In these circumstances, the Union can give 'directions to any State to observe such canons of financial propriety as may be specified'. These include reducing the salaries and allowances of government employees and requiring Money Bills passed by state legislatures to be 'reserved' for consideration by the President. This measure appears to have been included by the Drafting Committee to deal with circumstances in which financial profligacy by a state government risked jeopardising the Union's financial standing, but quite which circumstances would justify invoking article 360 were left ambiguous.[29] Unlike article 356, article 360 has never been invoked.

Finally, we turn to the office of the governor at the state level. The governor is an unelected nominee of the president provided for each state and one in whom the 'executive power of the State' is vested under article 154. This office has ill-specified discretionary powers and is often seen as a curious relic of colonialism. The Constitution specifies that the governor is to act in all functions on the advice of a Council of Ministers, with the Chief Minister at its head. While the intention of the Constituent Assembly was not to endow the governor's office with powers that undermined the operation of elected governments in the states, the Constitution leaves considerable scope for discretion.[30]

This discretion is particularly consequential at moments of government formation when elections have not provided any single party with an outright majority. In such circumstances, the governor can determine which party, and chief ministerial candidate, is able to test its majority first in the state legislature. The governor must also provide assent to any bill passed by a state legislature; he or she has the power also (under article 200) to reserve a bill

---

[28] Dr BR Ambedkar's remarks to Constituent Assembly cited in Government of India 1988, section 6.2.13.

[29] Sagar (2016).

[30] Narayanan, James, & Panda (2023).

for the consideration of the President or to return a bill to the state legislature for reconsideration (although they may not veto legislation if the bill is passed again by the House).

In terms of the powers of federal intervention, the governor's role has been highly consequential for the operation of article 356. Under article 356, the President may declare President's Rule if he or she is satisfied, 'on receipt of a report from the *Governor*', that there has been a failure of constitutional machinery.

As Narayanan, James and Panda write in a recent study of the governor's office,[31] the Constituent Assembly chose to retain the office of the governor despite some reservations that in doing so they were retaining an anti-democratic colonial legacy. They argue that the office of governor as incorporated in the Constitution was intended to protect the interests of the central government in its relationship with the states, in line with the Constituent Assembly's general preference for strong central government. However, in leaving the discretionary powers of the governor ill-specified, the Constituent Assembly failed to provide safeguards for scenarios in which the governor – usually a political appointee by the centre – is caught between the interests of the centre and a state.[32] As they conclude:

> Thus, various constitutional provisions relating to the Governor came to carry a hidden risk of a Governor disregarding the advice of the State Government or even acting completely at the Centre's behest thereby threatening the federal and democratic fabric of the Constitution.[33]

4. CONSTITUTIONAL AND LEGAL BASIS FOR INTERVENTION

This section reviews the constitutional and legal bases for intervention. Article 355 of the Constitution sets out the '[d]uty of the Union to protect States against external aggression and internal disturbance' and 'to ensure that the Government of every State is carried on in accordance with the provisions of this Constitution'. Article 356 makes provisions in the 'case of failure of constitutional machinery in the States', while article 357 covers the exercise of legislative powers during a proclamation issued under article 356.

The question of *who* may use this legal power is clearer than the substantive conditions under which it may be invoked. The power of intervention is

---

31 Narayanan, James, & Panda (2023).

32 Narayanan, James, & Panda (2023) at 34.

33 Narayanan, James, & Panda (2023) at 35.

granted to the President of the Republic of India, who is an indirectly elected head of state. Under article 74 of the Constitution, the President is bound to act on the advice of the Union Council of Ministers (the union cabinet).[34] The conditions which might meet the definition of a situation 'in which the government of the State cannot be carried on in accordance with the provisions of the Constitution' are, however, not specified.

Several Supreme Court judgments, as well as the Sarkaria Commission on Centre-State Relations, have reviewed the grounds and procedures for declarations of President's Rule. This followed the frequent recourse to the provision between the late 1970s to mid-1990s by Union governments to dismiss opposition-ruled state governments, often on spurious grounds. Neither of the principal Supreme Court judgements to scrutinise the operation of President's Rule – *State of Rajasthan & Ors. Etc. Etc. v Union of India Etc. Etc.* (1977) *('Rajasthan')* or *SR Bommai v Union of India 1994 ('Bommai')* – offered clear guidance as to what constitutes appropriate circumstances for the invocation of article 356. While the *Bommai* case led to clearer procedures for judicial scrutiny of the evidence on which the President has taken a decision, the bench did not specify the types of intervention likely to be considered appropriate.

The Sarkaria Commission in its 1988 report did identify four categories that might constitute a constitutional failure, though it noted that such a categorisation could not be watertight as many situations would contain multiple elements. The four categories it proposed were as follows:

1) Political crisis caused by the inability of any party to demonstrate a majority in state legislature. In this scenario, there would be alternatives to President's Rule, such as the governor calling fresh elections or establishing a caretaker government for a short period until elections are held. President's Rule should be a last resort only in circumstances where it is not possible to form a caretaker government or hold elections without delay.
2) Internal subversion caused by a state government deliberately governing in a fashion that disregards the Constitution or law; flouts principles of responsible government 'to substitute them for some form of dictatorship'; or 'foments a violent revolution with or without the connivance of a foreign power'.
3) Physical breakdown when a state government is unable or unwilling to respond to an internal disturbance or natural calamity, and this 'endangers the security of the state'.

[34] Government of India 1988, section 1.3.27.

4) Non-compliance with constitutional directions of the Union Government, when a state government fails to comply with directions issued under the executive power of the Union Government or during a national emergency; or if the state fails to inform the Union Government of public disorder that endangers the security of the state in such a way as to impede the exercise of executive power by the Union Government.

The Commission also listed several examples of the improper deployment of article 356. These were cases in which there was maladministration by an elected government enjoying majority support in the state legislative assembly; where a ministry resigns or loses support in the legislature but the governor does not give other parties the opportunity to demonstrate a majority; when used to resolve internal differences within political parties or to respond to 'financial exigencies'; and when responding to serious allegations of corruption. It noted that much of the criticism of the clause to date flowed from the concern that its application had been determined to 'suit the political interests of the party in power in the Union'.[35]

However, the government did not accept the Commission's recommendations regarding the substantive conditions under which article 356 could be invoked, and nor have these been codified by Supreme Court judgments.[36]

5. PROCEDURES OF INTERVENTION

This section examines procedures for intervention and whether these ensure proper checks and balances. Such checks and balances come from Parliament and via the courts, especially after the principle of judicial review was confirmed by the 1994 *Bommai* ruling. To some extent, presidents may also serve as a check. Clause 3 of article 356 provides that a proclamation of President's Rule must be laid before both houses of parliament and will cease to operate after two months if it has not been approved by both houses. Once approved, a proclamation expires after six months unless formally approved again.

Up until the *Bommai* ruling, the two checks provided by Parliament and the courts functioned weakly.[37] The Sarkaria Commission observed that the *Rajasthan* case exposed the 'inadequacies' of both the parliamentary and

---

35 Government of India 1988, section 6.4.02–6.6.02.

36 Sagar (2016).

37 In the original Constitution of 1950, article 356 included a clause that exempted the article from review by any court: 'Notwithstanding anything in this Constitution, the satisfaction of the President mentioned in Clause (1) shall be final and conclusive and shall not be questioned in any Court on any ground.' This clause was removed under the 44th amendment to the Constitution in 1978.

judicial checks envisaged in the Constitution. On the parliamentary side, the Supreme Court found that if, in the two months before parliamentary approval is given (or not), an irreversible decision such as dissolving the state legislature has been taken, this cannot be revoked following a parliamentary vote. On the judicial side, even though the bar to judicial review had been removed via constitutional amendment, this provision would be relatively meaningless as a recourse to justice against a *malafide* invocation of article 356 unless the Union executive was obliged to publish the 'material facts and grounds' on the basis of which a proclamation was made. Without the publication of these grounds, the Court was precluded, under article 74 of the Constitution, from inquiring into advice tendered by ministers to the President.[38]

In the *Bommai* judgment, the Supreme Court confirmed that the use of article 356 is subject to judicial review.[39] It underlined that the President's satisfaction that a 'situation has arisen in which the Government of the State cannot be carried on … in accordance with the provisions of the Constitution' must be based on 'objective material'. Judicial review of the use of article 356 will 'necessarily involve' scrutiny of this material and the 'legitimacy of inference drawn from such material'. While the Court agreed that article 74 prevents it from reviewing the advice of ministers, this does not prevent judicial review of the 'material on the basis of which the advice is given'. The judgment also discussed closing the loophole identified by the Sarkaria Commission around parliamentary approval, though it did not go so far as to require prior parliamentary approval of a proclamation. The judgment simply directed that if a proclamation is not approved by Parliament within two months, the suspended state legislative assembly will come back into power and fresh elections need not be held.

The *Bommai* judgment (whose important political context will be described in section 5) also recognised federalism as part of the basic structure of the Indian Constitution. The *Bommai* judgment held that the declaration of President's Rule was unconstitutional in cases where a government had lost its majority but an alternative political formation had not yet been allowed to test its strength on the floor of the state legislative assembly. It also stated that the central government could not dismiss an elected state government on the grounds that it was unable to provide stable governance.

Since *Bommai*, the courts have started to scrutinise President's Rule much more closely. In 1996, a high court (in Allahabad) for the first time ruled the imposition of President's Rule illegal (in Uttar Pradesh) and ordered the

---

[38] Government of India 1988, section 6.6.11–6.6.25.

[39] The 44th Constitutional Amendment, 1978, had removed the earlier clause 5 of article 356, which precluded judicial review.

state assembly to resume.[40] Sagar notes that subsequent judgments such as *Rameshwar Prasad v Union of India 2006* (ruling that the declaration of President's Rule in Bihar was unconstitutional) have scrutinised the formulation of the governor's report or the President's justification for suspending or dissolving a legislative assembly. The court has also stated that it could reverse unjustified action and directed the Union to employ floor tests (rather than subjective judgment) to determine whether a state government enjoys the support of the state legislature.[41]

For some observers, a stronger check on the use of President's Rule has come (in Parliament) from the regionalisation of the party system from the late 1980s onwards and the rise of coalition government in the 1990s. Sadananand[42] and Swenden[43] (for example) have argued that the presence of regional parties in coalition governments (1989–2014) has helped to reduce the arbitrary application of President's Rule.[44] Yet (as was the case in Uttar Pradesh as well as several other instances), regional parties in coalition government were also the protagonists in calling for the application of article 356 against their regional opponents.[45]

The most that can be argued is that the presence of regional parties fragmented parliamentary coalitions.[46] In some instances, regional parties did help to block attempts to apply President's Rule.[47] Sadananan goes further

---

40 Sadanandan A 'Bridling central tyranny in India' (2012) 52(2) *Asian Survey* 247 at 255.

41 Sagar (2016).

42 Sadanandan (2012).

43 Swenden W 'Centre-state bargaining and territorial accommodation: Evidence from India' (2016) 22(4) *Swiss Political Science Review* 491.

44 Sadanandan (2012); Swenden (2016).

45 For example, in 1998 Jayalalithaa, the leader of the Tamil Nadu party, AIADMK, was a member of the BJP-led National Democratic Alliance (NDA) government. Jayalalithaa pushed the BJP to use article 356 to remove her state rival, the DMK, from office. The BJP ultimately refused and Jayalalithaa withdrew from the NDA coalition, precipitating the fall of the government and fresh national elections. See Rudolph LI & Rudolph SH 'Redoing the constitutional design: From an interventionist to a regulatory state' in Kohli A (ed) *The success of India's democracy* Cambridge: Cambridge University Press (2001) 127 at 152.

46 In February 1999, for example, the NDA government failed to gain parliamentary support for the imposition of President's Rule in Bihar. See 'What is the SR Bommai case, and why is it quoted often?' *The Hindu* (18 May 2018) available at https://www.thehindu.com/news/national/what-is-the-sr-bommai-case-and-why-is-it-quoted-often/article61834854.ece (accessed 27 January 2025).

47 For example, in 2000, the BJP-led NDA sought to apply President's Rule to dismiss the Communist Party of India (Marxist) state government of West Bengal.

and argues that the rise of regional parties enabled a much stronger assertion of institutional safeguards, such as those provided by the President and the courts. He suggests that national parties, in an era of coalition, were also wary of antagonising future potential regional allies by recourse to President's Rule. All in all, the opportunistic nature of the coalition system served as a check on federal overreach during this era of political fragmentation.

As Sadananan notes, the President serves as a theoretical check on the usage of article 356. As the constitutional head of state, he or she is expected to act on the advice of the Council of Ministers (the Prime Minister and cabinet). In the era of coalition government of the 1990s and 2000s, the presidency also gained the space to serve as what Rudolph and Rudolph describe as the 'guardian of fairness and constitutional balance'.[48]

During the Emergency, Prime Minister Indira Gandhi had tried to assert parliamentary supremacy over the Presidency. After the Emergency, however, the new non-Congress Janata government introduced an omnibus constitutional amendment in 1978. This included a new clause providing the President with the ability to return legislation or a recommendation by the Council of Ministers for reconsideration. This was a 'suspensory veto', meaning that while the President could return matters for reconsideration, he or she could not veto them altogether if advised to approve them by the Council of Ministers.[49]

The coalition era (1989–2014) saw presidents intervene in partisan efforts to apply article 356. For instance, in 1997, the minority United Front government (led by Prime Minister IK Gujral) forwarded a governor's report from Uttar Pradesh recommending the imposition of article 356 after a coalition partner withdrew from the Bahujan Samaj Party–Bharatiya Janata Party (BSP–BJP) government (despite the fact that the BJP Chief Minister, Kalyan Singh, had been able to win a vote of confidence in the state legislature). The President returned this recommendation for reconsideration. The central government's recommendation of President's Rule had been influenced by the interests of the United Front Defence minister, himself the leader of another regional party in Uttar Pradesh, and of the Congress Party, which supported the United Front from outside and hoped to gain political mileage from the instability in the UP.[50] The government withdrew the recommendation. Similar presidential

This move was supported by the NDA coalition ally and the West Bengal regional party, the Trinamool Congress, but opposed by other regional parties in the NDA coalition (the Telugu Desam Party from Andhra Pradesh and the DMK from Tamil Nadu, which had joined the NDA after the departure of the AIADMK). See Sadanandan (2012) at 261.

48 Rudolph & Rudolph (2001) at 140.

49 Rudolph & Rudolph (2001) at 140.

50 Rudolph & Rudolph (2001) at 52.

interventions occurred in 1998 and in 2007 (the latter during the Congress-led United Progressive Alliance central government).

Under the new dominant-party system that has been in place since the BJP's national parliamentary majority (2014–2024), it is the courts rather than the regional parties or the President that have served as safeguards against federal intervention. This is evident in the way in which the two attempts by the BJP government in 2016 to exercise article 356 in Arunachal Pradesh and Uttarakhand were each struck down by the courts.[51] As Swenden and Saxena argue, these post-2014 decisions by the Supreme Court suggest that the *Bommai* judgment served to establish important precedents that the courts have continued to follow in the era of the more centralised dominant-party system.[52]

6. POLITICS OF INTERVENTION

To date, President's Rule has been invoked 134 times. Every state in India (with the exceptions of Chhattisgarh (formed in 2000), Himachal Pradesh and Telangana (formed in 2014)) has at some time come under President's Rule. Recourse to it peaked between the 1970s and mid-1990s. Since the mid-1990s, however, there has been a reduction in its arbitrary application on politically motivated grounds. At the same time, despite the less frequent resort to President's Rule, the office of the governor (and in union territories the lieutenant governor) has been politicised to enhance the centre's powers of intervention. Furthermore, President's Rule continues to be used by governors to threaten state governments. It is also frequently demanded by parties in opposition at the state level to protest against the actions of state governments. While recourse to it has undoubtedly declined, the idea of President's Rule has become an accepted part of political life in centre–state relations in India.

The changing political dynamics of federal intervention are best understood when seen historically across four main periods of Indian political life:

- In 1952–1977, the Indian National Congress (INC) dominated national (and for a time, regional) political life in the first dominant-party system.
- Next, in 1977–1989, the Congress Party's dominance declined but it was still able to form national governments due to the absence of a viable polity-wide opposition.

---

[51] The two cases were Supreme Court of India Arunachal Pradesh Legislative Assembly *Nabam Rebia v Deputy Speaker* (2016) 8 SCC 1 and Uttarakhand High Court *Harish Rawat v Union of India* (2016) SCC Online Utt 502.

[52] Swenden W & Saxena R 'Policing the federation: The supreme court and judicial federalism in India' (2022) 10(1) *Territory, Politics, Governance* 12.

- Thereafter, the period 1989–2014 was an era of coalition government in New Delhi, one in which political regionalisation meant that no national party (Congress or BJP) proved able to form a parliamentary majority.
- Finally, 2014–2024 is the period of the second dominant-party system, during which the BJP has governed with an outright parliamentary majority and since 2024 has been the dominant party in a coalition government.

Table 5.1 presents an overview (as summarised by the Sarkaria Commission) of the main categories of federal intervention across these periods.

In the first decade of the dominant-party era, the Congress Party under Prime Minister Jawaharlal Nehru ran most state governments as well as the national government. It resorted to President's Rule in just a handful of cases. In 1951 (Punjab), it was used to try and resolve internal conflict within the Congress Party. In Andhra Pradesh in 1954 it was used to prevent opposition parties from testing their majority on the floor of the house, and in 1959 it was used to suspend one of the few opposition-ruled state governments (the Communist-led government of Kerala) following mass protests.

From the late 1960s, under Prime Minister Indira Gandhi, as Congress ceded power to opposition parties in state elections, there was more frequent resort to President's Rule. It continued to be used to manage internal party dissent (for example, in Haryana in 1967, Andhra Pradesh in 1973 and Uttar Pradesh in 1973) as well as to prevent opposition parties from attempting to form state governments. It is worth noting that the Sarkaria Commission, in its review of all instances of President's Rule up to 1988, classified 15 of 32 instances of President's Rule between 1967–77 as 'inevitable' or, in other words, justifiable. Most of these were cases of instability caused by the resignation of chief ministers or defections, as these often involved the need to pass a budget before elections could be held.

The second period (1977–1989) saw a substantial increase in the use of President's Rule, usually motivated by egregiously partisan motives (see Figure 5.1). The end of the Emergency saw the election of the first non-Congress government in 1977.[53] One of the first moves by the Janata Party coalition government was to threaten nine Congress-led state governments with dismissal on the grounds that the Janata Party had lost its parliamentary majority in those states during the general elections.

---

[53] Under article 352 of the Constitution, Indira Gandhi declared a state of national emergency in June 1975 which lasted until March 1977, on the grounds of a threat to the internal security of the nation. During this period, constitutional rights to free speech and assembly were suspended, elections were not held, opposition leaders were arrested and the freedom of the media and judiciary was curtailed.

Table 5.1 Categories of President's Rule (PR) application outlined in Sarkaria Commission report (1988)

Category	Description	Examples
PR when the ministry (state government) commanded a majority in state legislature	Used to deal with intra-party problems or respond to alleged maladministration by an elected state government	Punjab (1951), after the Congress Party decided the Congress Party chief minister should resign with no alternative leader immediately re-elected; Andhra Pradesh (1973): PR declared to deal with a Congress Party split in the state over the bifurcation of Andhra Pradesh and Telangana; Punjab (1983), when the chief minister resigned and called for PR in view of the national security situation with the Akali agitation
PR proclaimed without floor test	Where a chief minister or ministry had resigned but other parties were not given the chance to test their majority in legislative assembly	Uttar Pradesh (1968): the Samyukta Vidhayak Dal government resigned but the opposition was not given the chance to test its majority; Kerala (1979): after several parties withdrew support for the chief minister the opposition claimed a majority but the governor recommended PR because the resulting ministry was unlikely to be stable
PR 'inevitable'	A variety of circumstances, including: where an alternative political formation was unable to prove a majority in the legislature; where no caretaker government could be formed pending fresh elections; where a budget needed to be passed in an unstable legislature; where extensive defections undermined the stability of government; and where the state government was unable to manage law and order	PR was deemed 'inevitable' in 26 of the 75 cases considered by the Sarkaria commission. The vast majority of these cases related to the absence of a stable majority government; only one (Punjab 1987) related to a breakdown of law and order

Source: Summary of Annexure VI.4, Cases of President's Rule – Categorywise, Chapter VI.

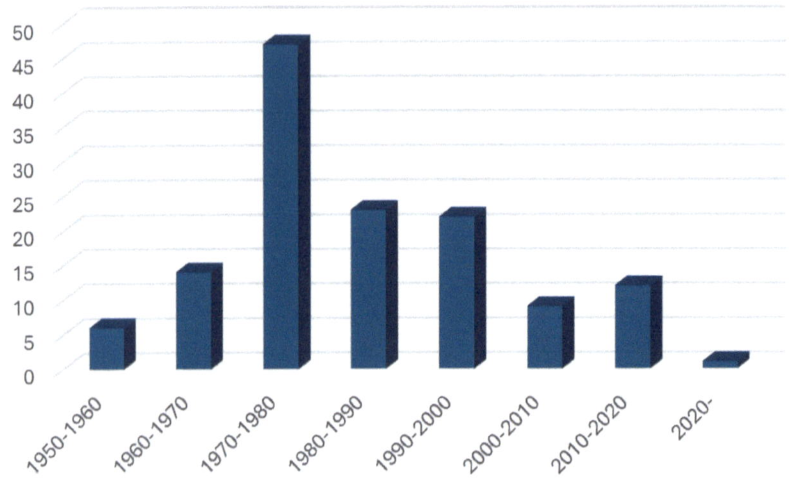

Source: Graph based on figures in Swenden (2016) and Adeney (2007), with post-2016 data from https://www.worldstatesmen.org/India_states.html. The post-2016 data includes the imposition of President's Rule in Arunachal Pradesh and Uttarakhand, later ruled illegal by the courts.

Figure 5.1 *Frequency of imposition of President's Rule*

The Union Home Minister sent a letter to the chief ministers of these states calling on them to advise their governors to dissolve their state assemblies and call fresh elections. This was justified, he argued, on the grounds of 'the most unprecedented political situation arising out of the virtual rejection, in the recent Lok Sabha elections, of candidates belonging to the ruling party in various States', with 'the resultant climate of uncertainty … causing grave concern'.[54] In response, six of the states filed a case to the Supreme Court, arguing that the Home Minister's letter was illegal and seeking an injunction against imposition of article 356. The court in *Rajasthan* held that the matter was beyond judicial review (this was prior to the 44th constitutional amendment). The consequence of this judgment was that the Janata government proceeded to dismiss the nine state governments. When Congress returned to power in 1980, it retaliated by dismissing nine Janata-led state governments.

These unambiguous abuses of President's Rule reflected a deeper deterioration in centre–state relations, and it was against this backdrop that the Commission on Centre–State Relations (otherwise known as the Sarkaria

54 Cited in Government of India 1988, section 6.6.04.

Commission) was established in 1983. The Commission was forthright in its response to these abuses: 'In our opinion, these 18 cases are typical instances of wholesale misuse of article 356 for political purposes, extraneous to the one for which the power has been conferred by the Constitution.'[55] This period, from 1977 to the early 1980s, was the lowest point in terms of the abuse of President's Rule.

A course correction took place in the period of political regionalisation and coalition government from 1989 to 2014. As outlined above, the introduction of checks and balances was strengthened by the 1994 *Bommai* judgment which firmly established that President's Rule is subject to judicial review and also laid down firmer principles governing its use.

The *Bommai* case was originally brought before the Supreme Court by the former chief minister of the state of Karnataka, SR Bommai, to contest the imposition of President's Rule in his state in 1989. His government had been dismissed in April 1989 following a series of defections from his party, but the governor denied him the opportunity to test his support in the legislature.[56] By the time the Supreme Court judgment was delivered in 1994, the case also referred to an additional five applications of article 356. These included two cases (Meghalaya and Nagaland in northeast India) which challenged the imposition of President's Rule when appropriate floor tests had not been carried out in the state assemblies. The three other cases involved the dismissal of BJP-ruled state governments, in Madhya Pradesh, Himachal Pradesh and Rajasthan, on the grounds of law-and-order concerns following the demolition of the Babri Masjid (mosque) in Ayodhya in December 1992 (a totemic cause for the Hindu nationalist BJP).

Justices Sawant and Kuldip Singh Jr, two of the judges in the *Bommai* case, underlined the significance of the checks and balances on article 356 for protecting the Constitution:

> The Constitution is essentially a political document and provisions such as Article 356 have a potentiality to unsettle and subvert the entire constitution scheme. The exercise of powers vested under such provisions needs, therefore, to be circumscribed to maintain the fundamental constitutional balance lest the Constitution is defaced and destroyed ... Democracy and federalism are the essential features of our Constitution and are part of its basic structure.

---

55 Government of India 1988, section 6.6.10.

56 *The Hindu* (2018).

They argued that the frequent dissolution of assemblies via recourse to article 356 risked creating 'disenchantment in the people with the process of election and thus with the democratic way of life itself'.[57]

The *Bommai* judgment pronounced invalid the proclamation of President's Rule in the cases of Karnataka, Meghalaya and Nagaland. However, it upheld the constitutionality of the dissolution of the legislatures of Madhya Pradesh, Himachal Pradesh and Rajasthan on the grounds that the President had reason to conclude that the BJP governments in these states could not govern in accordance with the Constitution following the destruction of the Babri Masjid. The governments could not disassociate themselves from the action and its consequences, and nor could they uphold a ban on the Hindu nationalist volunteer organisation the Rashtriya Swayamsevak Sangh, since many ministers were members.

After the *Bommai* ruling, the use of President's Rule fell dramatically. However (and as the rest of this section will show), under the second dominant-party system which coalesced under the BJP at the centre since 2014, the institutional safeguards against politically motivated federal intervention that were put in place following the *Bommai* ruling have been severely tested.

Following 2014, recourse to President's Rule has been less successful. In 2016, the courts rejected two attempts to apply President's Rule in Arunachal Pradesh and Uttarakhand. However, the office of the governor became much more politicised, and threats to invoke President's Rule continue to be made. In addition, in one of the most consequential cases for Indian federalism, the constitutional clause governing the differential autonomy granted to the Muslim-majority state of Jammu and Kashmir (article 370) was annulled in 2019. Furthermore, the state was bifurcated into two centrally administered union territories while under President's Rule (Jammu and Kashmir had been placed under President's Rule following the BJP's resignation from the governing coalition in the state).

As discussed in section 3, the office of governor has always been subject to politicisation because of the ill-defined scope of the discretionary powers granted to it by the Constitution. However, the potential for abuse of office has been greater in periods of one-party political dominance. Since 2014, the governor's office under the BJP dominant-party system has come under increasing scrutiny. There are several reasons for this.

First of all, governors have played a decisive role in enabling the formation of BJP-led ministries in states where the BJP did not emerge from state elections with a simple majority. In states including Manipur (2017), Goa (2017) and Meghalaya (2018), the process followed by governors in sequencing which

57 *Bommai.*

party or alliance was first invited to conduct a floor test visibly enabled the formation of BJP-led governments.

Second, in various opposition-ruled states, governors have openly entered the political fray, often using the threat of President's Rule to express their displeasure with actions taken by state governments. One example of this came in 2022, following the election of an Aam Aadmi Party state government led by Bhagwant Singh Mann in Punjab. In March 2023, a dispute between the chief minister and the governor made its way to the Supreme Court after the governor refused to summon the legislative assembly for the budget session.

In this case, the Supreme Court reminded the governor that he was 'duty-bound' to summon the legislature, but it also reprimanded the chief minister for the 'tone and tenor' of his social media communications about the governor's queries. The Court warned that 'political differences ... have to be worked out with a sense of sobriety and maturity', otherwise 'the effective implementation of constitutional values is liable to be placed in jeopardy'.[58]

By September 2023, the governor was threatening to send a report to the President recommending the imposition of article 356 on the grounds that he had written 22 letters to the chief minister about 'corruption, rampant drug abuse, and illegal mining' and had not received any proper replies. In an interview, the governor stated:

> If these things keep going on, then constitutional crises will develop. If he doesn't give me proper replies as per the Constitution, and if this continues, then I will have to take a decision to send a report to the President of India under article 356 about the failure of the constitutional mechanism in the State, seeking advice about what should be done under such circumstances.[59]

Partisanship in the invocation of President's Rule is also evident in instances of the non-declaration of President's Rule. The clearest recent example arises from the ethnic conflict in the BJP-ruled state of Manipur. This began in 2023 and led to the deaths of more than 150 people and the displacement of thousands more.[60] While opposition parties and a chief minister from a neigh-

58 Chadha K 'Governors vs CMS' (16 March 2023) *Tehelka* available at https://tehelka.com/governors-vs-cms/ (accessed 27 January 2025).

59 'Chief Minister is duty bound to reply to Governor's queries' *The Hindu* (18 September 2023). In other opposition-ruled states, such as Kerala, chief ministers have accused governors of holding up the ratification of legislation. In Delhi and in Puducherry, chief ministers have accused the respective lieutenant governors of undermining and interfering with the running of their governments. See Chadha (2023).

60 'Manipur violence: Mass burial for victims of India ethnic clashes' (15 December 2023) *BBC* available at https://www.bbc.co.uk/news/world-asia-india

bouring state called for the introduction of President's Rule, the governor made no recommendation.[61]

The institutional checks and balances provided by article 356 and President's Rule have yet to be tested in relation to either breakdowns in the relations between governors and their chief ministers or cases of the non-imposition of President's Rule in a state politically aligned with the centre despite a breakdown in law and order. However, the landmark Supreme Court judgment in December 2023 on the abrogation of article 370 governing Jammu and Kashmir's autonomous status did address the legitimacy of making such a significant constitutional change while the state was under President's Rule.

Petitioners in this case had queried the legitimacy of the original proclamation of President's Rule on the basis that no other political formation had been given the opportunity to test their majority. The Court ruled that since no material relief could be given (because President's Rule had already been lifted), the most substantive question was whether the abrogation of article 370 breached the 'constitutional limitations on the exercise of power' under President's Rule.[62] On this point, the Court found that there was no constitutional obstacle to the exercise of power under article 356 even if it creates 'irreversible' consequences.[63] Thus while the Supreme Court upheld the major tenets of the *Bommai* ruling, it did nothing to strengthen the checks and balances available to constrain the exercise of power under President's Rule.

7. CONCLUSION

This chapter has explored the history and practice of federal intervention in India since the promulgation of its Constitution in 1950. It has demonstrated that article 356 – on 'President's Rule' – has been invoked far more often than the Constitution's architects originally envisaged and for purposes that extend way beyond the limited uses they had had in mind. From the late 1960s up until the mid-1990s, President's Rule became a routine tool in the hands

-67724692 (last accessed January 31st 2024).

61 '"Expected President's Rule": Mizoram chief minister on manipur violence' (20 January 2024) *NDTV* available at https://www.ndtv.com/india-news/expected-presidents-rule-says-mizoram-chief-minister-lalduhoma-on-manipur-violence-4895359 (accessed 31 January 2024).

62 Supreme Court of India Judgment of Chief Justice of India, DY Chandrachud, on Writ Petitions concerning abrogation of Article 370 of the Constitution of India (11 December 2023) Writ Petition (Civil) No. 1099 of 2019 at 113–114 available at https://www.legalbites.in/landmark-judgements/case-review-supreme-court-verdict-on-article-370-abrogation-980543 (accessed 31 January 2024).

63 Judgement of Chief Justice of India (December 2023) at 152.

of Union governments to destabilise and even dismiss opposition-ruled state governments. Following the Supreme Court's 1994 *Bommai* ruling, and in the period of political regionalisation, a system of firmer checks and balances was established around the promulgation of President's Rule. Despite this tightening of checks and balances, there has been no fundamental challenge to the legitimacy of federal intervention. Article 356 continues to be used when no single party can demonstrate a majority in a state legislative assembly, or where law and order is threatened (as happened with the communal violence that erupted following the destruction of the Babri Masjid in Ayodhya in 1992). Furthermore, a Supreme Court judgment on the article 370 abrogation in December 2023 underlined that there are few checks and balances on the exercise of power *after* the promulgation of President's Rule.

Since 2014 and the transition to a new second dominant-party system, the robustness of the checks and balances around the powers of federal intervention has been further tested. The final sections of the chapter revealed the growing politicisation of the office of governor (particularly the use of article 356 as a threat). This reflects the extent to which federal intervention has been normalised as a method for dealing with partisan opponents, even as the most egregious abuses of President's Rule have been reined in.

In the 2024 general elections, the BJP fell shy of a majority and formed a coalition government in which a number of regional parties (and particularly the Telugu Desam Party from Andhra Pradesh and Janata Dal (United) from Bihar) play a crucial role. There are parallels with the previous era (1977–1989) in which the country's dominant party came under challenge from a range of different parties, which were unable to form a coherent polity-wide opposition. In those circumstances, as today, centre–state relations have become *the* political battleground. While today it may be more difficult to misuse President's Rule, there remain many other mechanisms for federal intervention. As well as the politicisation of the office of the governor, central investigative agencies such as the Enforcement Directorate (under the Ministry of Finance) have been used to conduct investigations into sitting opposition chief ministers.

The further frontier in terms of intervention sits at the state level. Much less is known, or publicly debated, about the routine powers of intervention wielded by state governments vis-à-vis municipal governments. As calls grow to reform the governance of Indian cities – the growth engines of the economy – the time is ripe for a further examination of the vertical powers of intervention between the second and third tiers of government.

BIBLIOGRAPHY

Books

Adeney K *Federalism and ethnic conflict regulation in India and Pakistan* New York: Palgrave Macmillan (2007)
Austin G *The Indian Constitution: Cornerstone of a nation* Oxford: Oxford University Press (1966)
Birch AH *Federalism, finance and social legislation in Canada, Australia and the United States* Oxford: Clarendon Press (1955)
Khosla M *India's founding moment: The constitution of a most surprising democracy* Cambridge: Harvard University Press (2020)
Narayanan S, James K, & Panda L *Heads held high: Salvaging state governors for 21st century India* New Delhi: Navi Books (2023)
Purushotham S *From Raj to republic: Sovereignty, violence, and democracy in India* Stanford: Stanford University Press (2021)
Sengupta A *The colonial constitution* New Delhi: Juggernaut Books (2023)
Sultan N *Waiting for the people: The idea of democracy in Indian anticolonial thought* Cambridge: Harvard University Press (1994)
Thiruvengadam AK *The constitution of India: A contextual analysis* Oxford; Portland, Oregon: Hart Publishing (2017)
Tillin L *Indian federalism* New Delhi: Oxford University Press (2019)
Wheare KC *Federal government* London; New York: Oxford University Press (1963)

Chapters in Books

James K & Arora B 'The judicial journey of Indian federalism' in Madhava M (ed) *Continuities and discontinuities: Politics and society in contemporary India* Hyderabad: Orient Blackswan (forthcoming)
Rudolph LI & Rudolph SH 'Redoing the constitutional design: From an interventionist to a regulatory state' in Kohli A (ed) *The success of India's democracy* Cambridge: Cambridge University Press (2001) 127–162
Sagar R 'Emergency powers' in Choudhry S, Khosla M & Mehta PB (eds) *The Oxford handbook of the Indian Constitution* Oxford: Oxford University Press (2016) 213–31
Singh MP 'The federal scheme' in Choudhry S, Khosla M, & Mehta PB (eds) *The Oxford handbook of the Indian Constitution* Oxford: Oxford University Press (2016)

Journal Articles

Arora B & Kailash KK 'Beyond quasi federalism: Change and continuity in Indian Federalism' (2018) 6(2) *Studies in Indian Politics* 297–302
Dardanelli P, Kincaid J, Fenna A, et al. 'Conceptualising, measuring, and theorising dynamic de/centralisation in federations' (2019) 49(1) *Publius* 1
Elangovan A 'Provincial autonomy, Sir Benegal Narsing Rau, and an improbable imagination of constitutionalism in India, 1935–38' (2016) 36(1) *Comparative Studies of South Asia, Africa and the Middle East* 66–82

Idiculla M 'Unpacking local self-government: The uncertain power of cities in the Indian Constitution' (2020) 53(1) *Law and Politics in Africa, Asia and Latin America* 30–50
Sadanandan A 'Bridling central tyranny in India' (2012) 52(2) *Asian Survey* 247–69
Swenden W & Saxena R 'Policing the federation: The supreme court and judicial federalism in India' (2022) 10(1) *Territory, Politics, Governance* 12–31
Swenden W 'Centre-state bargaining and territorial accommodation: Evidence from India' (2016) 22(4) *Swiss Political Science Review* 491–515
Tillin L 'Building a national economy: Origins of centralised federalism in India' (2021) 51(2) *Publius* 161–85

Internet Sources

'"Expected President's Rule": Mizoram chief minister on manipur violence' (20 January 2024) *NDTV* available at https://www.ndtv.com/india-news/expected-presidents-rule-says-mizoram-chief-minister-lalduhoma-on-manipur-violence-4895359 (accessed 31 January 2024)
'Manipur violence: Mass burial for victims of India ethnic clashes' (15 December 2023) *BBC* available at https://www.bbc.co.uk/news/world-asia-india-67724692 (last accessed January 31st 2024)
'What is the SR Bommai case, and why is it quoted often?' *The Hindu* (18 May 2018) available at https://www.thehindu.com/news/national/what-is-the-sr-bommai-case-and-why-is-it-quoted-often/article61834854.ece (accessed 27 January 2025)
Acahrya P & Bose N 'BMC completes 18 months without corporators; no elected reps in 24 municipal bodies in state' *The Indian Express* (20 September 2023) available at https://indianexpress.com/article/cities/mumbai/bmc-completes-18-months-without-corporators-no-elected-reps-in-24-municipal-bodies-in-state-8932683/ (accessed 27 January 2025)
Brand Bengaluru Committee *Greater Bengaluru Governance Bill* (20 July 2024) available at https://bbmprestructuring.wordpress.com/wp-content/uploads/2024/07/gbg-final-submission_with-bill__july-2024-1.pdf (accessed 5 December 2024)
Chadha K 'Governors vs CMS' (16 March 2023) *Tehelka* available at https://tehelka.com/governors-vs-cms/ (accessed 27 January 2025)

Case Law

Supreme Court of India Arunachal Pradesh Legislative Assembly *Nabam Rebia v Deputy Speaker* (2016) 8 SCC 1
Supreme Court of India Judgment of Chief Justice of India, DY Chandrachud on Writ Petitions concerning abrogation of Article 370 of the Constitution of India (11 December 2023) Writ Petition (Civil) No. 1099 of 2019
Supreme Court of India *Kuldip Nayar v Union of India* (2006) AIR 2006 SC 3127, Appeal (civil) 217 of 2004, 22 August 2006
Supreme Court of India *SR Bommai v Union of India* (1994)
Supreme Court of India S*tate of Rajasthan & Ors. Etc. Etc. vs Union of India Etc. Etc.* (1977)
Uttarakhand High Court *Harish Rawat v Union of India* (2016) SCC Online Utt 502

Legislation

Andhra Pradesh Municipalities Act, 1965
Karnataka Municipal Corporations Act, 1976
Kerala Municipalities Act, 1994
Maharashtra Municipal Corporations Act, 1949
Mumbai Municipal Corporation Act, 1888

Reports

Sarkaria RS & Ramasubramaniam KA (for the government of India) *Commission on centre-state relations* New Delhi: Government of India Press (1988)

6. Italy: federalism and intervention

Alice Valdesalici

1. THE ITALIAN REGIONAL SYSTEM IN CONTEXT

More than 20 years ago, Italy was seen as championing the movement towards federalisation. It introduced the most significant 'federalising' constitutional reform that the Western world had seen in decades. At present, however, the implementation of this reform remains a work in progress and, for a decade or more, a counter-wave of centralisation has become the prevailing trend.

Italian regionalism is characterised by an asymmetrical design, both as a matter of constitutional law and in terms of use of powers transferred to the regions. Of the 20 regions, 5 have a special status: Sicily, Sardinia, Aosta Valley, Friuli-Venezia Giulia and Trentino-South Tyrol.[1] Through bilateral negotiation, each of these has developed a different system of powers. Although laid down in the 1948 Constitution, regionalisation has only developed since the 1970s. In 1999 and 2001, constitutional reforms were approved that considerably increased the powers and political autonomy of ordinary regions, but these also confirmed the two-track asymmetry between ordinary and special regions.

One of the most important changes has concerned the distribution of legislative and administrative powers between the state (that is, the central government) and the regions. The introduction of new criteria for the distribution of power between the state and regions sparked controversy. The Constitutional Court has been playing a key role in redefining their respective competencies, often leaning towards a more centralistic approach. Fiscal federalism was considered one of the milestones of the 2001 new constitutional framework, though in practice it has remained largely unimplemented. Furthermore, there is no constitutionally guaranteed institutional representation of regional interests

[1] The last one, however, is divided in the two autonomous provinces of Trento and Bolzano. These are comparable to special regions in terms of their competences, thus taking the place of the region in their respective territories.

at the central level. The existing intergovernmental cooperative mechanisms remain weak, enjoying no more than a consultative role.

This trend has been sharply accelerated by economic and financial crisis which has led to the state imposing numerous austerity measures. These have not only challenged regional and local autonomy, but also bolstered the move towards re-centralisation. Paradoxically, while intended to rationalise public finances, the new measures actually undermine progresses made in regionalisation. All in all, the implementation of the federalising reform is (to say the least) stagnating.

Against the background set out above, this chapter examines the different forms and procedures of executive intervention by a higher level of government (either national or subnational) in singled-out entities at lower government levels, whether subnational or local. While acknowledging the distinct scenarios that can lead to intervention in Italy, the analysis focuses on those pertaining to matters of security or failure to comply with certain legal obligations. This analysis proceeds on the understanding that, in Italy, such instruments ends up shaping intergovernmental dynamics in significant ways and ultimately contributes to the transformation of the power structure formally entrenched in the Constitution.

2. EVOLUTION OF THE LEGAL FRAMEWORK AND RATIONALE FOR FEDERAL INTERVENTION

The Italian legal system recognises that central government has the power to intervene in subnational and local levels of government. In the 1948 Constitution, no provision was made for the state to exercise a right of intervention in the powers of regions and local authorities. Nonetheless, while from the 1970s onward regions were established and vested with competences, these were accompanied by the adoption of national provisions which allowed the state to substitute for territorial entities in the exercise of their prerogatives. Under certain conditions, the national executive may exercise a substitutive power in relation to administrative functions attributed either to the regions or to local authorities. The state was also granted substitutive power of a preventive nature in cases of regional inaction in the exercise of allocated legislative functions (though at that time of a concurrent nature only).

The earliest cases involved failures by the regions to fulfil their European Union (EU) obligations or failures in the exercise of their administrative functions (either own or delegated ones). It was only following the administrative decentralisation initiated at the end of the 1990s (with the 'Bassanini' laws) that a general rule of the substitutive power allows for state intervention vis-à-vis regions and local authorities in the exercise of the administrative functions.

However, this occurred through ordinary law[2] and represented a trade-off: to make up for allowing the decentralisation of powers, the central government insisted on retaining interventionary powers so as to avoid losing control entirely.

This system underwent revision as a result of constitutional reform in 2001. This reform effected profound changes to the relations between the state, regions and local authorities, primarily through an extension of the legislative power vested with regional governments. While regions were vested with exclusive legislative powers, the new residual clause meant that all matters not expressly listed in article 117 fell under the exclusive legislative competence of the regions. The allocation criteria for administrative functions were also renewed. In terms of the new article 118 of the Constitution, administrative functions are given in the first place to municipalities, as the territorial governing bodies closest to citizens. Only where deemed necessary for uniform implementation were these functions vested in provinces, metropolitan cities, regions or the state (in this order) pursuant to the principles of subsidiarity, differentiation and proportionality.

Evidence of this development can be found in constitutional jurisprudence. In a key decision,[3] the Constitutional Court declared that when the substitutive power is provided for in relations between the state and regions on matters belonging to the latter, the state must act in compliance with specific conditions. This is necessary because intervention interferes with constitutionally entrenched political autonomy. With the 2001 constitutional reform, territorial autonomies – and in particular regional governments – acquired vast competencies (also of a legislative nature). Given the fact that there are regions which belong to a political-representative circuit that is additional to and different from the political direction of the government of the Republic (that is, the national government), the result is an augmented pluralism in both institutions and sources of law. Nevertheless, according to the constitutional case law,[4] autonomy cannot imply any power to deviate from the common path defined by the Constitution, as based on the sharing of values and principles insensitive to the territorial dimension.

Over the years, however, interventionary powers have experienced a gradual expansion. This had an impact on the Italian regional system, and contributed to the undermining of the principle of separation in favour of a federal system organised around the principles of collaboration and, above all, coordination.

---

2 Law 59/1997 and Legislative Decree 112/1998.

3 Judgment 177/1988.

4 Judgment 219/2013.

The aftermath of the revision of Title V of the Constitution clearly demonstrates that even the most pronounced forms of regional (legislative) autonomy are not immune to the overarching influence of competencies exclusively assigned to the state.[5] A similar observation certainly applies to concurrent competencies (such as the coordination of public finance).[6] Here, the Constitutional Court has consistently ruled that the financial and organisational autonomy of regions recedes when confronted with measures that must be uniform across the country and are fundamental principles of the subject matter.[7] In the constitutional order emerging from the 2001 reform, the state maintains a distinct position, as is evident from article 5 of the Constitution, which enshrines the fundamental principles of the unity and indivisibility of the Italian Republic.

This position is amplified by recurrent references to unitary instances throughout the Constitution. These include the call to comply with the Constitution and the constraints deriving from EU and international obligations, and are listed as limits to regional legislative autonomy.[8] While the need to protect the legal and economic unity of the system is also recognised.[9] These unitary instances necessarily postulate the existence of a subject, the state, which is tasked with giving effect to them.[10]

Within this renewed territorial scenario, three different forms of intervention are constitutionally enshrined to counterbalance the increase in autonomy: the extraordinary power of substitution;[11] legislative substitution for the case of regional non-compliance in the implementation of EU law;[12] and the power to dismiss and/or remove the political bodies of the regions.[13] These intervention instruments manifest in various forms and concern various actors (national vs subnational levels of government, parliament rather than government) and distinct types of powers. The latter may in fact involve a temporary substitution of higher levels in the execution of actions, which could be either of administrative or legislative nature. Also, these may affect the governing bodies of the targeted entities, ordering their dissolution or removal.

---

5 Article 117(2), Constitution.
6 Article 117(3), Constitution.
7 See, for instance, judgments 169/2007, 417/2005 and 36/2004.
8 Article 117(1).
9 Article 120(2).
10 Judgment 274/2003.
11 Article 120, Constitution.
12 Article 117(5), Constitution.
13 Article 126, Constitution.

3. THE EXTRAORDINARY SUBSTITUTIVE POWER

3.1 Constitutional and Legislative Grounds for Intervention

Pursuant to article 120 of the Constitution, the national executive may act in substitution for regions, provinces and municipalities if these fail to comply with international or EU law, in cases of serious danger to public safety and security or whenever action is necessary to preserve legal and economic unity (and guarantee a basic level of civil and social rights). This form of intervention does not entail a permanent takeover of legislative and administrative powers by the central (*rectius*, the higher level of) government. The allocation of these powers persists, as specified by articles 117 and 118, respectively (the latter articulates only the guiding principles for this allocation). It rather determines a temporary takeover of the exercise of these powers, occurring only when certain unitary needs emerge.

The provision under review was enshrined in the Constitution in 2001 as a novel governmental power. Classified by the Constitutional Court[14] as an 'extraordinary' power, it is to be invoked solely in cases of 'serious institutional emergencies',[15] where there is a threat to 'essential, general, and unitary interests'.[16] However, the vagueness of the constitutional provision has given rise to various interpretative issues about its application.[17]

Understanding the rationale behind article 120 can shed light on its purpose. It can be traced back to the fundamental principles of unity and indivisibility of the Italian Republic entrenched in article 5 of the Constitution, though, according to the Constitutional Court,[18] the provision is a 'safeguard clause' that upholds the fundamental needs of equality, security and legality. These needs

---

[14] Judgment 43/2004.

[15] Judgment 43/2004.

[16] Judgments 236/2004 and 388/2004.

[17] To give but a few examples, questions have been raised about the admissibility of state interventions of a legislative nature or interventions that go beyond constitutional provisions; the need for inertia as a prerequisite for intervention; the interpretation of the cases, exhaustively listed, that legitimise substitute power; the coordination with the provision of article 117(5), on the non-fulfilment of EU obligations; the meaning of the reference to the principle of subsidiarity contained in the final part of article 120(2); the survival of a regional power of intervention in local authorities; and the territorial scope of enforceability of the provision. For detailed discussion, see Groppi T 'Nota a sentenza n. 43 del 2004' (2004) *Forum di quaderni costituzionali* available at https://www.forumcostituzionale.it/wordpress/ (accessed 1 March 2025).

[18] Constitutional Court, Judgment 236/2004.

could remain unmet or severely compromised due to the failure or improper exercise of competencies allocated to subnational and local governments under articles 117 and 118. Hence, there is an inseparable connection between the assignment of a competence to a territorial entity and the acknowledgement of the intervention power, which is aimed at ensuring that the unity and coherence of the system are preserved.[19]

In essence, the provision outlined in article 120(2) serves as a unifying element within the constitutional framework governing the allocation of powers (that is, articles 117 and 118 of the Constitution). The primary objective is to ensure that, even under pathological circumstances, the central authority retains the capacity to intervene in safeguarding unitary interests, notwithstanding the decentralisation of powers that is in place. Decentralisation cannot stand in the way of the protection of essential values: even within a system that values territorial autonomy, there are interests that transcend the boundaries of individual territorial entities. Since the central authority is entrusted with safeguarding the overall welfare of citizens, it inherently retains the prerogative to intervene when necessary in areas that extend beyond its jurisdiction.[20]

3.1.1 The territorial scope of enforceability

While there is no doubt about the enforceability of article 120 with regard to ordinary regions and local entities within their territories, the situation becomes more intricate when considering special regions, including the two autonomous provinces of Trento and Bolzano (hereinafter 'special regions').[21]

Special regions are supposedly granted more autonomy than ordinary regions. Prior to the 2001 reform, they were entitled to much broader legislative and administrative powers than ordinary regions. While the latter had legislative authority over a limited number of subjects,[22] and only within the framework outlined by a national law, special regions enjoyed much broader jurisdiction, with their legislative powers being listed in their autonomy statutes and, in most fields, they themselves being vested with exclusive competences.

This fundamental difference was (in theory) eliminated by the 2001 constitutional reform. This elevated the ordinary regions (in terms of

---

19 Constitutional Court, Judgment 236/2004.

20 De Michele A 'L'art. 120 della Costituzione e il suo ruolo nella riforma del Titolo V' (2008) 5 *Le Istituzioni del Federalismo* 623 at 634; Michetti M 'Titolo V e potere sostitutivo statale. Profili ricostruttivi ed applicativi' (2020) 3 *dirittifondamentali.it* 328.

21 The Trentino-South Tyrol Region is subdivided into the two autonomous provinces of Trento and Bolzano/Bozen, which are comparable to a special region in terms of competences and thus political autonomy.

22 Article 117, Constitution.

legislative power) to the same level as the special regions. The sources of law underlying them do, however, remain different. The legislative powers of the special regions are as a rule not regulated by the national Constitution but rather through the regions' autonomy statutes as well as a number of enactment decrees. The autonomy statutes take the form of national constitutional laws but are applicable only to the territory of the special region of concern. Similar considerations pertain to the enactment decrees: these have quasi-constitutional status and apply only within the regional territory, despite taking the form of national government decrees.[23] Furthermore, where the 2001 constitutional reform provides ordinary regions with a greater degree of autonomy, this is also extended to the special regions ('favour clause').[24]

The uncertainty regarding the applicability of article 120(2) to special regions is resolved by case law. In its Decision 236/2004, the Constitutional Court stipulates that the application of article 120(2) could not be suspended vis-à-vis special regions, not even by virtue of the 'favour clause'. There is in fact a direct correlation between the provisions governing the distribution of competencies[25] and the provision regarding the power of substitution.[26] The latter acts as a 'safeguard mechanism' for the former, ensuring that decentralisation and autonomy do not jeopardise vital interests. Given this correlation, the idea that article 120 is inapplicable to special regions must be dismissed. Conversely, it must be inferred that the power of substitution may also extend to them, albeit subject to certain limitations.

A distinction must indeed be made between the powers entrusted by the respective statutes of autonomy and those that passed because of the 2001 reform (that is, by virtue of the 'favour clause'). The specific rules of intervention prescribed by their statutes (or by the enactment decrees) apply to the former group, whereas for the latter the actual enforceability of article 120(2) is theoretically possible, though substantially conditioned. In fact, the actual transfer to special regions of the additional functions, attracted by virtue of the 'favour clause', is subordinated to the approval of the above-mentioned enactment decrees. This implies that even the rules governing the substitution power are essentially contingent upon the effective transfer of powers, meaning that article 120 of the Constitution remains inoperative regarding them until the enactment decrees are approved.

23 Such decrees are de facto adopted by a joint commission in which the state and the region are equally represented. This complicated procedure for their adoption gives such decrees quasi-constitutional value.

24 The so-called favour clause pursuant to article 10, Constitutional Law 3/2001.

25 Articles 117 and 118.

26 Article 120(2).

3.1.2 The functional scope: administrative vs legislative interventions

While it was evident from the outset that article 120(2) of the Constitution legitimised substitutions of an administrative nature, the permissibility of state interventions of a legislative nature has been a subject of prolonged debate. The ambiguity stems from the vague and indeterminate nature of the constitutional provision, which allows for conflicting interpretations on this matter. Even the law that implements article 120 (Law 131/2003) fails to provide a clear-cut answer to this uncertainty. Not surprisingly, scholars are divided on the matter. Some regard it as illegitimate, while others argue that it falls within the purview of article 120.[27] One of the main points of contention revolves around the rule that a substitutive intervention must not exceed its own authority.[28] However, an exploration of the established practice and the constitutional jurisprudence on it resolves the dispute.

Take, for instance, the case from the Apulia region. Regional elections were to be held in September 2020, and the national government wanted all voters to be guaranteed the possibility of expressing the so-called double gender preference (so to ensure compliance with article 117(7) on gender equality in regional electoral laws).[29] The laws of the regions Liguria and Apulia did not provide for such an institution, so the Prime Minister sent a note inviting them

---

27 For discussion in favour of this view, see Luciani M 'Le nuove competenze legislative delle Regioni a statuto ordinario. Prime osservazioni sui principali nodi problematici della l. cost. n. 3 del 2001' (2001) available at https://www.associazionedeicostituzionalisti.it/old_sites/sito_AIC_2003-2010/materiali/convegni/aic200201/luciani.html (accessed 9 February 2026); Gianfrancesco E 'Il potere sostitutivo' in Groppi T & Olivetti M (eds) *La Repubblica delle autonomie* Torino: G Giappichelli Editore (2003) at 239; Salerno GM 'La disciplina legislativa dei poteri sostitutivi tra semplificazione e complessità ordinamentale' in AA VV (eds) *Il DDL la Loggia* Federalismi.it (2002) at 47 ff. Contra: *ex plurimis*, Mainardis C 'Il nuovo regionalismo italiano e i poteri sostitutivi statali: una riforma costituzionale con (poche) luci e (molte) ombre' (2001) 6 *Le Regioni* 1357; Rescigno GU 'Attuazione delle direttive comunitarie e potere sostitutivo dello Stato' (2002) 4 *Le Regioni* 753; Veronesi G 'Il regime dei poteri sostitutivi alla luce del nuovo art. 120, comma 2, della Costituzione' (2002) 5 *Le Istituzioni del Federalismo* 742.

28 In this debate, the discussion of the sources of law appropriate for the purpose is prolific, in particular in relation to the use of law decrees and the need to respect the constitutional requirements for its use (that is, extraordinary circumstances of necessity and urgency). See, for example, Dickmann R 'L'esercizio del potere sostitutivo con decreto-legge per garantire l'espressione della doppia preferenza di genere in occasione delle elezioni regionali in Puglia del 2020' (2020) 4 *Forum di Quaderni Costituzionali.*

29 The 'double-gender preference' is a mechanism used in some electoral systems to promote gender equality. It allows voters to choose two candidates as long

to introduce it. The invitation was promptly accepted by the Liguria region, which, after two decades of inertia, equipped itself with its own electoral law. There was no response from the Apulia region, so the Prime Minister forwarded a 'formal act of warning' on 23 July, inviting the region to adapt its rules by 28 July. After the very short deadline had expired (perhaps not unexpectedly), the national executive adopted Decree-Law 86/2020, through which the double-gender preference was introduced in Apulia's regional elections.

The national government intervention to impose double-gender preference in the regional elections of September 2020 channels itself into the only available loophole: that is, the exercise of substitutive powers under article 120(2) of the Constitution, justified on the basis of the need to protect the 'legal unity of the Republic' or to ensure, throughout the national territory, effective gender equality in access to elected offices.[30]

Despite all legal and political perplexities raised by this case, what emerges as pertinent for this chapter is the implicit acknowledgement (also confirmed by case law) of forms of legislative substitution by the national government, provided they adhere to the circumstances and limitations outlined in the constitutional provision. In a later judgment,[31] the Court unambiguously affirmed that the exercise of state substitute power under article 120 of the Constitution can be manifested also through the enactment of legislative measures.

3.1.3 Legitimising grounds for intervention

With the ambiguity that characterises the entire provision, article 120 enumerates the pathological circumstances under which the national government may legitimately resort to the power of substitution. This list, deemed exhaustive, essentially encompasses three distinct situations: non-compliance with EU law and international acts and treaties; serious danger to public safety and security; the need for protection of legal unity and economic unity and, in particular, protection of the essential levels of services concerning civil and social rights.

The rationale is that when there are serious 'constitutional emergencies' that challenge essential interests of the Republic, the central government may legitimately intervene to safeguard them, on condition that the responsible level of government has proved unable to intervene or is unable to intervene adequately. According to the Constitutional Court, simple inertia or inadequate

as one is a female and the other is a male, thus favouring balanced gender representation in elected offices.

30 Cosulich M 'Ex malo bonum? Ovvero del decreto-legge n. 86 del 2020 che introduce la doppia preferenza di genere nelle elezioni regionali pugliesi' (2020) *Federalismi.it*.

31 Judgment 233/2019.

compliance is an insufficient ground for intervention: the serious and exceptional circumstances listed in article 120(2) must also be present.[32] Yet while the mandatory nature of the listed circumstances is to be understood as a guarantee of the constitutional allocation of powers, their vague formulation undermines the intended purpose of the provision by de facto granting the national government significant and discretionary leeway.

The listed hypotheses can be divided into two different categories. The first includes interests under the responsibility of the state (that is, non-compliance with international acts and treaties and EU law; serious danger to public safety and security; and protection of essential levels of services concerning civil and social rights). The second category includes interests vested *ex rerum naturae* in the state as ultimately responsible for preserving the unity and indivisibility of the Republic under article 5 of the Constitution (that is, legal and economic unity).[33]

Interventions intended to address any failure by regional or local governments to comply with international norms and treaties or European law partly overlap with the provision of article 117(5), albeit with differences concerning the authorities empowered and targeted by the intervention (see section 4 below). As for serious dangers to public safety and security, these include situations that disrupt public peace or involve disorderly conduct, as well as serious natural events or major phenomena of organised crime. In these circumstances, substitution serves to safeguard crucial interests in the maintenance of 'orderly civic coexistence'.[34]

As regards the protection of legal and economic unity, the former relates to ensuring a minimum of regulatory uniformity throughout the national territory, while the latter addresses measures and behaviours of territorial entities that conflict with constitutional principles and national directions on economic policy, public finance, and the tax system. Among these, the protection of essential levels of service involves the obligation on territorial authorities to comply with such essential levels set by state law, pursuant to the state's exclusive legislative competence under article 117(2) of the Constitution. Therefore, this intervention aims to ensure equal conditions for exercising and fulfilling fundamental rights throughout the territory, regardless of the place of residence.

---

32 Judgment 165/2011.

33 Michetti M (2020) at 337 and 356.

34 Judgment 290/2001.

3.2 Procedure for Intervention

Pursuant to article 120(2), the state law shall ensure that the power of substitution is exercised in accordance with the principles of subsidiarity and loyal cooperation. While substitutive power might appear to contradict the principle of subsidiarity, the two principles coexist and complement each other.[35] Article 120 legitimises only temporary deviations to address inefficiencies or lack of use of powers delegated to territorial authorities, and as such it is viewed as the 'lesser harm' from the perspective of subnational or local autonomy. When circumstances such as those outlined in article 120 arise, particularly those concerning legal and economic unity, the alternative would entail permanently transferring administrative functions to a more inclusive level of government for all territorial entities, rather than activating temporarily and geographically limiting waivers. In this way, the reference to subsidiarity serves as a guarantee of the temporary nature of the intervention; the government cannot permanently appropriate the function but must 'return' it to the *ex lege* entitled entity once the latter is ready to resume its exercise.[36]

Loyal cooperation is another principle that guides intervention under article 120. As a rule, the principle should underpin intergovernmental relations, especially when the interests and competencies of diverse authorities intersect. Specifically, this principle influences how this power should be wielded, emphasising the necessity to activate collaborative mechanisms. To achieve this, the implementing legislation of article 120(2) incorporates various instruments. First, it empowers the affected entity to prevent intervention by addressing the underlying issue. Second, it outlines mechanisms to ensure the entity's involvement in the adoption of intervention measures, if it is unwilling or unable to act directly (see below). The guarantee of a form of collaboration cannot be completely precluded, but the entity involvement varies in intensity depending on the urgency of the situation at stake.

In regard to the effectiveness of this guarantee, the Constitutional Court not only took on the task of scrutinising the adequacy of the legislative remedies but also asserted the existence of minimum procedural standards that cannot be ignored, even in instances where the law remains silent.[37] The demand for

---

[35] For an in-depth investigation of the link between federal intervention and subsidiarity, see further Papa S *La sussidiarietà alla prova: i poteri sostitutivi nel nuovo ordinamento* Milan: Giuffrè Editore (2008).

[36] Police A 'Sussidiarietà e poteri sostitutivi: la funzione amministrativa nello Stato al plurale' in Chieffi L & di S Luca GC (eds) *Regioni ed enti locali dopo la riforma del titolo V della Costituzione fra attuazione ed ipotesi di ulteriore revisione* Torino: G Giappichelli Editore (2004) at 315.

[37] See Constitutional Court judgments 313/2003; 43/2004; 227/2004.

loyal cooperation, in the eyes of the Court, necessitates 'participatory' procedures, wherein the entity under scrutiny is empowered to fulfil its obligations and thereby prevent the need for substitution. In other words, a recognition of inaction is not enough: the activation of these mechanisms is necessary.[38]

In line with the previously discussed guiding principles, the procedure for exercising the substitution power under article 120 of the Constitution is outlined in Law 131/2003. Pursuant to article 8, the President of the Council of Ministers, on the proposal of the minister in charge of the matter at stake, shall grant the region an appropriate term for adopting any measures deemed necessary. If the term expires without results, the Council of Ministers decides either on the enforcement of the measures or on the appointment of an ad hoc commissioner. The president of the region attends the meeting of the Council. In the event of an emergency, where delaying the intervention would jeopardise the constitutional interests outlined in article 120 (public safety and security, legal and economic unity), the Council of Ministers is authorised to implement the necessary measures. Simultaneously, the Council must notify the Permanent State-Regions Conference, as it retains the right to request a review of the case.

4. REGIONAL NON-IMPLEMENTATION OF EU AND INTERNATIONAL AGREEMENTS

4.1 Constitutional and Legislative Grounds for Intervention

Article 117(5) of the Constitution prescribes that 'Regions and Autonomous Provinces of Trento and Bolzano' (*omissis*)

> are responsible for the implementation of international agreements and EU measures, subject to the rules set out in state law, which regulate the exercise of subsidiary powers by the state in the case of non-performance by the Regions and autonomous Provinces themselves.

The provision bestows a power of substitution on the national authority in the event of any failure by the regions in implementing and executing international agreements and EU acts. The implementing regulations of article 117(5) are included in Law 234/2012 ('General rules on the participation of Italy in the formation and implementation of the legislation and policies of the policies of the European Union'). The general rule (article 40) is that regions shall provide for the transposition of European directives in matters within their own jurisdiction. However, article 41 stipulates that the state may adopt measures

[38] See, inter alia, Constitutional Court judgments 227/2004; 43/2004; 367/2007.

to implement EU acts and remedy any inertia of the regions, even when these acts normally fall under regional legislative competence.

The purpose of this tool is to forestall any breaches of EU law. It functions as a preventive mechanism, with national authorities responsible for supervising the implementation of EU legislation throughout the regions. To this end, the national executive provides regular updates (every six months) to the national parliament regarding the results of this monitoring process.

Furthermore, Law 234/2012 stipulates that state measures take effect only after the expiration of the EU legislation implementation deadline, and these are limited in application to regions and/or autonomous provinces that have not enacted the required implementing laws. Also, these measures cease to be effective once regional or provincial inaction is resolved. They constitute a power which is temporary in nature and that expires upon the removal of the triggering cause, namely the failure of one or more subnational governments to meet their obligations.

4.2 Procedure for Intervention

From a procedural viewpoint, the national law mandates a particular form of involvement by territorial entities in the decision-making process: the national acts to be adopted in substitution must undergo prior examination by the Permanent State-Regions Conference.

Normally, the domestication of EU law in national law is done by law, so as a rule the national executive plays only a monitoring role. However, in urgent cases, this obligation may be fulfilled by an act of the Council of Ministers. Pursuant to article 37, the President of the Council of Ministers or the Minister for European Affairs may propose to the Council of Ministers the adoption of measures, including urgent ones, other than the European delegation law and the European law, as long as these are necessary in the face of legislative acts of the EU, judgments of the Court of Justice of the European Union, or the initiation of infringement procedures against Italy involving state obligations to comply.[39]

In these circumstances, if the EU obligations fall within matters of legislative or administrative competence of the regions, the President of the Council of Ministers or the Minister for European Affairs informs the entities concerned and assigns a deadline to take action, and, if necessary, requests that the matter be submitted for consideration to the Permanent State-Regions

---

39 The precondition is, of course, that the deadline for doing so is prior to the date of presumed entry into force of the European delegation law or the European law relating to the reference year.

Conference, to agree on the initiatives to be taken. In case of failure to comply, the President of the Council of Ministers or the Minister for European Affairs shall propose to the Council of Ministers fitting initiatives for the purpose of exercising the substitutive powers referred to, respectively, in articles 117(5) and 120(2) of the Constitution.

5. DISSOLUTION OF REGIONAL COUNCILS

5.1 Constitutional and Legislative Grounds for Intervention

In Italy, dismissal of elected representatives is possible, but only under specific circumstances, such as the functional incapacity of the governing bodies (article 126(3) of the Constitution), or where imposed as a sanction by the national government (article 126(1)). This sanction is particularly relevant to the purposes of the book, since it introduces a form of intervention that entails the dissolution or removal of the political bodies of the regions, where acts contrary to the Constitution or serious violations of the law have been committed, or where reasons of national security so require.[40]

This provision grants the central authority the power to act against regional political bodies and to dissolve or remove them, if the conditions specified in article 126 are met. This distinguishes this form of intervention from that provided for under Article 120, where intervention primarily takes the form of substitution, either in relation to acts or activities of territorial entities or to their failure to act (inertia).

Intervention under article 126 addresses two foundations of the republican architecture, affecting both ordinary and special regions. First, there is the need to preserve the (constitutionally entrenched) political autonomy of subnational governments as the element characterising 'the very essence of the Italian state as a regional state'.[41] Second, that autonomy must necessarily align with the framework dictated by the fundamental principles of the unity and indivisibility of the Republic.[42] In other words, following the 2001 constitutional reform, regions have acquired broad powers (including legislative powers) which necessarily respond to a political-representative circuit that is additional to, and supposedly different from, the political and administrative direction expressed by the national government. In any case, the provision can be traced back to the instruments made available to the national authority to protect the unitary

---

40 Instead, the dissolution for political reasons (and thus involving the system of government) is referred to the region. After all, regions are given the competence to determine (in their statutes) their own systems of government.

41 Judgment 229/1989.

42 Article 5, Constitution.

principle, which is there to 'ensure the satisfaction of interests that transcend the regional sphere and involve the entire national community'.[43]

Given this stance, the recourse to the sanctioning power available under article 126 (against apex regional bodies) is legitimate only in the face of 'truly exceptional situations',[44] such as the ones brought about by acts contrary to the Constitution, serious violations of the law or reasons of national security. In no case should the dissolution of the regional council and the removal of the president of the region stem from an intergovernmental conflict concerning choices of political discretion, unless these are linked to specific obligations legitimately incumbent on the regional system by the Constitution or laws which have been found to be violated.

5.2 Procedure for Intervention

According to article 126 of the Constitution, dismissal is accomplished by means of a decree of the President of the Republic. However, this requires an opinion of a parliamentary commission of 20 senators and 20 deputies, as well as a preliminary deliberation of the Council of the Ministers called for by the Prime Minister.

In this regard, the Constitutional Court, in Judgment 219/2013, clarified the relationship between the different bodies involved in these procedures. The Court stipulated that, in this area, the role of the executive as responsible for general political direction is decisive. Accordingly, only the Government of the Republic is in a position to make the preliminary assessment (inevitably marked by margins of discretion) of the gravity of the violations suffered by a particular region in terms of article 126 and also of the magnitude of the resulting prejudice. However, as a guarantee of regional autonomy, the provision stipulates that the decision has to come in the form of a motivated decree of the President of the Republic, to be adopted only after the opinion of the parliamentary commission for regional issues.[45]

The motivation of the decree by the President not only strengthens the position of the region under sanctioning intervention, but also clarifies that the head of state acts in his/her capacity as representative and guarantor of national unity – not only in terms of the territorial unity of the state, but, above

---

43 D'Atena A *Diritto regionale* Torino: G Giappichelli Editore (2010) at 308.

44 Judgment 50/1959.

45 For detailed discussion, see Petrillo C *Aspetti problematici della 'nuova' disciplina dello scioglimento sanzionatorio del Consiglio regionale* (2013) *Consulta Online* available at https://giurcost.org/contents/giurcost/studi/petrillo2.pdf (accessed 1 March 2025).

all, in terms of the cohesion and harmonious functioning of the political powers and guarantees that make up the constitutional structure of the Republic.[46]

This approach ensures a balance between the various and paramount interests that underpin the exercise of this sanctioning power. First, to safeguard the regional system from an overly expansive authority, a 'violation of the law' must be challenged. This might be either a visible breaching of the obligations arising from primary or statutory laws that regional autonomy is subject to, or the council and the president of the region are expected to adhere to. Second, a violation is not sufficient in itself: the severity of the violation in terms of its effects must also be assessed. Third, both the President and the Government of the Republic must be involved, with the latter being required to countersign the presidential decree of dissolution. Finally, the input of Parliament has to be secured, though only at an advisory level.[47]

While the scope of article 126 is formally restricted to regions with ordinary statutes, similar provisions also exist in the autonomy statutes of special regions (that is, article 48 of the statute of the Valle d'Aosta Region; article 49-bis of the statute of the Trentino-Alto Adige Region; article 50 of the statute of the Sardinia Region; and article 22 of the statute of the Friuli-Venezia Giulia Region). Only in Sicily does article 8 of the statute make the dissolution of the regional assembly contingent on a resolution of the national parliament.

6. INTERVENTION IN LOCAL GOVERNMENT: LEGISLATIVE BASIS AND PROCEDURES

With regard to local government, the rules of intervention on the acts or organs thereof are found in a national law, the Consolidated Text on Local Authorities (TUEL). In both instances, the distinctive attributes of the constitutional provisions of articles 120 and 126 are taken up with adaptations.

With regard to the first group of interventions, the law foresees three different cases. The first concerns a failure or delay by municipalities or provinces in the fulfilment of acts required by law (regional substitutive control). Pursuant to article 136 of TUEL, this power is vested in the region and also encompasses the possibility of appointing a commissioner *ad acta*. Conversely, the power of substitution is up to the national executive with reference to the functions and tasks incumbent on local authorities, in the event of inactivity involving non-compliance with EU obligations or a danger of serious prejudice to national interests.[48] In such case, the President of the Council of Ministers,

[46] Judgment 1/2013.
[47] Judgment 219/2013.
[48] Article 137, TUEL.

following the proposal of the minister responsible for the matter, grants the entity an appropriate period within which to comply.

The procedure follows that prescribed under article 120, though the actors change. Here, proceedings are not in the hands of the Council but at the discretion of the President of the Council of Ministers, following a proposal put forward by the minister responsible for the subject matter. A deadline is assigned. If this expires with no action, the Council of Ministers, after hearing the targeted entity, appoints a commissioner who acts in substitution. In cases of urgency, the Council of Ministers may directly proceed to the appointment of a commissioner, though this decision can be challenged by the State-City and Local Government Conference.

Under article 138 of TUEL, the Council of Ministers is granted the authority for the extraordinary annulment of any illegitimate acts performed by local authorities. This power is exercised at the discretion of the Council to safeguard the unity of the legal system, acting upon a proposal from the Minister of the Interior, after consultation with the Council of State. The annulment is formalised through a decree issued by the President of the Republic. Unlike cases under article 126, no justification is required.

The second group of interventions concerns all those cases in which the governing bodies are affected, that is, are either dissolved or dismissed before the end of their term. Of particular concern to this chapter are those involving violations of law or security threats (as analysed below).

The mayor or the president of a province can be removed for various reasons: acts against the Constitution; persistent violations of the law; concerns regarding public order; and failure to comply with obligations concerning the management of municipal waste.[49] In the event of the mayor's removal, both the council and executive bodies are also dissolved. In such circumstances, individual members of the council and the executive may also be subject to removal.

The law also stipulates the dissolution of the council, if it performs acts contrary to the Constitution, or for serious and persistent violations of the law.[50] In addition, it identifies situations of financial crisis, including the failure to approve the budget;[51] the financial rebalancing measures;[52] the financial statements;[53] financial distress;[54] as well as the failure to comply with

49 Articles 141(1)(b) and 142, TUEL.
50 Article 141(1)(a), TUEL.
51 Article 141(1)(c), TUEL.
52 Article 193(3), TUEL.
53 Article 227(2)bis, TUEL.
54 Article 247, TUEL.

the obligations to submit a rebalanced budget;[55] and instances where general urban planning tools are not approved.[56]

The third scenario entails infiltration by organised crime. This is recorded when concrete, unambiguous and relevant evidence of politicians' connection with organised crime emerges and/or forms of conditioning of administrative activity are found to be in place (article 143).

Municipal and provincial councils are dissolved by decree of the President of the Republic, following a proposal from the Minister of the Interior. Mayors and presidents of provinces (as well as individual members of their councils or executives) may be removed by decree of the Minister of the Interior. If the mayor is removed, early elections are called; if the council is dissolved, a commissioner is appointed, who is given all powers vested in the governing bodies while waiting for the first round of elections.

Similar provisions on the bodies responsible for deciding on dissolution can be found in the autonomy statutes governing special regions. The major difference lies in the fact that special regions have jurisdiction over local governments in their territories.

7. INTERVENTION BEYOND THE BLACK LETTER OF THE CONSTITUTION

Since the approval of article 120(2), scholars have debated whether the scenarios of intervention outlined in the Constitution are to be regarded as exhaustive, or whether the state can legitimately exercise substitutive powers over and above those derived from this provision. Article 120 and its implementing regulations are also unclear as to whether ordinary regions can intervene as substitutes for local authorities within their territories. In this specific realm of regional action, the national government has filed numerous appeals to the Constitutional Court (its stance is that such action is not allowed to the regions).

Besides underscoring an overall acknowledgement of a diminished scope for regional autonomy compared to the pre-2001 reform era, this circumstance was rooted primarily in two (equally erroneous) assumptions. First, the allocation to the national level of the exclusive legislative competence to determine 'fundamental functions of local authorities' was considered as inclusive of the power of substitution. Second, article 120(2) was initially interpreted in broad terms as encompassing every conceivable form of intervention permitted within the Italian legal system.[57]

---

55 Article 262, TUEL.

56 Article 141(1)(b), TUEL.

57 For detailed discussion, see Staderini F, Caretti P, & Milazzi P *Diritto degli enti locali* Padua, Veneto: Cedam (2019) at 38.

Later, the Constitutional Court embraced a more expansive interpretation of this provision.[58] Determinant in this regard is Judgment 43/2004. Here the Court asserts that article 120(2) should not be construed as exhausting all the avenues for intervention (consolidating them solely within the national government). Instead, the accepted interpretation leans in the opposite direction: the mechanisms explicitly enshrined within the Constitution encompass only a segment of the broader spectrum of tools available to one level of government vis-à-vis another.[59] In this regard, the Constitution recognises and regulates only an extraordinary, additional, substitutive power which is attributed to the national executive, one which can be exercised only within the prerequisites for and the protection of the interests expressly indicated therein. However, in so doing, it does not preclude the admissibility of other interventions.[60]

In the absence of specific constitutional provisions, the legal foundations for such additional forms of intervention are found in the combined scope of articles 117 and 118, which delineate the allocation of legislative and administrative competencies. Article 118 stipulates that administrative functions are vested in municipalities, unless, to ensure their uniform exercise, they are assigned to metropolitan cities, provinces, regions or the state, based on the principles of subsidiarity, differentiation and adequacy. As a result, while the general rule favours the level of government closest to citizens, an element of flexibility is brought in to guide the assignment of functions across different levels. Since this concrete allocation can only be grounded in law (principle of legality), it follows that it is the national or regional law that makes the relevant choices, depending on whether the matter falls pursuant to article 117 under the legislative competence of the state or the region.[61]

Within this framework, even the provisions allowing for (exceptional) substitution of one level of government by another (for the execution of specific acts or activities such as those not promptly carried out by the designated authority but deemed necessary for the sake of unitary interests) inevitably align with the same logical scheme.[62] Consequently, their execution must be entrusted to the authority responsible for the matter, whether at the national or

---

[58] Several judgments of the Constitutional Court deal with this issue, such as 53/2003; 69/2004; 74/2004; 112/2004; 173/2004; 227/2004; 167/2005.

[59] Article 91(8) of Veneto's regional law on tourism provides for the appointment of a *commissioner ad acta* in the event of a claim of inaction by municipalities.

[60] For an in-depth investigation of this judgement and its implications, see Dickmann R 'La Corte riconosce la legittimità dei poteri sostitutivi regionali' (2004) *federalismi.it*; Merloni F 'Una definitiva conferma della legittimità dei poteri sostitutivi regionali (2004) 4 *Le Regioni* 1074 at 1074 ff.

[61] See Judgment 43/2004.

[62] See Judgement 43/2004.

regional level.[63] If this were not the case, the consequences could be absurd. To avoid the undermining of unitary interests that require the performance of certain acts or activities, in the face of inaction limited to one or more entities, the national or regional authority would have no other means than to place the function at a higher level of government, ensuring its 'unitary exercise' under article 118(1) of the Constitution. Such a consequence would be clearly disproportionate and in contradiction with the principle of subsidiarity.[64]

Put simply, both national and regional law (including sectoral legislation) can prescribe forms of interventions in correlation with the allocation of administrative functions and in the specific hypotheses for which these might be necessary, so long as they comply with the prerequisites and conditions identified by the Constitutional Court as early as in Decision 177/1998.[65]

First, this power can be exercised only in relation to activities lacking discretion in the *an* (though not necessarily in *quid* or *quomodo*). This applies, for instance, when such activities are bound by law to peremptory deadlines, or when the nature of the tasks to be carried out is such that their omission would gravely imperil the fulfilment of fundamental functions or the pursuit of essential interests for which the ultimate responsibility lies with the state.

Second, the interventions concerning the activities of another level of government must be provided for and regulated by law. At the same time, these powers must be conceived as instrumental to the execution or fulfilment of obligations linked to constitutionally protected interests, as their exercise limits subnational or local autonomy. Only under these circumstances is the higher level permitted, as an exception, to transcend the constitutionally guaranteed separation of competencies.

Third, the power of substitution may be exercised only by a governmental authority.

Fourth (and finally), the intervention must be assisted by substantive and procedural guarantees which align with the fundamental constitutional values that govern intergovernmental relations. These include a specific emphasis on the principle of loyal cooperation, which is crucial in scenarios where the principle of separation is not (exceptionally) applicable.[66] Compliance with the proportionality rule is also essential, and applies both to the conditions legitimising the intervention and to the content and scope of such power, so as

63 Constitutional Court, Judgment 43/2004.

64 See further De Michele (2008) at 634 and 669.

65 For an examination of ordinary powers of intervention, see Mainardis C *Poteri sostitutivi statali ed autonomia amministrativa regionale* Milano: Giuffrè Editore (2007).

66 See judgments 153/1986 and 294/1986.

to prevent substitution from resulting in an unjustified restriction of regional autonomy.[67]

That the national government has intervened and asserted substitutive power over local governments does not necessarily imply a reservation in favour of the state for regulating the power of substitution vis-à-vis local governments. Rather, it must be acknowledged that

> the regional law, intervening in matters of regional competence and regulating the exercise of administrative functions assigned to municipalities (or other local authorities), is entitled to provide for substitutive powers in the head of regional bodies, for the performance of obligatory acts or activities, in the case of inaction or non-fulfilment by the competent body, in order to safeguard unitary interests that would be jeopardised by the inaction or non-fulfilment itself.[68]

Simply put, if there are the conditions for the exercise of the national government's power of substitution against a local authority, the region may also exercise its power of substitution in matters of regional competence.[69]

8. THE POLITICS OF INTERVENTION

Italy lacks either databases or summary reports that comprehensively collect all legal acts where the interventions analysed in this chapter are regulated, or all cases in which these powers have been used. While there is some (partial) monitoring of municipalities, data are often outdated.[70] As a result, the politics of intervention in Italy can be understood only through the direct observation of single situations, or the examination of notable cases that have attracted media and scholarly attention. The latter typically includes two groups of potential case studies: those that are relevant because they involve a significant number of entities, and those that become notable because they contribute to clarifying interpretative doubts about the constitutional provisions (as in the Apulia Region case discussed below).

This section's analysis of the politics of intervention takes place within these limits. Initially, a few qualitative assessments regarding the use made of intervention powers are discussed. The following two subsections present a detailed examination of two case studies that have gained public attention due to the involvement of a significant number of entities.

---

[67] See judgments 77/1986 and 294/1986.

[68] Judgment 43/2004.

[69] Judgment 249/2009.

[70] For example, the website https://www.openpolis.it/ dedicates several articles to the topic, but the data dates to 2021.

An important preliminary observation is that the legitimacy of legislative substitution took a long time to be accepted. The first judicial decision to that effect was made in 2020 with reference to the Apulia Region. The issue is crucial, as uncertainty surrounding legislative substitution has delayed the resolution of critical situations such as the waste crisis and the failure to comply with health-care recovery plans.

It should be noted here that the Sicilian waste management system has been under pressure since the late 1990s due to problems such as poor organisation, infrastructural deficiencies, and low levels of separate waste collection. Over time, the situation has deteriorated because of the persistent failure to enforce national laws on waste management. It was only in 2015 that the process for activating the substitution power under article 120(2) was initiated in view of the need to ensure essential service levels and safeguard the legal unity clause.

While the health-care crisis will be examined below (in section 8.1), it is worth noting that the observation of the politics of intervention in this field is symptomatic of the intricate dynamics characterising state–region relations in Italy and of the profound asymmetry that marks them. Health care mirrors the deep socio-economic divide between the northern and southern, or central, regions (excepting Tuscany). The latter ended up under national tutelage in the years of the economic-financial crisis, while the northern regions managed to sustain sound budgetary conditions and consolidate their autonomy in health-care matters.[71]

Generally speaking, what is apparent in the national landscape is a trend towards the erosion of regional autonomy and a concurrent bolstering of the national level of government. This shift can be attributed to monumental historical, economic and legal factors such as the economic-financial crisis, European and monetary integration and the globalisation of markets. Cultural factors also play a role, including various manifestations of illegality and incompetence within political spheres and of certain public administrations (noting that these issues are not confined solely to the southern regions).[72]

The above-mentioned cases underscore the intricate, multifaceted nature of the interventions required to address pathological situations. These involve interventions related to infrastructural and financial resources, as well as comprehensive service reorganisation, thereby necessitating a close interplay between administrative and legislative powers that highlights their mutual interdependence. Practice shows that the notion of legislative substitution

---

[71] See further Neri S & Mori A 'Crisi economica, politiche di austerità e relazioni intergovernative nel Ssn. Dalla regionalizzazione al federalismo differenziato?' (2017) 2 *Autonomie locali e servizi sociali* 201 at 217.

[72] Brancati B 'Tensione nei rapporti tra Stato e Regioni sul tema della sanità (a margine del decreto-legge n. 35/2019)' (2019) 5 *Osservatorio costituzionale* 104.

cannot be dispensed with, if interventions under article 120(2) are to be properly equipped to achieve their goals. Without it, already difficult situations may easily deteriorate to the point where the more extreme forms of intervention provided for under article 126 become necessary.

At the same time, the uncertainty which surrounds the legitimacy of legislative substitution has constrained the use of the substitution power, especially with regard to the regions. The causes are multiple and include political, administrative and financial matters. One notable factor is the significant administrative (and financial) resources required for substitution activities. National public administrations often lack both the necessary infrastructure and the trained personnel to successfully manage such efforts. Alongside this, there is also the fact that while article 120(2) legitimises a temporary deviation from the constitutional allocation of competencies, it does not provide (as a rule) any extraordinary tools to facilitate the solution of the problems encountered.[73]

Interventions that enjoy robust support from the EU are more successful. Wastewater treatment and collection is a useful example. Interventions in this field affected some 737 urban agglomerations across the country, with Italy condemned in several EU court judgments for failure to fulfil the obligations provided under the Urban Waste Water Directive 1991/261. As a first step, the national government intervened by appointing an extraordinary commissioner for each entity.[74] This did not yield satisfactory results, and was followed by the appointment of a single extraordinary commissioner for all cases,[75] together with an expansion of the special powers conferred on the extraordinary commissioner.[76] These changes have led to a significant improvement in the situation, reducing the number of agglomerations under intervention, although it remains high (i.e., over 100).[77]

Similar challenges arose with regard to the clean-up of 200 illegal landfills found to be in infringment of EU laws. As a response, amendments were made

---

[73] Pajno S 'Un bilancio dei poteri sostitutivi straordinari a vent'anni dalla entrata in vigore della legge cost. n. 3 del 2001' (2022) 20 *Federalismi.it* 129 at 129.

[74] Article 7, d.l. 133/2014.

[75] Article 2, d.l. 243/2016.

[76] See further Extraordinary Commissioner for the Purification and Refuse of Wastewater available at https://commissariounicodepurazione.it/ (accessed 8 November 2024).

[77] According to the most recent official update at the end of 2023, the number stands at 116. See Italian Government Ministry of the Environment and Energy Security 'Procedura infrazione – P.I. 2017/2181' available at https://www.mase.gov.it/pagina/procedura-infrazione-pi-20172181 (accessed 23 January 2025).

in 2015 to Law 234/2012. The new provisions mandated the development of a timeline of the actions and activities to be implemented; they also acknowledged the possibility of activating substitution power at the first sign of non-compliance. In 2017 a single extraordinary commissioner was appointed by the national government to deal with all cases. This solution sought to minimise delays, yielding remarkable outcomes. By 3 October 2023, only eight sites in Italy still needed attention, a considerable improvement on the initial 200 illegal landfills that were placed under infringement procedure.[78]

The next sections focus on two case studies. These combine an examination of the legal framework for intervention with an exploration of the surrounding politics. The first case concerns the failure of certain regions to comply with health-care recovery plans, while the second concerns the dissolution of municipalities due to infiltration by organised crime.

8.1 Regional Non-compliance with Health-care Recovery Plans

The need to enforce regional compliance with health-care recovery plans stands out as one of the prevalent forms of intervention in the Italian regions. Such intervention is necessary to ensure that the regions provide essential levels of services, particularly in the field of health-care. Given the pivotal role of health care within regional competences, frequent intervention risks eroding regional autonomy. This is especially significant as health-care expenditure in ordinary regions accounts (on average) for more than 75 per cent of total regional spending.[79]

Historically, public health-care spending in Italy has had a fluctuating pattern, with periods of growth alternating with periods of significant contraction. Between 2002 and 2003, there was an overall decrease in the deficits arising within regional health systems. At the same time, there was a consolidation of residual deficits in certain regions, such as Liguria and Piedmont in the North and Lazio, Molise, Campania, Abruzzo, Sardinia and Sicily in the centre and

---

[78] See further Italian Government 'Commissario Unico per la bonifica delle discariche e dei siti contaminati Presidenza del Consiglio dei Ministri' available at https://www.commissariobonificadiscariche.governo.it/it/ accessed 23 January 2025).

[79] The case of special regions is different. Here, health-care expenditure amounts on average to 44 per cent of overall special region expenditure, due to a higher amount of non-health-care expenditure. There is much variation: in Valle d'Aosta, it is 24 per cent; in Sardegna, 46.5 per cent; and in Sicily, above 56 per cent. See Corte dei conti *Relazione sulla gestione finanziaria delle Regioni/Province autonome* (2022) at 15 available at https://www.camera.it/temiap/2022/04/19/OCD177-5473.pdf (accessed 9 October 2023).

the South. In the following years, the deficits in the latter regions surged considerably, necessitating remedial action.

Recovery plans are the tools established by Law 311/2004 to restore the balance of the budget in regional health-care services. Regions have a duty to ensure the health and well-being of their citizens, while maintaining a balanced budget, and conducting comprehensive spending reviews. If the structural deficit exceeds 5 per cent of ordinary financing, including the region's increased own health revenues (hospital or pharmaceutical co-payments), or if the deficit does not exceed 5 per cent but neither fiscal automatic measures nor other resources from the regional budget can guarantee its full coverage,[80] the region shall submit a three-year recovery plan for approval by the Council of Ministers, at the proposal of the Minister of Economy. This procedure embodies the principle of loyal cooperation between state and regions. Implementation of the plan is monitored quarterly, and the plan remains in force over the three years, but limitations can be softened upon achievement of intermediate targets.

In cases of non-compliance, a commissioner *ad acta* is appointed by the national executive. The latter's task is to take the steps the defaulting administration should have taken (but did not) to ensure compliance with the recovery plan. The commissioning of a territorial entity is one of the institutional formulae for the exercise of substitution power. It is never an automatic consequence of the recovery plan, but only a last resort.[81] If this also proves ineffective, the national executive appoints one or more commissioners responsible for implementing the plan, and these work alongside the commissioner *ad acta*. The commissioning of regional health care is triggered as a sanction that the national government imposes on the regions for non-compliance with economic-deficit recovery plans. In cases of severe financial distress in the health sector, Decree 149/2011 also provides for the dissolution of the regional assembly and the removal of the president of the region under article 126 of the Constitution.

The disqualifying effect covers any action of the commissioned entity: not only must regional laws not encroach on fields reserved for the recovery plan, but any overlap with the powers and mandate of the commissioner must be

[80] In fact, before the plan is approved, some measures automatically take effect, namely: raising the IRAP and regional surtax on IRPEF (by 0.15 and 0.30 percentage points, respectively); the automatic freeze on the turnover of health-care personnel; and the ban on non-obligatory expenditures for the same period.

[81] Patanè A 'La difficile "metabolizzazione" regionale del ruolo del Commissario ad acta nell'attuazione dei piani di rientro e la ferma posizione della Corte costituzionale' (2018) 1 *Corti supreme e salute* 17 at 30.

avoided.[82] Because of this broad understanding, regional bodies are completely disempowered from making decisions on health matters. This disempowerment runs for at least three years, and is often extended to a period of ten years.[83] In line with this case law, in Judgment 91/2012 the Constitutional Court also endorses the ability of an inter-institutional agreement to prevail over conflicting provisions of regional law, thereby severely narrowing the scope of regional (legislative) autonomy.[84]

For the moment, ten regions have experimented with recovery plans. Some, such as Sardinia and Liguria, managed to emerge from the intervention regime almost immediately, while Piedmont needed to endure a longer period. Others continue under commissioner status.[85] Among the latter, interventions have predominantly targeted single hospitals or other health-care facilities, rather than addressing the entire regional health-care structure. Currently, 39 hospitals or health-care facilities in 8 different regions remain under commissioner status. The fact that in several territories the commissioner status affects only a few of the existing health-care facilities is due to the complex array of factors behind this phenomenon (including cases where corporate dynamics take precedence over regional or national political considerations). In Lombardy, for instance, 5.7 per cent of health-care facilities in the region are under commissioner status, while in Piedmont this figure is 11.1 per cent. Slightly higher values, but still referring to isolated episodes, are to be found in Liguria (16.7 per cent), Emilia-Romagna (16.7 per cent) and Lazio (20 per cent).[86]

While in some cases it was the contraction of resources, *rectius* of national funding for health care, that caused the regional inaction and thus legitimised the intervention, there are instances where the situation has become deeply rooted. In these cases, substitution has become the norm, making it extremely difficult to break out of this vicious cycle.

Calabria provides perhaps the most notable example.[87] Here, the entire health-care sector has been under commissioner status for 15 years. Due to the

---

[82] Judgment 247/2018.

[83] Ciolli I 'Poteri sostitutivi statali, piani di rientro e vincoli di bilancio in materia sanitaria: Tra disuguaglianze e tentativi di emarginazione della decisione politica' (2021) 1 *Rivista di diritto delle autonomie territoriali* 39 at 53.

[84] Cerruti T 'I piani di rientro dai disavanzi sanitari come limite alla competenza legislativa regionale' (2013) 4 *Rivista AIC* at 1.

[85] The institutional website of the Ministry of Health indicates that in 2019–2020 as many as seven regions were subjected to the discipline of recovery plans.

[86] 'Le aziende sanitarie e i commissariamenti nel 2023' (16 May 2023) *Openpolis* available at https://www.openpolis.it/le-aziende-sanitarie-e-i-commissariamenti-nel-2023/ (accessed 9 October 2024).

[87] Brancati (2019).

severity of the situation, the national government enacted Decree-Law 35/2019. This act removed health-care management from the regional government for 18 months, and specific regulations were adopted to address this particularly dire circumstance. While these measures are considered legitimate for their purpose of remedying the extremely critical situation due to the health-care deficit, the Constitutional Court stipulates that

> [t]he actual compliance of the measures adopted with the pursued aim of 'reorganisation of the health service' and especially the protection of 'compliance with the essential levels of care in the health sector' as well as the absence of counterproductive effects ... have to be carefully monitored by the state, and assessed in concrete terms, when applying the measures themselves.

It is precisely in considering this warning that the Court found the subsequent governmental decree to be unlawful, deeming it inadequate and disproportionate to the purpose. In addition, the substitution itself has lost the temporary nature that was originally inherent to it.[88]

How best to evaluate these experiences? From a financial viewpoint, the utilisation of recovery plans for more than a decade has demonstrated their capacity to mitigate health-care deficits. However, while some regions (such as Liguria, Sardinia and Piedmont) have swiftly achieved budgetary equilibrium without the need to resort to the appointment of a commissioner, others (such as Lazio, Campania and Puglia) have experienced a much slower pace of fiscal realignment. In most of these regions (including Lazio and all southern regions except Basilicata), recovery plans remain in effect and commissioner oversight has now persisted uninterruptedly for more than a decade. Interestingly, research on the topic indicates that services have improved in regions subject to these plans.[89] However, it is noteworthy that the gap in health-care performance between regions has simultaneously widened.[90]

---

[88] See Judgment 168/2021.

[89] Bordignon M, Coretti S & Turati G 'I Piani di Rientro della sanità regionale: quali risultati finora?' (2019) *Osservatorio sui Conti pubblici italiani* available at https://osservatoriocpi.unicatt.it/cpi-archivio-studi-e-analisi-i-piani-di-rientro-della-sanita-regionale-quali-risultati-finora (accessed 4 November 2023). See also Bordignon M, Coretti S, Piacenza M & Turati G 'Hardening sub-national budget constraints via administrative subordination: The Italian experience of regional recovery plans' (2020) 29(11) *Health Economics* 1378.

[90] Chisari G & Lega F 'Impact of austerity programs: Evidence from the Italian national health service' (2023) 36(2) *Health Services Management Research* 145.

8.2 The Dissolution of Municipalities due to Organised Crime

Instances of intervention in local governments are abundant. This is not solely due to the sheer number of municipalities (there are 7,896 municipalities in Italy). It is also because the majority of interventions materialise with respect to administrative activities that typically fall within the purview of local authorities (and particularly municipal administrations), hence making them the primary target of such interventions. Furthermore, it is important to acknowledge that both the state and the regions are empowered to intervene in local authorities' affairs, effectively multiplying the actors involved in the process. Partly because of the plurality of entitled subjects and the available options for intervention, there is a lack of comprehensive data, except for the most resounding and numerically significant case studies.

Among the different intervention mechanisms, commissioner status stands out as especially important. It is not only widely utilised (notably in sectors such as waste and water management), but also ranks among the most intrusive tools from the perspective of local (as well as regional) autonomy, thus representing a sort of *tertium genus* between substitution on single acts and the dissolution of governing bodies.

Interventions resulting in the dissolution or removal of local government governing bodies are also common. Political reasons (such as no-confidence motions against the mayor, or the simultaneous resignation of the majority of municipal council members), as well as not-directly-political reasons (such as the ones resulting in the failure of the governing bodies to function, e.g., mayoral death or resignation) are the most recurrent causes, amounting altogether to 82.60 per cent of all cases.

However, two other major causes are frequently observed and are of relevance to this chapter. These are financial crisis (5.9 per cent)[91] and organised crime infiltration (7.5 per cent).[92] The latter will be the subject of in-depth exploration in this section, as intervention due to a failure to comply with certain legal obligations is one of the foci of this book. Dissolution for infiltration by organised crime was introduced in Italy in 1991 and is currently regulated in the Consolidated Text of Local Authorities.[93] It is an extraordinary preven-

---

[91] This can occur in various circumstances: failure to approve the budget; failure to approve financial rebalancing measures; failure to approve the financial statement; situation of financial distress; and non-compliance with the obligation to present a rebalanced budget.

[92] 'Come e perché si arriva allo scioglimento di un comune in Italia' (19 July 2021) *Openpolis* available at https://www.openpolis.it/parole/come-e-perche-si-arriva-allo-scioglimento-di-un-comune-in-italia/ (accessed 5 November 2023).

[93] Article 143 et seq.

tive measure to be applied only when there is a real danger that the activity of a municipality or another local government is under the control of mafia clans.

To make the case, and to establish the influence of criminal organisations on local government, the Minister of the Interior must appoint a special investigative commission. The commission conducts a thorough examination of the administrative activities, after which the prefect forwards the results to the provincial committee for public order for its opinion. Then, it is the Minister of the Interior, who decides whether to dismiss the case or to submit the proposal for dissolution to the Council of Ministers. The latter deliberates on that. In addition, in cases where there is suspicion of influence-peddling by administrative staff, other measures can be taken, including the suspension or reassignment of the officials in question.

The dissolution decree is an act of the President of the Republic (to which is attached the reports of the minister and the prefect). The presidential decree also specifies the composition of the extraordinary commission to be entrusted with the management of the entity for a maximum of 18 months, extendable under exceptional circumstances to 24 months. At the end of this period, the commissioner status must end and new elections be called. Although extensions from 18 to 24 months are intended to be an exception, in practice these are quite frequent: out of 36 cases in 2022, 26 were granted extensions. Only one case saw the termination of commissioner status after 28 months, while the other nine cases are scheduled to expire at the end of 2023 or beginning of 2024. Extensions for these may or may not be issued in the coming months.[94]

For the moment, the infiltration phenomenon mainly involves small (less than 10,000 inhabitants) and medium (under 50,000) municipalities. The majority of cases are concentrated in the southern regions, and notably Calabria, Campania, Sicily and Apulia. However, recent years have seen municipalities from the central and northern regions becoming involved. Between 1991 and 2021, a total of 360 entities were placed under commissioner status for mafia infiltration. In 2022, there were a total of 36 cases, with 11 of these being new ones. This figure aligns with the average number of cases per year over the past 30 years (11.75), but shows a slight decrease compared to 2021 when 14 municipalities were subjected to commissioner status. With 34 instances, 1993 saw the highest number of cases in a single year. While the number is not particularly large in absolute terms (considering that there are nearly 7,900

[94] 'Quali e quanti sono i comuni commissariati in Italia' (19 July 2021) *Openpolis* available at https://www.openpolis.it/parole/quali-e-quanti-sono-i-comuni-commissariati-in-italia/ (accessed 5 November 2024); 'I comuni commissariati per mafia nel 2022' (1 August 2023) *Openpolis* available at https://www.openpolis.it/parole/quali-e-quanti-sono-i-comuni-commissariati-in-italia/ (accessed 5 November 2023).

municipalities in Italy), this phenomenon ends up affecting 1.3 per cent of the Italian population.

9. CONCLUSION

This chapter examined executive interventions of higher-level over lower-level governments in Italy, focusing on interventions that are grounded either in matters of security or result from failures to comply with legal obligations. The Italian example has two particularly interesting aspects. First, the territorial system underwent a revision process back in 2001, one which altered national, subnational and local government relations and at the same time introduced new constitutional rules for intervention. The second arises from the vague nature of the rules and the broad interpretation of them that took root over time. These two features have contributed to the gradual expansion of intervention powers as a matter of practice, to the extent that their analysis is key in understanding the functioning of intergovernmental relations and dynamics in Italy.

Within the new territorial scenario, three different forms of intervention have been constitutionally enshrined to counterbalance the increase in subnational and local autonomy: the extraordinary power of substitution (article 120 of the Constitution); the power of legislative substitution in the case of regional non-compliance in the implementation of EU law (article 117(5)); and, finally, the power to dismiss or remove the political bodies of the regions (article 126). As demonstrated, these interventions manifest in various forms, in terms of involved actors (national vs subnational levels of government, parliament rather than government), and types of powers (legislative vs administrative, substitution for a single act vs commissioner status). Also, it has been shown that these interventions may affect the governing bodies of the targeted entities by ordering their dissolution or removal.

These tools also reveal potential overlaps. Interventions under article 117(5) partly overlap with the provision under article 120 allowing intervention in case of non-compliance with international acts and treaties and EU law, though significant distinctions also exist. The prevailing scholarly opinion is that the two provisions regulate two different hypotheses of intervention that are meant to cope with either non-fulfilment or inadequate fulfilment of EU and international obligations. In the first case (article 117(5)) the substitution operates exclusively at the legislative level and thus affects only the regions, while the second one (article 120(2)) stages an administrative substitution that can be seen vis-à-vis subnational as well as local levels of government.[95] Another distinction lies in the objectives pursued. The first case emphasises the unitary principle, while the unitary nature of the European and international state responsibility takes precedence in the second case.

The risk of overlap also emerges in regard to the interventions envisaged under articles 126 and 120, even though these differ in terms of their preconditions, purposes, and effects. Regarding their purposes, the former option provides for the deprivation of functions, leading eventually to the possibility of dissolving regional autonomy, whereas the latter is intended not to deprive regional bodies of the exercise of their functions but only to implement a temporary takeover of their exercise. There is only a temporary and materially restricted limitation of regional autonomy. The activation procedure itself is intentionally designed to provide stronger guarantees for autonomy, as it mandates adherence to the principles of subsidiarity and loyal cooperation.

The preconditions for the exercise of articles 120 and 126 are also different. Despite potential overlaps in certain circumstances, it is crucial to note that the activation of article 126 requires either a serious violation of laws or of the Constitution, or a compression of national security. The constitutional jurisprudence has clarified that for such intervention to be legitimate, a 'truly exceptional situation' affecting 'values and principles insensitive to the territorial dimension' is required.[96] These violations must be of such gravity that they pose a threat to unitary instances that are a manifestation of inalienable values and principles.

Nevertheless, the condition of the 'protection of legal and economic unity' under article 120 could be a consequence of the regional failure to comply with provisions of the law or of the Constitution. The same could be said for noncompliance with international or European norms, which can easily amount to acts *contra* the Constitution. Also, the hypothesis of public safety (*ex* article 120) could in some circumstances overlap with national security (*ex* article 126). However, if the former can be ascribed to public order, the latter pertains to more disruptive phenomena (for example, secessionist attempts) that do not necessarily compromise public safety. But the opposite is also true: cases could arise where a threat to national security erodes public safety (such

---

95 Caretti P 'L'assetto dei rapporti tra competenza legislativa statale e regionale, alla luce del nuovo Titolo V della Costituzione: aspetti problematici' (2001) 6 *Le Regioni* 1223 at 1228; Mainardis (2001) at 1357 and 1392; Caravita B *La Costituzione dopo la riforma del Titolo V. Stato, Regioni e autonomie fra Repubblica e Unione Europea* Torino: G Giappichelli Editore (2002) at 138.

96 Judgment 219/2013.

as when a regional council fosters seditious movements for the purpose of violent secession).[97]

In addition to the vagueness and complexity of the constitutionally provided instruments, the pervasiveness of such tools has to be considered. Among the various intervention mechanisms, commissioner status is particularly significant. It is extensively utilised, especially in sectors such waste and water management, but also in health care, and is one of the most intrusive tools regarding local and regional autonomy. Ideally, it should serve as an intermediate measure between substitution on single acts and the dissolution of governing bodies. However, it often results in a de facto deprivation of autonomy, and all too frequently for an indefinite period of time.

Furthermore, this normative apparatus does not preclude the possibility that other forms of intervention may also be put in place, provided that these are regulated by law and that the constitutional principles of loyal cooperation and subsidiarity are safeguarded. It is thus not possible to create an exhaustive list of the existing forms of intervention in Italy, to the extent that this analysis is limited to its main and recurring types.

This affects the understanding of the politics of intervention and their impact on intergovernmental dynamics and equilibrium to such an extent that, rather than offering firm conclusions, this chapter can only advance some tentative remarks on the impact of these powers on the territorial system. This is due not only to the lack of data collection and effective monitoring tools (see section 8), but also to matters of legislative design, specifically the proliferation of intervention tools and the vagueness of the relevant constitutional provisions. On top of that, the observations on the politics of intervention (section 9 above) highlight at least two factors demonstrating that these tools have a powerful – and if not transformative, then strongly conditioning – effect on intergovernmental dynamics.

A first factor concerns regional autonomy. The delay in legitimising legislative interventions and the organisational and financial burdens of the required interventions in many circumstances have reduced the use of the substitute power under article 120. However, the case of health-care clearly reveals a regional system under strain. Suffice it to say that health-care spending in ordinary regions accounts to a significant share of the regional budget (on average, more than 75 per cent), and thus also constrains of political autonomy, since autonomy in spending decisions is considered a key indicator of autonomy *tout court*. Furthermore, health-care systems or health-care facilities under commissioner status currently affect more than a third of Italian regions.

---

97 Salerno (2002).

At the same time, the health-care cases highlight the inadequacy of the intervention tools provided in Italy, especially when complex, structural problems must be addressed (the case of health care in Calabria is emblematic, as is that of waste emergency). These problems are partly attributable to long-standing regional regional (as well as local) mismanagement, but also stem from the duration and pervasiveness of the commissioner status, which contrast with the *extrema ratio* nature of intervention powers. In other words, the extraordinary nature of these measures, as provided for by law, has gradually given way to a practice that effectively alters the distribution of competences guaranteed at the constitutional level. This points to the need to rethink not only specific intervention tools but also the regional system as a whole, in order to identify new conditions of equilibrium in intergovernmental dynamics.

Finally, a second factor must be noted, which intersects with another key and determining element of such dynamics in systems informed by the federal principle, namely, the relations with local entities. The system of local autonomies is one of the most emblematic elements distinguishing Italy's decentralised model from that of mature federations. According to theorical approaches to federalism, federal states typically adhere to a common paradigm when it comes to local entities: local governments are creatures of subnational governments, whereas non-federal countries follow a different pattern in which local entities depend on the national government.

The politics of national intervention in local government observed in the Italian case challenge this paradigm and appear to confirm the hybrid nature of the Italian system, that is, a system in which relations with local governments cannot be situated within either of the two models. Indeed, the legal framework and the constitutional case law allow for interventions by both national and regional governments, although in practice the national level assumes a pervasive role, even with respect to local autonomy. This is due to its central role in cases of dissolution, as well as in instances of non-compliance with European law – issues which, as shown by the analysis above (section 8), give rise to particularly far-reaching interventions that strongly condition the federal – or rather regional – equilibrium.

BIBLIOGRAPHY

Books

Caravita B *La Costituzione dopo la riforma del Titolo V. Stato, Regioni e autonomie fra Repubblica e Unione Europea* Torino: G Giappichelli Editore (2002)

D'Atena A *Diritto regionale* Torino: G Giappichelli Editore (2010)

Mainardis C *Poteri sostitutivi statali ed autonomia amministrativa regionale* Milano: Giuffrè Editore (2007)

Papa S *La sussidiarietà alla prova: i poteri sostitutivi nel nuovo ordinamento* Milano: Giuffrè Editore (2008)
Staderini F, Caretti P & Milazzo P *Diritto degli enti locali* Padua, Veneto: Cedam (2019)

Chapters in Books

Gianfrancesco E 'Il potere sostitutivo' in Groppi T & Olivetti M (eds) *La Repubblica delle autonomie* Torino: G Giappichelli Editore (2003)
Police A 'Sussidiarietà e poteri sostitutivi: la funzione amministrativa nello Stato al plurale' in Chieffi L & di S Luca GC (eds) *Regioni ed enti locali dopo la riforma del titolo V della Costituzione fra attuazione ed ipotesi di ulteriore revisione* Torino: G Giappichelli Editore (2004)
Salerno GM 'La disciplina legislativa dei poteri sostitutivi tra semplificazione e complessità ordinamentale' in AA VV (eds) *Il DDL la Loggia* Federalismi.it (2002)

Journal Articles

Bordignon M, Coretti S, Piacenza M & Turati G 'Hardening sub-national budget constraints via administrative subordination: The Italian experience of regional recovery plans' (2020) 29(11) *Health Economics* 1378–99
Brancati B 'Tensione nei rapporti tra Stato e Regioni sul tema della sanità (a margine del decreto-legge n. 35/2019)' (2019) 5 *Osservatorio costituzionale* 104
Caretti P 'L'assetto dei rapporti tra competenza legislativa statale e regionale, alla luce del nuovo Titolo V della Costituzione: aspetti problematici' (2001) 6 *Le Regioni* 1223–1232
Cerruti T 'I piani di rientro dai disavanzi sanitari come limite alla competenza legislativa regionale' (2013) 4 *Rivista AIC*
Chisari G & Lega F 'Impact of austerity programs: Evidence from the Italian national health service' (2023) 36(2) *Health Services Management Research* 145–52
Ciolli I 'Poteri sostitutivi statali, piani di rientro e vincoli di bilancio in materia sanitaria: Tra disuguaglianze e tentativi di emarginazione della decisione politica' (2021) 1 *Rivista di diritto delle autonomie territoriali* 39–76
Cosulich M 'Ex malo bonum? Ovvero del decreto-legge n. 86 del 2020 che introduce la doppia preferenza di genere nelle elezioni regionali pugliesi' (2020) *Federalismi.it*
De Michele A 'L'art. 120 della Costituzione e il suo ruolo nella riforma del Titolo V' (2008) 5 *Le Istituzioni del Federalismo* 623–96
Dickmann R 'L'esercizio del potere sostitutivo con decreto-legge per garantire l'espressione della doppia preferenza di genere in occasione delle elezioni regionali in Puglia del 2020' (2020) 4 *Forum di Quaderni Costituzionali*
Dickmann R 'La Corte riconosce la legittimità dei poteri sostitutivi regionali' (2004) *federalismi.it*
Mainardis C 'Il nuovo regionalismo italiano ed i poteri sostitutivi statali: una riforma con (poche) luci e (molte) ombre' (2001) 6 *Le Regioni* 1357–1423
Merloni F 'Una definitiva conferma della legittimità dei poteri sostitutivi regionali (2004) 4 *Le Regioni* 1074–83
Michetti M 'Titolo V e potere sostitutivo statale. Profili ricostruttivi ed applicativi' (2020) 3 *dirittifondamentali.it* 328

Neri S & Mori A 'Crisi economica, politiche di austerità e relazioni intergovernative nel Ssn. Dalla regionalizzazione al federalismo differenziato?' (2017) 2 *Autonomie locali e servizi sociali* 201–220
Pajno S 'Un bilancio dei poteri sostitutivi straordinari a vent'anni dalla entrata in vigore della legge cost. n. 3 del 2001' (2022) 20 *Federalismi.it* 129–62
Patanè A 'La difficile 'metabolizzazione' regionale del ruolo del Commissario ad acta nell'attuazione dei piani di rientro e la ferma posizione della Corte costituzionale' (2018) 1 *Corti supreme e salute* 17–38
Rescigno GU 'Attuazione delle direttive comunitarie e potere sostitutivo dello Stato' (2002) 4 *Le Regioni* 753
Veronesi G 'Il regime dei poteri sostitutivi alla luce del nuovo art. 120, comma 2, della Costituzione' (2002) 5 *Le Istituzioni del Federalismo* 742

Legislation

Law 177/1988
Law 59/1997
Legislative Decree 112/1998

Case Law

Judgments 290/2001; 53/2003; 274/2003; 313/2003; 36/2004; 43/2004; 69/2004; 74/2004; 112/2004; 173/2004; 227/2004; 167/2005; 417/2005; 169/2007; 367/2007; 219/2013; 233/2019

Internet Sources

'Come e perché si arriva allo scioglimento di un comune in Italia' *Openpolis* (19 July 2021) *Openpolis* available at https://www.openpolis.it/parole/come-e-perche-si-arriva-allo-scioglimento-di-un-comune-in-italia/ (accessed 5 November 2023)
'I comuni commissariati per mafia nel 2022' (1 August 2023) *Openpolis* available at https://www.openpolis.it/parole/quali-e-quanti-sono-i-comuni-commissariati-in-italia/ (accessed 5 November 2023)
'Le aziende sanitarie e i commissariamenti nel 2023' (16 May 2023) *Openpolis* available at https://www.openpolis.it/le-aziende-sanitarie-e-i-commissariamenti-nel-2023/ (accessed 9 October 2024)
'Quali e quanti sono i comuni commissariati in Italia' (19 July 2021) *Openpolis* available at https://www.openpolis.it/parole/quali-e-quanti-sono-i-comuni-commissariati-in-italia/ (accessed 5 November 2024)
Bordignon M, Coretti S & Turati G 'I Piani di Rientro della sanità regionale: quali risultati finora?' (2019) *Osservatorio sui Conti pubblici italiani* available at https://osservatoriocpi.unicatt.it/cpi-archivio-studi-e-analisi-i-piani-di-rientro-della-sanita-regionale-quali-risultati-finora (accessed 4 November 2023)
Corte dei conti *Relazione sulla gestione finanziaria delle Regioni/Province autonome* (2022) available at https://www.camera.it/temiap/2022/04/19/OCD177-5473.pdf (accessed 9 October 2023)
Extraordinary Commissioner for the Purification and Refuse of Wastewater available at https://commissariounicodepurazione.it/ (accessed 8 November 2024)

Groppi T 'Nota a sentenza n. 43 del 2004' (2004) *Forum di quaderni costituzionali* available at https://www.forumcostituzionale.it/wordpress/ (accessed 1 March 2025)
Italian Government 'Commissario Unico per la bonifica delle discariche e dei siti contaminati Presidenza del Consiglio dei Ministri' available at https://www.commissariobonificadiscariche.governo.it/it/ (accessed 23 January 2025)
Italian Government Ministry of the Environment and Energy Security 'Procedura infrazione – P.I. 2017/2181' available at https://www.mase.gov.it/pagina/procedura-infrazione-pi-20172181 (accessed 23 January 2025)
Luciani M 'Le nuove competenze legislative delle Regioni a statuto ordinario. Prime osservazioni sui principali nodi problematici della l. cost. n. 3 del 2001' (2001) available at www.associazionedeicostituzionalisti.it (accessed 1 March 2025)
Petrillo C *Aspetti problematici della 'nuova' disciplina dello scioglimento sanzionatorio del Consiglio regionale* (2013) *Consulta Online* available at https://giurcost.org/contents/giurcost/studi/petrillo2.pdf (accessed 1 March 2025)

7. Kenya: the framework and practice of national intervention in counties

Henry Gichana

1. INTRODUCTION

This chapter discusses the framework and practice of interventions in Kenya. The first section introduces Kenya's federal-type multilevel governance system, referred to as 'devolution', highlighting the historical, political and social contexts for its adoption as well as its key features. The second explores potential rationales for the legal entrenchment of intervention powers in Kenya's constitutional framework. The third section elaborates upon the legal framework for intervention, setting out the constitutional and legislative basis for interventions, the grounds, the requirements and the entities involved in the process. The fourth details the procedures for interventions, paying attention to whether these procedures provide adequate and effective checks and balances to prevent abuse of the powers of intervention. The fifth section discusses the implementation of interventions, including the politics underlying the practice of interventions in Kenya. The chapter then makes conclusions and recommendations regarding interventions in Kenya.

2. KENYA'S SYSTEM OF DEVOLUTION IN BRIEF

Kenya's multilevel system of government was adopted after a lengthy constitution-making process that culminated in a majority of Kenyans endorsing, via a referendum, a devolved system of government. The system features largely federal-type arrangements within a constitutional framework that also embraces some otherwise typically unitary features.[1] Thus, while the system established under the Constitution of Kenya, adopted in 2010, is labelled as

[1] See Bosire CM *Devolution for development, conflict resolution, and limiting central power: An analysis of the Constitution of Kenya 2010* (Unpublished LLD thesis, University of the Western Cape, 2013) at 156.

'devolutionary', it may be classified as semi-federal. Consequently, subnational governments in Kenya enjoy a constitutionally defined margin of autonomy.

The system has two levels of government: the national and the county levels. Article 1 of the Constitution specifically indicates that the people's sovereign power is exercised at two levels: the national and the county level (which is made up of 47 counties).[2] This power is then delegated to the national executive and Parliament at the national level, and to the executive structures and legislative assemblies at the county government level.

At the subnational level, a county government is made up of a county executive, consisting of the county executive committee (CEC), headed by a governor and a county assembly (CA), the members of which represent wards[3] and special interest groups.[4] Although counties function as the principal subnational unit, the Constitution requires each county government to decentralise its functions and the provision of its services.[5] However, all tiers created by the county are subject to, and report to, the respective county governments.

As to the nature of relations between the two levels of government, and hence to Kenya's approach to the federal concept of self-rule, the Constitution states, in terms that are somewhat similar to the South African Constitution (on which Kenya's system was largely modelled), that they are 'distinct and interdependent'.[6] On this basis, the Constitution enjoins both levels of government to perform their functions and exercise their powers in a manner that respects the functional and institutional integrity, as well as the constitutional status and institutions, of the other level of government.[7] All of this points to the conferment of a degree of autonomy on county governments and to the parity of constitutional status of the two levels of government.

However, in addition to, and as an extension of, the 'interdependent' qualification of the distinctiveness of the two levels above, the Constitution requires that they 'conduct their mutual relations on the basis of consultation and

[2] Article 6(1), Constitution of Kenya (2010). The demarcation of the boundaries of the counties, however, coincided with those of pre-existing districts.

[3] Areas into which a county is divided for purposes of representation in the county assembly.

[4] Article 176(1), Constitution of Kenya (2010), as read with articles 177 and 179. Special interest groups in the assembly include women, persons with disabilities and youth.

[5] Article 176(2), Constitution of Kenya (2010).

[6] Article 6(2), Constitution of Kenya (2010).

[7] Article 189(1)(a), Constitution of Kenya (2010); section 4 of the Intergovernmental Relations Act (IGRA) 2 of 2012 lists these as part of the core principles governing intergovernmental relations and the operation of intergovernmental relations structures under the Act.

cooperation'.[8] This means that they are not independent of each other in the execution of their functions and the exercise of their powers; rather, they are required to liaise with each other for the purposes of, among other things, coordinating policies and administration.[9]

In terms of the shared-rule component of Kenya's system of devolution, various mechanisms have been built into the system to secure the participation of the county sphere in national decision-making. Institutionally, this has been accomplished by adopting a bicameral parliament consisting of two houses, the National Assembly and the Senate.[10] The National Assembly represents constituencies and special interests, and is generally charged with deliberating on and resolving issues of concern to the people.[11] The Senate, for its part, represents the counties at the national level and works to protect the interests of counties by, among other things, deliberating on and approving bills concerning counties.[12]

In terms of the legislative process, the Constitution requires that both houses concur on any bill that concerns county governments.[13] The Senate's participation in the legislative process serves to enhance the system of checks and balances at the national level in favour of county governments, while ensuring the participation of the people (via counties) in national decision-making.[14] Importantly, in the context of this chapter, the Senate plays a critical role in providing checks and balances to the exercise of powers of intervention by the national government. The details are discussed below.

3. RATIONALE FOR LEGAL ENTRENCHMENT OF POWERS OF INTERVENTION

While the legal entrenchment of powers of intervention in Kenya may be attributed largely to the federal origins and constitutional modelling of the multilevel system that was eventually adopted in Kenya (devolution within a unitary framework, rather than federalism), it may also, arguably, find explanation in circumstances unique to Kenya.

---

8 Article 6(2), Constitution of Kenya (2010). See also section 4(h), IGRA.

9 Article 189(1)(c), Constitution of Kenya (2010).

10 Article 93(1), Constitution of Kenya (2010).

11 Article 95(1) and (2), Constitution of Kenya (2010).

12 Article 96(1) and (2), Constitution of Kenya (2010).

13 Article 110(4) and (5), Constitution of Kenya (2010); article 110(1) defines 'a bill concerning county government' as including 'a Bill referred to in Chapter Twelve affecting the finances of county governments'.

14 Committee of Experts on Constitutional Review *Final report of the Committee of Experts on Constitutional Review* (2010) at 114–15.

The rationale hence may also lie in, among other things, the history of Kenya's overall governance objective of nation-building: here the emphasis was on national unity as well as (and more importantly) the socio-political experience of Kenyans, given Kenya's post-colonial, highly centralised system of governance, one that revolved around an imperial presidency – hence raising the need to place checks and balances on the exercise of political power. This history shaped the debates around constitutional reform and the content of Kenya's current constitution.

Given the system's federal origins, the powers of intervention it prescribes find justification in federal theories which maintain that national supervision – including through the imposition and enforcement of fiscal responsibility laws – ensures subnational fiscal and financial discipline.[15] This may explain the adoption of intervention powers in the constitutional framework of countries such as South Africa, on which Kenya's multilevel governance framework was modelled.

Additionally, Kenya's overarching focus on nation-building and national unity at independence, as well as their continuation post-independence as national values and goals, may also explain the lack of discomfort with incorporating powers of intervention in the Constitution of Kenya of 2010. Opposition to federalism and a preference for a unitary state (for the sake of nation-building) characterised Kenya's independence ruling party's approach to post-independence governance.[16] This approach prevailed throughout the pre-2010 constitutional dispensation. Hence, it is arguable that the subconscious need to preserve elements of unitary governance in the system of devolution may have informed the retention of powers of intervention in the adopted constitutional model.

Lastly, and importantly, Kenya's experience with centralisation and the ensuing need to guard against the abuse of unchecked power may explain the retention of intervention powers in the constitutional model that was adopted. Kenya's post-colonial centralisation of power, and the resulting increased concentration of state power in the office of the President, led to the diminution of democratic space, the exclusion of the people from political decision-making (which in turn resulted in exclusionary policies), the marginalisation of communities in the distribution of resources and development and the lack of downward accountability to the people by the government and public officials.[17]

---

[15] Liu L & Webb SB 'Laws for fiscal responsibility for subnational discipline: International experience' (2011) World Bank Policy Research Working Paper.

[16] Muigai G & Juma D *Power, politics & law: Dynamics of constitutional change in Kenya, 1887–2022* Nakuru: Kabarak University Press (2022) at 171–173.

[17] Constitution of Kenya Review Commission *The final report of the Constitution of Kenya Review Commission* (2005) at 234. See also Ghai Y

The distrust that Kenyans have developed regarding the grant of absolute or unfettered political power to any institution of government hence could also explain the retention of intervention in subnational governments as a means of enhancing checks and balances and ensuring accountable governance.

4. CONSTITUTIONAL AND LEGISLATIVE FRAMEWORK FOR INTERVENTION

National intervention in Kenya forms only a part of the broader mechanisms that have been built into the devolved framework to facilitate the accountability of county governments. The Constitution and the legislative framework have erected a system of controls targeted at ensuring the accountability of county governments. This system consists of three sets of control mechanisms: those that are internal to the county level of government and aimed at ensuring fiscal responsibility and accountability at the county level without intrusion from the national government (internal systemic controls);[18] those that, while external to the county level, emanate from neutral or evenly placed sources (supportive controls);[19] and those that emanate from the national government and typically involve the national government's exerting itself in the county sphere of government (external fiscal controls).

While the first two are classic federal-theory compliant, in the sense that they are autonomy-enhancing, the last is the most intrusive, as it necessarily involves the limitation of county autonomy or the full assumption of county functions.[20]

The Constitution envisages the intervention of the national government in counties in four instances: where a county is unable to perform its functions;[21] where a county fails to operate a financial management system that complies

'Devolution: Restructuring the Kenyan state' (2008) 2 *Journal of Eastern African Studies* 221 at 215.

18 Internal systemic controls include county-executive-level self-regulation through mechanisms such as internal audit units; executive accountability to county assemblies; and horizontal accountability through the requirement of public participation.

19 Supportive controls include independent commissions and offices, the mandates of which work to support systems of internal control at the county level. These include the offices of the Controller of Budget, the Auditor-General and the Commission on Revenue Allocation.

20 Steytler N & De Visser J *Local government law of South Africa* South Africa: LexisNexis (2016) Chapter 15 at 5.

21 Article 190(3)(a), Constitution of Kenya (2010).

with the expenditure control measures prescribed under national legislation;[22] where a county registers a serious material breach or persistent material breach of legislative measures aimed at ensuring transparency and expenditure control;[23] and where there are exceptional circumstances warranting the suspension of a county government.[24] Although the Constitution does not specify what amounts to, or qualifies as, an exceptional circumstance in the latter case, the County Governments Act (CGA) indicates that where a county's engagements are deemed to be against the common needs and interests of its citizens, this would constitute a basis for suspension.[25]

In terms of the legislative framework, Parliament has enacted the CGA, the Public Finance Management Act (PFMA) (including its regulations) and the Intergovernmental Relations Act (IRA) to give effect to the constitutional provisions relating to the intervention of the national government in counties.

Each of the grounds for intervention above is discussed in the subsections below.

4.1 Inability to Perform Functions

Where a county is unable to perform its functions,[26] the Constitution requires national legislation to authorise the national government to take appropriate measures to assist it to resume full responsibility for the functions.[27] In this case, the Cabinet Secretary for Finance is required to prepare a recovery plan, in consultation with the county government, to secure the county's ability to resume its functions.[28]

However, although justified in the circumstances, the recovery plan provides binding budget parameters for the county, determines revenue measures and tariff rates necessary for financial recovery and allows for the liquidation of specific county assets. Nonetheless, the intervention directly limits the fiscal autonomy of the affected county government.[29] Moreover, where a recovery plan may not resolve the issue, or where it actually fails to do so, the national government is allowed to assume responsibility for the performance

22 Article 190(3)(b), Constitution of Kenya (2010).
23 Article 225(3)(a), Constitution of Kenya (2010).
24 Article 192(1)(b), Constitution of Kenya (2010).
25 CGA, section 123(1) as read with article 192(1)(b) of the Constitution.
26 What amounts to an inability to perform a function is, however, not presently defined or detailed in law.
27 Article 190(5)(c), Constitution of Kenya (2010).
28 Section 99(1)(c) and (3), PFMA.
29 Sections 99(4)(d)–(e) and 99(5)(a), PFMA.

of the affected functions,[30] a situation that involves a complete limitation of the autonomy of the county.

While this form of intervention significantly limits the autonomy of county governments, it is worth noting that the objective is to work towards capacitating the specific county to resume full functionality.

4.2 Failure to Operate a Financial Management System that Complies with National Legislation

The national government's obligations and powers when undertaking an intervention on the grounds of a failure by a county to operate a financial management system that complies with national legislation are the same as those under the above form of intervention.[31] The lumping together of these forms of intervention under the Constitution does not help to provide clarity on them. National legislation has not done much to provide clarity on what amounts to a failure to operate a compliant financial management system, or on how this form of intervention is to be implemented.[32]

Nevertheless, what is clear from section 101 of the PFMA concerning this intervention is how it may be terminated. Circumstances under which the intervention may be ended include where the Joint Intergovernmental Technical Committee (Joint Committee), which is charged with reviewing interventions under the PFMA, is satisfied that the county government is able and willing to fulfil its obligation,[33] or where it finds that the county government is operating a financial management system that complies with legislation.[34]

4.3 Material Breach of Legislative Measures on Transparency and Expenditure Control

In addition to the two forms of intervention above, the cabinet secretary in charge of finance (through the National Treasury)[35] is allowed to intervene to

---

30 Article 190(4)(b), Constitution of Kenya (2010).

31 Article 190(4)(a)–(b) and 190(5)(b) and (d), Constitution of Kenya (2010).

32 See, for example, section 93(3), PFMA.

33 Section 101(1)(b), PFMA.

34 Section 101(1)(d), PFMA. The Committee consists of the Cabinet Secretary for Finance; the Cabinet Secretary responsible for intergovernmental relations; a representative of the county government or county-government entity concerned; a representative of the Intergovernmental Budget and Economic Council; and a representative of the Commission on Revenue Allocation. It can also invite or enlist any other persons to assist it in performing its functions.

35 Section 13(1)(f), PFMA.

stop the transfer of funds to a county government in instances where a county is in serious or persistent material breach of legislative measures aimed at ensuring transparency and expenditure control.[36] Factors that may indicate that a county is in serious or persistent material breach include where a county has failed to make payments as and when due, or has defaulted on financial obligations for financial reasons; a county is more than 60 days late in submitting its annual financial statements to the Auditor-General (AG); the Controller of Budget (CoB) has raised material issues in its quarterly report; the AG has withheld an opinion or issued a disclaimer as a result of inadequacies in the county's records; or the AG has identified a serious financial problem in the opinion issued.[37] The consequences of the stoppage of transfers, as well as the limitations imposed on the fiscal autonomy of the counties when a recovery plan is imposed,[38] impact on the overall autonomy of county governments.

4.4 Actions Deemed to be Against the Common Needs and Interests of Citizens

Intervention that is triggered as a result of actions that are deemed to be against the common needs and interests of citizens entails the suspension of a county government where it is found to engage in actions that are deemed to be against the common needs and interests of the citizens of the county.[39] In such a case, any person is allowed to petition the President, by a petition supported by at least 10 per cent of a county's registered voters, to suspend the county government.[40] The President is then required to first submit a report on the petition to the National and County Government Co-ordinating Summit for its approval,[41] before nominating a commission of inquiry, with the Senate's approval, to investigate the allegations.[42] The commission's report is considered by the Senate and, where approved, the President is obligated to suspend the county for a period of 90 days, with the Senate reserving the right to terminate the suspension.[43] Upon the suspension of the county, the Constitution

---

36 Constitution of Kenya (2010), article 225(3) as read with section 93 of the PFMA.

37 Section 94(1), PFMA.

38 PFMA, section 99(1)(c) and (3) as read with sections 99(4)(d)–(e) and 99(5)(a).

39 CGA, section 123(1) as read with article 192(1)(b) of the Constitution.

40 CGA, section 123(1) as read with article 192(1)(b) of the Constitution.

41 CGA, section 123(3).

42 CGA, section 123(4) as read with article 192(2) of the Constitution.

43 CGA, section 123(11), (12) and (13) as read with article 192(4) and (5) of the Constitution.

requires arrangements to be made for the performance of the county's functions and, unless the suspension is lifted, for elections to be conducted for the county within 90 days.[44]

Given that the county assembly stands prorogued with an interim county management board (ICMB) – appointed by the President with the Senate's approval, and taking over all the powers and functions of the CEC during the period of suspension – this form of intervention is the most intrusive in a county's autonomy.[45]

5. PROCEDURES FOR INTERVENTION AND CHECKS AND BALANCES AGAINST THEM

For the first three forms of intervention, the Public Finance Management Act establishes a Joint Intergovernmental Technical Committee (Joint Committee), which is made up of the cabinet secretaries for finance and intergovernmental relations, as well as representatives of the Commission on Revenue Allocation (CRA), the Intergovernmental Budget and Economic Council (IBEC), and the county concerned. The Joint Committee is charged with undertaking quarterly reviews of any interventions to gauge the progress made in the resolution of the identified problem, as well as with assessing the effectiveness of the recovery plan adopted.[46] The Joint Committee is required to submit reports on the progress, as well as a final intervention report, where appropriate, to the Cabinet Secretary for Finance, the county executive member for finance, the relevant county assembly, the IBEC and the Senate.[47] This is critical in ensuring that the national government's powers of intervention are checked, to ensure that a county's autonomy is restored once the problem underlying the intervention has been sufficiently addressed.

Procedures, checks and balances specific to each of the forms of intervention are discussed further below.

5.1 Inability to Perform Functions and Failure to Operate a Compliant Financial Management System

In terms of procedure, where it has been found that a county is unable to perform its function or that it does not operate a financial management system that complies with national legislation, the Cabinet Secretary for Finance is required, before intervening, to:

44 Constitution of Kenya (2010), article 192(3) as read with (6).
45 CGA, section 124(1) as read with sections 125(1) and 127(1).
46 PFMA, section 100(1) and (3).
47 PFMA, section 100(4).

1) notify the county government as well as the cabinet secretary for intergovernmental relations of the finding and the intention to intervene;
2) consult the county governor to obtain the county government's cooperation in the development and implementation of a recovery plan, including the approval of a budget and legislative measures giving effect to the recovery plan;
3) prepare an appropriate recovery plan in consultation with the county government; and
4) notify the CoB, Senate, Joint Committee and the AG of the findings and the contents of the recovery plan.[48]

This cooperative approach to the initiation of the intervention is important in ensuring that the constitutional objective of capacitating the affected county towards its full resumption of its functions. In addition, the imperative to notify the various stakeholders under (d) above serves to facilitate transparency as well as incentivise the Cabinet Secretary to ensure that the recovery plan aligns with and is suited to the problem identified. Additionally, the fact that the national government is required to take only necessary measures[49] and that the Senate is allowed to bring the intervention to an end[50] serves to provide checks on the exercise of this power of intervention by the national government which secure the autonomy of county governments.

Besides the above safeguards, which apply to both forms, interventions that are based on an inability to perform functions have a further safeguard. The cabinet secretary for intergovernmental relations must seek Parliament's approval before escalating the intervention to an assumption of responsibility for county functions.[51] This is critical in protecting against national government overreach and usurpation of county functions.

5.2 Material Breach of Legislative Measures on Transparency and Expenditure Control

Procedurally, the Cabinet Secretary for Finance has a number of obligations when he or she stops the transfer of funds to a county government on the grounds that the latter is in serious or persistent material breach of its obligations or financial commitments. The Cabinet Secretary is required, within seven days of stopping the transfer, to inform the county government's

48 PFMA, section 99(1) as read with section 93(3).
49 Article 190(5)(b), Constitution of Kenya (2010).
50 Article 190(5)(d), Constitution of Kenya (2010).
51 Section 121(4), CGA.

accounting officer, the cabinet secretary in charge of intergovernmental relations, the county's CEC member in charge of finance, the CoB, the CRA and the IBEC.[52] Alternatively, the Cabinet Secretary is obligated to inform the county's CEC for finance and then request the AG to assess the county's financial state to determine the reasons for the breach and submit a report within 30 days to the Cabinet Secretary and the CEC member.[53]

The first obligation – to inform the various entities, including intergovernmental organs as well as independent constitutional bodies – is important in that it facilitates transparency, encourages objectivity, and discourages arbitrariness in the initiation of this form of intervention. Moreover, the CoB is required to investigate the basis for intervention and present a report to Parliament within 14 days of the stoppage of funds. Also, the option for the Cabinet Secretary to involve the AG allows for the intervention not only to react to symptoms that may point to breach but, importantly, to objectively examine the underlying issues that would then inform the solution explored as part of the intervention.

In addition, the Constitution puts in place various measures aimed at checking how this intervention is implemented. For instance, an intervention stopping the transfer of funds is required to be approved by both Houses of Parliament within 30 days, failing which it lapses.[54] As part of the approval process, the affected county government is required to be given a chance to appear before the relevant parliamentary committee to state its case and answer the allegations against it.[55] This allows Parliament access to alternative explanations of allegations by the National Treasury to inform its decision-making.

Given the devastating effect that the stoppage of funds may have on the operations of counties (especially seeing as the bulk of their expenditure is funded by transfers), the Constitution prohibits the stoppage of more than 50 per cent of funds due to the county, and also requires such stoppage not to exceed 60 days unless renewed by Parliament.[56] Additionally, the requirement for the CoB to be informed, to investigate the circumstances underlying the decision to stop funds, and to submit a report to Parliament before Parliament approves the commencement of the intervention,[57] as well as the requirement for the CoB to submit a further report when Parliament is considering a renewal of the intervention,[58] serves to ensure that objective assessments of

---

[52] Section 96(2), PFMA.
[53] Section 96(3), PFMA.
[54] Article 225(5)(b), Constitution of Kenya (2010).
[55] Article 225(7)(b), Constitution of Kenya (2010).
[56] Article 225(4), (5)(a) and (6), Constitution of Kenya.
[57] Section 96(2) and (3), PFMA.
[58] Section 98(1) and (2), PFMA.

the circumstances are made and that Parliament is provided with an objective basis for its decision-making when checking the national government's use of these powers.[59]

It is worth noting that the National Treasury is required to release to the affected county all funds held during the period of stoppage within a period of 15 days where a request to renew the stoppage of funds has been declined by Parliament.[60] This ensures that all funds that were due to a county government are eventually released.

In addition to these measures, the courts have played an important role in preventing the abuse of this power. A case in point is an attempt by the Senate in 2014 to direct the CoB to withhold approval of funds to counties whose governors had failed to appear before its committee to respond to financial management queries raised in the CoB reports;[61] here, the court found this to be unlawful for not having been initiated by the National Treasury.[62]

5.3 Actions Deemed to Be Against the Common Needs and Interests of Citizens

The Constitution puts measures in place to check the President's ability to suspend a county government. First, it requires that an independent commission of inquiry be set up to investigate any allegations against a county upon which a suspension is petitioned.[63] Even where the President is satisfied by the commission's report that the allegations are justified, the Constitution requires the Senate to authorise the decision to suspend the county.[64] Additionally, even after the Senate has authorised such a suspension, the Constitution reserves the Senate's right to terminate the suspension at any time.[65] Moreover, the law requires that the Senate approves members appointed to the ICMB appointed to run the affairs of the county during the pendency of the suspension.[66] To avoid a situation where a county's operations are indefinitely grounded on account of the suspension, the Constitution imposes a maximum period of 90 days upon the expiry of which elections are required to be held to put in

59 See also section 98, PFMA.
60 Section 98(4), PFMA.
61 *Council of Governors & 6 others v Senate*, Judgment of the Court of Appeal [2015] eKLR at paras 2 and 156.
62 *Council of Governors* at paras 165–167 and 183(k).
63 Article 192(2), Constitution of Kenya (2010).
64 Article 192(2), Constitution of Kenya (2010).
65 Article 192(4), Constitution of Kenya (2010).
66 Section 126(2), CGA.

place a new government for the suspended county.[67] All these measures are key in safeguarding the long-term autonomy of county governments.

6. THE POLITICS OF INTERVENTION IN KENYA

With respect to the forms of interventions discussed above, the practice has so far presented a variety of circumstances. To begin with, there have been no reported cases of a county being unable to perform its functions; hence, there have been no grounds to justify an intervention on this basis. However, there have been various scenarios that would have justified interventions on the two grounds relating to a county's financial affairs, and only one instance justifying intervention by suspension of a county. Notwithstanding the circumstances in the latter cases, the national government has been unable to intervene, arguably due to political reasons or to ignorance of and/or indifference to its legal obligations in this respect.

6.1 Interventions Related to a County's Financial Affairs

Despite the elaborate system of fiscal controls provided through both the internal systemic controls and the mechanism of supportive controls, counties have generally performed poorly in their audit outcomes (although these have improved over time). While the audit outcomes for 2018/2019 were the best for the counties over the years, only two county governments obtained an unqualified audit opinion, whereas a majority (36) still received qualified opinions (with four receiving adverse opinions while the last five got disclaimers).[68]

Moreover, the CoB has consistently reported cases of counties exceeding the regulatory threshold for personnel emoluments; having consistently high pending bills;[69] failing to deposit all collected or unspent county own source revenue (OSR) into the county revenue fund (using OSR at source);[70] failing to establish and/or effectively operationalise internal audit units and audit committees;[71] failing to establish and/or fully operationalise the County Budget Economic Forums;[72] and having high levels of travel expenditure, even during the period that saw restrictions on movement as a result of the Covid-19

---

67 Article 192(5) and (6), Constitution of Kenya (2010).

68 Muwonge A, Williamson TS, Owuor C, & Muratha K *Making devolution work for service delivery in Kenya* Chicago, Illinois: World Bank (2021) at 75.

69 See the CoB end-of-year reports for 2019/20 at 402; 2017/18 at 311; 2016/17 at 318; 2015/16 at 321. See also CoB (2019) at 67.

70 CoB (2020) at 402; CoB (2018) at 312.

71 CoB (2019) at 69; CoB (2019) at 313; CoB (2018) at 312.

72 CoB (2019) at 69; CoB (2019) at 313; CoB (2016) at 320.

pandemic.[73] These issues have also been highlighted in audit opinions issued by the AG.[74]

All of the above indicates that there are problems of financial management at the county level that have remained unaddressed by the systems of internal and supportive controls, hence necessitating the triggering of national intervention. More specifically, there has been inaction over a failure by counties to run compliant financial management systems. Although reports by the CoB and AG consistently show that counties are openly violating national laws in their financial management (in relation to thresholds for staff expenditure and procurement regulations), the national government has never initiated this form of intervention to ensure compliance. This may be the reason why counties do not feel obliged to address instances of non-compliance identified in the annual AG reports.

There has also been national inaction over what otherwise qualify as serious or persistent material breaches by counties. Despite the existence of factors such as huge recurrent eligible pending (unpaid) bills, the raising of material issues in the CoB reports, the issuance of qualified opinions by the AG that identify serious financial problems and consistent adverse findings in counties,[75] the national government has never invoked its intervention powers to stop the transfer of funds. All that it has managed to do over the years is

73 CoB (2021) at 452–453.

74 Office of the Auditor-General *Report of the Auditor-General on County Executive of Mombasa for the year ended 30 June 2019* (2020) at 5; Office of the Auditor-General *Report of the Auditor-General on County Executive of Machakos for the year ended 30 June 2019* (2020) at 3; Office of the Auditor-General *Report of the Auditor-General on County Executive of Kirinyaga for the year ended 30 June 2019* (2020) at 6; Office of the Auditor-General *Report of the Auditor-General on County Executive of Kiambu for the year ended 30 June 2019* (2020) at 14; Office of the Auditor-General *Report of the Auditor-General on County Executive of Kakamega for the year ended 30 June 2019* (2020) at 6; Office of the Auditor-General *Report of the Auditor-General on County Assembly of Nairobi City for the year ended 30 June 2019* (2020) at 3–4; Office of the Auditor-General *Report of the Auditor-General on County Assembly of Mombasa for the year ended 30 June 2019* (2020) at 4; Office of the Auditor-General *Report of the Auditor-General on County Assembly of Makueni for the year ended 30 June 2019* (2020) at 3–4; Office of the Auditor-General *Report of the Auditor-General on County Assembly of Kisumu for the year ended 30 June 2019* (2020) at 2–3; Office of the Auditor-General *Report of the Auditor-General on County Assembly of Kakamega for the year ended 30 June 2019* (2020) at 4.

75 World Bank *Kenya accountable devolution program: Annual report 2018* Washington, DC: World Bank Group at 7 available at http://documents.worldbank.org/curated/en/519061588168487358 (accessed 1 March 2025).

issue directives through the National Treasury to counties to pay pending bills under the threat of initiating a stoppage of transfers.[76] The threat of intervention through stoppage seems to have been selected largely because triggering it would involve little political inconvenience; in addition, the PFMA sets a low threshold for the initiation of such a measure.

While the threats are reported to have compelled some counties to act in clearing up eligible pending bills,[77] the national government's reluctance to fully apply its powers in actualising the intervention on these grounds as well as other grounds only encourages non-compliance and defeats the ends of achieving accountable subnational fiscal autonomy.

6.2 Interventions Due to Actions against Citizens' Interests

The power to suspend a county has only been invoked once, in the case of Makueni County in 2015. This followed disagreements between the governor and members of the county assembly (MCAs) that crippled the operations of the county government and led, inter alia, to an assassination attempt on the governor.[78] The governor had, among other things, declined to formally assent to a county assembly law establishing a county ward development fund, one under which the MCAs had allocated themselves almost the entire development budget, along with powers to oversee the implementation of projects within their wards.[79] This was in addition to a failure by the governor to approve funds for foreign trips for the MCAs, as well as salaries and allowances that exceeded national ceilings.[80] In both instances, the governor insisted on the constitutional and legal invalidity of the actions of the county assembly.

---

[76] 'Settle all pending bills by end of month, President Kenyatta orders accounting officers' (1 June 2019) *Business Times* available at https://businesstimes.co.ke/settle-pending-bills-end-month-president-kenyatta-orders-accounting-officers/ (accessed 21 November 2021); National Treasury and Planning *The budget summary for the fiscal year 2021/22 and the supporting information* (29 April 2021) at 33–34 available at https://www.treasury.go.ke/wp-content/uploads/2021/06/FY-2021-22-Budget-Summary.pdf (accessed 1 March 2025).

[77] Kenya Institute for Public Policy Research and Analysis (KIPPRA) 'Pending bills: Will the private sector survive?' (29 July 2020) *KIPPRA* available at https://kippra.or.ke/pending-bills-will-the-private-sector-survive/ (accessed 21 November 2021).

[78] Kenya Law 'Petition for the suspension of the government of Makueni County' (2019) *Kenya Law* available at http://kenyalaw.org/kenyalawblog/suspension-of-the-government-of-makueni/ (accessed 7 November 2023).

[79] Kenya Law (2019).

[80] Kenya Law (2019).

Although the President eventually declined to suspend the county, as had been recommended by a commission of inquiry following a petition by the residents of Makueni County, the whole process of inquiry and the stakes involved served to rein in MCAs and facilitate the restoration of order in the county.[81] This constitutes the only recorded formal process of intervention initiated by the national government. Although it was not seen through, its success lay in the fact that the initiation of the process made real the possibility of the MCAs losing their seats and failing to be re-elected – thereby compelling them to back down and adopt a more collaborative approach with the county executive.

7. CONCLUSION

Given the scope of the autonomy that the Constitution extends to counties, Kenya's legal framework provides a comprehensive array of controls whose enforcement has the capacity to secure the functional, financial and institutional accountability of county governments. While the imperative of autonomy for county governments demands that deference be given to internal systems of control, supportive controls and, where these fail, national government measures aimed at providing support to strengthen the capacity of counties to self-regulate and ensure their own accountability, the mechanism of intervention is crucial. It helps not only in serving as a deterrent to poor fiscal management practices at the county level but also in remedying deteriorating levels of accountability at the county level.

While mechanisms of intervention constitute a legitimate and justified limitation on the overall autonomy of counties, their application is balanced by various checks and balances that serve to protect the autonomy of counties while at the same time allowing room for corrective measures aimed at facilitating the continued accountability of county governments. Notable in this regard is the role played by the courts, which, as demonstrated in this chapter, have been instrumental in ensuring that while the law is interpreted to ensure the accountability of county governments, the implementation of control measures is not used as a pretext for violating the autonomy, institutional integrity and constitutional status of county governments.

However, despite the comprehensiveness of the framework for controls and its potential to secure the accountable exercise of autonomy, the implementation of this framework has been far from satisfactory. Systems of internal

---

[81] Muasya P 'How Kibwana spanked Makueni's rebel MCAs' (2017) *The Sunday Standard* available at https://www.standardmedia.co.ke/entertainment/county-riftvalley/article/2001234702/how-kibwana-spanked-makuenis-rebel-mcas (accessed 1 March 2025).

control have largely been ineffective in securing fiscal prudence at the county level, as evidenced by the reports of the CoB and AG. Moreover, these systems have been ineffective in resolving issues identified through the systems of supportive control, given the recurrence of the identified financial management issues. Although these circumstances demand that external fiscal controls be applied to ensure the effectiveness of the systems of internal and supportive controls and the facilitation of accountable fiscal autonomy, the national government has been reluctant to initiate and implement such controls.

Various reasons may be advanced to explain the national government's reluctance to use its powers of intervention. First, this may be partly attributable to the intermediate superintending oversight role played by the Senate, which renders the national government complacent by providing an appearance of national action relating to the accountability of county governments. However, the lack of enforcement powers on the part of the Senate makes its role in this respect ineffective.

Second, even though the implementation of devolution began more than a decade ago in 2013, the lack of political will at the national level to embrace the transition to genuine multilevel governance has undermined the letter and spirit of devolved governance. This has led to stagnation in the governance culture and a failure to put in place frameworks, systems and resources to facilitate effective monitoring and operationalisation of the law on interventions.

Third, this reluctance means that the national level has been unable to fully comprehend and brace itself for the political consequences of intervention, especially in counties affiliated with the ruling party. As such, fear of the political consequences of intervention may also underlie the reluctance to intervene. Consequently, counties seem to experience minimal limitations to their overall margin of autonomy, all of which comes at the expense of their functional, financial and institutional accountability.

BIBLIOGRAPHY

Books

Muigai G & Juma D *Power, politics & law: Dynamics of constitutional change in Kenya, 1887–2022* Nakuru: Kabarak University Press (2022)

Muwonge A, Williamson TS, Owuor C & Muratha K *Making devolution work for service delivery in Kenya* Chicago, Illinois: World Bank (2021)

Steytler N & De Visser J *Local government law of South Africa* South Africa: LexisNexis (2016)

Journal Articles

Ghai Y 'Devolution: Restructuring the Kenyan state' (2008) 2 *Journal of Eastern African Studies* 221–26

Liu L & Webb SB 'Laws for fiscal responsibility for subnational discipline: International experience' (2011) World Bank Policy Research Working Paper

Case Law

Council of Governors & 6 others v Senate, Judgment of the Court of Appeal [2015] eKLR

Legislation

Constitution of Kenya, 2010

County Governments Act 17 of 2012

Intergovernmental Relations Act 2 of 2012

Public Finance Management Act 18 of 2012

Reports

Committee of Experts on Constitutional Review *Final Report of the Committee of Experts on Constitutional Review* (2010)

Constitution of Kenya Review Commission *The final report of the Constitution of Kenya Review Commission* (2005)

Internet Sources

'Settle all pending bills by end of month, President Kenyatta orders accounting officers' (1 June 2019) *Business Times* available at https://businesstimes.co.ke/settle-pending-bills-end-month-president-kenyatta-orders-accounting-officers/ (accessed 21 November 2021)

Kenya Institute for Public Policy Research and Analysis (KIPPRA) 'Pending bills: Will the private sector survive?' (29 July 2020) *KIPPRA* available at https://kippra.or.ke/pending-bills-will-the-private-sector-survive/ (accessed 21 November 2021)

Kenya Law 'Petition for the suspension of the government of Makueni County' (2019) *Kenya Law* available at http://kenyalaw.org/kenyalawblog/suspension-of-the-government-of-makueni/ (accessed 7 November 2023)

Muasya P 'How Kibwana spanked Makueni's rebel MCAs' (2017) *The Sunday Standard* available at https://www.standardmedia.co.ke/entertainment/county-riftvalley/article/2001234702/how-kibwana-spanked-makuenis-rebel-mcas (accessed 1 March 2025)

Reports

Controller of Budget (CoB) Reports 2021, 2020, 2019/20, 2018, 2017/18, 2016/17, 2015/16

National Treasury and Planning *The budget summary for the fiscal year 2021/22 and the supporting information* (29 April 2021) available at https://www.treasury.go.ke/wp-content/uploads/2021/06/FY-2021-22-Budget-Summary.pdf (accessed 1 March 2025)

Office of the Auditor-General *Report of the Auditor-General on County Executive of Mombasa for the year ended 30 June 2019* (2020)

Office of the Auditor-General *Report of the Auditor-General on County Executive of Machakos for the year ended 30 June 2019* (2020)

Office of the Auditor-General *Report of the Auditor-General on County Executive of Kirinyaga for the year ended 30 June 2019* (2020)

Office of the Auditor-General *Report of the Auditor-General on County Executive of Kiambu for the year ended 30 June 2019* (2020)

Office of the Auditor-General *Report of the Auditor-General on County Executive of Kakamega for the year ended 30 June 2019* (2020)

Office of the Auditor-General *Report of the Auditor-General on County Assembly of Nairobi City for the year ended 30 June 2019* (2020)

Office of the Auditor-General *Report of the Auditor-General on County Assembly of Mombasa for the year ended 30 June 2019* (2020)

Office of the Auditor-General *Report of the Auditor-General on County Assembly of Makueni for the year ended 30 June 2019* (2020)

Office of the Auditor-General *Report of the Auditor-General on County Assembly of Kisumu for the year ended 30 June 2019* (2020)

Office of the Auditor-General *Report of the Auditor-General on County Assembly of Kakamega for the year ended 30 June 2019* (2020)

World Bank *Kenya accountable devolution program: Annual report 2018* Washington, DC: World Bank Group available at http://documents.worldbank.org/curated/en/519061588168487358 (accessed 1 March 2025)

Theses

Bosire CM *Devolution for development, conflict resolution, and limiting central power: An analysis of the Constitution of Kenya 2010* (Unpublished LLD thesis, University of the Western Cape, 2013)

8. Malaysia: intervention under the guise of emergency powers?

Andrew Harding

1. INTRODUCTION

This chapter examines how federal power can intervene in state governments in Malaysian federalism. In keeping with the comparative nature of this edited volume, this chapter (to quote from the book's introduction) examines such intervention as 'driven by (1) the executive of a higher level of government; [one] which (2) targets a lower government level (subnational and/or local); (3) on grounds related to security or a failure to comply with legal obligations regarding their preservation of democracy and the rule of law or their financial and administrative performance'. The chapter focuses on state rather than local governments since local government authorities in Malaysia are not elected and do not enjoy anything beyond nominal independence.[1]

In view of the fact that Malaysia does not have specific provisions on federal intervention in state governments, and even lacks a federal power in terms of which to give directions to state governments, the focus is on the only relevant instrument: emergency powers. Although the case studies in this book are to exclude 'interventions that come as a result of countrywide emergencies', this implicitly covers emergencies that relate to a *specific state*. We will see that, of the six emergencies proclaimed in Malaysian history to date, two of these were authorised so as to apply to a specific state.

As the introduction observes, although intervention may be necessary in the interests of security, the maintenance of the constitutional order, effective governance, and so on, it is inevitably 'inconsistent with federalism's basic tenet of protecting self-government of own affairs against central government interference'. This paradox is fully present in the Malaysian case.

[1] Harding A *Local government in Malaysia: Responses to urban-rural challenges* European Union Horizon 2020 Project (2021a) at 31ff.

Powers of intervention are highly relevant in deciding if a 'federation' corresponds in practice with its formal description, given that all accepted definitions of federalism stress the autonomy and exclusivity of states in acting freely within their own areas of competence. However, Malaysia has often been recognised as a case of 'quasi-federalism',[2] with the Reid Commission that drafted the 1957 Constitution of the Federation of Malaya having accorded the states only what it called 'a measure of autonomy'.[3]

The following section of this chapter looks at the complex origins and nature of Malaysian federalism, while section 3 examines the importance of emergency powers, as activated in Sarawak in 1966 and Kelantan in 1977. Section 4 analyses the facts in terms of their impact on federalism; this is followed by a fifth and concluding section.

2. INTRODUCTION: MALAYSIA'S UNIQUE FORM OF FEDERALISM

The Federation of Malaya was created by the Federation of Malaya Agreement of 1948. In this agreement, all the various British-controlled territories in Malaya were brought together for the first time into a federal system. This federation included two crown colonies (the Straits Settlements of Penang and Malacca);[4] five 'unfederated' Malay states;[5] and four 'federated' Malay states.[6] It was this federation that, following the Reid Commission's Report, became independent in 1957 under the Constitution of the Federation of Malaya. The new basis for federation had been anticipated in the Federation of Malaya Agreement of 1957.

In 1963 the remaining British-controlled territories in Southeast Asia, namely Singapore, Sarawak and North Borneo (but excluding the Sultanate of Brunei), joined with the existing Federation of Malaya to form Malaysia. This followed the recommendations of the Cobbold Commission (1963), an Intergovernmental Committee Report (1962) and the signing of the Malaysia

---

2 Zahrin Z & Mohamed AM 'Revising the unitary vs federation classification' (2022) 18 *Journal of International Studies* 125; Harding A *The Constitution of Malaysia: A contextual analysis* Oxford: Hart/Bloomsbury (2021b) chapter 6.

3 Federation of Malaya Constitutional Commission *1956–7 Report* Kuala Lumpur: Government Printer (1957) at para 3.

4 Singapore was also one of the Straits Settlements but was not included in this federal arrangement, remaining a crown colony until 1963, when it joined Malaysia under the Malaysia Agreement of 1963.

5 That is, Johor, Kedah, Kelantan, Perlis and Terengganu.

6 That is, Negri Sembilan, Pahang, Perak and Selangor. See further Harding (2021b) chapter 1.

Agreement of 1963 (hereafter 'MA1963') by the governments of the three territories, the United Kingdom and the Federation of Malaya. The new federation came into effect on 16 September 1963. On 9 August 1965, Singapore left the federation by agreement to become an independent republic. North Borneo was renamed 'Sabah'.

MA1963 contained no provision for drafting a new constitution for a new federation. Instead, the existing federal constitution was amended in a manner already agreed by an Intergovernmental Committee Report in 1962 and the federation renamed 'Malaysia'. Under this pre-constitutional agreement, Sabah and Sarawak (the new states joining the federation) were given, in a number of respects, special status and powers compared to the existing 11 states. This was due to their ethnic composition, having a majority of indigenous people, and concerns about their protection under the new federal system.

Sabah and Sarawak (hereafter 'S&S') retained their own legal systems, including the judiciary and the legal profession, and also powers over immigration and land matters. Additionally, they were accorded a veto on any constitutional amendments that might affect them, something other states did not enjoy. These states on the island of Borneo are vastly different from West Malaysia in terms of both human and physical geography, ethnic pluralism, religious adherence and natural resources. They are also separated from Peninsular (or West) Malaysia by a large stretch of the South China Sea.[7]

The status of S&S has been ambiguous and problematic from the beginning. MA1963 created a two-tier federal system by bringing together territories, one of which was already a federation. The obvious question that came up was: Is this a *new federation*, or just the admission of new states into an *existing federation*?

Article 1 of the MA1963 stated:

> The Colonies of North Borneo and Sarawak and the State of Singapore shall be federated with the existing States of the Federation of Malaya as the States of Sabah, Sarawak and Singapore in accordance with the constitutional instruments annexed to this Agreement and the Federation shall thereafter be called 'Malaysia'.

Several things made the precise nature of this federation unclear. First, the federation had new terms and, if there was no new constitution, the constitution was renamed as that of Malaysia rather than the Federation of Malaya. Second, it had been stated repeatedly that MA1963 represented a 'partnership, not a take-over'. Third, that partnership was between the three new states and a federation (the Federation of Malaya) that immediately ceased to exist as a

7 Harding (2021b) at 142ff.

political entity,[8] having been replaced with a new federal entity whose territory and people included those of the three newly admitted states. Inevitably, therefore, the proposed equal partnership never really existed. Indeed, it is hard to see how it could have existed, given the primacy of what was in essence a highly centralised federation with a powerful central government which was also dominated by a coalition (initially called 'the Alliance', and after 1974, the 'Barisan Nasional') that was to remain in power from 1957 right up to 2018.

Thus, while S&S were assured on paper that they were entering a partnership in which their autonomy enjoyed special protection (in terms of their culture, religion and law), they were in fact folded into a federation of 14 (13 after Singapore's departure) rather than 4 (3 after Singapore's departure) subjects. This underlying reality was formally recognised in a 1974 constitutional amendment. Article 1(2) of the Federal Constitution was amended so as to list the states alphabetically, thereby removing or disallowing the special status of S&S as equal partners with 'Malaya'.

As a result of popular discontent and pressure from S&S leaders, the Constitution was further amended in 2022[9] so as to restore S&S's separate listing from the other states. They were designated as 'territories' rather than states, while the federation itself (in article 160) was designated as that federation established by the Federation of Malaya Agreement 1957 *and* MA1963.[10] A further amendment recognised that Merdeka (Independence) Day does not apply to S&S (it had achieved independence on a different date, 16 September 1963),[11] and also provided for a separate 'Malaysia Day'.

Sarawak has since then amended its constitution to redesignate its head of government as 'Premier' rather than 'Chief Minister',[12] the appellation normally used for the government heads of the states of Malaya. These amendments are, of course, symbolic, but in federal systems symbols are enormously important. It is expected by many in S&S that these symbolic changes will herald a real devolution of powers.

---

8 This is so because 'Malaya' exists as a region with its own legal system (statute law, judiciary and legal profession), but has no government or legislature. The government and legislature of the Federation of Malaya simply became those of the Malaysian Federation.

9 Act A1642/2022.

10 The listing of both federal agreements does not remove the ambiguity, of course; rather, it increases it.

11 Chin J 'Federal-east Malaysia relations: Primus inter pares?' in Harding A and Chin J (eds) *50 years of Malaysia: Federalism revisited* Singapore: Marshall Cavendish (2014) chapter 1.

12 Constitution of Sarawak (Amendment) Ordinance 2022.

3. REASONS FOR THE LACK OF POWERS OF INTERVENTION

The Constitution resulting from the amendments of 1963 lists federal powers, state powers, concurrent powers and the special powers of S&S in its Schedule 9. While many of the provisions on federalism appear to facilitate a cooperative form of federalism (as opposed to a sharp demarcation of state and federal powers),[13] there are, as indicated above, no provisions expressly allowing the federal government to intervene in state government matters or give directions to state governments.

It is interesting in this context to note that the conferring of such powers was not even discussed by the Reid Commission in the chapter of its Report regarding the states. The only relevant issue that concerned the Commission was the possibility of a state failing, after the coming into effect of the Federal Constitution, to implement in its own constitution the so-called essential provisions providing for parliamentary democracy along Westminster lines.[14] In paragraph 178 of the Report, the Commission stated:

> In pursuance of our duty to recommend 'a strong central government' with 'a measure of autonomy' to the States, we have made proposals in Chapter V designed to give the States a greater measure of autonomy in limited but important fields while retaining national control where the national interest as a whole requires it.

It did not occur to the Commission, apparently, that circumstances could arise in which the national interest might require active intervention, as opposed to a general vesting of appropriate powers in the federation. Nonetheless, the Commission proved to be correct: no such circumstances have in fact arisen in the 69 years since the Constitution was brought into effect. This outcome could be attributed to the high degree of centralisation the Constitution provides for, as well as the due execution of state powers, whether or not by a government of a different political complexion from the federal government.

Each of the states has its own constitution. Under Schedule 8 of the Federal Constitution, the state constitutions are required to conform to conventional Westminster norms in terms of internal state governance, embodying, like the federation itself, a constitutional monarchy (S&S have a 'Governor' as head of state rather than a traditional ruler, a Sultan, as elsewhere in the federation). Thus the state's chief executive is appointed by the head of state on the basis

---

13 Harding (2021b) at 133ff.

14 Article 71(4), Schedule 8, Constitution. The remedy here is that the federal legislature could enact these provisions with regard to a particular state. In the event, no such thing has happened.

of the latter's judgment as to which member of the (unicameral) state assembly commands the confidence of a majority of its members. At the federal level, the head of state is the *Yang di-Pertuan Agong* ('he who is lord of the state'), who is appointed by a Conference of Rulers (a *durbar*, or meeting of the nine sultans of the Malay states) on a five-year rotational basis.

Under the Federal Constitution, any unconstitutional actions by state governments or officials are subject to judicial review by the Federal Court, which also resolves any legal issues arising between the federal government and a state government.[15] Thus the judiciary polices the line between federal and state powers, and it is assumed that there is no need for the federal government to have powers equivalent, for example, to those under article 356 of the Indian Constitution providing for 'President's Rule'.[16]

4. EMERGENCY POWERS

One consequence of the federal nature of the Malaysian Constitution and its provisions is that the only way in which the federal government can interfere with the operation of state governments (apart from a suit to have an act or legislation struck down by the courts or by legislation that itself could be challenged by a state government) is via the exercise of emergency powers. These are provided in article 150:

(1) If the Yang di-Pertuan Agong is satisfied that a grave emergency exists whereby the security, or the economic life, or public order in the Federation *or any part thereof*[17] is threatened, he may issue a Proclamation of Emergency making therein a declaration to that effect.
(2) A Proclamation of Emergency under Clause (1) may be issued before the actual occurrence of the event which threatens the security, or the economic life, or public order in the Federation or any part thereof if the Yang di-Pertuan Agong is satisfied that there is imminent danger of the occurrence of such event.

Article 150 is quite extensive in its provisions, but an emergency proclamation gives the government power to legislate inconsistently with the Constitution, while also requiring Parliament to be summoned as soon as is practicable to ratify the proclamation.[18]

---

15 Article 128, Constitution.
16 See Chapter 5 of this volume.
17 Emphasis added.
18 See further Harding (2021b) at 100ff.

For our purposes, clause (8) of article 150 is highly pertinent. This clause was introduced by constitutional amendment in 1981, and states:

> In this Constitution –
>
> (a) the satisfaction of the Yang di-Pertuan Agong mentioned in Clause (1) and Clause (2B) shall be final and conclusive and shall not be challenged or called in question in any court on any ground; and
> (b) no court shall have jurisdiction to entertain or determine any application, question or proceeding, in whatever form, on any ground, regarding the validity of –
>   (i) a Proclamation under Clauses (1) or of a declaration made in such Proclamation to the effect stated in Clause (1);
>   (ii) the continued operation of such Proclamation;
>   (iii) any ordinance promulgated under Clause (2B); or
>   (iv) the continuation in force of any such ordinance.

From the perspective of federalism, article 150(8) raises a question of profound significance: Can emergency powers be used to give the federal government unchecked power to intervene in, or take over, a state government? If the answer is yes, then it is hard to see how Malaysia can be called a federation in any real sense of the term, since this would mean that the powers of state governments would exist only at the whim of the federal government. This would be true for S&S as for the other 11 states, notwithstanding MA1963 and the veto power on constitutional amendments enjoyed by S&S under article 161E(2).

However, this dire conclusion is based on the assumption that clause 150(8), introduced via constitutional amendment, represents a valid amendment. It may well be argued that it violates the Constitution's basic structure and should accordingly be struck down. Ultimately it is on the thin thread of this argument that the powers of the states to resist federal intervention depend. In some recent cases, the Malaysian judiciary has accepted (although not unanimously and only in *obiter dicta*) that the basic structure doctrine applies in Malaysia. It has yet to actually strike down a constitutional amendment on the ground of violating the Constitution's basic structure.[19]

However, supervening on this argument is the fact that the Constitution has now been amended (see above) to refer to the agreements prior to the

---

[19] Moreover, in a case decided at the High Court at Kuala Lumpur on 15 February 2024, it has been held that article 150(8) does not violate the Constitution's basic structure. See 'King's power to proclaim emergency cannot be reviewed by court, judge says' (15 February 2024) *The Star* available at https://www.thestar.com.my/news/nation/2024/02/15/kings-power-to-proclaim-emergency-not-justiciable-by-court-says-judge (accessed 27 January 2025).

Constitution as defining the federation itself. In principle at least, it appears to hold that the federal government, in pursuit of an emergency proclamation, could not – validly and consistently with the Federation of Malaya Agreement 1957 and MA1963 – abolish or interfere with the operation of a state government. It may be added that there was judicial support for use of that Agreement to interpret the Constitution even prior to the 2021 amendment.[20] The amendment cements beyond any argument the relevance of MA1963 to the interpretation of the Constitution.

In the next section, we will see that on two occasions the federal government has in fact used emergency powers to intervene (to drastic effect) in a state government.

5. POLITICS OF INTERVENTION

Article 150 has been invoked on six occasions in Malaysian history. On three of these, the proclaimed emergency covered the entire federation. This happened in 1964 (on the occasion of military operations by Indonesia in pursuit of its *konfrontasi* against Malaysia and Singapore),[21] in 1969 (due to a serious outbreak of inter-ethnic rioting) and in 2021 (to deal with the Covid-19 pandemic). In 2020, a government proposal for a federation-wide emergency was rejected by the *Yang di-Pertuan Agong*. Instead a proclamation was made, covering just two districts in which by-elections were to be held with a high risk of precipitating coronavirus infections.[22]

On two occasions, emergencies were proclaimed which were restricted to single states: Sarawak in 1966 and Kelantan in 1977. These are each discussed in depth below.

5.1 Sarawak (1966)

This episode, coming soon after the formation of Malaysia, was the first major test for federal–state relations and of intervention under the new federal arrangements.

---

20 *Robert Linggi v Government of Malaysia* (2011) 7 CLJ 373.

21 Harding A *Territorial governance in Southeast Asia* Oxford: Hart Publishing (2025) at 184.

22 Harding A 'Acting (or not acting) on (lawful or unlawful) advice in Malaysia: From Windsor to Kuantan and back again' (20 November 2020) *I-CONnect blog of the International Journal of Constitutional Law* available at https://www.iconnectblog.com/acting-or-not-acting-on-lawful-or-unlawful-advice-in-malaysia-from-windsor-to-kuantan-and-back-again/ (accessed 27 January 2025).

Datuk Stephen Kalong Ningkan had been the chief minister of Sarawak since Sarawak joined Malaysia. His party was a partner in the Alliance federal coalition government, but the leadership of the United Malays National Organisation (UMNO), the major force in the coalition, disliked his independent policy as chief minister. While chief minister, Ningkan sought to protect the interests of the indigenous Iban people (his own ethnic group) and also worked to retain British civil servants rather than recruiting personnel from West Malaysia.

As Cyrus Das put it in his 1993 study: 'The events leading to the emergency were inextricably tied up with the political moves at the federal level to oust [Ningkan] ... fierce local loyalties invariably created tension between the Centre and the State.'[23] As a result, attempts were made to oust Ningkan as chief minister, and the federal government even sent a special emissary, Datuk Syed Kechik, to Sarawak 'to procure the removal of Ningkan'.[24] Of the 42 members of the state assembly, 21 were taken to Kuala Lumpur and compelled to sign a letter to the state governor saying they had no confidence in Ningkan. As a result, the assembly was deadlocked. The governor dismissed Ningkan on the basis that he no longer commanded the confidence of a majority of the assemblymen, even though there had been no actual vote in the assembly, which was unable to meet without being summoned by the governor (acting on government advice).

Ningkan applied to the High Court for an order striking down his dismissal. This was granted on the basis that the governor had no power to dismiss the chief minister; that, in any case, 21 was not a majority of the assembly; and that no no-confidence motion had been passed.[25] Syed Kechik, the special emissary, told the federal government that Ningkan had to be brought down 'whatever the financial or constitutional cost'.[26] Accordingly, the federal government did not take measures to have an appeal filed by the defendants against the High Court decision, reasoning that it would take time to get the decision overturned. It was also unable to secure a vote in the assembly without Ningkan (now reinstated as chief minister) agreeing to advise the governor to summon it. Fearing that adherence of a Chinese party to Ningkan's side might consolidate his position in terms of the Constitution, the federal government

[23] Das CV *Government and crisis powers: A legal study on the use of emergency powers* Kuala Lumpur: Malaysian Current Law Journal Sdn. Bhd (1996) at 164.

[24] Das (1996).

[25] *Stephen Kalong Ningkan v Tun Haji Openg and Tawi Sli* [1966] 1 MLJ at 261.

[26] Das (1996) at 165.

went so far as to threaten that party that, if it supported Ningkan, the federal government would impose *continuing emergency rule* on the state.

As a result of these deliberations, the federal government proclaimed an emergency in Sarawak on the express basis of 'constitutional breakdown'. The emergency was in turn used to enact a law[27] allowing a temporary amendment to the state constitution to facilitate Ningkan's dismissal via a no-confidence vote in the assembly. The governor then dismissed Ningkan for a second time. But once again Ningkan challenged his dismissal. He claimed that the emergency itself was passed *in fraudem legis*. In response, the Federal Court held that emergency powers by their nature could not be subjected to judicial review.[28]

Ningkan appealed to the Judicial Committee of the Privy Council in London, which had jurisdiction over Malaysia up until 1985. The Privy Council (in a very odd judgment) entirely avoided the issue of the justiciability of emergency powers[29] but defined these powers so widely as to include cases of 'constitutional breakdown'. It then dismissed the *in fraudem legis* claim despite the ample evidence of constitutional malpractice adduced by Ningkan's counsel, Sir Dingle Foot QC. It added, quite gratuitously, that no outbreak or threatened outbreak of violence was needed to justify an emergency. The end result was that the Alliance got the new government it wanted and Ningkan never regained power.

In his 1986 study of this episode, Yash Ghai concluded that this was the 'clearest example of the manipulation of the Constitution by creating conditions which would justify the proclamation of an emergency'.[30] The overall practical and lasting effect was to lay down the ground rules for future manipulation of state governments by the federal government. As the introduction to this volume indicates, '[e]ven if these legally available powers are not or rarely invoked, they might have a "chilling effect" because interference hangs like a sword of Damocles over the heads of potential targets and thus already constrains their effective autonomy'. This exactly describes the situation that was established by this first precedent. Yet worse was to come.

---

27 Emergency (Federal Constitution and Constitution of Sarawak) Act 1966.

28 *Stephen Kalong Ningkan v Tun Haji Openg and Tawi Sli [No2]* [1967] 1 MLJ at 46.

29 *Stephen Kalong Ningkan v Government of Malaysia* [1968] 2 MLJ 238, Privy Council. Note that this case in 1968 came long before the insertion of the ouster clause in the federal constitution via article 150(8).

30 Ghai Y 'The politics of the constitution: Another look at the Ningkan litigation' (1986) 7 *Singapore Law Review* 147.

5.2 Kelantan (1977)

Kelantan is a highly Islamicised state in Northeastern Malaya. It has experienced a long and difficult conflict over control of the state between UMNO, the main ruling party (and cornerstone of the Barisan Nasional (BN) coalition at the federal level), and the Islamic party, PAS. In 1977, PAS held 22 of the 36 seats in the assembly and was a part of the ruling BN coalition. Its leader, Datuk Mohamed Nasir, was the chief minister of the state.

As a result of discord between UMNO and PAS, PAS left the coalition in 1977. Nasir, however, moved to support UMNO against the majority of his own party and, as a result, eight members of PAS crossed the floor of the assembly to join UMNO. Nasir was then expelled from PAS and a no-confidence vote passed against him. Following Westminster convention, he then requested a dissolution of the assembly. The Ruler of Kelantan was pressured by the federal government to ignore Nasir's request. He also demanded that PAS stand down or emergency powers would be invoked. The threat was similar to that used in the case of Sarawak. PAS refused and, as threatened, an emergency was proclaimed. Emergency law then suspended the state constitution and state government and also dismissed Nasir as chief minister, imposing rule over the state by the National Operations Council, under the direction of the Prime Minister.[31] Eventually, elections were held, and UMNO (together with the PAS dissidents) held power in the state from 1977 until PAS regained control in 1990.[32]

This use of emergency powers was very similar to that in the Sarawak case: the powers were used to resolve political tensions in favour of what was in effect the ruling party at the federal level. Yet it was also different in the important sense that it went further and put in place full federal rule in the state. This was a draconian measure to resolve a purely constitutional issue of control over the state government. The sword of Damocles thus appeared both larger and hanging by a thinner thread than had previously been the case.

It should be added that in neither of these instances did any violence actually occur. It is true that there were social tensions of a kind that could have erupted into violence, especially in Sarawak. But it is clear that had they done so, the responsibility would have been laid at the door of the federal government, not at that of the parties or leaders who had fallen out of favour with the federal government.

---

[31] The significance of 'NOC rule' is that this very method had been used pursuant to the 1969 emergency, which was still in effect in 1977. In effect, the measure placed Kelantan under military rule.

[32] Das (1996) at 174ff.

The problem in each of these two case studies is that emergency powers were used by the federal authorities in very specific ways. They were not used to resolve internal difficulties in the state (such as corruption, bankruptcy, insurgency, natural disaster or even actual or threatened breakdown of law and order). Instead, they were used to impose the party-political will of the Alliance-BN to secure a state government of its own choosing, irrespective of the electoral process and the results this yielded. Given that constitutional issues of the kind at play in these two instances are by no means unusual – and in fact have arisen in one or more states, and even at the federal level (2018), after every election since 2008 (as well as on other occasions between elections) – it is highly unconvincing to argue that the federal government was left with no alternative to that of draconian emergency intervention and that there were no constitutional means of resolving the issue.

The bottom line in terms of the Constitution seems to be that established by the Kelantan case. It has the following components:

- The federal government can impose emergency powers on a state without judicial interference.
- It can do so on the basis of 'constitutional breakdown' despite the fact that (i) the federal government itself created the situation through behind-the-scenes manipulation, and by intervening; (ii) the political issue could be resolved under the provisions of the state constitution; and (iii) there was no threat to public order or security.
- In pursuit of these powers, the federal government can suspend or amend the state constitution, dismiss the state government, impose federal rule and enact any law inconsistent with the state or federal constitutions.

In this regard, the 2013 'Lahad Datu' incident offers a striking comparison. Here, no emergency was proclaimed, despite the fact that a group of insurgents from the Philippines forcibly occupied a district of Sabah in support of the claim of an ancient sultanate (that of Sulu) to the state of Sabah and despite the fact that a military operation by Malaysian armed forces was needed to expel the insurgents, with this resulting in 72 dead, including 10 members of the Malaysian military and six civilians.[33]

It is also striking that various instances of manipulation of a state political system have occurred without the need for an emergency. For example, in Perak in 2009, the BN in power at the federal level secured the defection

[33] 'Sabah stand-off "turns deadly" as clashes break out' *BBC* (1 March 2013) available at https://www.bbc.com/news/world-asia-21628758 (accessed 27 January 2025).

of three assemblymen to bring about the fall of a government controlled by opposition parties, the Ruler having (not dismissed but) declared the position of Chief Minister vacant following his refusal to accede to requests for dissolution or for summoning of the assembly.[34] In this instance the Federal Court held that the Ruler had validly appointed the new chief minister, even though he had considered an expression of no confidence outside the assembly.[35]

The question then arises: How does the Malaysian constitutional and legal system deal with the kinds of issues that would in fact ordinarily justify federal intervention? We can answer as follows.

- Excess or abuse of powers: The courts police the line between state and federal powers and deal with unconstitutional and unlawful acts by state officials.[36]
- Financial issues: Fiscal matters are controlled by the treasury, and although there are political conflicts over finance, no state has ever been declared bankrupt.
- Corruption: Corruption in state governments is dealt with by the Malaysian Anti-Corruption Commission and the courts.[37]
- Breakdown of law and order: Criminal law and, if necessary, emergency powers may be invoked.

6. CONCLUSION

In nearly 50 years, emergency powers have never been used to intervene in a state government. State governments have changed hands on many occasions (and especially since 2008), and it appears now to be accepted that the federal government will regularly have to deal with state governments of a different political persuasion. This is simply a fact of life in the (since 2018) new, fragmented and transactional ecology of Malaysian political parties. Indeed, if the federal government did not co-operate peaceably with its opponents at the state level, attempts to replace the state government leadership with something closer to its wishes would simply undermine its own political position.

[34] Harding (2021b) at 121–3.

[35] *Datuk Nizar Jamaluddin v Datuk Seri Zambry Abdul Kadir* [2010] 2 MLJ 285.

[36] See, for example, *Iki Putra bin Mubarrak v Kerajaan Negeri Selangor* [2021] 2 MLJ 323.

[37] Fong DR 'Ex-deputy director of Sabah water dept given DNAA, fined RM30 million' (8 February 2022) *Free Malaysia Today* available at https://www.freemalaysiatoday.com/category/nation/2022/02/18/ex-deputy-director-of-sabah-water-dept-given-dnaa-fined-rm30-million/ (accessed 27 January 2025).

It is likely that due to the dissipation of dominant-party rule since 2018, overt manipulation of state governments is probably no longer politically possible, even if the legal position discussed in the two case studies above has alarming implications. It is now accepted that state elections are the right means to contest control over state governments, rather than dark dealings by government agents in smoke-filled rooms.

The real threat to democracy (at both levels of government) comes from parties' defection from coalitions, which (as occurred in 2020)[38] can effect a change in government without an election. This has happened at both state and federal levels. On the positive side, however, the anti-party-hopping law of 2022 has prevented the suborning of individual members by bribery or inducement, and has been replicated in most of the state constitutions.[39]

Despite the lack of recent instances of federal intervention via emergency powers, and despite the repeal of all existing emergency laws and proclamations in 2012, the use or abuse of emergency proclamations is not necessarily a thing of the past. In 2020 a federal emergency was (unprecedentedly) refused by the *Yang di-Pertuan Agong* in the middle of the pandemic because it would have meant that Parliament would in effect be suspended during the emergency, and the government did not appear to have a majority, or at least a certain majority, in Parliament.[40] Yet in early 2021, an emergency proclamation similar to the one refused just a few weeks previously was granted.

On these occasions it was clear that the *Yang di-Pertuan Agong* was obliged to consult his fellow Rulers before making a decision.[41] This suggests that the Rulers themselves represent the most realistically available check on the exercise of emergency powers. Certainly, as the heads of their states, they would be alive to the implications of emergency powers directed at a particular state and its government.

The constitutional system of Malaysia continues to evolve. Both the judiciary and the Rulers are exercising their powers to limit abuses by the government in ways which have not previously been in evidence. Citizens in S&S (in particular) are wary of federal power and demand greater autonomy. It may be that the risk to state autonomy implicit in emergency law is not now as great as it appeared to be in 1977 and beyond. At some levels and in some ways at least,

---

38 Harding (2021b) at 37.

39 Ostwald K 'Why Malaysia's Unity Government will (probably) survive' (2 May 2023) 36(223) *Perspective.*

40 *Robert Linggi v Government of Malaysia* (2011) 7 CLJ 373.

41 See *Robert Linggi.* The rotational monarchy at the federal level implies a convention that the *Yang di-Pertuan Agong* should consult the other rulers sitting in the Conference of Rulers before making any controversial decision.

state autonomy and the culture of federalism are proving to be more than just figments of constitutional imagination.

BIBLIOGRAPHY

Books

Das CV *Government and crisis powers: A legal study on the use of emergency powers* Kuala Lumpur: Malaysian Current Law Journal Sdn. Bhd (1996)
Harding A *Local government in Malaysia: Responses to urban-rural challenges* European Union Horizon 2020 Project (2021a)
Harding A *The Constitution of Malaysia: A contextual analysis* Oxford: Hart/ Bloomsbury (2021b)
Harding A *Territorial governance in Southeast Asia* Oxford: Hart Publishing (2025)

Chapters in Books

Chin J 'Federal-east Malaysia relations: Primus inter pares?' in Harding A and Chin J (eds), *50 years of Malaysia: Federalism revisited* Singapore: Marshall Cavendish (2014)

Journal Articles

Ghai Y 'The politics of the constitution: Another look at the Ningkan litigation' (1986) 7 *Singapore Law Review* 147
Ostwald K 'Why Malaysia's Unity Government will (probably) survive' (2 May 2023) 36(223) *Perspective*
Zahrin Z & Mohamed AM 'Revising the unitary vs federation classification' (2022) 18 *Journal of International Studies* 125–57

Reports

Federation of Malaya Constitutional Commission *1956–7 Report* Kuala Lumpur: Government Printer (1957)

Case Law

Datuk Nizar Jamaluddin v Datuk Seri Zambry Abdul Kadir (2010) 2 MLJ 285
Iki Putra bin Mubarrak v Kerajaan Negeri Selangor (2021) 2 MLJ 323
Robert Linggi v Government of Malaysia (2011) 7 CLJ 373
Stephen Kalong Ningkan v Government of Malaysia (1968) 2 MLJ 238, Privy Council
Stephen Kalong Ningkan v Tun Haji Openg and Tawi Sli (1966) 1 MLJ 261
Stephen Kalong Ningkan v Tun Haji Openg and Tawi Sli [No2] (1967) 1 MLJ 46

Legislation

Constitution of Malaysia, Act A1642/2022
Constitution of Sarawak (Amendment) Ordinance 2022

Internet Sources

'King's power to proclaim emergency cannot be reviewed by court, judge says' (15 February 2024) *The Star* available at https://www.thestar.com.my/news/nation/2024/02/15/kings-power-to-proclaim-emergency-not-justiciable-by-court-says-judge (accessed 27 January 2025)

'Sabah stand-off "turns deadly" as clashes break out' *BBC* (1 March 2013) available at https://www.bbc.com/news/world-asia-21628758 (accessed 27 January 2025)

Fong DR 'Ex-deputy director of Sabah water dept given DNAA, fined RM30 million' *Free Malaysia Today* (18 February 2022) available at https://www.freemalaysiatoday.com/category/nation/2022/02/18/ex-deputy-director-of-sabah-water-dept-given-dnaa-fined-rm30-million/ (accessed 27 January 2025)

Harding A 'Acting (or not acting) on (lawful or unlawful) advice in Malaysia: From Windsor to Kuantan and back again' (20 November 2020) *I-CONnect blog of the International Journal of Constitutional Law* available at https://www.iconnectblog.com/acting-or-not-acting-on-lawful-or-unlawful-advice-in-malaysia-from-windsor-to-kuantan-and-back-again/ (accessed 27 January 2025)

9. Nigeria: continuity and change in the law and politics of federal intervention

Rotimi Suberu

1. INTRODUCTION

The Nigerian federation has a long history of constitutionally embedded, but politically selective and corruption-prone, intervention by higher levels of government in the affairs of subnational administrations at regional (state) and local levels. The 1962 declaration of a state of emergency in the Western Region (one of the federation's three original regions) was particularly momentous, setting off the chain of events that culminated in the military's violent overthrow of the country's First Republic in 1966. Nigeria has witnessed multiple constitutional transformations and political transitions since this initial coup. These changes include the dissolution of the regions into multiple states (now 36 in number); a shift from parliamentary to presidential rule; the collapse of the country's second republic (1979–1983); the failure of its third democratic experiment (1993); and the inauguration of a Fourth Republic under the 1999 Constitution. Despite these changes, persistent intervention in lower tiers of the federation by higher levels of government has remained a standard feature of Nigeria's constitutional politics.

Nigeria experienced wide-ranging intergovernmental intervention and hyper-centralisation under military rule during the 1966–1979 and 1984–1999 periods. In addition, four specific forms of intervention have come to dominate Nigeria's intergovernmental landscape: federal proclamations of states of public emergency in subnational governments plagued by political infighting or constitutional crisis; federal impositions of states of emergency on subnational governments experiencing violent communal clashes or sectarian insurgencies; federal government orchestration of the impeachments of state governors; and rampant interference by subnational states in the affairs of local governments.

This chapter demonstrates that this intergovernmental intervention is deeply rooted in Nigeria's constitutional foundations, centralised federal structures and chronically contentious ethnic politics, and finds expression in the unresolved debates regarding an appropriate design and future for the federation. Successive tinkering with Nigeria's internal federal territorial morphology and institutional architecture has altered the structure, stakes and outcomes of intergovernmental intervention and come to routinise such interventionism, making it less likely to polarise and destabilise the entire federation.

After this introduction, the main part of the chapter begins with a discussion of the factors underlying Nigeria's relentless intergovernmental interventionism. The constitutional and statutory frameworks which regulate intergovernmental intervention are then analysed, prior to discussion of its actual procedures and political ramifications. The chapter's concluding section focuses on the theme of continuity and change in the evolution and practice of federal intervention in Nigeria.

2. INSTITUTIONAL AND STRUCTURAL RATIONALE FOR INTERVENTION

Many factors account for the pervasiveness of intergovernmental intervention in Nigeria's federal practice. These include the unitary foundations of the country's federalism; the centripetal transformation of the federation under military rule; the paucity, fragility or fragmentation of institutional firewalls (and the associated lack of societal restraints) against intergovernmental interventionism; and the interventionist imperatives that are inherent in Nigeria's combustible and ill-managed ethnic, regional and religious diversity.

Like other major post-colonial federations of the Global South, Nigeria did not evolve from the classical, American-style, bottom-up political process in which separate units came together to create a federal union. The Nigerian federation was established in 1954 under the aegis of British colonialism in a top-down fashion, one which involved the devolutionary creation of subnational governments by a central government. As the Nigerian Supreme Court stated in *Olafisoye v Federal Republic of Nigeria*, a federation can

> take its branches from the tree of unitary government. In such a situation, the historical ties may make it impossible for the federal constitution to entirely and totally strip off its relationship with unitarism. That could be the Nigerian experience for now.[1]

Federalism's unitary roots in Nigeria produced multiple centralising institutional structures and political dynamics. All of these enhanced the federal

---

1 *Chief Olafisoye v Federal Republic of Nigeria* (2004) 4 NWLR (Pt 864) at 580.

government's powers of intervention in relation to subnational governments. Nigeria's 'unitary federalism' engendered an expansive definition of the centre's legislative prerogatives; constituent units with limited autonomy to design their own constitutional institutions; fragile 'demos-constraining' (anti-majoritarian) institutions in the form of relatively weak second chambers and supreme courts; and an arrogation by the centre of the authority to reconfigure the federation's internal territorial configuration through the fragmentation, proliferation and control of subnational units of state and local governments.[2] The constitutional concentration of powers and resources in the central government, for instance, virtually elides the formal federalist division of powers, effectively providing the centre with expansive prerogatives that can be harnessed to eviscerate subnational state administrations. Subnational states themselves enjoy and exercise equally extensive powers in relation to local governments despite the pervasive rhetoric of three-tier (central, state and local) federalism.

Thus, despite some federalist features, Nigeria's 1960 Independence Constitution for the First Republic in many ways reflected central government hegemony. Examples were the inclusion of 44 diverse items on the exclusive list of federal legislative powers; the endowment of the centre with an additional 22 items of legislative power under the concurrent list; a provision that any alterations to a regional constitution cannot take effect unless it is approved by at least a two-thirds majority of all members in each house of the bicameral federal parliament; and another provision empowering the federal parliament to assume full legislative powers in any newly created region for a period of six months following the establishment of the region.[3] The inception of military rule in 1966 dramatically expanded and consolidated these centralising powers.

While the First Republic witnessed the excision of a Mid-Western region from the Western Region in 1963, the subsequent period of military rule produced a dramatic increase in the number of Nigeria's federating units. From just four regions at the onset of military rule in 1966, the number of states kept on growing: to 12 in 1967, 19 in 1976, 21 in 1987, 30 in 1991, and, by 1996, up to 36. While the 1963 creation of the Midwest region involved elaborate national constitutional amendments and a political referendum in the region, state reorganisation under the military was implemented by central executive fiat.

---

2 Suberu R 'De/centralization in Nigeria, 1954–2020' (2023) 33(5) *Regional & Federal Studies* 699; Stepan A 'Federalism and democracy: Beyond the US model' (1999) 10(4) *Journal of Democracy* 19.

3 Section 5(4) and (5), Constitution of the Federation of Nigeria, 1960.

The centre's fragmentation and proliferation of constituent units reflected and reinforced the prerogatives and interventionist powers of the central government since, as Diamond puts it, 'the greater the number of states, the weaker and less viable individual states will become, with the direct consequence that the centre would actually gather more powers and initiatives'.[4] Beyond fragmenting the Nigerian regions into smaller and weaker constituent units, however, the military implemented several other centripetal initiatives which further consolidated the centre's hegemony and capacity for interventionism.

The military consolidated Nigeria's oil-centric political economy, de-emphasising the First Republic's fiscal principle of regional derivation, under which large proportions of centrally collected revenues were to be returned to the region of production or consumption. Instead, the military expanded the powers of the centre to appropriate and redistribute the expanding oil revenues, while increasing the dependence of subnational state and local governments on federal revenue transfers. It reorganised local governments into the putative third tier (after the centre and the states) of the federal system 'as a way of reducing the strength of the states so that they will be more amenable to the unit-of-command principle of military organization'.[5]

The military also presided over a massive shift of legislative and coercive powers to the centre by assigning novel responsibilities (including the authority to enforce fundamental national objectives) to the centre; by placing under the centre's exclusive control several matters (for example, arms, ammunitions, and explosives) that previously were under joint federal–state concurrent jurisdiction; and by denuding the regions of their powers to maintain local-level police forces. Consequently, the repertoire of exclusive federal legislative powers increased from 44 items under the pre-military 1960 Constitution to 67 and 68 items, respectively, under the post-military 1979 and 1999 constitutions. What is more, the military promoted Nigeria's transition from parliamentary to presidential governance, creating an institutional framework that would entrench political chief executives at federal and state levels as powerful repositories and activators of interventionist powers.

By supplanting the institution of judicial review, consolidating executive and legislative functions in the Supreme Military (later Armed Forces Ruling) Council and subsuming subnational governments within its unitary command structure, the military institutionalised and bequeathed a regime of intergovernmental intervention and integration with enduring ideological, constitutional, structural, fiscal, administrative and political dimensions.

---

[4] Diamond L 'Issues in the constitutional design of a third Nigerian republic' (1987) 86(343) *African Affairs* 211.

[5] Osaghae E 'The status of state governments in Nigeria's federalism' (1992) 22(3) *Publius* 188.

Ideologically, the military promoted federal government's relentless intervention in, and effective control of, subnational governments as a strategy for achieving the centripetal integration that could counter the centrifugal instability inherent in Nigeria's extraordinary cultural diversity. As Admiral Augustus Aikhomu, a deputy head of the military government, explained, 'Our understanding of a pragmatic approach to Nigerian federalism has been to use the advantages of centralised military administration to weaken the prospects for confederation' and 'to strengthen the powers and status of the national government provided that Nigeria avoided the dangers of disintegration'.[6]

Constitutionally, the military retained Nigeria's federalist designation as an indispensable foundation for inter-group security and unity. In practice, it asserted the central government's jurisdictional hegemony and functional supremacy, though granting 'limited autonomy' to subnational authorities.[7] Successive military administrations confined the authority of subnational states to residual matters only and precluded them from exercising jurisdiction over concurrent subjects without the permission of the military high command who were in control of the central government.

Structurally, the military reconfigured the federation both vertically (by establishing a putative third order of the federal system) and horizontally (by dissolving large regions into multiple states). Fiscally, the military entrenched a national distributable pool system. In this system, the most lucrative national revenues were pooled into a common Federation Account, which was then redistributed by the federal government vertically among the federal, states and local governments, and horizontally among the states and the localities. Administratively, according to Aikhomu, military governors were 'required to take directives from the central administration'. This included the issuance of 'yearly budget guidelines to the governors who were subsequently physically present at the headquarters to defend their budgets'. Furthermore, the central military government sent 'monitoring teams ... to the states to assess how faithfully the state governments implemented federal government directives and guidelines as well as the performance of the budgets. Also, in accordance with true military principles, defaulters were duly penalized.'[8]

Politically, the military incorporated into its decree-law the civilian-era provision which prohibited subnational governments from impeding or prejudicing the executive authority of the federation or endangering the continuance

---

6 Aikhomu A 'Federal–state relations under military government, 1985–1992' (1994) 1(1) *Nigerian Journal of Federalism* 11.

7 Babangida I 'Federalism and nation-building in Nigeria: The challenges of the twenty-first century' (1994) 1(1) *Nigerian Journal of Federalism* 2.

8 Aikhomu (1994) at 17.

of the federal government of Nigeria.[9] Furthermore, following the intra-military coup of 1975, state governors were relegated from the Supreme Military Council (the military's most important executive and decision-making organ) to the advisory Council of States. The shift reinforced the hierarchical nature of the military's political leadership over its more collegiate aspect, tightening political control, supervision and domination of the states by the centre. The constant redeployment of state governors by the military head of state was a major consequence of this shift.

Military rule compounded the fragility of legislative and judicial institutions, undermining their potential to act as checks on the executive's political interventionism. While the legislature was completely abrogated under military rule, the judiciary was emasculated through ouster clauses that precluded judicial review of the most important military decree-laws, policies and practices. With the end of military rule, civilian political chief executives largely inherited the accumulated prestige and prerogatives of their military predecessors, while legislative and judicial branches struggled to recover their intended institutional capacities, resources and powers. Although the Fourth Republic has seen remarkable episodes of legislative assertiveness and judicial activism, robust checks on executives have been the exception rather than the rule. Indeed, whatever judicial or legislative robustness exists has been largely confined to the national level (as distinct from the subnational level). The countervailing formal institutional powers required to police or restrain intergovernmental interventionism effectively are chronically weak in Nigeria.

Informal oversight by civil society could potentially go some way in compensating for the absence of strong formal legislative and judicial policing of executive-driven intergovernmental intervention. In Nigeria, any such civic constraints have been both fragile and fragmented. Because of the ethnic, regional and religious fault lines built into Nigerian society, civic actors have been unable to present coherent, united and principled perspectives on intergovernmental intervention. Instead, civic and media perspectives on intervention reflect sectional considerations, contestations, prejudices and even 'bigotry'.[10] Such a sectionalist approach to intergovernmental intervention underscores Nigeria's predicament as a 'conglomerate society of antagonistic cultural sections', and corroborates Chinua Achebe's thesis that 'Nigerians'

[9] Akande J *Emergency powers in newly independent African countries in the Commonwealth* (Unpublished PhD Thesis, University of London, 1971) at 354.

[10] Editorial Board 'Nigeria: State of emergency: An intensification of attack on already terrorized masses' (7 June 2013) *Workers Alternative*.

greatest weakness' is 'their inability to face grave threats as one people instead of as competing religious and ethnic interests'.[11]

When they escalate into violent internal conflicts, the sectional fault lines that prevent cohesive and principled civic responses to intergovernmental intervention provide a convenient political rationale for security-focused central intervention. Indeed, as the UN human rights Special Rapporteur Agnes Callamard put it, contemporary Nigeria is a 'pressure cooker of internal conflict and generalized violence', with the military deployed to assist the regular national police in internal security operations across the 36 states of the federation.[12] Although it has been able to avoid a recurrence of its disastrous 1967–1970 civil war, the Nigerian federation is plagued by major threats to national security, public order and political stability in virtually all of its six geopolitical zones.

Rural banditry, the Islamist Boko Haram insurgency and ethnic and/or religiously inflected clashes between farmers and herders plague the Northwest (populated by Muslim Hausa-Fulani), the Northeast (Kanuri and other Northern Muslims) and the ethno-religiously diverse North-central zones, respectively. Biafran revivalist gunmen, aiming to restore the defunct secessionist Biafra Republic which instigated the 1967–1970 war, continue to ravage the Ibo Southeast. Similarly, violent agitators for subnational control of oil resources remain active in the oil-rich Niger Delta communities of the South-South zone. Even the relatively peaceful Yoruba southwest has not been immune from the national epidemic of ethnoreligious, communal and criminal violence. The crisis has killed tens of thousands and displaced millions of Nigerians during the Fourth Republic.

Nigeria's security crisis is symptomatic of a deeper structural flaw: the kleptocratic nature of its federal governance. This has fostered monumental and tragic levels of corruption, economic mismanagement and fraud, 'feeding political polarization, ethnic resentment, citizen alienation, and an increasingly virulent Islamic terrorist movement in the north'.[13] Essentially, contemporary Nigeria's federal governance revolves around the unproductive distribution

---

11 Achebe C 'The high price of patience' (27 July 1993) *New York Times*; Joseph R *Democracy and prebendal politics in Nigeria* Cambridge: Cambridge University Press (1987) at 52–3.

12 United Nations Office of the High Commissioner for Human Rights 'Nigeria needs urgent action to end "pressure cooker" of violence claiming thousands of lives, says UN rights expert' (3 September 2019) available at https://www.ohchr.org/en/press-releases/2019/09/nigeria-needs-urgent-action-end-pressure-cooker-violence-claiming-thousands (accessed 27 January 2025). See also 'Kidnappers are wreaking havoc in Nigeria' (18 January 2024) *The Economist.*

13 Diamond L 'Democracy's deepening recession' (2 May 2014) *The Atlantic.*

of oil rents and other centrally collected revenues among the diverse ethnic elite cartels that are in control of national and subnational governments. This governance model fails to generate or expand productive socio-economic opportunities for the country's impoverished mass-based ethnic constituencies. Federal military and police intervention to contain the attendant violent agitations and social disorders has engendered debates about its efficacy, constitutionality and legality.

3. CONSTITUTIONAL AND LEGAL GROUNDS FOR INTERVENTION

Constitutional and legal frameworks for intergovernmental intervention in Nigeria consist of two broad categories: (1) the constitutional, statutory and regulatory provisions for declaring a state of public emergency in subnational jurisdictions; and (2) other constitutional provisions that concentrate or centralise powers and resources, thereby enabling mostly intrusive, abusive or corruptive intergovernmental intervention *sans* emergency rule.

3.1 Constitutional, Statutory, and Regulatory Provisions on Emergency Rule

These provisions are to be found mainly in section 305 of the 1999 Constitution (a recasting of the emergency provisions in the 1960 and 1963 constitutions of the First Republic); in the Emergency Powers Act of 1961 (as modified); and in various emergency regulations made pursuant to the Constitution and the Act. These provisions (and especially section 305 of the 1999 Constitution) work to conflate, rather than separate, emergency rules and the rules regulating intervention.

Section 305 of the 1999 Constitution empowers the President to issue by instrument published in the official federal gazette 'a proclamation of a state of emergency in the federation or any part thereof ... only when' any of the following conditions exist: (a) 'the federation is at war'; (b) 'the federation is in imminent danger of invasion or involvement in a state of war'; (c) 'there is actual breakdown of public order or public safety in the federation or any part thereof' requiring 'extraordinary measures to restore peace and security'; (d) 'there is a clear and present danger of an actual breakdown of public order and public safety in the federation or any part thereof' requiring extraordinary action; (e) 'there is an occurrence or imminent danger … of any disaster or natural calamity'; (f) 'there is any other public danger which clearly constitutes a threat to the existence of the federation'; or (g) the President receives a request from the governor of a state, supported by a resolution of two-thirds of members in the state legislature, asking 'the president to issue a proclamation of a state of emergency in the state when there is' an imminent danger or actual breakdown of public order or safety within 'the boundaries of the state'.[14]

The enumeration of seven different conditions for proclaiming emergency rule under the 1999 Constitution contrasts significantly with the 1960 Independence Constitution of the First Republic. The 1960 document defined a 'period of emergency' as any moment involving one of the following three circumstances: (a) 'the federation is at war'; (b) 'there is in force a resolution of each house of [the bicameral federal] parliament supported by the votes of not less than two-thirds of all members of the House declaring that democratic institutions in Nigeria are threatened by subversion'; or (c) 'there is in force a resolution passed by each house of parliament declaring that a state of public emergency exists'.[15]

The federal government's invocation of the latter clause to impose emergency rule in the Western Region in 1962, following a scuffle on the floor of the regional legislature, was a brazen abuse of emergency powers that presumably could have been avoided by a more rigorous stipulation of the conditions for emergency rule. Yet legal scholars described the more elaborate provisions of the 1999 Constitution as verbose, vacuous and ultimately ineffective in preventing abuse of emergency rule in the Fourth Republic.[16] For instance, the reference in section 305(f) of the 1999 Constitution to 'any other public danger' as a constitutional ground for imposing emergency rule is a vague clause prone to misuse.

What is more, the 1999 Constitution, like the 1960 Constitution before it, fails to specify what should happen to elected officeholders at the subnational level under emergency rule. Instead, the vague and open-ended emergency rules described above can be (and, indeed, were) interpreted by the central government as implicitly giving it sweeping emergency and interventionist powers, including the power to remove elected subnational officeholders. In essence, the conditions and limits for exercising emergency powers under the Nigerian constitutions are ill-defined and not sufficiently specified to protect states from unwarranted central intervention.

In Nigerian constitutional law, a state of emergency primarily enables the central government to extend its authority beyond matters in the exclusive and concurrent lists of legislative powers, thereby supplanting the residual powers traditionally reserved to the regions (as the Nigerian federating units were called before the 1967 state reorganisation) or states (as the federal subunits have been known since 1967) under Nigeria's federal practice. The Emergency

---

[14] Constitution of the Federal Republic of Nigeria, 1999.

[15] Section 65, Constitution of the Federation of Nigeria, 1960.

[16] Alabi M 'Emergency powers in Nigeria: Legal and constitutional issues' (2005) 5(4) *The Constitution* 1.

Powers Act of 1961 provides a sweeping authorisation for the federal executive to make 'such regulations as appear to him to be necessary or expedient for the purpose of maintaining and securing peace, order and good government in Nigeria or any part thereof'.[17]

A reenactment of the authoritarian colonial-era emergency orders-in-council, the Emergency Powers Act provides that regulations made under the Act may, 'without prejudice to the generality of powers conferred' by the Act, include provisions on the following: the detention, deportation and exclusion of persons from Nigeria or any part thereof; the taking of possession of any property; the entering and search of any premises; applying, suspending or amending any law; apprehension, trial and punishment of persons; maintaining essential supplies and services; and empowering specific authorities or persons to make appropriate orders, rules and supplementary provisions necessary for the purposes of the emergency regulations.[18]

These broad powers are arguably consistent with the constitutional provision which allows any federal 'law that is reasonably justifiable in a democratic society' to restrict, or derogate from, most fundamental human rights 'in the interest of public order and safety' and 'during periods of emergency'.[19] The only major restrictions to the wide-ranging regulatory powers that the Emergency Act confers upon the central executive involve the requirement that the regulations be laid before the national legislature for approval within two months of their coming into operation, and the prohibition of any regulations 'for the trial of persons in military courts'.[20]

From the First to the Fourth Republic, the various regulations made pursuant to the 1961 Emergency Powers Act have extended beyond the provisions explicitly envisaged to include orders that speak to the omnibus nature or 'generality' of the Act. In particular, both during the 1962 Western Nigerian emergency and (more recently) under the Fourth Republic, the Emergency Powers Act has been invoked to replace elected subnational executives and legislatures with a centrally appointed administrator. This supplanting persists despite the provisions of section 11(4) of the 1999 Constitution. While this states that the national legislature may assume the functions of a state legislature if the latter 'is unable to perform its functions by reason of the situation prevailing in that state', it also explicitly stipulates that 'nothing in this section shall be construed as conferring on the National Assembly power to remove the Governor or Deputy Governor of the state from office'. However, the Constitution's open-ended construction of emergency powers, and the unwillingness or inability of

---

17 Section 3(1), Emergency Powers Act of 1961; Akande (1971) at 58.
18 Section 3(2), Emergency Powers Act of 1961.
19 Section 45, 1999 Constitution; section 28, 1960 Constitution.
20 Section 3(2), Emergency Powers Act of 1961.

the Nigerian Supreme Court (see below) to pronounce on the constitutionality or legality of the 1961 Emergency Powers Act, has fostered a climate of constitutional uncertainty around, and political abuse of, the permissible boundaries of emergency rule.

During the Fourth Republic, the extensive scope of the central executive's regulatory prerogatives under the Emergency Powers Act provoked considerable debate. Two contending perspectives dominated this discourse. For many legal scholars and observers, the Emergency Powers Act ceased to be a federal law following its non-inclusion in the Laws of the Federation of Nigeria in 1990, when the country's Law Review Commission simply indexed the Act as 'omitted' and 'spent'.[21] The Commission has powers to omit from the federal codebook all enactments which have been repealed or are seen to have expired by effluxion of time. From this perspective, the Emergency Powers Act is extinct and obsolete and cannot qualify as an existing law, one that the President is empowered (under section 315 of the 1999 Constitution) to modify in order 'to bring that law into conformity with the provisions of the Constitution'.

However, adopting a different perspective, the federal government issued the Emergency Powers Act (Modification) Order 2004 precisely in order to bring the Emergency Powers Act into conformity with Nigeria's shift from a parliamentary to a presidential executive. According to this view, because it has not been explicitly repealed and was probably erroneously omitted by the Law Commission, the Emergency Powers Act qualifies as an existing federal law which the President may validly invoke in times of emergency.[22] Thus, formal declarations of emergency rule under the Fourth Republic continued to invoke the Emergency Powers Act 1961 (as modified), together with section 305 of the 1999 Constitution, and the National Assembly did not deem it necessary to enact a new law on emergency rule.

Of more moment, however, is the extensive opportunity that Nigeria's constitutional design provides for intergovernmental intervention outside the framework of formal emergency rule.

3.2 Non-Emergency Provisions for Intergovernmental Intervention

Multiple provisions of the 1999 Constitution either explicitly authorise or implicitly enable federal encroachments and interventions in subnational affairs and residual powers even without the proclamation of a public emergency.

---

[21] Alabi (2005) at 15.

[22] Idornigie P 'Partial declaration of state of emergency' in Azinge E (ed) *State of emergency in Nigeria: Law and politics* Lagos: Nigerian Institute of Advanced Legal Studies (2013) 368.

Section 5(3) of the 1999 Constitution, for instance, prohibits using the executive powers of a state to 'impede or prejudice the exercise of the executive powers of the federation', to 'endanger any asset or investment of the Government of the federation in that state' or to 'endanger the continuance of a federal government in Nigeria'. Under Nigeria's previous constitutional practice, a determination by the federal parliament that subnational executive authority is being used to prejudice, impede or endanger federal authority would empower Parliament to exercise subnational residual legislative powers.[23] As already indicated, section 11(4) of the 1999 Constitution re-enacts that interventionist rule by empowering the National Assembly to make laws 'for the peace, order and good government' of any state governments 'at any time when' the House of Assembly of the state 'is unable to perform its functions'.

Subnational state–local relations in Nigeria are much more prone to interventionism than federal–state relations. The constitutional basis for interventions by state governments in local governments lies in section 7(1) of the 1999 Constitution. This 'guaranteed ... the system of local government by democratically elected local government councils', while empowering each state government to 'ensure their existence under a law which provides for the establishment, structure, composition, finance and functions of such councils'. The broad powers that section 7 confers upon the state governments in relation to local governments seem to belie Nigeria's ambitious constitutional design of a three-level federal structure. In addition to providing for elected local councils, the 1999 Constitution entrenches the boundaries of Nigeria's 774 local government areas, enunciates a separate schedule of 'functions of a local government council' and provides for the effective inclusion of local governments in the federal revenue-sharing system.[24]

To reiterate, the military promoted the autonomy of local government as part of a constitutional scheme to weaken state governments and consolidate federal government hegemony. Under the Nigerian system of military federalism, the army abandoned its disastrously controversial constitutional project to impose a full-fledged unitary system in Nigeria and instead effectively consolidated and entrenched the system of 'unitary federalism'.[25] Thus, the Nigerian military's foundational decree-law empowered the 'Federal Military Government' to 'make laws for the peace, order, and good government of Nigeria or any part thereof with respect to any matter whatsoever'.[26]

[23] Sections 66 and 80, 1960 Constitution.

[24] Sections 3(6) and 162, and Fourth Schedule, 1999 Constitution.

[25] Wodu N 'Nigeria's unitary federalism' (16 December 2020) *Council on Foreign Relations.*

[26] See Suberu R *Federalism and ethnic conflict in Nigeria* Washington, DC: United States Institute of Peace Press (2001) at 31.

Nigeria's post-military basic laws, including the 1999 Constitution, perpetuate this all-inclusive, intrusive and interventionist construction of federal powers by endowing the centre with an exclusive mandate to establish and regulate 'authorities for the federation or any part thereof [in order] to promote and enforce the observance of the fundamental objectives and directive principles contained in this constitution', including the 'fundamental obligations of government' to advance 'the security and welfare of the people'.[27] The legacy of military rule has had a powerfully centralising impact on the law, politics and procedures of intergovernmental intervention in Nigeria.

4. PROCEDURES FOR INTERVENTION

Under section 305 of the 1999 Constitution, any presidential proclamation of a state of emergency affecting the federation or any part thereof must be approved by a 'resolution supported by two-thirds majority of all the members of each house of the National Assembly'. The approval must be obtained 'within two days [of the proclamation] when the National Assembly is in session, or within ten days when the National Assembly is not in session'.

Under the First Republic, the renewable term for emergency rule could extend to one year in each instance. A proclamation of a state of emergency under the 1999 Constitution, however, 'shall cease to have effect … after a period of six months has elapsed since it has been in force' unless it is extended 'from time to time for a further period of six months' by a resolution supported by a two-thirds majority in the National Assembly. In addition, a presidential proclamation of a state of emergency can be revoked at any time by a presidential instrument published in the Federal Gazette, or by majority vote from each house of the national assembly.

Two of the four categories of intervention practised in Nigeria are the emergency regimes imposed in response to (1) subnational political fiascos or (2) ethno-religious violence. Both these regimes explicitly invoked, as their constitutional and legal grounds, the emergency provisions of section 305 of the 1999 Constitution (or section 65 of the 1960 Constitution), along with regulations pursuant to the 1961 Emergency Powers Act. The remaining two categories of intervention discussed in this section involve: (3) central government's orchestration of the impeachment of state governors and (4) state governments' subversion of local government autonomy. These latter categories entirely lacked any constitutional or legal justifications beyond the enormous opportunities for political abuse inherent in Nigeria's overcentralised federation and weak rule of law. Procedures across the four categories of interventions

---

27 Sections 13–24 and Item 60, Second Schedule.

entailed varying processes, including (or not including) different opportunities for legislative and judicial oversight of the executive's implementation of the powers of intervention.

4.1 Emergency Rule Imposed in Response to Subnational Political Fiascos

Impositions of emergency rule in the Western Region (May–December 1962) and in Ekiti (October 2006–April 2007) and Rivers (March–September 2025) states were the three major instances of federal intervention provoked by political infighting in a subnational unit. In all three cases, the federal government replaced the elected regional or state governments with a federal administrator.

In line with the provisions of the 1960 Constitution and the Emergency Powers Act 1961, the federal parliament on 29 May 1963 approved the declaration of a state of emergency in Western Nigeria, along with 13 emergency regulations, including the appointment of an administrator for the region with powers to issue restriction orders on leading regional political figures, among other prerogatives. The declaration was litigated before the Supreme Court in *Williams v Majekodunmi*, *Adegbenro v Attorney General of the Federation & Others* and *Akintola v Governor of Western Nigeria and Adegbenro*.[28] The Court opined that it could not go behind Parliament to inquire as to whether a state of public emergency actually exists; that Parliament can validly authorise 'reasonable' restriction orders whether during an emergency period or not; and that the ceremonial governor of the Western Region erred in purporting to remove the incumbent regional premier (Akintola) and appoint a new premier (Adegbenro) on the basis of a petition extraneously signed by a majority of the regional legislators, rather than by an actual confidence vote emanating from proceedings on the floor of the regional legislature. The Court 'ingeniously evaded' an opinion on whether even a legitimately proclaimed state of emergency could validly authorise the removal of a regional government.[29] The Court argued that proffering such an opinion would prejudge determination of the separate question on whether Adegbenro, the plaintiff seeking the opinion, was validly designated as the premier of the Western Region.

Across all these decisions, the Supreme Court refused to adopt any position that would invalidate the proclamation of emergency rule in the Western Region. However, in a determination in *Williams v Majekodunmi*, the Court

---

[28] See further Sawer G 'Emergency powers in Nigerian and Malayan federalism' (1964) 6(1) *Malaya Law Review* 83; Davies SG 'Nigeria – some recent decisions on the constitution' (1962) 11(4) *International & Comparative Law Quarterly* 919.

[29] Sawer (1964) at 93.

opined that while it was not in its purview or province to determine whether a state of emergency actually exists, it could decide whether or not certain acts are reasonably justifiable during an emergency. The Court then upheld Chief Rotimi Williams's claim that the restriction order placed on him, pursuant to the emergency regulations, was not justifiable as far as he was concerned individually. Williams (a noted lawyer and legal adviser to the conflict-ridden ruling party in the Western Region) had played an actively non-partisan, mediatory role in the crisis leading up to the declaration of emergency rule in the region.

Legislative oversight, rather than judicial arbitration, proved to be the defining feature of emergency rule in Ekiti. While it overwhelmingly approved the presidential proclamation, the National Assembly inveighed against the federal executive's complicity in the impeachment saga, which necessitated federal intervention, including the emergence of three different claimants (the governor, deputy governor and speaker of the state legislature) to the governorship of the state. The Assembly condemned the federal executive's 'use of the Economic and Financial Crimes Commission [EFCC] and other security agencies to intimidate members of the state assembly in the exercise of their legislative functions'.[30] Invoking section 11 of the Constitution, it also resolved that 'all laws for the governing of Ekiti State during the period of emergency shall be enacted by the National Assembly'.[31] This was a riposte to the federal executive's position, which suggested that its federally appointed administrator

> will not need any new laws for the administration of the state. But if he does it will be in the form of regulation which he will submit to the president for consideration by the federal executive council and promulgated by the president for the state.[32]

Because general elections in the state and the rest of the federation coincided with the six-month emergency period, the National Assembly called on the President 'to ensure that the 2007 elections will be free and fair and on schedule'.[33] What is more, following the expiration of the six-month term of the emergency administration in April 2007, the National Assembly did not approve the President's request for a re-authorisation of emergency rule in Ekiti. Instead, the Assembly resolved that the erstwhile speaker of the suspended state legislature should assume the leadership of the state until the inauguration of a newly elected state government in May 2007. In rejecting the

---

30 Senate, Federal Republic of Nigeria, Votes and Proceedings, 26 October 2006 at 500–1.
31 Senate (2006) at 501.
32 Senate (2006) at 498.
33 Senate (2006) at 498.

executive's proposal to extend emergency rule in Ekiti, the National Assembly demonstrated its determination to act, in the words of Senate President Ken Nnamani, as 'an independent legislature that ... cannot be made another department of the federal executive'.[34]

4.2 Emergency Rule Arising from Ethnic and/or Religious Violence

Communal or sectarian violence in northern Nigeria prompted the federal imposition of emergency rule on three occasions during the Fourth Republic. These took place in the Plateau State (May–November 2004); in the 15 local governments across Borno, Niger, Plateau and Yobe states (December–June 2012); and in the Borno, Adamawa, and Yobe (BAY) states (May 2013–November 2014).

Of these cases, only the emergency rule in Plateau involved the suspension of the elected state executive and legislature and their replacement with a presidentially appointed federal administrator. The President accused Plateau's political leadership in general, and the state governor in particular, of variously instigating, exacerbating, mismanaging and neglecting 'what has now become a near mutual genocide' between Plateau's Christian and Muslim ethnic communities, with this involving significant spillovers (in the form of internal refugees and reprisal attacks) in several other states of the federation.[35] Furthermore, according to the President, it was imperative to remove the Plateau State House of Assembly 'as the formal legislative body of the state with immediate effect' because

> [h]aving a State Assembly in position under a state of emergency is incongruous and may not allow for the expeditious actions that the Administrator will need to put the state back into a situation of peace, harmony, security for all, and maintenance of law and order.[36]

While reaffirming its authority (under section 11 of the Constitution) to enact any 'new laws to govern Plateau State during the emergency period', the National Assembly overwhelmingly approved the President's proclamation of emergency rule in Plateau, appointment of a federal administrator for the state, and promulgation of eight different emergency regulations (on curfews, processions and meetings, and reporting, restriction and detention of persons, and so

---

[34] Senate, Federal Republic of Nigeria, Votes and Proceedings, 24 April 2007 at 1187.

[35] House of Representatives, Federal Republic of Nigeria, Votes and Proceedings, 19 May 2004 at 651.

[36] House of Representatives (19 May 2004) at 652.

on).[37] Plateau's legislators, however, mounted a legal challenge in the Supreme Court to the President's suspension of the state's elected government. Here, the Court, in *Plateau State & Another v Attorney General of the Federation & Another*, ruled the challenge incompetent because it was instituted during the six-month emergency administration by the suspended legislators without the authorisation of the incumbent, centrally imposed, administration in the state.[38] That the emergency administration could not possibly have authorised a legal action against its own validity did not stop the Court from dismissing the action as lying outside its jurisdiction to adjudicate disputes between the federation and a state.

Ben Nwabueze, Nigeria's preeminent legal scholar, excoriated the Court's decision as 'misconceived and untenable', seeing it as symptomatic of the judiciary's 'sheer timidity [and] lack of courage', and concluding that 'the decision is one based, not on law or the demands of justice, but rather on judicial policy, the policy of judicial avoidance of hypersensitive constitutional issues'.[39] Nonetheless, six months of emergency rule in Plateau brought relative peace to the state, thereby allowing for the restoration of Plateau's elected political leadership in November 2004.

The most unremarkable and non-contentious case of emergency proclamation in Nigeria's history was that imposed on 15 local government areas across four northern Nigerian states at the end of December 2011. There are three main reasons for this.

First, major flashpoints of violent insecurity which took place at or near the federal capital during the second half of 2011 preceded the proclamation, thereby justifying for a broader national audience the urgency and legitimacy of emergency rule. These incidents included massive attacks by terrorists linked to Boko Haram on the United Nations headquarters in Abuja in August and on a Catholic Church in Madalla, Suleija (near Abuja) on Christmas Day. As a result of these actions, the proclamation was unanimously and expeditiously approved by the National Assembly, which also commended the President's responsiveness in declaring the emergency.

Second, instead of the previous practice of imposing emergency rule across entire regions or states of the federation, the December 2011 proclamation targeted only 15 specific localities that were associated with violent Islamist terrorism or communal clashes. This specificity appeared to underscore

---

37 House of Representatives, Federal Republic of Nigeria, Votes and Proceedings, 25 May 2004 at 661.

38 Suit No. SC. 113/2004.

39 Nwabueze B *How President Obasanjo subverted Nigeria's federal system* Ibadan: Gold Press (2007) at 232, 238–9.

the political innocuousness, objectivity and even non-partisanship of the proclamation.

Finally, emergency rule did not involve the suspension or displacement of the political and administrative structures in the 15 local government areas (LGAs), thereby further alleviating suspicions of political motivation or manipulation. Instead, the President asked the administrations in the LGAs 'to carry out any order, instruction, or regulation as may be issued by me from time to time during the period of emergency'.[40] Specifically, he asked the LGAs 'to give maximum cooperation to the law enforcement agencies' that he had 'directed to put appropriate measures in place to ensure the protection of lives and properties'.[41] Yet the security measures, including expanded military deployments and the closure of national borders contiguous to the affected localities (in order to curtail cross-border terrorism), failed to curb the violent activities of Boko Haram or prevent a further iteration of federal emergency rule in northern Nigeria in May 2013.

Although it adopted the politically benign practice of not imposing a federal administrator on emergency areas, the May 2013 proclamation of emergency rule in the northeastern Borno, Adamawa and Yobe (BAY) states became deeply contentious. Ultimately, it created deep schisms not only between the affected states and the federal government but also between the federal executive and the legislature. The main problems were the protracted nature of this iteration of emergency rule, its failure to improve security in the northeast and its assimilation into ethno-regional North–South struggles for the control of the presidency in the 2015 elections.

After initially proclaiming and obtaining legislative approval for six months of emergency rule in May 2013, the President extended the emergency in November 2013, in May 2014 and again in November 2014. He justified these extensions by claiming that, while emergency rule had produced some progress in the war against Boko Haram in the BAY states, the security challenges in these areas remained daunting. Although the National Assembly approved the extensions of the emergency of November 2013 and May 2014, it did not authorise a further extension in November 2014.

The Assembly had become increasingly sceptical of the effectiveness and sincerity of the President's emergency proclamations. Citing the infamous abduction of more than 250 schoolgirls in Chibok (Bornu State) in April 2014, it noted that insecurity in the BAY states had actually worsened (rather than

---

40 House of Representatives, Votes and Proceedings, 8 January 2012 at 470–1.

41 'Address by His Excellency, President Goodluck Ebele Jonathan, on the occasion of the declaration of a state of emergency in certain states of the federation in order to restore public order, peace and security in the federation' (31 December 2011) *Vanguard*.

improved) during the emergency. The Assembly condemned the harsh effects of emergency rule on the local population in the northeast, and also criticised its over-centralising implications for Nigerian federalism. It demanded detailed and regular briefings from the security agencies on the situation in the BAY states. Instead of re-imposing emergency rule, the Assembly urged the presidency to take measures to improve the morale and resources of the security personnel engaged in the military campaigns against Boko Haram. It also suggested the implementation of more creative socio-economic and political solutions for winning the hearts and minds of local populations in the emergency areas.[42]

The National Assembly's positions and reservations echoed the sentiments of the governors of the BAY states. These had persistently urged the Assembly to 'discard' the President's request for an extension, claiming that the federal government's approach to the insurgency 'requires a redefinition rather than an extension' of government policy.[43]

Ultimately, it was the perceived impact that a further six-month extension of emergency rule in November 2014 could have on the general elections (to be held early in 2015) that led members of the National Assembly to end the emergency in the BAY states. President Jonathan's decision to seek re-election in the 2015 elections, after five years in office, was unpopular in the North, where leading politicians wanted a northern Muslim to succeed Jonathan (a Christian from the South-South) in accordance with Nigeria's informal practice of regional and zonal rotation of the powerful presidency. Jonathan's ultimately unsuccessful re-election bid resulted in massive defections from the ruling People's Democratic Party (PDP) to the opposition All Progressives Congress (APC) (which controlled the BAY states). The defectors included 5 governors and 79 national legislators.[44] The strong perception among the affected opposition governors, in particular, was that perpetuating emergency rule in the BAY states would disenfranchise thousands of opposition voters and simply 'help the ruling party combat dissent and not armed insurgency'.[45]

42 See, for example, Senate, Votes and Proceedings, 15 May 2014 and 20 May 2014.

43 Jegede M 'Jonathan's plea for emergency rule extension' (16 May 2014) *Sahara Reporters*.

44 Owen O & Usman Z 'Briefing: Why Goodluck Jonathan lost the Nigerian presidential election of 2015' (2015) 114 (456) *African Affairs* 455; LeVan C 'Reciprocal retaliation and local linkage: Federalism as an instrument of opposition organizing in Nigeria' (2018) 117(466) *African Affairs* 1.

45 'Emergency rule extension in North East' (14 November 2014) *News Herald* available at https://newsheralddotme.wordpress.com/2013/11/14/emergency-rule-extension-in-north-east (accessed 14 February 2024).

4.3 Federal Interference in the Impeachments of State Governors

The informal, unconstitutional and illegal use of powerful federal agencies (so-called federal might) to interfere in subnational affairs represents a distinct form of federal intervention in Nigeria. These agencies include the presidentially appointed and controlled national electoral commission, anti-corruption agencies and police, military and other security agencies. These have all too often been deployed by the federal executive to manipulate subnational elections; to intimidate (including abducting, detaining or even deporting) state governors or other high-profile subnational politicians; to conduct massive internal security operations in the states without invoking formal emergency powers; and to orchestrate the impeachment of state governors.

Seven governors faced impeachment under the presidential system. These were: Balarabe Musa (impeached in Kaduna State in June 1981); DSP Alamieyeseigha (Bayelsa, December 2005); Rashidi Ladoja (Oyo, January 2006); Peter Fayose (Ekiti, October 2006); Joshua Dariye (Plateau, November 2006); Peter Obi (Anambra, November 2006); and Murtala Nyako (Adamawa, July 2014). The National Assembly aborted the federal executive's attempt in 2014 to orchestrate the impeachment of Rotimi Amaechi of Rivers State by invoking section 11 of the 1999 Constitution 'to take over the State Assembly'.[46] The impeachments had two commonalities: they were directed at governors who were widely perceived to be opponents or non-loyalists of the federal executive; and they entailed flagrant violations of the letter and spirit of the Constitution, often with the active complicity of the federal executive.

The Constitution (section 188) enunciates the procedures for removing governors (or their deputies), processes which do not entail any roles for the federal government. The procedures have four main stages: (1) the presentation to the speaker of the state legislative assembly of a written notice signed by at least one-third of the members of the legislature alleging official 'gross misconduct' by the governor; (2) a motion, within 14 days of the presentation (and circulation) of the notice, by at least two-thirds of the legislators supporting the investigation of the alleged misconduct; (3) within seven days of the motion, the appointment by the chief judge, acting on the request of the speaker, of an independent seven-member panel to investigate the allegation and submit a report within three months of its appointment; and (4) if the report confirms the allegation of gross misconduct, and two-thirds of the legislators adopt the report, the governor will stand removed.

The second term of the Obasanjo presidency (2003–2007) saw multiple violations of the impeachment process. These included the instigation and

46 LeVan (2018) at 13.

stage-managing of impeachment processes by the federal executive rather than by the state legislatures; the use of the EFCC, a federal agency notorious for its politically selective anti-corruption programme, as the main author or source of the charges of gubernatorial misconduct; the resort to impeachment as a strategy for removing the constitutional immunity of the governors in order to enable their prosecution for corruption by the EFCC; the use of federal security agencies (that is, the police, state security services, and even the military) to coerce state legislators into endorsing the impeachments; suspensions of recalcitrant legislators in bids to achieve the majorities required for impeachment; the appointment of openly partisan members to, and the unduly hasty conduct of the work of, a panel of investigation; and

> tampering with the offices of the speaker of the House of Assembly and of the chief judge, sittings at odd times of the day, acting on an interim report of a panel of investigation, or even acting without a report at all. To make matters worse, the federal government was complicit in all this mess.[47]

Although the Constitution explicitly prohibits judicial review of impeachment proceedings, Nigeria's appellate and supreme courts intervened to remedy these violations, arguing that judicial oversight is ousted only if the constitutional provisions on impeachments are respected. Thus, in cases such as *Hon. Michael Dapianlong & Ors v Chief (Dr) Joshua Chibi Dariye & Ors* and *Hon. Muyiwa Inakoju & Ors v Hon. Abraham Adeolu Adeleke & Ors*, the courts invalidated and reversed the arbitrary impeachments of state governors.[48]

4.4 Arbitrary State Interference in Local Governments

A long-standing feature of Nigeria's federal practice (dating back to at least the First Nigerian Republic) is the capricious intervention of regional and state governments in the politics and administration of local governments. It is particularly remarkable that such interference has persisted, and even deepened, despite the grand rhetoric of three-tier federalism, the judiciary's policing of federal–state–local relations and multiple attempts by the federal government to liberate the localities from the stranglehold of the states.

With the help of pliant and passive legislative houses, state governors have routinely manipulated, delayed or completely supplanted local government elections; replaced elected councils with appointed caretaker or management committees; and truncated or tinkered with the tenures of such councils. State

---

[47] Lawan M 'Abuse of powers of impeachment in Nigeria' (2010) 48(2) *Journal of Modern African Studies* 317.

[48] Lawan (2010).

governments circumvented the entrenchment of the boundaries of Nigeria's 774 local government areas by creating and proliferating so-called Local Council Development Areas (LCDAS). The states usurped some of the most important local government functions (such as the construction and maintenance of roads, the establishment and maintenance of markets and motor parks and control and regulation of outdoor advertising and boarding). State governments also hijacked federal revenue transfers to the local authorities, while appropriating or expropriating independent sources of local revenues such as tenement rates, signage fees and licences and motor-park taxes.[49]

The ambiguity of the constitutional provisions for local government autonomy facilitated the 'kleptocratic capture of local government' by state governments.[50] The multiplicity of entirely legal institutions available to the states for controlling local governments contributed to this capture. The most prominent of these institutions is the constitutionally mandated State Joint Local Government Account (SJLGA). All federal and state revenue transfers to local governments in a state are to be consolidated into this account, from which they are then disbursed to each local authority by the state government. Other institutions of state control of localities include the State Independent Electoral Commission, Local Government Service Commission, and office of the auditor-general of local government. All in all, the states were often able successfully to defy repeated attempts by the courts and the federal government to protect the localities from gubernatorial capture and predation.

In judgments such as *Attorney General of Plateau State & ors v Goyol & ors*, *Eze v Governor of Abia State* and *Governor Ekiti State & Ors v Olubunmo & Ors*, Nigerian federal courts inveighed against and invalidated state governments' dissolution of elected local councils.[51] But final judicial determinations often came after the expiration of the councillors' tenures, with the courts typically resorting to asking the offending state governments to pay the councillors the emoluments due to them during the unserved portions of their tenures. Such outcomes reinforced the rent-seeking nature of Nigerian office-holding while leaving the offending governors and legislatures unsanctioned for their assaults on local democracy.

For its part, the federal presidency and legislature implemented several measures to try and protect the localities from intervention by the states. The measures included deploying the office of the attorney-general of the

---

[49] Suberu R 'Nigeria' in Steytler N (ed) *Forum of Federations handbook on local government in federal systems* New York: Palgrave Macmillan (2024).

[50] Page M & Wando A *Halting the kleptocratic capture of local government in Nigeria* Washington, DC: Carnegie Endowment for International Peace (2022).

[51] See, respectively, (2007) 16 NWLR (Pt. 1059) 57; (2014) 14 NWLR (Pt. 1426) 192; and (2016) LPELR-48040(SC).

federation and the police high command to enforce judicial decisions on local government autonomy; suspending federal revenue transfers to states which unconstitutionally created new local government areas or dissolved elected local councils; enacting a law to monitor payments into, and disbursements from, the SJLGA; issuing an anti-money laundering policy that regulated cash withdrawals from the SJLGA; and formulating constitutional reform proposals for insulating local governments and state legislatures from gubernatorial control.

In May 2024 the federal government instituted legal proceedings in the Supreme Court to challenge, and to obtain multiple reliefs against, state governments' 'gross misconduct' in relentlessly subverting the autonomy of local governments. In its landmark judgment of July 2024, *Attorney General of the Federation v Attorney General of Abia State & Ors*, the Court voided the governance of local government areas other than by democratically elected councils and declared that federal revenue transfers must be paid directly, and only, to elected local councils (this, controversially, bypassed the SJLGA mandated by the Constitution itself and as maintained by state governments).[52] Many of the federal measures that were designed to protect the localities from state interference were found to be *ultra vires*. They were discredited by the centre's own paternalistic relations with subnational governments and selective targeting of opposition states or governors, or were systematically frustrated by the governors. The state governors of the Fourth Republic successfully dismantled, and often vehemently denounced, the military's legacy of three-tier federalism.[53]

5. POLITICS OF INTERVENTION

With few exceptions, powers of intervention in Nigeria have been politically abused and have proved to be ultimately dysfunctional with regard to federalism and constitutionalism. While it is arguable that the centre's extraordinary powers of intervention under military rule helped to restructure an unwieldy regional federalism and secure the federation's territorial integrity, the military's hyper-centralisation was corrosive of the country's long-term political stability and developmental progress. Noted observers of Nigerian politics celebrate the pre-military era as the golden period of federalism, while critiquing the military's political legacy as one of bastardised, denatured and truncated federalism.[54] Given the impact of the unbalanced and lopsided pre-military

---

52 *AG Federation v AG Abia & Ors*, SC/CV/343/2024.

53 Suberu (2024).

54 Adamolekun L 'The Nigerian federation at the crossroads: The way forward' (2005) 35(3) *Publius* 383.

federalism in polarising and destabilising the federation during and following the imposition of emergency rule in the Western Region in 1962, however, such idealisation of Nigeria's unwieldy regional federalism seems exaggerated.

Similarly, while most of Nigeria's impeached governors were guilty of serious financial misconduct, the federal government's intervention in their impeachment was itself corruptive, selective and abusive in nature. As Lawan puts it, 'The Federal Government merely capitalized on the misconduct of the governors to get rid of opponents and non-loyalists among them. It was in this process that the constitutional provisions on impeachment suffered unprecedented breaches.'[55] State intervention in local government contributed to the corruption, capture and collapse of the local government system, thereby fuelling 'democratic backsliding, communal conflict, and poverty', while provoking calls for 'removing local government from the constitution'.[56]

The uses of emergency powers were especially illustrative of the politicisation and pathologies of intergovernmental intervention in Nigeria. Most scholarly assessments describe the implementation of emergency rule in Nigeria as unconstitutional, illegal, politically motivated and selective, ineffective, counterproductive and ultimately redundant.[57]

Criticism of the unconstitutionality of emergency rule has focused on those cases (Western Nigeria, Ekiti, Plateau and Rivers) where emergency powers were invoked to remove elected subnational governments. 'Nowhere in the constitution', one critic claims, 'is the president [or federal government] granted powers to remove elected officers from office'.[58] The constitutionally prescribed procedures for removing elected office-holders involve impeachments (for political chief executives) and recalls (for legislators), rather than emergency rule. Furthermore, according to this critique, inasmuch as nationwide emergency rule would not constitutionally suspend the national government, emergency rule at the subnational level should not lead either to the displacement of elected subnational authorities. In addition, to reiterate, section 11(4) of the 1999 Constitution explicitly prohibits the National Assembly from removing state chief executives when the Assembly constitutionally assumes the function of a state legislature that is 'unable to perform its functions by reason of the situation prevailing in that state'. Yet, as already indicated, the vague, open-ended and ill-defined construction of general emergency powers under the Constitution more or less implicitly (rather than explicitly) abets the abuse of these powers.

---

55 Lawan (2010) at 333.

56 Page & Wando (2022) at 1, 34.

57 See the collection of essays in the volume edited by Azinge (2013).

58 Alabi (2005) at 1.

In addition to its alleged unconstitutionality, the practice of emergency rule in Nigeria is arguably illegal, particularly as it also violates ordinary law. The presumed illegality of recent emergency rule stems from its invocation of the (arguably obsolete) Emergency Powers Act of 1961. However, the inability or unwillingness of the Nigerian National Assembly to craft a new statutory framework for emergency rule may reflect the historical opprobrium and negativity surrounding the legacy of politicised emergency rule in Nigeria.

From its first implementation in 1962 (in the Western Region) to its application to the BAY states in 2013–2014, emergency rule has elicited credible allegations regarding its political selectivity and partisan motivation. For instance, the central government invoked emergency rule because of a commotion in the regional legislature of Western Nigeria in 1962, even though (outside the premises of the legislature) the region, including the capital city of Ibadan, 'was certainly in a state of profound peace'.[59] However, the centre did not invoke emergency powers when the same region descended into violent lawlessness in 1964–1965 (which culminated in the military coup of January 1966). In 1962, emergency rule effectively prevented a political faction in opposition to the centre from taking over the regional government, while re-imposing emergency rule in 1964–1965 would have undermined a pro-centre regional administration that the federal government had helped to regain power following the end of emergency rule in December 1962. Similarly, Nigeria's opposition-controlled northeastern BAY states perceived federal emergency rule in their jurisdictions as ethno-politically selective (since several other states that were not placed under emergency rule were plagued by the same security challenges as the BAY states).[60]

Owing to its political instrumentalisation, emergency rule has often not achieved its ostensible purpose of securing public order and security. The failure of 18 months of emergency rule in the BAY states was especially notable. Beyond being ineffective, however, emergency rule often proved to be entirely counterproductive, complicating and aggravating, rather than ameliorating, the crisis in the emergency area and alienating the local population from the centre's anti-insurgency campaign. According to Shehu Sani, the leader of a civil society coalition in northern Nigeria (and soon-to-be federal Senator), the 'state of emergency has turned the affected states into evil dungeons of impunity, unlawful arrests, extrajudicial killings, and unlawful detentions … [which] undermine all its objectives, if it has any'.[61]

---

59 Sawer (1964) at 90.

60 Nwabufo F 'Yobe rejects emergency rule' (13 May 2014) *The Cable*; Tukur S 'Governor Nyako accuses Jonathan administration of genocide against northern Nigeria' (19 April 2014) *Premium Times*.

61 News Herald (2014).

A final damning criticism of emergency rule is that it is redundant. Given the vast powers and resources of the federal government, the President may, for instance, exercise extraordinary powers on behalf of law, security and order without necessarily imposing emergency rule. Indeed, despite the country's deteriorating internal security situation and the deployment of the military in security operations across Nigeria, formal emergency rule was not imposed anywhere in the federation between 2015 and 2024. By early (January–February) 2025, Nigeria had witnessed a decade of civilian governance without the proclamation of federal emergency rule anywhere in the federation.

6. CONCLUSION

Despite Nigeria's multiple constitutional and institutional transitions, intergovernmental intervention has remained a rampant, politicised and deeply contentious feature of the country's federal practice. At the same time, Nigeria has witnessed important changes in the constitutional framework, structural context and political ramifications of intervention.

Intervention is a pervasive and persistent feature of Nigeria's federal practice. It has assumed multiple forms and spanned the country's regime alternations from the First Republic through military rule to the Fourth Republic. The pervasiveness and persistence of intervention, to reiterate, reflects structural and institutional features embedded both in Nigeria's foundations and evolution as a top-down, coming-together and ethno-politically contentious federation. To the extent that these features remain ingrained in Nigeria's federalism, intervention is likely to persist as a part of federal practice in, and the politics of, the country.

The persistent politicisation of intervention in Nigeria is consistent with the country's over-centralisation of powers and resources. It is this which allows political executives to wield enormous personal neo-patrimonial powers of intervention with relatively limited institutional checks and civic oversight. While the legislature and judiciary have constrained the politicisation of intervention in many instances, their oversight can hardly be described as robust. Legislative and judicial oversight has been weak, intermittent and prone to corruption and ethno-political fragmentation.

Despite its pervasiveness, intervention remains ethno-politically contentious, provoking scholarly critiques and political agitation for federal constitutional reforms. The 1962 crisis in the Western Region underscored how prone to abuse emergency rule was. It also revealed the flagrant flaws of a tripartite ethno-regional federalism in which infighting and instability in any one unit could polarise politics and destabilise the entire federation. The unhappy experience of the First Republic led to the reformulation of the constitutional provisions on emergency rule and prompted the dissolution of the regions into smaller constituent units. Yet contemporary agitation around 'the need to retrieve and preserve the federal system', restructure 'the constituent units of the federation' and decentralise government's 'coercive forces' all reflect new constitutional concerns and contestations about the over-centralisation of the federation and the centre's overwhelming powers of intergovernmental intervention.[62]

Expanded opportunities for federal intervention were created by the expansion of central powers following the military overthrow of the First Republic. These included empowering the federal president with the right to unilaterally proclaim a state of emergency before seeking legislative ratification. Indeed, presidential proclamations of a state of emergency involved several measures (including the publication of the emergency proclamation in the Federal Gazette, national broadcasts justifying the emergency and the deployment of the military to the emergency area) that effectively nudged the legislature to ratify the proclamations. Thus, all presidential proclamations of emergency rule were, in the first instance, expeditiously and overwhelmingly approved by the national legislature.

At the same time, the increase in the basic threshold for the legislature's ratification of emergency rule (from a simple majoritarian parliamentary resolution in the First Republic to the requirement of approval of two-thirds of assembly members since the inception of a presidential constitution in 1979), the restriction of each iteration of emergency rule to six months and the formal separation of powers between the executive and the legislature all imposed real limits on the execution of presidential emergency rule. Overall, as is evident in the legislature's refusal to re-authorise emergency rule in Ekiti and the BAY states, emergency rule was easier to initiate, but somewhat more difficult to sustain or extend, under Nigeria's military-sponsored presidential constitution.

The military was largely successful in its aspiration to use state re-organisation to facilitate federal cohesion and intervention. Nigeria's multi-state framework fundamentally recalibrated the structural context for emergency rule, making such rule less likely to disrupt the entire federal system. Imposing emergency rule on a few states out of a 36-state federation had a less destabilising impact than imposing emergency rule in one of just three large regions. Federal intervention, in general, and emergency rule, in particular, benefited from the flexibility and fluidity arising from having a multiplicity of players in the federal structure.

The military's reconstruction of Nigerian constitutional institutions may also be working to normalise federal intervention in other ways. The fragmentation of regions has transformed states into weak units lacking sufficient

62 Nwabueze (2007) at 391–443; Alabi (2005) at 17.

autonomous powers and resources to sustain an independent local government system, thereby encouraging intervention by state governments in the functioning and funding of the localities (despite the military's intention to insulate them from the states). At the same time, the proliferation of states as arenas of inter-group competition for federally distributed resources multiplies the number of local-level conflicts. Though not nationally polarising, these conflicts create enough local-level security challenges to compel the centre's coercive law and order intervention. Such intervention is increasingly being undertaken without the formal declaration of emergency rule, thereby further routinising and institutionalising the practice of federal intervention. Despite such normalisation, however, intergovernmental intervention will remain politically contentious in Nigeria, because it often erodes the federal democratic norms and institutions required to manage the country's extraordinary diversity.

BIBLIOGRAPHY

Books

Azinge E (ed) *State of Emergency in Nigeria: Law and politics* Lagos: Nigerian Institute of Advanced Legal Studies (2013)

Joseph R *Democracy and prebendal politics in Nigeria* Cambridge: Cambridge University Press (1987)

Nwabueze B *How President Obasanjo subverted Nigeria's federal system* Ibadan: Gold Press (2007)

Page M & Wando A *Halting the kleptocratic capture of local government in Nigeria* Washington, DC: Carnegie Endowment for International Peace (2022)

Suberu R *Federalism and ethnic conflict in Nigeria* Washington, DC: United States Institute of Peace Press (2001)

Chapters in Books

Idornigie P 'Partial declaration of state of emergency' in Azinge E (ed) *State of emergency in Nigeria: Law and politics* Lagos: Nigerian Institute of Advanced Legal Studies (2013) 368–99

Suberu R 'Nigeria' in Steytler N (ed) *Forum of Federations handbook on local government in federal systems* New York: Palgrave Macmillan (2024)

Journal Articles

Adamolekun L 'The Nigerian federation at the crossroads: The way forward' (2005) 35(3) *Publius* 383–405

Aikhomu A 'Federal–state relations under military government, 1985–1992' (1994) 1(1) *Nigerian Journal of Federalism* 11

Alabi M 'Emergency powers in Nigeria: Legal and constitutional issues' *The Constitution* (2005) 5(4) 1–22

Babangida I 'Federalism and nation-building in Nigeria: The challenges of the twenty-first century' (1994) 1(1) *Nigerian Journal of Federalism* 2
Davies SG 'Nigeria – some recent decisions on the constitution' (1962) 11(4) *International & Comparative Law Quarterly* 919–36
Diamond L 'Issues in the constitutional design of a third Nigerian republic' (1987) 86(343) *African Affairs* 211
Lawan M 'Abuse of powers of impeachment in Nigeria' (2010) 48(2) *Journal of Modern African Studies* 317
LeVan C 'Reciprocal retaliation and local linkage: Federalism as an instrument of opposition organizing in Nigeria' (2018) 117(466) *African Affairs* 1–20
Osaghae E 'The status of state governments in Nigeria's federalism' (1992) 22(3) *Publius* 188
Owen O & Usman Z 'Briefing: Why Goodluck Jonathan lost the Nigerian presidential election of 2015' (2015) 114 (456) *African Affairs* 455–71
Sawer G 'Emergency powers in Nigerian and Malayan federalism' (1964) 6(1) *Malaya Law Review* 83–99
Stepan A 'Federalism and democracy: Beyond the US model' (1999) 10(4) *Journal of Democracy* 19–34
Suberu R 'De/centralization in Nigeria, 1954–2020' (2023) 33(5) *Regional & Federal Studies* 699–724

Legislation

Constitution of the Federal Republic of Nigeria, 1999
Constitution of the Federation of Nigeria, 1960
Emergency Powers Act of 1961
House of Representatives, Federal Republic of Nigeria, Votes and Proceedings, 19 May 2004
House of Representatives, Federal Republic of Nigeria, Votes and Proceedings, 25 May 2004
House of Representatives, Federal Republic of Nigeria, Votes and Proceedings, 8 January 2012
Senate, Federal Republic of Nigeria, Votes and Proceedings, 15 May 2014
Senate, Federal Republic of Nigeria, Votes and Proceedings, 20 May 2014
Senate, Federal Republic of Nigeria, Votes and Proceedings, 26 October 2006
Senate, Federal Republic of Nigeria, Votes and Proceedings, 24 April 2007

Case Law

AG Federation v AG Abia & Ors, SC/CV/343/2024
Attorney General of Plateau State & ors v Goyol & ors, Eze v Governor of Abia State and *Governor Ekiti State & Ors v Olubunmo & Ors* (2007) 16 NWLR (Pt. 1059) 57; (2014) 14 NWLR (Pt. 1426) 192; and (2016) LPELR-48040(SC)
Chief Olafisoye v Federal Republic of Nigeria (2004) 4 NWLR (Pt 864)
Plateau State & Another v Attorney General of the Federation & Another Suit No. SC. 113/2004

Internet Sources and Others

'Address by His Excellency, President Goodluck Ebele Jonathan, on the occasion of the declaration of a state of emergency in certain states of the federation in order to restore public order, peace and security in the federation' (31 December 2011) *Vanguard*

'Emergency rule extension in North East' (14 November 2014) *News Herald* available at https://newsheralddotme.wordpress.com/2013/11/14/emergency-rule-extension-in-north-east (accessed 14 February 2024)

'Kidnappers are wreaking havoc in Nigeria' (18 January 2024) *The Economist*

Achebe C 'The high price of patience' (27 July 1993) *New York Times*

Diamond L 'Democracy's deepening recession' (2 May 2014) *The Atlantic*

Editorial Board 'Nigeria: State of emergency: An intensification of attack on already terrorized masses' (7 June 2013) *Workers Alternative*

Jegede M 'Jonathan's plea for emergency rule extension' (16 May 2014) *Sahara Reporters*

Nwabufo F 'Yobe rejects emergency rule' (13 May 2014) *The Cable*

Tukur S 'Governor Nyako accuses Jonathan administration of genocide against northern Nigeria' (19 April 2014) *Premium Times*

United Nations Office of the High Commissioner for Human Rights 'Nigeria needs urgent action to end "pressure cooker" of violence claiming thousands of lives, says UN rights expert' (3 September 2019) available at https://www.ohchr.org/en/press-releases/2019/09/nigeria-needs-urgent-action-end-pressure-cooker-violence-claiming-thousands (accessed 27 January 2025)

Wodu N 'Nigeria's unitary federalism' (16 December 2020) *Council on Foreign Relations*

Theses

Akande J *Emergency powers in newly independent African countries in the Commonwealth* (unpublished PhD Thesis, University of London, 1971)

10. South Africa: the origins, uses and effectiveness of intervention powers

Yonatan T. Fessha, Lisa Draga and Jaap De Visser

1. INTRODUCTION

Intervention in South Africa may be understood as the exercise of a power that gives senior levels of government the authority to interfere in the powers and functioning of lower levels of government. The Constitution provides for intervention in both provincial and local government. The national executive has the power to intervene in the provinces, while the provincial executive may intervene in local government. The national executive may also intervene in local government, but only when the provincial government fails to do so and under certain conditions.

This chapter examines the law and politics of intervention in South Africa. It commences by setting out the constitutional context, with its focus on the federal features of the South African form of government. It then moves to explore the grounds for intervention, followed by the forms of intervention. The discussion shifts thereafter to the procedural safeguards the Constitution provides to protect lower levels of government from unwarranted intervention by senior levels. The role of the judiciary in regulating interventions is also examined, after which the chapter concludes by discussing the politics of intervention.

2. CONSTITUTIONAL CONTEXT AND RATIONALE FOR ENTRENCHING POWERS OF INTERVENTION

Section 40 of the Constitution of South Africa provides that national, provincial and local governments are 'distinctive, interdependent and interrelated'. 'Distinctiveness' emphasises the autonomy enjoyed by each sphere of government, while their interrelatedness and interdependence mean that no sphere exists purely independently of another. They 'do not tread on each other's toes' and 'they understand that all of them perform governmental functions for the benefit of the people of the country as a whole'.[1] The Constitution explicitly requires all spheres of government to act in the spirit of cooperative government rather than in competition with each other. As the Constitutional Court stated in its *First Certification* judgment, the Constitution has rejected competitive federalism and chosen instead to adopt 'cooperative government'.[2]

Chapter 3 of the Constitution is dedicated to outlining the normative principles of cooperative government. Section 41(1) lists the principles of cooperative government and intergovernmental relations to which all spheres of government and organs of state must adhere. The principles may be categorised broadly as principles that promote and emphasise national unity, respect for autonomy and a duty to cooperate. The first half of the principles of cooperative government stress the need to promote national unity: the three spheres of government must 'preserve the peace, national unity and indivisibility of the Republic',[3] must work collectively to 'secure the wellbeing of the people of the Republic'[4] and must maintain loyalty 'to the Constitution, the Republic and its people'.[5] The second part of the principles reaffirms the distinctiveness of each sphere and promotes respect for autonomy: the three spheres of government must 'respect the constitutional status, institutions, powers and functions of government in the other spheres',[6] and they must 'not assume any power or functions except those conferred on them in terms of the constitution'.[7] Furthermore, they have to 'exercise their powers and perform their functions in a manner that does not encroach on the geographical, functional or institutional integrity of government in another sphere'.[8]

Chapter 7 of the Constitution sets out a framework for national and provincial supervision and support of local government. Section 154(1) provides that 'national government and provincial governments, by legislative and other measures, must support and strengthen the capacity of municipalities to manage their own affairs, to exercise their powers and to perform their function'. Section 155(6)(a) tasks provincial government with monitoring and supporting local government based within its borders through 'legislative or other

---

1 *Independent Electoral Commission v Langeberg Municipality* 2001 (3) SA 925 (CC) 26.

2 *In Re: Certification of the Constitution of the Republic of South Africa, 1996* 1996 (10) BCLR 1253 (CC) 290.

3 Section 41(1)(a), Constitution.

4 Section 41(1)(b), Constitution.

5 Section 41(1)(d), Constitution.

6 Section 41(1)(e), Constitution.

7 Section 41(1)(f), Constitution.

8 Section 41(1)(g), Constitution.

measures'. The Constitutional Court conceives of the monitoring power as 'the antecedent or underlying power from which the provincial power to support, promote and supervise [local government] emerges'.[9] Steytler and De Visser explain that monitoring entails the exposure of legislative non-compliance and reveals whether support or, indeed, intervention is necessary.[10] Together with sections 100 and 139 of the Constitution – which authorise intervention in provincial and local governments, respectively – these provisions convey what the Constitutional Court in the *First Certification* judgment described as a 'hands-off – hands-on' relationship between local government and the other two spheres of government. It is hands-off in the sense that national and provincial government must respect the integrity and autonomy of local government; it is hands-on in the sense that national and provincial government, using the process set out in section 139 of the Constitution, must intervene where local government functions in a 'deficient or defective' way.[11]

The background to the original inclusion of intervention powers in the Constitution is twofold. First, provincial intervention in municipalities had always been part of the architecture of local government even before local government's elevation to constitutional status. It was a common feature in ordinances applicable to local government before the advent of democracy. The concept was thus not new but was carried forward into the constitutional dispensation and also made applicable to provinces. Second, the drafters of the Constitution were acutely aware that the capacity of provincial and local governments to fulfil their obligations would to be varied, given the challenges of underdevelopment, the abysmal governance record of the former homelands and the great expectations surrounding service delivery and redistribution. Furthermore, the drafters feared that provincial and local government autonomy could be used to pursue overtly regional, parochial or personal interests. In short, it was envisaged that there would be a need for correcting, supporting and stabilising provincial and local government institutions that fail to meet their obligations to their citizens.

The rationale for the 2003 constitutional amendments to the regime for interventions in local government was more targeted in approach. By then, it had become clear that financial mismanagement was the Achilles' heel of local government. A regime akin to 'bankruptcy', which minimises political

---

9 *Ex parte Chairperson of the Constitutional Assembly: In re Certification of the Constitution of the Republic of South Africa 1996* 1996 (4) SA 744 (CC) (*'Certification of the Constitution'*) at para 372.

10 Steytler N & De Visser J *Local government law of South Africa* South Africa: LexisNexis (2007) at 15–19.

11 *Certification of the Constitution* at para 373.

discretion in deciding whether or not to intervene, was thus necessary to retain potential lenders interested in loaning money to municipalities.

3. GROUNDS FOR INTERVENTION

Under South African law, the consent of the government which is being subjected to intervention is not a requirement: the national or provincial government may unilaterally declare intervention. This sets the South African approach apart from other countries where intervention, at least with regard to certain grounds and conditions, requires the consent or request of the level of government which is subject to intervention.

Again, unlike in other federations, where intervention seeks to address problems related to national security or human rights, intervention in South Africa is aimed largely at allowing senior levels of government to deal with dysfunctionality and poor performance at lower levels of government. Senior levels of government may intervene when their immediate lower level of government fails to fulfil an executive obligation.[12] That, however, is not the only ground for intervention. Finance-related concerns at the municipal level may also trigger interventions;[13] in fact, these concerns are the only issues that can ultimately form the basis for national government intervention in municipalities.[14] The failure by municipalities to fulfil an executive obligation does not trigger national intervention – it triggers only provincial intervention. Yet finance-related dysfunctionality at provincial level is not among the grounds that can be used as the basis for national government intervention in the provinces. This indicates that municipalities face a more intrusive intervention regime.

The grounds for intervention are broadly formulated and centre on the term 'failure to fulfil an executive obligation'. What, then, is an executive obligation, and when is a government deemed to have failed to fulfil it? What kind of financial emergencies trigger intervention by another sphere of government? Definitions are critical. A wide interpretation might lead to an undermining of the autonomy of subnational governments; a narrow interpretation might safeguard that autonomy, yet at the price of shielding dysfunctional governments from intervention. The following section focuses on the failure to fulfil an executive obligation as one of the grounds for intervention.

---

12 Sections 100(1) and 139(1), Constitution.

13 Sections 139(4) and 139(5), Constitution.

14 Section 139(7), Constitution.

3.1 Failure to Fulfil an Executive Obligation

In the Constitution, neither section 100 nor section 139 defines the term 'executive obligation'. It is also unclear from the Constitution, or any other legislation, when a provincial or local government is deemed to have failed to fulfil such an obligation. In *Mnquma Local Municipality and Another v Premier of the Eastern Cape and Others*,[15] the court defined executive functions in local government as 'the residue of functions of government after legislative and judicial functions are taken away'.[16] Executive functions are therefore functions that are neither legislative nor judicial in nature; however, not all executive obligations may be the subject of intervention. According to the court, '[e]xecutive obligations must not be confused with statutory obligations or duties that are aimed at ensuring the effective performance by local government of its executive obligations'.[17] As the court put it:

> It could never have been the intention, within the framework of the system of government established by the Constitution, that the failure by a mayor to table a time schedule within the prescribed time limit, or the failure to include an annual performance report in the annual report, would on its own constitute an executive obligation that would empower intervention as envisaged by sub-section (1).[18]

Only obligations that originate from the Constitution are potentially a subject of intervention.[19]

The failure to fulfil an executive obligation arises when the concerned government is unable or unwilling to take appropriate executive action. This

---

15 *Mnquma Local Municipality and Another v Premier of the Eastern Cape and Others* [2009] ZAECBHC 14 (5 August 2009).

16 *Mnquma* at para 55.

17 *Mnquma* at para 62. Section 155(7) of the Constitution allows national and provincial government to regulate the exercise of executive authority by municipalities for the purposes of ensuring that municipalities perform their functions effectively. The national government has done so by adopting a number of municipality-related statutes, including the Municipal Structures Act 117 of 1998 and the Municipal Systems Act 32 of 2000. The failure to comply with any of these obligations does not constitute a failure to fulfil an executive obligation.

18 *Mnquma* at para 62.

19 The court has made it clear that 'obligations arising from other sources such as contracts' cannot be regarded as executive obligations. According to the court, 'the statutory duty of a municipality to pay over an employee's deducted tax to the Revenue Services, or the contractual obligation to pay bond instalments, are not executive obligations'. See *Member of the Executive Council for Local Government, Mpumalanga v Independent Municipal and Allied Workers Union* 2002 (1) SA 76 (SCA) at para 64.

must be established objectively before it can trigger an intervention. As much was confirmed in *City of Cape Town v Premier, Western Cape and Others*,[20] where the court stated that intervention may be triggered only when there is 'an omission or an inaction by the municipality and not positive misconduct'. Furthermore, the court emphasised that it must be an ongoing, rather than a past, failure; in other words, '[i]intervention would not be appropriate where a past omission had already ceased'.[21]

There is nothing in the Constitution which states that the failure to fulfil an executive obligation has to be so serious that a municipality (or provincial department) has collapsed. One may argue that the relevant sphere of government does not have to wait for a total collapse before intervening.[22] At the same time, the principle of cooperative government, which requires each sphere to respect the integrity of other spheres of government, suggests that the discretion to intervene must be used sparingly. This also means that the nature of the failure of an executive obligation should at least influence the nature of the appropriate steps that the intervening authority takes. As the court notes, the fact that there are many complaints against a municipality, or that 'there were so many failures', does not on its own indicate the existence of the conditions for intervention. The same can be said for the seriousness of the failure to fulfil executive obligations. According to the court,

> the danger with this approach is that a large number of what may constitute failures that are not serious and could easily have been resolved in another manner, are thrown together to justify the dissolution of a Municipal Council.[23]

Failure to fulfil an executive obligation is the most commonly invoked ground for intervention. On many occasions, however, the list of alleged failures to fulfil executive obligations does not in fact reveal a failure to fulfil executive obligations, but points instead to finance-related concerns.

3.1.1 Appropriate steps: forms of intervention

Both sections 100 and 139 of the Constitution state that the national and provincial government may intervene 'by taking appropriate steps' when there is a failure to fulfil an executive obligation. The Constitution does not provide a

---

[20] *City of Cape Town v Premier of the Western Cape and Others (5933/08)* 2008 ZAWCHC 52; 2008 (6) SA 345 (C) (1 September 2008) at para 79.

[21] *City of Cape Town v Premier of the Western Cape and Others* at para 79.

[22] Department of Provincial and Local Government *Intervening in provinces and municipalities: Guidelines for the application of sections 100 & 139 of the Constitution* (2007).

[23] *Mnquma* at para 97.

definition of 'appropriate steps'. In *Mnquma*, the court, albeit within the context of provincial intervention, stated that the appropriateness of an intervention must be assessed in the light of the nature of the executive obligation implicated, the interests of those impacted by the municipality's inability or failure to fulfil such obligation and the interests of the particular municipality. Due consideration must be given to the principles of cooperative governance. This involves balancing, on the one hand, the constitutional mandate that the integrity of local government is to be respected as far as possible with, on the other, the constitutional demand for effective governance. It also requires consideration of whether the type of intervention 'would be effective and commensurate with the nature and/or the extent of the failure to fulfil the obligation concerned'.[24] The Constitutional Court has endorsed this reasoning in *Mnquma*,[25] explaining that appropriate steps are steps 'fitting or reasonably capable of resolving the issue of non-fulfilment of the executive obligation, or suitable in the sense that they fit the situation'.[26]

A number of appropriate steps are identified by the Constitution. Section 100 lists two: the issuing of a directive to the provincial government (section 100(1)(a)) and the assumption of the relevant provincial government's responsibility (section 100(1)(b)). Section 139(1) lists three 'appropriate steps'. These are the issuing of a directive along the same lines as those contemplated in section 100(1)(a), taking over the responsibilities of the relevant municipal government and dissolving the municipal council.[27] It must be noted that the appropriate steps that a national executive may take when intervening in provinces do not include the dissolution of the provincial legislature. The constitutional amendment that introduced the dissolution of municipal councils as one of the appropriate steps left section 100 – which regulates national government

24 *Mnquma* at para 75.

25 *Premier, Gauteng and Others v Democratic Alliance and Others; All Tshwane Councillors who are Members of the Economic Freedom Fighters and Another v Democratic Alliance and Others; African National Congress v Democratic Alliance and Others* 2021 (12) BCLR 1406 (CC) *('Premier, Gauteng')* at paras 81 to 84.

26 *Premier, Gauteng* at para 8.

27 The list of 'appropriate steps' provided by the Constitution is not exhaustive; that is, 'appropriate steps' other than those explicitly provided in the constitutional text are not excluded. Court proceedings, for example, could be regarded as 'appropriate steps'. This was confirmed by the court in *Mnquma* at para 63 where it indicated that 'court proceedings are not excluded from steps that may constitute "appropriate steps"'.

intervention in provinces – unchanged. The reason for this distinction is not evident.[28]

Issuing a directive is the least intrusive form of intervention. It simply involves the rather soft measure of sending a directive to the provincial or municipal executive that sets out the extent to which the province or municipality has failed to meet the executive obligation. The directive also has to lay out any steps which the provincial or municipal government must follow to remedy this failure. While the intervening authority thus issues instructions as to the actions that should be taken, it is not involved in the actual execution of those instructions – that is left to the relevant government subjected to intervention.

The notably more intrusive form of intervention occurs when the intervening authority assumes responsibility. In this situation, the intervening authority takes over, and carries out, the executive obligation of the organ of state which is alleged to have failed to perform. This is clearly a significant intrusion in the autonomy of the relevant sphere of government, which is why the scope of this form of intervention is limited by additional requirements. According to section 100 of the Constitution, national intervention in provinces by way of assuming responsibility is permitted to the extent to which it is necessary to

> maintain essential national standards or meet established minimum standards for the rendering of a service, maintain economic unity, maintain national security or prevent the province from taking unreasonable action that is prejudicial to the interests of another province or to the country as a whole.[29]

The same requirements are enumerated in section 139 of the Constitution. The only difference between sections 100 and 139, however, is that 'national security' does not appear as one of the considerations in delimiting the extent to which a provincial executive assumes the responsibility of a municipality.[30]

While assumption of responsibility is intrusive, it is not as intrusive as the provincial power to dissolve a municipal council. That is why section 139 permits such a form of intervention only in 'exceptional circumstances', which is an acknowledgement that 'the dissolution … is the more drastic and far-reaching

---

28 Perhaps this differentiation represents a deliberate hierarchy in which the provincial government's authority is more closely guarded against national intervention than the local government's is in the case of provincial intervention.

29 Section 44 of the Constitution lists the same requirements that the national government must meet before it intervenes in the exclusive legislative jurisdiction of the provinces.

30 This may be based on the premise that municipal authority by nature is little likely to undermine national security.

of the three forms of intervention authorised by [section 139(1)]'.[31] Nonetheless, the Constitution does not define 'exceptional circumstances'. National government guidelines deem exceptional circumstances to exist when there is 'failure of the intervention … due to the Council's unwillingness to resolve the problems'.[32]

3.1.2 Successive steps?

One of the key issues in the interpretation of the appropriateness of the intervention is whether the steps may be used only in succession. In other words, the question is whether assumption of responsibility is possible only after a directive has failed, and whether dissolution is possible only after a failed assumption of responsibility. It could be argued that less intrusive forms of intervention should be given a chance before undertaking an intervention that involves a more serious encroachment on the autonomy of the relevant sphere of government.

In answering this question, a distinction must be made between national intervention in provincial government, on the one hand, and provincial intervention in local government, on the other. With regard to the former, the Constitutional Court determined that 'the appropriate steps' are successive steps. Based on the premise that the issuing of a directive in terms of section 100(1)(a) and the assumption of responsibility for the relevant obligation of the provincial government in terms of section 100(1) (b) 'have not been formulated in the alternative', it held that both steps 'deal with one process'.[33] This means that the issuing of a directive under section 100(1)(a) is a necessary precursor to the taking over of any provincial responsibilities under section 100(1)(b).[34] This is confirmed in practice. For example, when the national government intervened in Limpopo and North West in 2011 and 2018, it assumed responsibility in the two provinces only after the directives it issued did not yield the desired result.

With regard to provincial interventions in local government, a 2003 constitutional amendment made it clear that the steps are not necessarily successive. Among other things, in section 139(1) of the Constitution, the amendment replaced the conjunction 'and' with 'or' when listing the appropriate steps that a provincial government takes when intervening in a municipality.[35] The Constitutional Court has also rejected the view that the steps are

---

31 *Mnquma* at para 76.

32 Department of Provincial and Local Government (2007) at 29.

33 *Certification of the Amended Text of the Constitution of the Republic of South Africa, 1996* 1996 ZACC 24 (4 December 1996) at para 120.

34 *Certification of the Amended Text of the Constitution of the Republic of South Africa* 1997 (1) BCLR 120.

35 *Mnquma* at para 72.

necessarily successive.[36] It emphasised that the appropriateness of an intervention does not automatically hinge on the sequence of the steps adopted under section 139(1); rather, the focus is on what is a 'suitable' form of intervention, that is, one which is an appropriate fit for the given circumstances. It is therefore possible for more drastic forms of intervention to be used without first employing the less intrusive forms of intervention. What is important is that serious attention should be given to using other less invasive types of intervention before resorting to the drastic form of intervention.[37]

This does not mean, however, that the less intrusive forms of interventions must be employed first when they are not as effective as the drastic form of intervention.[38] The practice with provincial interventions is that most of them have come in the form of assumption of responsibility, and that, in many of these cases, the provincial governments did not first issue a directive.[39]

The court in *Mnquma* has also specifically rejected the view that dissolving a municipal council must be preceded by another (now-failed) intervention step. According to the court, '[e]xceptional circumstances may lie in the nature of the problem that may be experienced in a municipality and the fact that any other form of intervention would not be appropriate'.[40] The existence of exceptional circumstances should be determined on a case-by-case basis. What is clear is that this is a step that should be resorted to not 'easily' but 'only after careful consideration has been given to the facts and circumstances of each particular case with due regard to the principles that underlie the position of local government in the constitutional framework'.

3.2 Financial Interventions

Prior to 2003, the constitutional provisions on intervention did not mention finance-related concerns as specific grounds for intervention. However, in practice, governance and service delivery failures very often manifest themselves in financial problems, such as the failure to pass a budget or honour financial commitments. A comprehensive amendment of section 139 of the Constitution introduced finance-related grounds for intervention. According to the National Treasury, which sponsored the amendment, this was justified by 'the increasing financial troubles observed in municipalities and the need

---

36 *Premier, Gauteng* at paras 81 to 84.
37 *Mnquma* at para 78.
38 *Mnquma* at para 78.
39 South African Human Rights Commission (SAHRC) (2014) at 29.
40 *Mnquma* at para 77.

to respond systematically to the finance problem'.[41] In particular, the Treasury wanted the law to provide for a mandatory intervention 'in the event of serious financial problems in a municipality'.[42] Although the power to intervene in municipalities on financial grounds is a power reserved primarily to the provincial government, the national government may intervene in municipalities when a provincial government is unable to, or does not, intervene in these finance-related matters.

Section 139 of the Constitution provides a number of finance-related circumstances that can trigger intervention in municipalities. The first is when a municipality fails to approve a budget or impose revenue-raising measures.[43] According to section 160(2)(b) and (c) of the Constitution, the responsibility for approving a budget and imposing rates, taxes, levies and duties lies with the municipal council. Furthermore, in terms of the Municipal Financial Management Act (MFMA), a municipality is required to approve its budget before the start of the budget year, which begins on 1 July.[44] Along with budget approval, the municipality must also pass a resolution imposing any municipal taxes and setting municipal rates. Failure to approve the budget and impose revenue-raising measures by the first day of the budget year constitutes a violation of the municipality's obligation under the Constitution and legislation.

In addition to the failure to approve budgets or impose revenue-generating measures, financial emergencies may form the basis for intervention in municipalities. This is the case, according to section 139(5) of the Constitution, where a municipality experiences a financial crisis that results in a serious or persistent material breach of its obligations to provide basic services or meet its financial commitments, or where it admits that it is unable to meet its obligations or financial commitments.[45] The Constitution is not the only source of the list of financial grounds that trigger provincial intervention in municipalities. According to section 136 of the MFMA, a serious financial problem in a municipality can also trigger a provincial government intervention.[46] The Constitution does not indicate when a financial problem becomes a

---

[41] Ledger T & Rampedi M *Mind the gap: Section 139 interventions in theory and practice* (2 October 2019) *Public Affairs Research Institute* available at https://pari.org.za/wp-content/uploads/2019/10/20191002_MindTheGap_Report_Ledger_Rampedi_v8.pdf (accessed 1 March 2025).

[42] Ledger & Rampedi (2019) at 3.

[43] Section 139(4), Constitution.

[44] Section 16(1), MFMA.

[45] Section 139(5), Constitution.

[46] Section 136 of the MFMA lists factual finance-related circumstances that constitute a serious financial problem.

financial crisis,[47] but the distinction clearly seems to relate to the extent of the municipality's financial difficulties. This explains why intervention in serious financial problems is discretionary, whereas intervention in a financial crisis is mandatory. It perhaps also explains why the Minister of Finance is in charge of managing an intervention in response to a financial crisis in a municipality, as opposed to the Minister of Local Government, who handles interventions arising from financial problems.[48]

3.2.1 Appropriate steps: forms of intervention

Section 139(4) sets out the non-exhaustive steps that the provincial executive may take when a municipal council has failed to approve a budget before the commencement of the new financial year or approve 'any revenue-raising measures necessary to give effect to the budget'. The specified steps are the dissolution of the municipal council; the appointment of an interim administrator until a new municipal council is formally elected; and the approval of 'temporary budget or revenue-raising measures' to ensure the municipality continues to operate. The provincial executive has no discretion, and must intervene where the jurisdictional prerequisites for invoking a section 139(4) intervention are present.[49] However, the provincial executive retains discretion as to the form of the intervention, subject only to the requirement that the chosen measures are 'appropriate'. The Supreme Court of Appeal emphasised that the chosen measures must be capable of remedying the particular municipal failure that gave rise to the need for a section 139(4) intervention.[50]

When it comes to financial problems or financial crisis, a provincial government may take a number of steps. If the failure to fulfil an executive obligation stems from a financial problem, the first step would be to impose a financial recovery plan on the relevant municipality. This is not the most intrusive form of intervention, because the municipality is responsible for the implementation of the plan: only if the municipality fails to implement the plan may the provincial executive resort to a more intrusive form of intervention. This could include assuming responsibility or dissolving the municipal council. The reasons for the non-implementation of the recovery plan would influence the course of action the provincial government has to take. In instances of simple lack of capacity, intervention should be limited to assuming responsibility through the appointment of an administrator responsible for the implementation of the financial recovery plan. If the issue does not concern capacity, the

---

47 Section 136, MFMA.

48 Section 139, MFMA.

49 *Premier of the Western Cape and Others v Overberg District Municipality and Others* 2011 (4) SA 441 (SCA) *('Premier v Overberg')* at para 19.

50 *Premier v Overberg* at para 19.

intervention may involve dissolving the municipal council.[51] Where an intervention is precipitated by a financial crisis under section 139(5), the relevant provincial executive must 'impose a recovery plan'. This plan must stabilise the municipality so that it can deliver basic services and honour its financial commitments. The provincial executive must develop this plan in line with a framework set out in the MFMA.

It may be that a municipality cannot, or will not, introduce legislative measures aimed at ensuring the success of the plan, for instance where the council does not approve a budget or any other revenue-generating measure needed to implement the plan. Under these circumstances, the provincial executive is compelled to dissolve the municipal council and appoint an administrator until a newly elected council is formally declared. The provincial executive must, in addition, 'approve a temporary budget or revenue-raising measures or any other measures' aimed at accomplishing the objectives of the recovery plan. Where the circumstances do not demand dissolution of the municipal council, the provincial executive must assume responsibility for executing the recovery plan to the extent that the municipality is unable or unwilling to do the same. The municipality is bound by the contents of the plan. However, this binding effect exists 'only to the extent necessary' to resolve the financial crisis the municipality finds itself in. The provincial executive may thus not over-prescribe how the municipality should act.[52]

4. REVIEW OF INTERVENTION: POLITICAL AND LEGAL SAFEGUARDS

Before an intervention may be deemed legitimate, the failure to fulfil an executive obligation – or, more generally, the presence of any of the financial grounds for intervention – must be established as juridical fact. The intuition or subjective view of the intervening government that there is a financial emergency or a failure to fulfil an executive obligation is not sufficient. That is to say, the national or provincial decision to intervene is reviewable in court under the principle of legality and is subject to legal and political safeguards.

[51] This is provided that the plan contains 'suggestions for the adoption of a budget and revenue-raising measures with regard to spending limits and revenue targets, budget parameters for a specified period, and specific revenue-raising measures that are necessary for financial recovery'.

[52] Steytler N 'Interventions in municipalities: Amendment to section 139 of the Constitution' (n.d.) Dullah Omar Institute available at https://dullahomarinstitute.org.za/multilevel-govt/local-government-bulletin/archives/volume-5-issue-2-may-2003/vol-5-no-2-2003-interventions-in-municipalities-amendment-to-section-139-of-the-constitution.pdf (accessed 1 March 2025).

4.1 Political Safeguards

4.1.1 Notice and approval

The intervening executive must provide written notice of an intervention to the National Council of Provinces (NCOP), the second chamber of the national parliament. The NCOP must in turn decide whether or not to approve the intervention. The duration of the required notice period, as well as the time within which the NCOP must make a determination, varies according to the nature of the intervention. Where an intervention is triggered by an assumption of responsibility under sections 100 or 139(1)(b), the notice must reach the NCOP within 14 days of the commencement of the intervention.[53] The NCOP then has 180 days in which to decide. An intervention ends where the NCOP disapproves or fails to reach a decision within the requisite period. In practice, the requirements of notice have not always been adhered to. It is not uncommon for the provincial executive to fail to meet the 14-day deadline prescribed in section 139(2).[54]

In the case of a provincial intervention in a municipality, written notice of the intervention must also be given to the national minister responsible for local government. This must be done within 14 days of the start of the intervention. A failure to notify the minister within the requisite time results in an automatic end to the intervention, thus opening up to legal challenge any actions taken thereunder.[55] The minister must decide, within 28 days, whether to approve the intervention.[56] Again, the period in which notice must reach the minister and a decision be made varies according to the nature of the provincial intervention. Should the minister disapprove, all responsibilities are restored to the municipal council.[57] Decisions of the provincial executive prior to the disapproval remain valid, however.[58]

In practice, the minister, as happens with the NCOP, is not always notified in time.[59] Furthermore, the minister often has insufficient time to apply

---

[53] Section 100(2)(a), Constitution.

[54] See De Visser J & November J 'Overseeing the overseers: Assessing compliance with municipal intervention rules in South Africa' (2017) 9 *Hague Journal of the Rule of Law* 109; Ledger & Rampedi (2019) at 9.

[55] De Visser & November (2017) at 19–20.

[56] Section 139(2)(a)(i) and (b)(i), Constitution.

[57] Department of Provincial and Local Government (2007), Part 2, section 3.3.2(c) at 22.

[58] Department of Provincial and Local Government (2007), Part 2, section 3.3.2(c) at 22.

[59] De Visser & November (2017) at 18–19.

his or her mind to the issue of whether an intervention is justified,[60] to the issue of whether the correct sub-provision under section 139 was invoked and to a proper assessment of the structure of the suggested intervention.[61] Interventions are rarely refused outright within the 28 days.[62] According to a senior national government official, some provinces proceed with interventions even without the minister's response.[63]

The NCOP is empowered to veto the minister's approval, but may not veto a refusal.[64] Where the minister disapproves, the provincial executive must nevertheless notify the NCOP and provincial legislature of the requested intervention.[65] The veto power has been invoked inconsistently – and, arguably, far too infrequently – by the minister and the NCOP. Of the 33 provincial interventions between 2010 to 2015, merely two were vetoed.[66] However, it appears that many of these interventions may have been unlawful.[67] The fact that the minister and NCOP rarely veto interventions, even though there are clearly problems with many of them, reflects poorly on the intergovernmental checks and balances surrounding interventions. It seems that, in the face of evident municipal dysfunction, the minister and NCOP are hesitant to override interventions on the basis of procedural non-compliance.[68]

---

60 See Chair of Select Committee – COGTA, Human Settlements, Water & Sanitation *Section 139 interventions: A critical reflection on its application, successes & challenges (the role of the NCOP)* (10 September 2020) at 19; Parliamentary Monitoring Group 'Workshop on section 139 interventions in municipalities and general observations' (5 November 2019) available at https://pmg.org.za/committee-meeting/29249/ (accessed 1 March 2025); Ledger & Rampedi (2019) at 9.

61 Ledger & Rampedi (2019) at 9.

62 Ledger & Rampedi (2019) at 9.

63 November (2015) at 70. See also De Visser & November (2017) at 21; Mohale DM *Placement of municipalities under administration: A comparative case study of Masilonyana and Nala local municipalities in the Free State Province in South Africa* (Unpublished Master's thesis, University of Witwatersrand, 2013) at 125.

64 Johnstone S *The veto power to terminate provincial interventions in terms of section 139(2)(b) and 139(3)(b) of the Constitution* (Unpublished Master's thesis, University of the Western Cape, 2014) at 20.

65 Department of Provincial and Local Government (2007), Part 2, section 3.3.2(c).

66 Johnstone (2014) at 29–31, 46. These were either interventions under section 139 of the Constitution or section 136 of the MFMA.

67 Johnstone (2014) at 31.

68 In regard to the NCOP, see Hoffman-Wanderer Y & Murray C 'Suspension and dissolution of municipal councils under section 139 of the Constitution: Aantekeninge' (2007) 1 *Journal of South African Law* 141; Johnstone (2014) at 64.

4.1.1.1 Intergovernmental checks and balances for financial intervention and dissolution

The intergovernmental checks and balances for financial interventions and council dissolutions are different from those for assumptions of responsibility. Where a municipality is dissolved under section 139(1)(c) the minister, NCOP and provincial legislature must receive immediate notice.[69] The clock for evaluating the dissolution starts ticking from the date of receipt of notice, with the window for approval ending 14 days thereafter. The Constitutional Court held that this timeframe allows impacted parties to make representations to both the minister and NCOP. This 'plainly illustrates' that during the 14 days 'the dissolution is inchoate'.[70] Absent a veto by the minister or NCOP, the dissolution takes effect at the expiry of this period.

In the case of a financial intervention (in response to the failure to adopt a budget, or to a financial crisis), the provincial executive must notify the minister, the NCOP and the provincial legislature all within seven days of the commencement of the intervention.[71] In contrast to the assumption of responsibility and dissolution, the approval of the minister or the NCOP is not required.

The role of the NCOP and minister under section 139 has been described as a 'legal and political' safeguard.[72] The reason is that the approval by both is supposed to filter out potentially vexatious and frivolous attempts by the executive to invoke section 100 and 139.[73] The requirement of NCOP approval is meant to ward against abuse of power by the intervening executive,[74] safeguard the integrity of provincial and local government[75] and aid the efficiency with which the intervention operates.[76] The involvement of the NCOP in the intervention process is linked to the fact that it is regarded as the torchbearer of provincial interests.[77] The NCOP's role as an advocate for and guardian of provincial interests finds reflection in its makeup as a body composed of delegates from the nine provinces.[78] This means that the NCOP, as a structure, is

---

69 Sections 139(3)(a)(i) and (ii), Constitution.

70 *Premier, Gauteng and Others* at para 179.

71 Section 139(6), Constitution.

72 *Mnquma* at para 82.

73 De Visser J 'Provincial intervention the principles and rules' (1999) 1(2) *Local Government Law Bulletin* 12.

74 Murray C, Bezruki D, Ferrell L, et al. *Interim report: Speeding transformation: NCOP's role in the oversight process* (n.d.) available at https://www.ndi.org/sites/default/files/1215_sa_ncoprole22001_5.pdf (accessed 1 March 2025).

75 Hoffman-Wanderer & Murray (2007) at 11.

76 Mohale (2013) at 111.

77 Section 42(4), Constitution.

78 Section 60, Constitution.

best placed to safeguard the integrity of the provincial government in the event of a national intervention.

The NCOP is also a platform where local government interests are protected, albeit not as strongly as with regard to provinces. Section 67 of the Constitution provides that a maximum of 'ten part-time representatives designated by organised local government … represent the different categories of municipalities'. These representatives 'may participate, when necessary' in NCOP proceedings but may not vote. Consequently, local government representatives can be involved in NCOP discussions concerning a provincial intervention but have no vote on any formal determinations in regard to such an intervention. This distinction in voting status highlights the NCOP's role as a body that, by constitutional design, serves provincial interests first and foremost. Mathenjwa argues that since local and provincial government are two distinct spheres,[79] it is not 'readily possible' for representatives of the provincial government to effectively represent the interests of local government.[80] These two spheres may differ on their understanding of how best to restore a municipality to proper functioning, with the NCOP being more likely than the local government to favour a provincial perspective on what would work best.

4.1.2 Review

Sections 100 and 139 of the Constitution both provide that the NCOP must 'review the intervention regularly'.[81] The NCOP may 'make any appropriate recommendations' to the intervening executive.[82] The Constitution thus requires that the NCOP frequently examine interventions from the date of their approval until they end. The NCOP's review function has been characterised as protective.[83] That is, it must guard against overly intrusive, ill-defined or improperly executed interventions.[84] The NCOP's review function is thus key to ensuring that the unstable province or municipality is restored as quickly as

[79] Section 40(1) of the Constitution makes it clear that the government consists of three distinctive spheres of government.

[80] Mathenjwa MJ 'Challenges facing the supervision of local government in South Africa' (2014) 1 *Journal of South African Law* 140 at 146.

[81] Sections 100(2)(c) and 139(2)(c), Constitution.

[82] Sections 100(2)(c) and 139(2)(c), Constitution.

[83] In regard to section 100, see Murray et al. (n.d) at 11 and 56; Mdledle TP *Evaluating the role of the NCOP in reviewing national government interventions in provincial governments: A case study of the 2011 interventions in the Eastern Cape and Limpopo provinces* (unpublished LLM thesis, University of the Western Cape, undated) at 12. In regard to section 139, see De Visser (1999) at 12; Hoffman-Wanderer Y & Murray C (2007) at 26.

[84] De Visser (1999) at 12.

possible.[85] The review goes beyond merely keeping a close watch over the process to prevent potential exploitation by the intervening executive: the NCOP must promote cooperative intergovernmental relations.[86] It also may advise on the management of the intervention.[87] The ultimate purpose of NCOP review is to assess whether the goals of intervention have been achieved. Regular reporting by the intervening executive is thus 'critical' to the process,[88] as the NCOP itself has noted.[89]

Some intervening provincial executives have failed to provide the NCOP with regular reports on the status of interventions.[90] Where reports have been provided, they have often contained 'poor information' about interventions.[91] There are thus clear indications that the NCOP has not always exercised effective oversight of provincial interventions. For example, civil society reports that it identified poor oversight of the national intervention in the provincial education department of the Eastern Cape.[92] The intervention here was characterised by irregular, insufficient and vague reporting by the national executive to the NCOP,[93] as well as prolonged neglect by the NCOP of its oversight duty.[94] The NCOP's poor oversight has been attributed to the absence of clear

---

85 Equal Education *Submission to the Joint Constitutional Review Committee on Section 100: National intervention in provincial administration* (2016) at 29.

86 South African Local Government Association *SALGA municipal support and intervention model* (2020) at 3.

87 De Visser (1999) at 12.

88 Parliamentary Monitoring Group 'Joint workshop with national and provincial legislatures on the application of section 139 of the Constitution and the need for legislation in terms of section 139(8)' (1 November 2010) available at https://pmg.org.za/committee-meeting/12254/ (accessed 23 November 2023).

89 Parliament & South African Local Government Association *National Council of Provinces Local Government Week 2018 – Land use: Towards integrated spatial planning 8–10 May* (2018) at 146.

90 Department of Cooperative Governance *Application of section 139 of the Constitution* (23 July 2019) available at https://static.pmg.org.za/190723application.pdf (accessed 1 March 2025) at 9.

91 Murray, et al. (n.d) at 20.

92 Equal Education (2016) at 34–35.

93 Equal Education *Presentation of submission on amending section 100 of the Constitution* (2020) at 7 and 9; Equal Education (2016) at 34–35.

94 Equal Education *EE & EELC submission to the Select Committee on Education & Recreation on the section 100(1)(b) intervention in the Eastern Cape* (2016) at 3 and 15; Equal Education (2016) at 34–35; Equal Education (2020) at 7 and 9.

guidelines on how it should undertake a review.[95] Indeed, the Constitution provides no detail on how the NCOP is to discharge this essential mandate.[96]

With respect to interventions in local government, the provincial legislature represents a further check on the provincial executive. Sections 139(2)(a)(iii) and (3)(a)(ii) of the Constitution instruct the provincial executive to notify the provincial legislature of the intervention. The provincial legislature's role or power is not defined, arguably because the provincial executive is any event accountable to the provincial legislature. However, there is little evidence to show that provincial legislatures are indeed overseeing the actions of the provincial executive under section 139 of the Constitution.[97]

There is no procedure for continuous review of financial interventions, that is, those prompted by budgetary issues or a financial crisis.[98] This poses the risk that the provincial or national executive could evade review by deliberately crafting an intervention under these provisions instead of the more cumbersome ones.[99] Murray and Hoffman-Wanderer argue, on the basis of the principle of cooperative governance, that the NCOP should exercise a formal review of financial interventions under section 139(4) and (5).[100] The Constitution, so they argue, not only authorises but demands NCOP review of financially related interventions.[101] While this position is attractive from the perspective of cooperative governance, it seems to go too far in 'reading in' an intergovernmental check which the legislator left out. It must be assumed that the omission of the NCOP review of financial intervention was deliberate and that the text of the Constitution should hence prevail over what otherwise perhaps would have been desirable.

95 Department of Cooperative Governance *Local government: A chronology of the past 21 years* (2021) at 113–14; Department of Cooperative Governance (2019) at 8; Department of Cooperative Governance *Intergovernmental Monitoring, Support and Intervention Bill: 5th National Municipal Managers Forum* (30 April 2013) at 7; Ledger & Rampedi (2019) at 22 and 28.

96 The Constitution does, however, make room for the NCOP to establish rules on how it conducts its business (see sections 70(1) and 70(2) of the Constitution). The NCOP revised these rules in 2021. Rule 237(5) of Parliament of the Republic of South Africa *Rules of the National Council of Provinces* 10th ed (December 2021) relates to section 100. More specifically, Rule S238(5) requires the NCOP to review whether it is necessary to continue with an intervention under section 139.

97 Department of Cooperative Governance (30 April 2013) at 7.

98 De Visser J 'Applying the new section 139 intervention powers: Issues arising from practice' (2005) 7(1) *Local Government Bulletin* at 9.

99 De Visser (2005) at 9–10.

100 Hoffman-Wanderer & Murray (2007) at 13.

101 Hoffman-Wanderer & Murray (2007) at 13–14.

4.2 Legal Safeguards: Judicial Enforcement of Interventions

So far, the focus of this discussion has been on legal safeguards against overzealous national or provincial executives. However, there is a contrary legal risk: a national or provincial executive which is reluctant to intervene. Communities and local businesses infuriated by crumbling municipalities and unwillingness by provincial governments to intervene have successfully used litigation to force provinces to do so. The national government has similarly been compelled by court order to skip over the provincial government and intervene in this way.[102] The community-driven litigation that resulted in the Eastern Cape High Court order compelling the Eastern Cape provincial executive to dissolve the Makana Municipality has been hailed as an illustration of 'accountable democracy and constitutionalism' at work.[103]

Yet while this is valid, this type of judicial involvement does not guarantee fruitful government intervention. Successful intervention requires synergy among an array of role-players possessing the correct skills and bringing a strategic focus to issues spanning the short, medium and long term.[104] By its very nature, litigation does not automatically produce such a synergy.[105] As Wright, Dube and du Plessis argue, court-ordered provincial interventions run the risk of coming up against a lacklustre provincial executive, or one that might itself be struggling to stay afloat financially; it may also lack the resources for successfully executing an intervention.[106] A court victory is then unlikely to translate into improved service delivery in the long term. The eMalahleni Local Municipality in Mpumalanga serves as a cautionary tale in this respect.

Save eMalahleni Action Group made legal history in 2019 when it became the first community-based group to secure a court order against the provincial

---

102 De Visser J 'Local government in intergovernmental relations' in Kariuki P, Reddy P & Wissink H (eds) *Subnational governance and development in South Africa post-1994: Prospects and challenges* (2021) at 32.

103 Abdullah I & Hofmeyr A 'Failing municipalities – hope in sight?' (11 March 2020) *Cliffe Dekker Hofmeyr* available at https://www.cliffedekkerhofmeyr.com/news/publications/2020/dispute/dispute-resolution-alert-11-march-Failing-municipalities-hope-in-sight.html (accessed 1 March 2025).

104 Research Unit of the Parliament of the Republic of South Africa *Overview of municipalities under section 139 intervention as it relates to service delivery* (2020) at 16.

105 Wright J, Dube F & Du Plessis A 'Judicial enforcement of mandatory provincial interventions in municipalities in South Africa' (2022) 55 *VRÜ Verfassung und Recht in Übersee* 105 at 121.

106 Wright, Dube & Du Plessis (2022) 105 at 123.

executive to intervene under section 139(5).[107] The group had pressed for such an intervention to secure the 'superior skills' of the National Treasury's Municipal Financial Recovery Service (MFRS) in resolving the municipality's dire financial challenges. Only the MFRS is permitted by law to draft a financial recovery plan for a municipality where an intervention was triggered by a financial crisis. The MFRS in eMalahleni's case, however, proved incapable of delivering on its mandate as a consequence of resource and capacity constraints. This left Save eMalahleni highly dissatisfied with the recovery plan the MFRS had produced and resulted in threats by the group that it would return to court.[108]

Continued malfeasance in the municipality later forced Mpumalanga's member of the executive council (MEC) for Cooperative Governance and Traditional Affairs to appoint forensic investigators. The final forensic report, dated November 2021, was never made public but was leaked in the media. The leaked report exposed huge fraud, corruption and tender irregularity within the municipality.[109] This was reflected too in the Auditor-General's 2020–2021 financial report, which revealed that eMalahleni had ZAR 444 million in unauthorised expenditure and ZAR 618 million in irregular expenditure in this period.[110] The Auditor-General also referred certain spending irregularities in the municipality to the Public Protector (an independent state institute established by the Constitution to support and safeguard democracy) for further investigation.[111]

---

[107] Glasser MD 'South African municipalities in financial distress: What can be done' (2020) 24 *Law, Democracy & Development* 413 at 427. The order was by consent of the parties.

[108] Public Affairs Research Institute *Mind the gap: Section 139 interventions in theory and in practice* (2019) at 21–3.

[109] Yende SS 'Forensic report revealing Emalahleni municipality's R26m corruption gathering dust one year on' (31 July 2023) *City Press* available at https://www.news24.com/citypress/news/forensic-report-revealing-emalahleni-municipalitys-r26m-corruption-gathering-dust-one-year-on-20230731 (accessed 3 December 2023).

[110] Auditor-General South Africa 'Emalahleni' available at https://mfma-2021.agsareports.co.za/municipality/6-emalahleni (accessed 3 December 2023).

[111] Auditor-General South Africa *Consolidated general report on local government audit outcomes: MFMA 2021–2022* (2023) at 46 available at https://www.agsa.co.za/Portals/0/Reports/MFMA/2021-22/MFMA%20Report%202021-22%20FINAL%20-%2031%20May%202023.pdf?ver=2023-05-31-072950-280 (accessed 1 March 2025).

Thus, even after the provincial intervention,[112] eMalahleni Municipality remained incapable of supplying 500,000 of its residents with clean drinking water. The municipality has four water treatment works and eight waste water treatment works: not one of these had met compliance standards since 2020.[113] eMalahleni bears testimony, then, to just how much of a defeat a victory in the courts can be.

There is also the danger of courts being exploited for ulterior political motives through litigation aimed at government intervention.[114] Bronstein and Glaser point out that the service delivery woes of local government are intractable and that there are hence no quick fixes. They warn, too, that even the best-run municipalities inevitably suffer some form of delivery failure that can serve as cannon fodder for politically driven groups seeking to muscle out their opponents through the courts.[115] Where courts are called upon to compel government intervention, they are susceptible to becoming pawns in such political gamesmanship.

Moreover, provincial interventions, in and of themselves, represent a significant inroad into democratic governance. It is therefore less than ideal for judges, as non-elected officials, to deliberate on provincial interventions that may have sweeping ramifications far beyond the appreciation of the courts.[116] Courts are, however, mandated to uphold the provisions of the Constitution, which includes ordering mandatory interventions where circumstances demand as much. Whether such court-ordered remedies can be effective, though, is open to debate.

---

112 Department of Cooperative Governance and Traditional Affairs 'Provincial intervention in local government in terms of section 139 of the Constitution and the Municipal Finance Management Act' (29 March 2022) available at https://www.cogta.gov.za/index.php/2022/03/29/provincial-intervention-in-local-government-in-terms-of-section-139-of-the-constitution-and-the-municipal-finance-management-act-as-of-february-2022/ (accessed 3 December 2023).

113 Kretzmann S & Gilili C 'Emalahleni is failing to provide clean drinking water to 500 000 people' (22 September 2022) *Groundup* available at https://www.groundup.org.za/article/people-have-to-use-their-social-grants-to-boil-tap-water-so-that-it-is-safe-to-drink/ (accessed 3 December 2023).

114 Bronstein V & Glaser D 'Intervention in South African municipalities: Dangers and remedies' (2023) 140(1) *The South African Law Journal* 95 at 117.

115 Bronstein & Glaser (2023) at 117.

116 Wright, Dube & Du Plessis (2022) 105 at 122.

5. THE POLITICS OF INTERVENTION

The first intervention in a municipality (Butterworths Transitional Local Council) took place in 1998. At the time – the first years of democracy in South Africa – such interventions were few and far between, but over the past decade they have increased dramatically in number. Given the levels of dysfunctionality and corruption in many municipalities, this is not surprising. In fact, some argue that even more interventions are necessary. As for interventions in provinces, these began only much later in 2011, when the national government intervened in Limpopo, Gauteng and the Free State.[117] In 2018, it intervened in the North West province.

Both trends are counterintuitive because one would have thought that intervention would have been common in the early days of democracy when the new system was introduced and subnational governments were struggling to establish themselves as viable sites of government. It would be expected that intervention would become less common as subnational governments gained experience and institutions took shape. Quite the opposite happened in South Africa.

A close look at the performance of provincial and local governments reveals that dysfunctionality at the provincial and municipal level did not emerge 15 years into democracy. In fact, professionalisation was not given the attention it deserves and 'newly appointed, inexperienced staff were overwhelmed by the technical challenges of making numerous contradictory and often inequitable institutional systems (such as payrolls, conditions of service, and asset registers) work properly'.[118]

The underlying political reality is that the ruling party at national government level, the African National Congress (ANC), has also controlled most provincial governments since 1994. The ANC wanted to avoid the image of being associated with failed subnational government structures, and so the national government, no doubt due to the ANC's concern about the optics of intervention, engaged in 'informal intervention' that involves the provision

[117] Lethoko M, Musandiwa J & Njoko BM 'Social control theory and public financial accountability: Changing from section 100(1)(a) to section 100(1)(b) intervention in Limpopo' (2018) 53(3) *Journal of Public Administration* 707. These interventions took place in 2011.

[118] Powell D & Phindle N 'Implementations of provincial and local government in post-apartheid South Africa' in Steytler N & Ghai Y (eds) *Kenyan-South African dialogue on devolution* Cape Town: Juta (2015) 393.

of 'active support'. To avoid political embarrassment, formal declarations of interventions were not used.[119]

What is also surprising is that the vast majority of interventions are initiated under section 139(1) of the Constitution. There have not been many finance-related interventions, despite the fact that the financial woes of municipalities are well documented. In the overwhelming majority of cases, provinces have invoked section 139(1) when a section 139(5) financial-crisis-related intervention was called for.[120] This may be because financial interventions require the National Treasury's involvement, while section 139(1) interventions are conducted under the auspices of provincial departments responsible for local government. The existence of two separate regimes, overseen by separate departments, thus sparked interdepartmental rivalry. Ultimately, the incorrect use of the constitutional provisions casts doubt on the utility of the 2003 constitutional amendments that explicitly provided for financial interventions.

Claims of politically motivated intervention surface now and again, but are difficult to prove. In 2005, the provincial government of KwaZulu-Natal dissolved the council of the Abaqulusi Municipality despite the recommendation of its own commission of enquiry into the affairs of the municipality, which concluded that the conditions for intervention did not exist. Evidently, the ANC-led provincial government was determined to intervene in the municipality by dissolving the council as it was controlled by the opposition, in this case the Inkatha Freedom Party (IFP).[121]

The uncomfortable truth about interventions in South Africa is that, in many cases, the local governments that are subjected to them emerge from them in worse repair than they were in to begin with.[122] There are reports of municipalities which, after being under provincial administration for years, have seen the money they owe their creditors double; likewise, municipalities have relapsed into dysfunctionality not long after the end of interventions that brought some positive change.

Capacity constraints seem to be at the heart of the problem. A government report on section 139 interventions reveals that provincial governments frequently lack the budgetary and staff resources to effectively discharge their mandate to monitor and support local government under provincial intervention. A deficit in skills and institutional knowledge within the provincial

119 Steytler N 'National cohesion and intergovernmental relations South Africa' in Steytler N & Ghai Y (eds) *Kenyan–South African dialogue on devolution* Cape Town: Juta (2015) 303.

120 Ledger & Rampedi (2019) at 8.

121 Mathenjwa (2014).

122 SAHRC (2014) at 29.

government also undermines its ability to offer effective oversight and assistance.[123] More often than not, the provinces rely entirely on a single administrator to execute the intervention. The administrator does not have a team of experts on which to rely in addressing the myriad challenges of the relevant sphere of government; instead, he or she may have to rely on municipal personnel who lack the necessary skills or, worse, are part of the problem in the first place. Administrators also often encounter personnel of the organ of state who resist the intervention, which may then undermine the effectiveness of the intervention. There are reports of 'resistance and obstructive tendencies by municipal councils and municipal staff to the extent of non-cooperation and illegal activities such as destroying records and giving illegal instructions to other municipal officials against the functions of the administrator'.[124]

A further problem relates to the indispensable political backing that administrators require in order to turn around an ailing provincial department or municipality. They may have the initial backing of national and provincial political structures, but as they start taking unpopular decisions, such as charging errant staff or tightening financial controls, support may turn into opposition. This is often when interventions are stymied or lose their momentum.

6. CONCLUSION

Interventions are not only conceptually integrated in South Africa's system of intergovernmental relations but are also, sadly, a common phenomenon. The Constitutional Court has made it clear that interventions represent the 'hands-on' part of the relationship between spheres of government. Unlike the case in many other federations, interventions in South Africa are aimed at addressing problems in subnational government performance rather than security or public order matters.

To shield legislative powers from intervention, the Constitution presents 'failure to fulfil an executive obligation' as a key ground for intervention. With respect to local government, where the council exercises both legislative and executive powers, the singling out of these obligations has been particularly difficult.

The fact that interventions are reviewable under the principle of legality has resulted in court cases that shape the interpretation of the constitutional provisions on intervention. Principles such as that an intervention must be aimed at an ongoing failure, that the measure must be reasonably capable of addressing

[123] Department of Cooperative Governance (2021) at 113; Department of Cooperative Governance *Narrative report on interventions and the development of supplementary legislation for section 139 of the Constitution* (2013) at 2–3.

[124] SAHRC (2014) at 29.

the failure, and that dissolution may be appropriate when the council itself is the problem have taken firm root in the country's jurisprudence.

While interventions in provinces are limited to the 'failure to fulfil an executive obligation', a constitutional amendment in 2003 introduced a raft of financial interventions to the framework for intervention in municipalities. The failure to adopt a budget or the existence of a financial crisis were added as specific triggers, thus underscoring the focus on interventions on governance and performance. The amendment also introduced the possibility that the national government can 'leapfrog' over the provincial government and intervene directly in a municipality when a provincial government fails to do so. This signalled a break with the hitherto 'dualistic' nature of interventions, whereby only the provincial government could intervene in municipalities. In practice, provincial governments seemed to prefer the 'classic' intervention under section 139(1) and have only recently started to use the financial interventions.

Sections 100 and 139 of the Constitution both contain an intricate scheme of intergovernmental checks and balances meant to keep overzealous national and provincial executives in check. The NCOP, as the chamber bringing together all three spheres of government, plays a particularly important oversight role. In practice, the checks are not always adhered to or carried out, and the NCOP's oversight leaves much to be desired. This has resulted in interventions that were arguably unlawful being permitted to continue. The reverse legal argument has also emerged and reached the courts, namely the review of the absence of an intervention where circumstances on the ground clearly demand one. Community-based organisations have succeeded in forcing national and provincial governments to intervene. However, the jury is out on whether these legal victories ultimately translate into improved service delivery.

The political undertones of interventions have become more pronounced as politics in South Africa diversifies and different parties and coalitions govern different levels of government. There is little evidence of widespread overt political abuse and, where abuse has occurred, the courts were sometimes there to end it. However, there is no doubt that political factors influence the practice of intervention, not least of all because a successful intervention comes with painful measures for which the intervening body requires firm political support.

All in all, interventions are an integral part of intergovernmental relations in South Africa. Given the parlous state of affairs in many subnational governments, they are likely to remain a regular occurrence. National and provincial governments will have to continue walking the tightrope between, on the hand, respecting the institutional integrity of organs of state in another sphere and, on the other, respecting the rights of communities and residents to dignity and basic services.

BIBLIOGRAPHY

Books

Steytler N & De Visser J *Local government law of South Africa* South Africa: LexisNexis (2007)

Chapters in Books

De Visser J 'Local government in intergovernmental relations' in Kariuki P, Reddy P & Wissink H (eds) *Subnational governance and development in South Africa post-1994: Prospects and challenges* Democracy Development Programme (2021)

Powell D & Phindle N 'Implementations of provincial and local government in post-apartheid South Africa' in Steytler N & Ghai Y (eds) *Kenyan-South African dialogue on devolution* Cape Town: Juta (2015) 393–418

Steytler N 'National cohesion and intergovernmental relations South Africa' in Steytler N & Ghai Y *Kenyan–South African dialogue on devolution* Cape Town: Juta (2015) 303–23

Journal Articles

Bronstein V & Glaser D 'Intervention in South African municipalities: Dangers and remedies' (2023) 140(1) *The South African Law Journal* 95–125

De Visser J 'Provincial intervention the principles and rules' (1999) 1(2) *Local Government Law Bulletin* 12

De Visser J 'Applying the new section 139 intervention powers: Issues arising from the practice' (2005) 7(1) *Local Government Bulletin* 9–10

De Visser J & November J 'Overseeing the overseers: Assessing the compliance with municipal intervention rules in South Africa' (2017) 9 *Hague Journal of the Rule of Law* 109–33

Glasser MD 'South African municipalities in financial distress: What can be done' (2020) 24 *Law, Democracy & Development* 413–41

Hoffman-Wanderer Y & Murray C 'Suspension and dissolution of municipal councils under section 139 of the Constitution: Aantekeninge' (2007) 1 *Journal of South African Law* 141–145

Lethoko M, Musandiwa J & Njoko BM 'Social control theory and public financial accountability: Changing from section 100(1)(a) to section 100(1)(b) intervention in Limpopo' (2018) 53(3) *Journal of Public Administration* 707–17

Mathenjwa MJ 'Challenges facing the supervision of local government in South Africa' (2014) 1 *Journal of South African Law* 140–50

Wright J, Dube F & Du Plessis A 'Judicial enforcement of mandatory provincial interventions in municipalities in South Africa' (2022) 55 *VRÜ Verfassung und Recht in Übersee* 105–25

Case Law

Certification of the Amended Text of the Constitution of the Republic of South Africa 1997 (1) BCLR 120
Certification of the Amended Text of the Constitution of the Republic of South Africa, 1996 1996 ZACC 24 (4 December 1996)
City of Cape Town v Premier of the Western Cape and Others (5933/08) 2008 ZAWCHC 52; 2008 (6) SA 345 (C) (1 September 2008)
Ex parte Chairperson of the Constitutional Assembly: In re Certification of the Constitution of the Republic of South Africa 1996 1996 (4) SA 744 (CC)
In Re: Certification of the Constitution of the Republic of South Africa 1996 1996 (10) BCLR 1253 (CC) 290
Independent Electoral Commission v Langeberg Municipality 2001 (3) SA 925 (CC) 26
Member of the Executive Council for Local Government, Mpumalanga v Independent Municipal and Allied Workers Union 2002 (1) SA 76 (SCA)
Mnquma Local Municipality and Another v Premier of the Eastern Cape and Others 2009 ZAECBHC 14 (5 August 2009)
Premier of the Western Cape and Others v Overberg District Municipality and Others 2011 (4) SA 441 (SCA) 19
Premier, Gauteng and Others v Democratic Alliance and Others; All Tshwane Councillors who are Members of the Economic Freedom Fighters and Another v Democratic Alliance and Others; African National Congress v Democratic Alliance and Others 2021 (12) BCLR 1406 (CC)

Legislation

Constitution of the Republic of South Africa, 1996
Local Government: Municipal Finance Management Act 56 of 2003
Parliament of the Republic of South Africa *Rules of the National Council of Provinces* 10th ed (December 2021)

Reports

Auditor-General South Africa *Consolidated general report on local government audit outcomes: MFMA 2021–2022* (2023) available at https://www.agsa.co.za/Portals/0/Reports/MFMA/2021-22/MFMA%20Report%202021-22%20FINAL%20-%2031%20May%202023.pdf?ver=2023-05-31-072950-280 (accessed 1 March 2025)
Chair of Select Committee – COGTA, Human Settlements, Water & Sanitation *Section 139 interventions: A critical reflection on its application, successes & challenges (the role of the NCOP)* (10 September 2020)
Department of Cooperative Governance and Traditional Affairs 'Provincial intervention in local government in terms of section 139 of the Constitution and the Municipal Finance Management Act' (29 March 2022) available at https://www.cogta.gov.za/index.php/2022/03/29/provincial-intervention-in-local-government-in-terms-of-section-139-of-the-constitution-and-the-municipal-finance-management-act-as-of-february-2022/ (accessed 3 December 2023)

Department of Cooperative Governance and Traditional Affairs 'Provincial intervention in local government in terms of section 139 of the Constitution and the Municipal Finance Management Act' (29 March 2022) available at https://www.cogta.gov.za/index.php/2022/03/29/provincial-intervention-in-local-government-in-terms-of-section-139-of-the-constitution-and-the-municipal-finance-management-act-as-of-february-2022/ (accessed 3 December 2023)

Department of Cooperative Governance *Application of section 139 of the Constitution* (23 July 2019) available at https://static.pmg.org.za/190723application.pdf (accessed 1 March 2025)

Department of Cooperative Governance *Intergovernmental Monitoring, Support and Intervention Bill: 5th National Municipal Managers Forum* (30 April 2013)

Department of Cooperative Governance *Local government: A chronology of the past 21 years* (2021)

Department of Cooperative Governance *Narrative report on interventions and the development of supplementary legislation for section 139 of the Constitution* (2013)

Department of Provincial and Local Government *Intervening in provinces and municipalities: Guidelines for the application of sections 100 & 139 of the Constitution* (2007)

Equal Education *EE & EELC submission to the Select Committee on Education & Recreation on the section 100(1)(b) intervention in the Eastern Cape* (2016)

Equal Education *Presentation of submission on amending section 100 of the Constitution* (2020)

Equal Education *Submission to the Joint Constitutional Review Committee on Section 100: National intervention in provincial administration* (2016)

Ledger T & Rampedi M *Mind the gap: Section 139 interventions in theory and practice* (2 October 2019) *Public Affairs Research Institute* available at https://pari.org.za/wp-content/uploads/2019/10/20191002_MindTheGap_Report_Ledger_Rampedi_v8.pdf (accessed 1 March 2025)

Murray C, Bezruki D, Ferrell L, et al. *Interim report: Speeding transformation: NCOP's role in the oversight process* (n.d.) available at https://www.ndi.org/sites/default/files/1215_sa_ncoprole22001_5.pdf (accessed 1 March 2025)

Parliament & South African Local Government Association *National Council of Provinces Local Government Week 2018 – Land use: Towards integrated spatial planning 8–10 May* (2018)

Parliamentary Monitoring Group 'Joint workshop with national and provincial legislatures on the application of section 139 of the Constitution and the need for legislation in terms of section 139(8)' (1 November 2010) available at https://pmg.org.za/committee-meeting/12254/ (accessed 23 November 2023)

Parliamentary Monitoring Group 'Workshop on section 139 interventions in municipalities and general observations' (5 November 2019) available at https://pmg.org.za/committee-meeting/29249/ (accessed 1 March 2025)

Research Unit of the Parliament of the Republic of South Africa *Overview of municipalities under section 139 intervention as it relates to service delivery* (2020)

South African Human Rights Commission (2014)

South African Local Government Association *SALGA municipal support and intervention model* (2020)

Internet Sources

Abdullah I & Hofmeyr A 'Failing municipalities – hope in sight?' (11 March 2020) *Cliffe Dekker Hofmeyr* available at https://www.cliffedekkerhofmeyr.com/news/publications/2020/dispute/dispute-resolution-alert-11-march-Failing-municipalities-hope-in-sight.html (accessed 1 March 2025)

Auditor-General South Africa 'Emalahleni' available at https://mfma-2021.agsareports.co.za/municipality/6-emalahleni (accessed 3 December 2023)

Kretzmann S & Gilili C 'Emalahleni is failing to provide clean drinking water to 500 000 people' (22 September 2022) *Groundup* available at https://www.groundup.org.za/article/people-have-to-use-their-social-grants-to-boil-tap-water-so-that-it-is-safe-to-drink/ (accessed 3 December 2023)

Steytler N 'Interventions in municipalities: Amendment to section 139 of the Constitution' (n.d.) *Dullah Omar Institute* available at https://dullahomarinstitute.org.za/multilevel-govt/local-government-bulletin/archives/volume-5-issue-2-may-2003/vol-5-no-2-2003-interventions-in-municipalities-amendment-to-section-139-of-the-constitution.pdf (accessed 1 March 2025)

Yende SS 'Forensic report revealing Emalahleni municipality's R26m corruption gathering dust one year on' (31 July 2023) *City Press* available at https://www.news24.com/citypress/news/forensic-report-revealing-emalahleni-municipalitys-r26m-corruption-gathering-dust-one-year-on-20230731 (accessed 3 December 2023)

Theses

Johnstone S *The veto power to terminate provincial interventions in terms of section 139(2)(b) and 139(3)(b) of the Constitution* (Unpublished Master's thesis, University of the Western Cape, 2014)

Mdledle TP *Evaluating the role of the NCOP in reviewing national government interventions in provincial governments: A case study of the 2011 interventions in the Eastern Cape and Limpopo provinces* (unpublished LLM thesis, University of the Western Cape, undated)

Mohale DM *Placement of municipalities under administration: A comparative case study of Masilonyana and Nalal local municipalities in the Free State Province in South Africa* (Unpublished Master's thesis, University of Witwatersrand, 2013)

11. Spain: the regulation and (rare) practice of central government's intervention in the State of Autonomies

Ignacio Molina and Mayte Salvador Crespo

1. INTRODUCTION

There is no consensus among experts, let alone politicians and the public, on whether Spain's multilevel government can be considered federal in nature.[1] The Constitution of 1978 is ambiguous on this point. According to its first two articles, 'national sovereignty is vested in the Spanish people' as a whole, and is thus not shared between the centre and the constituent parts. Moreover, the nation is designated as indissoluble and indivisible, even though there is also explicit recognition of the guaranteed 'right to autonomy of the nationalities and regions of which it is composed'. Article 137 adds that the state is organised territorially into local bodies (municipalities and provinces) and regional ones (autonomous communities), declaring that all of them 'enjoy self-government for the management of their respective interests'. Defining the territorial organisation of Spain as federal or not is thus in itself a politicised exercise; but over and above this, and irrespective of nominalism,[2] legal and political developments in the past 45 years have served to shape a specific Spanish model, the so-called State of the Autonomies (*Estado Autonómico*).

During that nearly half a century of political decentralisation, the experience of direct central government intervention in regional or local self-government has been rather limited. The range of cases to analyse is confined to a single example in an autonomous community (the dismissal of the Catalan

[1] Colino C 'Decentralisation in Spain: Federal evolution and performance of the Estado Autonómico' in Muro D & Lago I (eds) *The Oxford handbook of Spanish politics* Oxford: Oxford University Press (2020).

[2] See Sala G 'Federalism without adjectives in Spain' (2014) 44 *Publius* 109.

regional government, which was replaced by direct rule from Madrid for seven months between 2017 and 2018) and a single further case in a municipality (the dissolution of Marbella Local Council for just over a year, from 2006 to 2007). This small number of interventions – and the fact that they were imposed only briefly until the situation could be normalised – shows that suspension of self-government in Spain is considered an exceptional, last-resort measure.

Nevertheless, the traumatic circumstances surrounding both of these extreme cases should serve to ensure that both institutional actors (whether political or judicial) and scholars pay close attention to the motivation for intervention, the procedure employed in it, the controls applicable to it and for how long it is imposed. Catalonia is, after all, the second most populated region in the country. Since 2012, Catalan nationalist parties (which had a majority of seats in the regional parliament at the time, but without having reached 50 per cent of the vote) had embarked on a sovereigntist process of radical contestation of the constitutional system. But it was not until the autumn of 2017, after the unilateral declaration of independence by a tiny majority of the members of the Catalan parliament, that the central government requested authorisation from the Senate to take control of the regional powers in application of article 155 of the Constitution.[3]

A few years earlier, in 2006, the central government had also decided to intervene in Marbella (in Málaga), an internationally renowned municipality in the Andalusian Mediterranean coast, when it became clear that the local council was afflicted by systemic corruption. The intervention, applying article 61 of the 1985 law on local government *(Ley de Bases del Régimen Local)*, took place in the context of a major judicial operation that uncovered a web of criminal activities: bribery, embezzlement of public funds, prevarication and influence-peddling. The plot was carried out by, among others, the mayor, local councillors and municipal civil servants, as well as businessmen and even celebrities. Given its complexity and peculiarities, it was the paradigmatic example of the evils associated with the Spanish real estate bubble, which eventually burst during the great recession of 2008.[4]

Significantly, these two cases of central intervention are directly connected to the two major crises – economic and territorial – that hit the legitimacy of the Spanish political system hard in the first two decades of this century: the great recession (Marbella) and the independence conflict (Catalonia). An

---

[3] López-Basaguren A 'Claims for secession in Catalonia: Rule of law, democratic principle and federal alternative' in López-Basaguren A & San-Epifanio LE (eds) *Claims for secession and federalism* Cham: Springer (2019).

[4] Jiménez F 'Building boom and political corruption in Spain' (2009) 14(3) *South European Society & Politics* 255.

in-depth examination of these crises is therefore useful in gaining a better understanding of contemporary Spanish politics and institutions.

Accordingly, after this introduction, the analysis in this chapter is carried out over four sections. Section 2 explores the underlying rationale for the legal regulation of powers of intervention and section 3 deals with the constitutional and legal requirements that determine who can intervene against whom and under what circumstances. Section 4 examines the procedure and its controls (*ex ante* at the Senate and *ex post* at the Constitutional Court). Finally, in section 5, the chapter considers how powers have been used (or misused) in political practice.

2. RATIONALE FOR CENTRAL INTERVENTION IN THE 'STATE OF AUTONOMIES'

Complex centre–periphery dynamics are a distinctive feature of the Spanish political system.[5] Regional self-rule was linked to short periods of freedom in the early 20th century and rescinded by the dictatorship of General Franco (1939–1975). After its transition to democracy, Spain shifted from hyper-centralisation to a de facto federation in just five years. Catalonia and the Basque Country were the first territories to approve a Statute of Autonomy (1979) defining them as 'nationalities'. Between 1980 and 1983, Spain's other 15 regions were also granted such statutes.

According to the Regional Authority Index,[6] Spain's State of Autonomies makes it the second most decentralised country in the world, with only Germany ahead of it. Other regional self-rule indexes[7] rank the power enjoyed by the Spanish autonomous communities as equal to or greater than that of the German *Länder* and as only slightly below the Swiss cantons, Belgian regions or specific cases such as the Faroe Islands in Denmark. The powers of the autonomous regions are broad when seen from a legal and institutional perspective, and are guaranteed by the Constitutional Court, which has played a profound role in shaping the contours of the decentralisation process.[8]

[5] 'The independence conflict in Catalonia' (9 October 2019) *Real Instituto Elcano* available at https://www.realinstitutoelcano.org/en/work-document/the-independence-conflict-in-catalonia/ (accessed 1 March 2025).

[6] Hooghe L, Mark G, Schakel AH, et al. *Measuring regional authority: A postfunctionalist theory of governance (vol. 1)* Oxford: Oxford University Press (2016).

[7] Dardanelli P 'Conceptualising, measuring, and mapping state structures – with an application to Western Europe, 1950–2015' (2019) 49 *Publius* 271.

[8] Harguindeguy J-B, Rodríguez GS, & Díazet JC 'Between justice and politics: The role of the Spanish Constitutional Court in the State of Autonomies'

Subnational governments can effectively translate their preferences into distinctive policies and wide-ranging public spending.

Nonetheless, certain features of the model of territorial organisation could limit real autonomy. The central power's use of funding and basic legislation generates conflicts and may even lead to the erosion of regional powers. At the same time, the ineffectiveness of the Senate as a territorial house and, more broadly, the limited participation of autonomous communities in central decisions mean that a high level of self-rule (with either exclusive or concurrent competences) co-exists with low shared rule.

The tensions and grievances that are not uncommon in highly decentralised systems – combined with the governance imperfections typical of any federal model – are compounded in the case of Spain by the existence of powerful nationalist and pro-independence movements in Catalonia and the Basque Country. These two autonomous communities have been governed almost continuously since the 1980s by regional nationalist parties, in the process increasing tensions with the central government over the scope of their powers and economic resources.

Conflicts of jurisdiction between the central level of government and autonomous communities are resolved by the Constitutional Court (in terms of article 161(1)(a) and (c) of the Constitution). Over four decades, hundreds of constitutional procedures have tried to clarify who has legal competence in a particular policy dimension, with these conflicts of jurisdiction having been resolved peacefully through the Court's application of the provisions of the Constitution itself as well as those of the different Statutes of Autonomy.

But alongside this ordinary mechanism of conflict resolution by an arbiter, the Spanish Constitution includes an additional instrument, one envisaged for a different and exceptional scenario. This is article 155, which grants the central government a mechanism by which to force an autonomous community to comply with the law when it is in serious contravention of its constitutional obligations or acts in a way that significantly harms Spain's general interests.

It is, that is to say, an article designed to cover the theoretically unlikely event of disobedience, and was inspired by the 'federal coercion' ('*Bundeszwang*') mechanism provided in article 37 of the Basic Law of the Federal Republic of Germany. Although it is often said that article 155 is almost a literal translation of the German constitutional provision, there are significant differences between them, one of which is that the weak Spanish Senate is not comparable

---

(2018) 8 *Territory, Politics, Governance* 222.

to the strong *Bundesrat,* which, as the house of territorial representation, has to approve central intervention (the same is true in Spain).[9]

While the existence of central coercion mechanisms is not indispensable in decentralised states, it is common to find rules similar to article 155 in other European constitutions.[10] In the history of Spanish constitutionalism, though, there are no precedents for this article, which was included in the 1978 Constitution on the assumption that it would be applied only extremely rarely.[11]

The decision to include the possibility of intervention in the Constitution was influenced by the general assessment among historians of the problems caused during the Second Republic (1931–1936) by the lack of a similar mechanism. The aim was to provide a constitutional basis for possible temporary intervention by the central institutions of the state in the event of serious breaches of the law by the regional governments, yet without permanently violating the principle of territorial political autonomy. In October 1934, during the Second Republic, there was an armed insurgency in Catalonia, one linked to the declaration of 'a Catalan State within a Spanish Federal Republic' by the autonomous government at the time. The Spanish parliament approved the suspension of the self-government regime recognised by the 1932 Statute of Autonomy of Catalonia. This suspension was declared unconstitutional in 1936 by the 'Constitutional Court of Guarantees' that existed in the republican period.[12]

In 1978, the transition from a unitary autocratic state to a federal state in all but name, along with the recognition of strong political powers to the autonomous communities, raised questions about the peaceful coexistence of the

9 Garcés J 'Consideraciones sobre el artículo 155 de la CE como instrumento de coerción estatal' (2019) 18 *Cuadernos Manuel Giménez Abad* 42. Another difference is that article 37 of the German Basic Law can be activated only if the *Land* disregards constitutional and federal laws, while article 155 refers to non-compliance with any legal obligation. However, Germany does not require a prior request to the president of the *Land* before launching the intervention.

10 Bauer H 'Art. 37 GG' in Dreier C (ed) *Grundgesetz-Kommentar (vol. 3)* Tübingen: Mohr Siebeck (2015). In addition to article 37 of the German Basic Law, article 126 of the Italian Constitution, article 100 of the Austrian Constitution or article 234 of the Portuguese Constitution may be cited.

11 Albertí E 'Constitutional questions on the application of article 155 SC to the Catalan conflict' (2019) 9 *Catalan Social Sciences Review* 41.

12 Orfanel GG 'La prehistoria española del artículo 155 de la Constitución de 1978' in Sánchez AJ, López Guerra JL & García Ruiz JL, et al. (eds) *Constitución y desarrollo político: Estudios en homenaje a Jorge de Esteban* Valencia: Tirant lo Blanc (2013); Lafuente Balle JM 'El artículo 155 de la Constitución española (El acuerdo del Senado)' (2018) 103 *Revista de Derecho Político* 79.

principles of unity and autonomy. For this reason, including a mechanism of intervention in the Constitution reassured those who were concerned about a too-generous dispensation of autonomy to regional self-government. That is to say, in the event of insubordination by the autonomous communities, tools would be available for the central government to enable it to guarantee territorial integrity and ensure respect for the constitutional order.

The parliamentary session diaries that record the constituent debates on article 155 show that it was not easy to reconcile the positions of the different political actors. In particular, disagreements arose between, on the one hand, the two centre-right parties at the time (the Union of the Democratic Centre and the conservative People's Alliance, the precursor of today's People's Party, or PP), which favoured granting the central government broad powers to safeguard the unity of Spain, and, on the other hand, Catalan and Basque nationalists (with some support from nationwide left-wing parties), who defended a stronger self-government or even a plurinational state. In the end, a compromise was reached through the adoption of a regulation closer in service to the federal than to the regional regimes.

In a typical federation, the lines that define the boundary of authority between territorial levels are set out in the constitution, and thus an intervention will always be considered as exceptional and subject to strict controls. In fact, the design and application of article 155 is one of the features that distinguishes Spain from regionalised states in which the centre delegates some of its powers to regions but remains free to take them back whenever it considers it necessary to do so (something which can happen even if the devolution is ambitious, as in the case of the United Kingdom, with its frequent suspensions of the Northern Ireland Assembly and exercise of direct rule from London).

The text of article 155 as finally approved in the 1978 Constitution does not allow for the suspension of autonomy. What is provided instead is that certain competences or powers of the subnational government – powers which have to be clearly identified in the central government's proposal and approved by the Senate – temporarily cease to be exercised by the authorities of the autonomous community and are assumed by the centre through officials appointed ad hoc. The Constitution also allows for the adoption of mechanisms aimed at forcing the autonomous subnational authorities to comply with the law.

In addition, Spanish legislation provides for the possibility of intervening in local government bodies. When central government intervention in municipalities and provinces was regulated in 1985, many of the elements of article 155 (both substantial and procedural) served as the inspiration for it. As in the case of intervention in the autonomous communities, there is no possibility of a general and permanent suspension of self-government, since this would contravene the right to autonomy of local governments, which is guaranteed in articles 137 and 140 of the Constitution. However, the dissolution of municipal government, even if limited in time until the next local elections, is permitted. This may also occur in many other cases in Europe.[13]

3. REQUIREMENTS FOR TRIGGERING ARTICLE 155 AND DISSOLVING LOCAL GOVERNMENTS

As mentioned, the basis for central intervention in subnational governments is regulated in the Constitution in the case of the autonomous communities, and in legislation on local government in the case of municipalities, provinces and other local bodies. The requirements for intervention in the case of the autonomous communities are delineated in article 155 of the Constitution (see Box 11.1), which establishes who can use these powers (the central government with the approval of the Senate), against whom (the regional political authorities), on what grounds and by what procedure.

BOX 11.1 ARTICLE 155 OF THE SPANISH CONSTITUTION

1. If an Autonomous Community does not fulfil the obligations imposed upon it by the Constitution or other laws, or acts in a way seriously prejudicing the general interests of Spain, the Government, after lodging a complaint with the President of the Autonomous Community and failing to receive satisfaction therefore, may, following approval granted by an absolute majority of the Senate, take the measures necessary in order to compel the latter forcibly to meet said obligations, or in order to protect the above-mentioned general interests.
2. With a view to implementing the measures provided in the foregoing clause, the Government may issue instructions to all the authorities of the Autonomous Communities.

---

[13] According to a study by the European Committee on Local and Regional Democracy (CDLR) of the Council of Europe, at least 18 European countries have regulated the possible dissolution of local governments: Austria, Belgium (only Wallonia), Bulgaria, Croatia, Czech Republic, France, Germany (only Bavaria, Brandenburg and Hesse), Greece, Hungary, Italy, Lithuania, Luxembourg, Monaco, Poland, Portugal, Romania, Slovenia, and Spain. See CDLR 'Interim dissolution of the local/regional councils: Results of RRS No 10 LR-IC (2009) 12 Bil.' (6 October 2009) available at https://open.overheid.nl/documenten/ronl-archief-bf973662-6eea-4011-a0cb-7ce85a49f940/pdf (accessed 1 March 2025).

While the Constitution regulates the procedural or formal requirements in detail (see next section), it leaves substantive requirements relatively undetermined, albeit that the prerequisite of a serious situation is emphasised. Article 155 envisages that at least one of the two enabling conditions which are mentioned (non-compliance with obligations or prejudice to the general interests) must be met in order for it (the article) to be applied. That is to say, for the coercive mechanism to be activated, both conditions do not have to be met.

The first enabling condition arises when the autonomous community fails to comply with its constitutional or legal obligations (in regard to all types of laws, including the legislation of the autonomous community itself, international treaties and European Union (EU) law). It must be a serious legal breach. If this were not the case, it would be sufficient to respond to the autonomous community's non-compliance by means of the ordinary control mechanisms in articles 153 and 161 of the Constitution.[14] The case law of the Constitutional Court (in particular, Judgment 89/2019) has also established that the non-compliance must be 'flagrant, manifest and contumacious' and imputable to the higher bodies of the autonomous community (its parliament or government), and therefore not to the administrative levels.

The second enabling condition arises if the autonomous community acts in a way that seriously undermines the general interests of Spain, that is, it deliberately impacts on fundamental values protected by the Constitution, such as territorial integrity, security and public order or constitutional loyalty. Although the drafters of the Constitution took care to distinguish this second enabling condition from the first one above, most legal scholars take the view that this is, in fact, a distinction without a difference, given that there can be no harmful action against the general interests that does not logically entail a prior breach of constitutional and legal obligations.

García Roca[15] points out that the enabling factual condition can emanate from an 'imminent lawless action' or the identification of a 'clear and present danger', here paraphrasing the doctrine that the Supreme Court of the United

---

[14] Articles 153 and 161 state that control of autonomous communities shall be exercised by the Constitutional Court (in matters related to conflicts of jurisdiction, the constitutionality of regional legislation and, under some circumstances, regulatory provisions or acts without legal force); the ordinary courts (for administrative litigation in most matters related to administrative acts); the central government (in case of powers and functions of the state that have been just delegated to the regional level); and the Court of Audit (with regard to financial and budgetary matters).

[15] García Roca J 'Diez tesis sobre la intervención extraordinaria del Estado en las Comunidades Autónomas (artículo 155 CE) tras su aplicación en Cataluña' in Centro de Estudios Políticos y Constitucionales: Tribunal Constitucional (España)

States (US) adopted for determining the circumstances under which limits may be placed on fundamental freedoms.[16] In short, intervention in autonomous communities should be understood as something exceptional that occurs only when other, pre-existing mechanisms have not worked. The ideal would be to apply the ordinary measures of control of regional acts wherever possible and pursue this last resort only if the latter fail. However, these steps may be bypassed in urgent situations that make it impossible to wait for a solution by a court and where it is unlikely that the autonomous community would comply.

In the case of the Catalan conflict, attempts were made in its first years (2012–2017) to resolve it through ordinary judicial mechanisms. The Constitutional Court imposed successive jurisdictional controls establishing provisional measures of suspension (under article 161(2) of the Constitution);[17] it also issued incidental rulings, promoted by the central government, to secure enforcement of these judgments.[18] Such efforts proved ineffective in stopping resolutions, deemed unconstitutional, that the Parliament of Catalonia had passed since 2013, such as approving the right to self-determination or calling for a referendum on secession.[19] This continued non-compliance with judicial rulings, national laws, the Statute of Autonomy, the Standing Orders of the Parliament of Catalonia and other Catalan laws openly demonstrated Catalonia's intention to break with the state and 'its express rejection of the binding force of the Constitution itself'.[20]

It seems clear that a unilateral attempt at secession is no mere breach of a legal obligation, such as a refusal to implement an EU directive. The events in 2017 were serious, given that the autonomous community questioned the Constitution and the Statute of Autonomy in order to create a new constituent power, thereby breaking with the principles of unity, constitutional loyalty and

(eds) *El artículo 155 de la Constitución: XXIV Jornadas de la Asociación de Letrados del Tribunal Constitucional* Madrid: CEPC (2019).

16 *Schenck v United States* 249 US 47 (1919).

17 Article 161(2) states that the central government may contest before the Constitutional Court the provisions and resolutions adopted by the autonomous communities which shall bring about their suspension, but the Court must either ratify or lift the suspension within a period of not more than five months.

18 Casañas E 'The Constitutional Court of Spain: From system balancer to polarising centralist' in Aroney N & Kincaid J (eds) *Courts in federal countries: Federalists or unitarists?* Toronto: University of Toronto Press (2017); Roig E 'The Catalan sovereignty process and the Spanish Constitutional Court: An analysis of reciprocal impacts' (2017) 54 *Revista Catalana de Dret Públic* 24.

19 Ferreres V 'The Spanish Constitutional Court confronts Catalonia's right to decide' (2014) 10 *European Constitutional Law Review* 571.

20 See Constitutional Court judgments 42/2014 and, especially, 259/2015, legal reasoning 6.

national sovereignty.[21] Notwithstanding the seriousness of the situation, there has been consensus among scholars that, due to the anomaly of central government interference in the powers attributed to the democratically elected body of an autonomous community, its application has to be transitory and proportionate. That is to say, the limited use of the central government's extraordinary powers of intervention must be translated into autonomy-respecting measures.

Turning to intervention in local government, the substantive requirements are similar to those in the case of intervention in autonomous communities, although this is regulated not in the Constitution but in Law 7/1985 on the Basis of the Local Government. Article 61 of this law also sets out the procedural requirements that have to be followed. These matters are discussed in the following section.

BOX 11.2 ARTICLE 61 OF LAW 7/1985 (LAW ON THE BASIS OF THE LOCAL GOVERNMENT)

1. The Council of Ministers, on its own initiative and with the knowledge of the Governing Council of the Autonomous Community concerned or at its request and, in any case, with the prior favourable agreement of the Senate, may proceed, by means of a Royal Decree, to dissolve the bodies of the local governments in the event of a mismanagement seriously damaging the general interests that entails a breach of constitutional obligations.
2. Decisions or actions of the bodies of the local governments which give express or tacit coverage or support, repeatedly and seriously, to terrorism or to those who participate in its execution, glorify or justify it, and those which belittle or humiliate the victims or their families, shall in any case be considered decisions seriously damaging the general interests in accordance with the terms set out in the previous paragraph.
3. Once dissolution has been agreed, general electoral legislation shall apply, where appropriate, in relation to the calling of by-elections

---

[21] Several proceedings in the Constitutional Court and other national courts regarding the Catalan independence process have been challenged before the European Court of Human Rights (ECHR). So far, all the rulings of the Strasbourg Court have endorsed the Constitutional Court's decisions as 'proportionate and necessary', as the existing political and legal order in a democratic state cannot be amended 'by means other than those contained in the constitutional and legal rules in force'. See ECHR Decision *Costa i Rosselló and others v Spain* on the Admissibility of Application No. 29780/20, 27 February 2025.

and, in any case, the regulations governing the provisional ordinary administration of the local government.

As regards the substantive conditions for activation of the procedure by central state institutions, the main similarity between regional and local intervention is that, in both cases, what is required is serious harm to the general interest and a breach of constitutional obligations. However, there are also differences, given that article 155 refers only to disobedience of the legal order by regional political authorities with constitutional significance whereas local intervention may be triggered by causes of lesser importance, such as the 'ungovernability' of a municipality, or serious corruption.[22] Likewise, while article 155 aims to restore compliance with the Constitution and the laws, local intervention seeks rather to guarantee, for instance, the provision of essential public services and the normal functioning of local government.

A relevant, and controversial, example of the latter relates to internal security. In 2003, by means of the Organic Law for the Guarantee of Democracy in Local Councils and the Security of Councillors, a paragraph was added (article 61(2)) for the case of those municipalities, generally in the Basque Country and Navarre, with links to or sympathies towards terrorism.

4. PROCEDURES AND CONTROLS FOR CENTRAL GOVERNMENT INTERVENTION

Article 155 of the Constitution leaves the possible measures to be adopted by the central government when intervening in an autonomous community rather indeterminate, but it is detailed with regard to the procedure to be followed before the intervention is initiated. Here, article 189 of the Senate Standing Orders adds further detail. Five steps may be identified:

1) Prior requirement or complaint by the central government.
2) Response by the autonomous community.
3) Approval by the central government of proposed measures to be adopted.
4) Authorisation by the Senate.
5) Publication and entry into force of the applicable measures.

The central government's prior requirement to the president of the autonomous community is not subject to any form or deadline, but it seems logical that

---

[22] Francesch JLP, Cocciolo E & De Lorenzo JAE 'Disolución de los ayuntamientos en España y corrupción sistémica' (2007) 305 *Revista de Estudios de la Administración Local y Autonómica* 299.

it should clearly identify the misconduct being denounced, request that it be corrected and provide a deadline for replying.[23] The provision to include this previous complaint was conceived as a guarantee for the autonomous community, to favour a dialogue with the central government, aiming to prevent a sudden and unannounced application of the intervention. If the government believes that the circumstances for applying article 155 are met, it must first inform the autonomous community in detail, listing the causes that may warrant intervention and specifying the coercive measures it envisages in the event that this prior requirement is not heeded.

Article 155 makes it clear that this requirement must come from the central government as an institution, thus forcing it to be approved and legally formalised by its collective body, that is, by agreement of the Council of Ministers. It also makes it clear that the addressee of the complaint must be the president of the autonomous community. It must be notified in an official manner, with the Spanish prime minister signing the issuance of the complaint.

The autonomous community is obliged to reply so that it may be assessed whether it (the autonomous community) has complied with the request or not. This issue was problematic during its application in Catalonia in October 2017, because the deadline by which the president of the autonomous community has to respond is not regulated. The legal literature has underlined that, given the characteristics of the mechanism, this timeframe should be clearly set out in the text of the requirement. However, the fact is that, in the absence of regulation, the central government is free to set the deadline as it wishes.[24] It has also been pointed out that the deadline for replying cannot be equated with the time-limit for satisfactory implementation of the measures demanded, and that this time-limit should be reasonable and proportionate so as to make compliance possible.

Failure to reply is considered non-compliance and allows the central government to move on to the next step. However, if the request is answered ambiguously, or the autonomous community denies the factual content which is used to justify the complaint, the central government may reformulate its request and ask for additional responses.[25] The assessment of the response by the president of the autonomous community is the responsibility of the central government, which will have to decide whether or not to continue with the application of article 155.

---

[23] Lafuente Balle (2018).

[24] Calafell V 'La compulsión o coerción estatal (Estudio del artículo 155 de la Constitución Española)' (2000) 48(49) *Revista de Derecho Político* 99–146; Vírgala E 'La coacción estatal del artículo 155 de la Constitución' (2005) 73 *Revista Española de Derecho Constitucional* 55.

[25] Calafell (2000).

If the autonomous community changes its attitude after receiving the complaint, then the procedure may be terminated. This happened in 1989, which (prior to the independence process in Catalonia) was the only point in time that the central government had considered activating article 155. On that occasion, the Spanish prime minister, Felipe González, sent a complaint to the Canary Islands government, which was refusing the dismantling of tariffs managed by the autonomous community that had to be applied due to Spain's entry into the European Economic Community (which was therefore a serious breach of the 1985 Treaty of Accession). The president of the Canary Islands, Lorenzo Olarte, sent a text in response in which he did not recognise the non-compliance and announced that he would defend the autonomy of the region (which has its own economic and fiscal regime) in national and international courts. The Council of Ministers confined itself to approving a second request to the Canary Islands government, urging it again to comply with the law; a few days later, the Secretary of State for Finance (then Josep Borrell) travelled to the islands, where he reached an agreement that deactivated the process.

This precedent shows that the procedure can be modulated and even interrupted. It is up to the discretion of the central government to assess the extent to which the autonomous community's response to the complaint is satisfactory, before moving forward. Even in the event that the request has not been heeded by the region, the central government is not obliged to ask the Senate for authorisation to adopt measures of intervention if it thinks or foresees that the conflict could be resolved by a less drastic means. This is why article 155 uses the formula 'may take the measures' instead of 'shall take': it is an enabling provision rather an obligatory one.

In any case, if it is decided to go ahead after an unsatisfactory response from the autonomous community, the third step in the procedure is for the central government to approve the measures to be adopted. To this end, it meets again in the Council of Ministers and adopts another formal agreement where, after underlining that the complaint has been lodged and ignored by the autonomous community, it approves the intervention measures to be applied. There must be congruence between the content of the central government's first complaint (which identified the conduct likely to harm the general interest) and the scope of the instrument of coercion.[26]

The central government's agreement is then sent to the Senate for approval. This phase of the procedure is regulated in detail by article 189 of the Senate's Standing Orders (see Box 11.3) and is a decisive moment, since it is

---

26 Satrústegui M 'Un instrumento para la defensa del Estado: el artículo 155 de la Constitución'' in Alfonso LJP, Fernández JV, De la Quadra-Salcedo T, et al. (eds) *Los retos del Estado y la Administración en el siglo XXI* Valencia: Tirant lo Blanch (2017).

a constitutional prerequisite for the government to be able to apply the intervention at all. The Senate's role is important in both a positive and a negative sense. In the negative sense, the Senate is the only body that could prevent the central government from intervening in an autonomous community without just cause or a proper basis; in the positive sense, when the Senate grants its approval, it also acquires political responsibility for the entire process.

Bearing in mind that Spanish bicameralism is highly asymmetrical (the Congress is immensely more powerful than the Senate), it is interesting to note that article 155 entails the only parliamentary procedure in which the Senate has a superior and exclusive competence. In this sense, it is doubtful if the Senate's participation may be considered a safeguard for the autonomous communities, given that the Spanish upper house is not so much an effective body of territorial representation of subnational units as it is a chamber where the two large national parties (and especially the PP) have a greater ability to impose decisions than in Congress.

BOX 11.3 ARTICLE 189 OF THE STANDING ORDERS OF THE SENATE

1. If the Government, in the cases referred to in Article 155.1 of the Constitution, requires the Senate's approval for the adoption of the measures referred therein, it shall submit to the President of the House a letter indicating the content and scope of the proposed measures, as well as the justification that the relevant complaint has been lodged with the President of the Autonomous Community and that the latter has failed to comply with it.
2. The Bureau of the Senate shall refer this letter and the supporting documentation to the General Committee on Autonomous Communities, or shall create a joint Committee [made up of members of the two chambers: Congress and Senate].
3. The Committee [shall request] the President of the Autonomous Community to submit, within a fixed term, any background information, data and allegations it may consider relevant and to designate, if it deems it appropriate, the person who will represent it for these purposes.
4. The Committee shall formulate a reasoned proposal on whether it is advisable or not to grant the approval requested by the Government, with the conditions or the modifications which, where appropriate, should be made to the envisaged measures.

5. The Plenary of the House shall debate this proposal, with two turns pro and two turns against, of twenty minutes each, and speeches, lasting also twenty minutes, to be made by the Spokespersons of the Parliamentary Groups who wish to take the floor. Upon conclusion of the debate, the proposal presented shall be put to the vote. The approval of the resolution shall require the favourable vote by the absolute majority of the Senators.

When the Senate receives the request from the central government, the parliamentary process begins. The Senate's deliberation takes place first in committee and thereafter in a plenary session. The committee has to draw up a reasoned proposal as to whether the approval requested by the Council of Ministers is appropriate, as well as indicate any conditions or modifications to the planned measures which it considers necessary. This proposal is discussed in the plenary and the final resolution has to be approved by an absolute majority.

The president of the autonomous community concerned may make written submissions to the committee. The Standing Orders of the Senate suggest that it should not be the president of the autonomous community who directly intervenes in the process,[27] as it is stated that the president may designate a person to represent him or her. Be that as it may, in 2017 the Senate offered the president of the Catalan government, Carles Puigdemont, the opportunity to speak before the plenary, an opportunity he declined.

The Senate's resolution is a crucial step in launching the procedure and must undergo two stages of reasoning. First, the Senate must make a reasoned assessment of whether it is appropriate to apply article 155. Next, it must approve, reject or modify the measures proposed by the central government, verifying the congruence of the previous actions – the first complaint lodged with the president of the autonomous community and the subsequent agreement by the Council of Ministers – with the measures of intervention to be carried out. The resolution must also be adequately reasoned, cannot entail the suspension of autonomy and should comprise specific measures deemed necessary to restore both the constitutional order as well as self-government. In any case, the Senate is a political institution within the Spanish democratic system (where the parties are highly disciplined) and its decisions are adopted in accordance with the political majorities of the day.

The Senate's approval of the use of article 155 is a legally binding regulatory measure nature with legal force, and therefore it must also be published in the

27 Vírgala (2005).

Official State Gazette so as to enter into force. With this final step for triggering the intervention, it is then up to the central government to decide whether to make use of the Senate's authorisation, noting that the scope of its actions has to be aligned with the framework approved by the upper house. From that point on, the intervention itself may begin.

Given the characteristics of the Spanish Senate, its *ex ante* control of the intervention is not effective; much more relevant, however, is the *ex post* control exercised by the Constitutional Court.[28] Unlike the upper chamber, the Court does not follow a political logic,[29] and, moreover, it has the authority to impose limits on the coercion applied by the central government.[30] As such, it is useful to analyse its case law (namely judgments 89 and 90/2019). This is undertaken in the following section, which examines how the powers of intervention have been applied in practice.

As far as intervention in local governments is concerned, the procedure and controls are similar, albeit not identical. The most important similarities between article 155 and article 61 of the Law on Local Government are threefold: (i) it is only the central government that may use the powers of intervention, and thus the government of an autonomous community cannot do so against a local government in its region; (ii) prior approval by the Senate is necessary;[31] and (iii) there is *ex post* control by the Constitutional Court.

However, there are also three differences: (i) although the Council of Ministers is the only body that can decide to launch the intervention, the government council of the autonomous community where the municipality is located must be informed and can request the initiation of the procedure; (ii) authorisation is required not only from the Senate but also the National Commission of Local Administration (a permanent joint committee composed of top officials of the central government and representatives of local

---

28 See Helmich M 'Spain, Catalonia, and the supposed authority of the judiciary: On the self-constitutive moment in adjudication' (2020) 2 *Jus Cogens* 259–79 for a more theoretical examination of its role.

29 Nevertheless, there is a growing controversy over the politicisation of the judges of the Constitutional Court and the erosion of division of powers in the Spanish political system. See Casañas (2017); Arzoz X 'Functioning and independence of the Constitutional Court of Spain: Guarantees and challenges' (2019) 79 *Rechtspolitisches Forum*.

30 López-Laborda J, Rodrigo F & Sanz-Arcega E 'Is the Spanish Constitutional Court of the central government against the autonomous communities?' (2018) 29 *Constitutional Political Economy* 317.

31 The General Committee of the Autonomous Communities is called upon to report (article 56, letter 'n' of the Standing Orders of the Senate).

authorities); and (iii) the intervention is carried out by royal decree, which does not have the status of law.

Once the dissolution of the local council has been agreed to, the general electoral legislation is applicable, usually entailing the call for early elections.

5. HOW POWERS HAVE BEEN USED IN PRACTICE

Until the emergence of the Catalan conflict in 2012, article 155 of the Constitution was of interest only to academics. As mentioned, the article 155 procedure had been employed only once before, in 1989 against the government of the Canary Islands, and even then went no further than the initial complaint. Later, in 2002, the possibility of intervention in the Basque Country arose when the president of the regional government, Juan José Ibarretxe, made a bold proposal to reform the Statute of Autonomy, one which included the right to self-determination and envisaged a free association with Spain on an equal footing. Nevertheless, the so-called Ibarretxe Plan, which had been approved by the Basque Parliament in 2003, was debated in the Spanish Parliament under conditions of full institutional normality, before eventually being rejected in 2005 and thus raising no need for further action by the central government.

But the shift from theory to practice duly came, becoming especially marked from 2015 onwards when the Catalan government announced a self-determination referendum outside of the procedures established in the Constitution, the Statute of Autonomy of Catalonia and electoral legislation. In the autumn of 2017 the intervention process was triggered, as the Catalan regional government ignored the Constitutional Court's explicit order to suspend the secession vote (held on 1 October and characterised by low turnout, no guarantees of electoral integrity, and pressure by the national police).

As a result, the president of the Catalan government proclaimed – and then suspended – an independent republic in an ambiguous political declaration made in the Catalan regional parliament. Next, the central government, under Prime Minister Mariano Rajoy, initiated the article 155 procedure via a formal request asking President Puigdemont to clarify within five days whether or not he had made a unilateral declaration of independence. Puigdemont refused on two occasions to give a clear response to the request, and thus the Council of Ministers decided on the measures that it would propose for Senate approval.

Here, the central government emphasised that 'Catalonia's autonomy was not being suspended' – it was rather that 'the individuals who had placed the region outside the law were being dismissed', with their functions to be transferred to supervisory authorities appointed ad hoc. Moreover, the power to dissolve the Catalan parliament would be transferred to the Spanish prime minister, who would call for early elections. The regional administration, including the Catalan police force, would continue operating, albeit under direct rule from Madrid. Any regional acts or resolutions that contradicted such measures would be considered null and void, and disciplinary sanctions would be imposed on officials or employees who failed to comply. The interventionary measures would remain in force until a new Catalan regional government could be elected in regional parliamentary elections and take office.

The Senate authorised the measures after three days (in committee and in the plenary), with the Catalan government making written submissions in which it accused the central government of exceeding the limits of article 155. In a Senate vote on 27 October 2017 to approve the intervention, the major centre-right and centre-left parties (the PP and Spanish Socialist Workers' Party, or PSOE), as well as several small regionalist parties, voted in favour, while a left-wing group (Unidos Podemos) and all Catalan and Basque nationalists voted against.

At the same time as the Senate authorised the measures, the Catalan parliament held a session in which it approved a 'unilateral declaration of independence to establish a Republic as an independent state'. The declaration passed with 70 votes in favour out of 135 members. Following the Senate's resolution, Prime Minister Mariano Rajoy convened an extraordinary meeting of the

Table 11.1 *Resolution of the Senate to approve the activation of article 155 in Catalonia (27 October 2017)*

Vote	Party	Number
In favour	PP PSOE/PSC Ciudadanos UPN (Navarra regionalists) Foro (Asturias regionalists) Coalición Canaria	214 senators
Against	Unidos Podemos ERC (left-wing Catalan nationalists) PDeCAT (centre-right Catalan nationalists) PNV (centre-right Basque nationalists) EH Bildu (left-wing Basque nationalists) Compromís (Valencia nationalists)	47 senators
Abstention/absents	Nueva Canarias Some PSOE/PSC senators	4 senators

Council of Ministers that approved five royal decrees ordering, inter alia, the dismissal of the members of the regional government, the transfer of political leadership in the autonomous community to the Spanish deputy prime minister, the abolition of certain offices, the dissolution of the regional parliament and the holding of new regional elections within 54 days.

The activation of article 155 was challenged before the Constitutional Court by 50 deputies of Congress (all members of Unidos Podemos) and the Catalan parliament. As a result, there is now constitutional case law in Spain clarifying the meaning, legal nature and limits of the intervention measures adopted, as set out in judgments 89 and 90/2019 of the Constitutional Court[32] – the latter also provide a framework for use in any future applications of article 155.

The Court resolved (on the same day) the two appeals of unconstitutionality which had been brought against the resolution of the Senate's plenary session of 27 October 2017 authorising the intervention (its attendant measures had legal force and thus could be controlled by the Court). Both judgments distinguish between procedural and substantive issues, and the latter synthesises and reiterates the doctrine established in the former.

The appeals were dismissed almost in their entirety. The Court only partially accepted the appellants' allegations on a secondary issue: the central government's intention that any administrative act or rule adopted by the Catalan administration which did not have the prior authorisation of the supervisory authorities appointed by Madrid would not enter into force and have no legal effect. The Court declared as unconstitutional the paragraph of the resolution adopted by the Senate establishing such excessive control, on the grounds that it was contrary to the need to ensure legal certainty.

The judgments are particularly significant because they mark the first time that the Constitutional Court has had the opportunity to pronounce directly on the meaning and scope of article 155. The plenary of the Constitutional Court (that is to say, its 12 judges) unanimously affirmed that the Constitution recognises the coercive power of central institutions over the autonomous communities, a power which in extraordinary circumstances may limit their autonomy, yet it also recognised that autonomy is an authentic right and structural principle of the state: as such, the central government is not authorised to suppress or suspend a regional self-government indefinitely.[33] For this reason, article

---

[32] Both judgments of the Constitutional Court on 2 July 2019 were published in the Official State Gazette on 12 August 2019. They are available at the following locations: (1) 89/2019: https://www.boe.es/boe/dias/2019/08/12/pdfs/BOE-A-2019-11901.pdf; (2) 90/2019: https://www.boe.es/boe/dias/2019/08/12/pdfs/BOE-A-2019-11902.pdf (accessed 1 March 2025).

[33] Judgment 89/2019, Legal Ground 4, para (b).

155 must be understood as an exceptional, subsidiary remedy, and as a means of last resort.

Moreover, according to the Court, the sole causes that could justify the activation of the intervention are serious breaches of the constitutional order, and then only provided that other possible solutions to restore normal institutional functioning have been ineffective. The Court also insisted on the need for the measures to be adopted in a specified timeframe, one deemed necessary for re-establishing the legal order, rather than for an extended period.[34]

With regard to procedural issues, the Court maintained that all the conditions enabling the exercise of intervention were met and that the central government's request to the president of Catalonia was correctly formulated, as it identified which actions and institutions had violated Spain's territorial and constitutional unity. The Court also concluded that Puigdemont had not complied with the terms of the complaint in either of his replies. It stressed too that in his replies, the Catalan president neither denied the existence of the conditions enabling the application of article 155, nor affirmed his intention to comply with the request. In regard to the objection raised in the appeals about an alleged lack of coherence between the measures in the complaint and those approved by the Senate, the Court said that the final measures taken should not be confused with the actions contained in the complaint, which had aimed to avoid the use of coercion and hinged on the response of the president of the autonomous community.

Furthermore, the judgment dwelt on the Senate's role in approving the measures which the central government had proposed.[35] The Court found no formal defects in this regard, since the upper chamber was able to so decide in accordance with its Standing Orders; indeed, in the course of this it provided all the necessary guarantees and even offered the Catalan president the opportunity to speak to the plenary in person rather than through representatives (as was finally done, by way of two Catalan senators representing the autonomous community).

The most controversial parts of the judgments dealt not with procedural matters but the substantive measures taken and instructions given in application of article 155.[36] As noted, article 155 merely states that the measures taken must be those necessary to restore compliance with legal obligations and secure protection of the general interest. For this reason, the limits set by the Court are crucial for the future. The Court rejected the appellants' arguments,

---

[34] Judgment 89/2019, Legal Ground 4, para (d); Judgment 90/2019, paras (e) and (g).

[35] Judgment 89/2019, Legal Ground; Judgment 90/2019, Legal Ground 5.

[36] Judgment 89/2019, legal grounds 11–16; Judgment 90/2019, legal grounds 6–7.

which were based mainly on comparative law and the constituent debates. It stressed that neither the Constitution nor the Senate's Standing Orders specify the measures that may be applied, thus leaving a wide margin in regard to the most suitable measures to apply. The Court concluded that 'giving instructions' is a possibility contained in paragraph 2 of article 155 but is not a limit.[37] It was precisely this reasoning that enabled it to state that all of the measures were constitutional.

Nevertheless, the Court indicated that the measures could not be applied in a discretionary manner to any body or authority of the autonomous community, but only against those whose actions, in the opinion of the central government and the Senate, were directly related to the situation that had led to the intervention, namely the regional government and parliament. Moreover, under no circumstances would it be permissible to suppress regional parliamentary activity under the aforementioned constitutional provision.

Among the measures adopted, some were aimed at ensuring that the Catalan administration acted under the directives of central government officials: to this end, for example, the administration's actions were subjected to a system of prior notification or authorisation. Other measures related to public order and security; economic, financial, budgetary and tax management; and telecommunications and media communications.

Much more contested was the dismissal of the president of Catalonia and the rest of the governing council; these were replaced by the central government and the supervisory authorities that were created, or the attribution to the Spanish prime minister of the power to dissolve the regional Parliament and call new elections within a maximum period of six months (a competence that belongs to the President of the autonomous community).

Scholars have argued that while article 155 allows the central government to issue instructions, it does not cover the dissolution of the political organs of the autonomous communities.[38] However, in this instance the Court considered the dissolution 'absolutely necessary and proportionate' for the purposes of article 155.[39] This was in view of the fact that there was a clear desire by the regional government to place itself outside the Constitution and the Statute of Autonomy in order to create an independent state; as such, the dismissal was necessary and appropriate to the aim of re-establishing legality. It was not seen as excessive because it was the central government's response to a serious institutional crisis and was aimed at preventing the break-up of the

---

[37] Legal Ground 10.

[38] Albertí (2019).

[39] Judgment 89/2019, Legal Ground 12; Judgment 90/2019, Legal Ground 7, section (a).

state. Moreover, it was not an indefinite suspension or a permanent substitution because a maximum period of six months had been set.

The Constitutional Court also dealt with objections to certain measures directed at the Parliament of Catalonia that may have affected the democratic nature of the autonomous community and the right to political participation. In this regard, the Court cited the rulings and orders that were ignored by the Catalan parliament, maintaining that the regional legislature shared responsibility for the events that had led to the activation of article 155.

In addition, the Court pointed out that, when the central government came to exercise the functions of the executive of the autonomous community, the supervisory officials who were appointed by Madrid could not act as accountable authorities before the Parliament of Catalonia. For this same reason, the actions of the central government in this context could not be subject to political control by the regional parliament because the necessary relationship of trust between the two institutions would not be established, given that this was a provisional situation that arose as a result of coercive action.

The Court also endeavoured to demonstrate that the right to political participation had not been violated, since as a legally established right it could not protect the infringer of the legal system. It emphasised that

> the provision for an early dissolution of the Catalan Parliament, with a simultaneous call for elections, is objectively aimed at the need to set up a new regional assembly as soon as possible to put an end to the intervention.[40]

According to Spanish electoral law, the period from the call for elections to the day of voting lasts for 54 days.

Finally, the Court ruled that the assumption of command of the regional police by members of the national security forces did not constitute a violation of the distribution of powers between the centre and the autonomous communities, given that article 155 allows for the limitation of regional powers to the extent that the central government, with the approval of the Senate, considers it necessary.

In short, all the measures of the intervention passed the constitutionality check, except for the rule that deprived validity from regional administrative acts adopted without the authorisation of the central government or considered contrary to the measures of the intervention. This was in reference to the second paragraph of section E.3 of the Agreement of the Council of Ministers of 21 October 2017, which was declared unconstitutional and thus null and void.

In May 2018, following the early regional parliamentary elections on 21 December 2017, a new President of Catalonia was appointed from the same

---

[40] Legal Ground 13.

nationalist party as Carles Puigdemont. A few days later, coinciding with Pedro Sánchez's taking office as Spain's new Prime Minister, article 155 was lifted and regional autonomy restored.

Although article 155 has been applied only once so far, this during the Catalan independence crisis, it cannot be denied that the breach of the taboo surrounding its use may have larger, systemic implications for the Spanish territorial model. Indeed, since 2018 there have been at least two occasions when speculation has arisen about using it again: first, in 2020, following a plan by the government of Murcia to adopt a so-called parental pin in regional schools (this refers to a system in which parental permission is required before exposing children to materials on civic or sexual morals); and second, following the announcement of anti-abortion measures by the government of Castilla y León.

In both cases, it was the left-wing junior coalition member of the central government (Unidos Podemos and its heir, Sumar) which perceived a threat and sought to curb the policies of regional governments in which the right-wing populist party Vox had a stake. The socialist party, the majority partner in the central government, ruled against activating the intervention.

In the case of central government intervention in local governments, the relevant powers have likewise been used only once before. This was in April 2006, when the Council of Ministers responded to a request by the governing body of the autonomous community of Andalusia and – with the unanimous support of the Senate and National Commission of Local Administration – dissolved Marbella Local Council.

The central government decided to act in view of the extremely serious charges of corruption made against members of the local government and, in addition, the paralysis of the municipality and its services. In the case of Marbella, early elections were not called because, in terms of article 183 of Spanish Electoral Law 5/1985, this may be done only if the new local council were to have a term of office of more than one year before the next municipal elections (elections which, in Spain, take place on the same day every four years). This was not the case, and hence an interim managing committee was appointed until the next regular nationwide local elections were to be held.

To date, this is the only case in which a local government has been dissolved in Spain. Although it was uncontroversial and supported by both the citizens of the municipality and Spanish society in general, its implementation sparked debate as to whether it may have contradicted the principle of local autonomy guaranteed in article 137 of the Constitution. The Constitutional Court indirectly addressed the issue in Judgment 154/2015 of 9 July 2015, where it declared a provision of the 2002 Andalusian Urban Planning Law as unconstitutional. The latter granted the regional government the power to strip municipalities of their urban planning authority in cases of corruption (a measure applied in Marbella between 2006 and 2007 while the local council had been dissolved by the central government).

Marbella was a ground-breaking case that set a precedent for future dissolutions in Spain; as with article 155 and Catalonia, the mere existence of such precedent may have a chilling effect on the rest of the municipalities, which highlights the need to balance intervention with the protection of local autonomy. With this in mind, some scholars propose legal reforms that establish clearer procedures and more proportional measures.[41]

After Marbella, and as with Catalonia, there have also been further demands for dissolution. In 2007, the Popular Party urged the then socialist government to apply the intervention procedure in local councils governed by Basque Nationalist Action, a movement which it regarded as the heir of Batasuna, a party outlawed as a 'political complement to [the] terrorism' of Euskadi Ta Askatasuna (ETA). Another case took place in Santa Fe, Granada, in 2012, where the mayor, struggling with his lack of majority in the local council, himself issued a request to the Senate and Council of Ministers for the dissolution of the local government on the grounds of a year-long situation of 'ungovernability'. However, none of these requests were entertained, demonstrating that Spanish law and practice is cautious when it comes to dissolving democratically elected bodies.

6. CONCLUSION

The territorial governance of Spain – based on a variant of federalism – includes the possibility of central intervention in regional and local authorities in cases where the latter fail to fulfil their constitutional and legal obligations or act in a way that seriously harms the general interest. The mechanism established by article 155 of the 1978 Constitution, inspired by Germany's federal coercion model, was later extended to local governments by a 1985 law. During the five decades of contemporary democratic experience, intervention has occurred only twice: in Marbella (2006–2007) and Catalonia (2017–2018). The fact that there are at least two cases demonstrates that the instrument might be necessary; the fact that there are nonetheless only two such cases shows that intervention has been limited to extreme situations.

Thanks to these events and how political actors and institutions behaved during them, the nature of such interventions is now better understood. Constitutional Court judgments 89/2019 and 90/2019 on Catalonia (and, to

41 Calonge A & Orduña E *La disolución de los ayuntamientos: el caso singular de Marbella* Valencia: Tirant lo Blanch (2013); Francesch, Cocciolo & De Lorenzo (2007).

some extent, Judgment 154/2015 on Marbella) provide a model for their application in regard to (i) the dismissal of political leaders in the autonomous government concerned; (ii) the appointment of temporary officials from Madrid; (iii) the dissolution of the regional parliament (or the plenary of the local council); and (iv) holding elections promptly to restore normality. During the short period in which the intervention takes place, self-government is politically constrained, but the legal distribution of powers remains unchanged.

In theory, the main institutional actor is the Senate, which approves, calibrates and oversees the intervention. However, aside from its formal role, its political role is secondary given the characteristics of Spain's upper house. The Senate has almost no legislative or government oversight powers in other matters, and its composition does not reflect territorial decentralisation but rather the same parties which, via a highly majoritarian electoral system, are represented in the Congress. In reality, then, political leadership during the process falls, first and foremost, to the central government, as well as to the main opposition party, which supported the government's initiatives in both the Marbella and Catalonia cases. If such consensus did not exist between the two major parties, it would be doubtful if an intervention could be staged.

After the events of 2006 and 2017 (and in line with the Constitutional Court's case law), the central institutions, autonomous communities and municipalities now understand that the intervention model derived from article 155 is constitutional within certain strict limits and that, if necessary, it could be repeated. It is clear that both precedents will shape the actions of future central, regional and local governments in potential scenarios of constitutional conflict, and there is no clear line defining when such a situation may be considered extreme or intractable.

Nonetheless, a positive conclusion can be drawn about the relative solidity of Spain's federative territorial model. It is true that coercive powers may be a sword of Damocles hanging over subnational governments as potential targets of future intervention, thereby already constraining their effective autonomy. However, despite moments of temptation, the use of these powers has not been repeated. Twenty years after the Marbella intervention, and almost ten after the Catalan one, the consensus among parties and scholars remains that the dissolution of a democratically elected body should be regarded as a measure of last resort employed only under extreme circumstances. That said, it seems advisable that some of the limits introduced by the Constitutional Court should be incorporated in a reform of the current legal framework (particularly concerning the local level).

The conclusion is less clear when one looks at how both cases affected the underlying situations that triggered the intervention. In Marbella, there was indeed a change in the local political elite, and there have been no big scandals since then. However, the truth is that urban corruption in local governments across Spain merely decreased at the end of the real estate boom in 2008 but is still otherwise a widespread problem.[42] In Catalonia the activation of article 155 initially led to a slight intensification of support for secession (to about a half of Catalan society), but shortly afterwards, and possibly due to the PSOE's rise to power, first, at the national level, and later in Catalonia itself, the trend shifted. Catalan nationalism remains strong (securing about 43 per cent of the vote in the 2024 regional elections), though a significant portion of its support base has abandoned the unilateral approach – according to opinion polls by the Catalan government itself, support for breaking up Spain has dropped to 30 per cent of citizens.[43] At any rate, it is clear that federal coercion and the suspension of autonomy cannot, in themselves, be the remedy for corruption or separatism.

BIBLIOGRAPHY

Books

Calonge A & Orduña E *La disolución de los ayuntamientos: el caso singular de Marbella* Valencia: Tirant lo Blanch (2013)
Hooghe L, Mark G, Schakel AH, et al. *Measuring regional authority: A postfunctionalist theory of governance (vol. 1)* Oxford: Oxford University Press (2016)

Chapters in Books

Bauer H 'Art. 37 GG' in Dreier C (ed) *Grundgesetz-Kommentar (vol. 3)* Tübingen: Mohr Siebeck (2015)
Casañas E 'The Constitutional Court of Spain: From system balancer to polarising centralist' in Aroney N & Kincaid J (eds) *Courts in federal countries: Federalists or unitarists?* Toronto: University of Toronto Press (2017)
Colino C 'Decentralisation in Spain: Federal evolution and performance of the Estado Autonómico' in Muro D & Lago I (eds) *The Oxford handbook of Spanish politics* Oxford: Oxford University Press (2020)
García Roca J 'Diez tesis sobre la intervención extraordinaria del Estado en las Comunidades Autónomas (artículo 155 CE) tras su aplicación en Cataluña' in Centro de Estudios Políticos y Constitucionales: Tribunal Constitucional (España) (eds) *El artículo 155 de la Constitución: XXIV Jornadas de la Asociación de Letrados del Tribunal Constitucional* Madrid: CEPC (2019)

---

[42] Jiménez F, Villoria M, & Garcia Quesada M 'Badly designed institutions, informal rules and perverse incentives: Local government corruption in Spain' (2012) 10(4) *Lex localis: Journal of Local Self Government* 363.

[43] Centre d'Estudis d'Opinió (CEO) *Baròmetre d'Opinió Política 3/2024* Barcelona: Generalitat de Catalunya (2024) available at https://upceo.ceo.gencat.cat/wsceop/9528/Dossier%20de%20premsa_1112.pdf (accessed 1 March 2025).

López-Basaguren A 'Claims for secession in Catalonia. Rule of law, democratic principle and federal alternative' in López-Basaguren A & San-Epifanio LE (eds) *Claims for secession and federalism* Cham: Springer (2019)
Orfanel GG 'La prehistoria española del artículo 155 de la Constitución de 1978' in Sánchez AJ, López Guerra JL, García Ruiz JL, et al. (eds) *Constitución y desarrollo político: Estudios en homenaje a Jorge de Esteban* Valencia: Tirant lo Blanc (2013)
Satrústegui M 'Un instrumento para la defensa del Estado: el artículo 155 de la Constitución' in Alfonso LJP, Fernández JV, De la Quadra-Salcedo T, et al. (eds) *Los retos del Estado y la Administración en el siglo XXI* Valencia: Tirant lo Blanch (2017)

Journal Articles

Albertí E 'Constitutional questions on the application of article 155 SC to the Catalan conflict' (2019) 9 *Catalan Social Sciences Review* 41–64
Arzoz X 'Functioning and independence of the Constitutional Court of Spain: Guarantees and challenges' (2019) 79 *Rechtspolitisches Forum*
Calafell V 'La compulsión o coerción estatal (Estudio del artículo 155 de la Constitución Española)' (2000) 48(49) *Revista de Derecho Político* 99–146
Dardanelli P 'Conceptualising, measuring, and mapping state structures – with an application to Western Europe, 1950–2015' (2019) 49 *Publius* 271–98
Ferreres V 'The Spanish Constitutional Court confronts Catalonia's right to decide' (2014) 10 *European Constitutional Law Review* 571–90
Francesch JLP, Cocciolo E & De Lorenzo JAE 'Disolución de los ayuntamientos en España y corrupción sistémica' (2007) 305 *Revista de Estudios de la Administración Local y Autonómica* 299–324
Garcés J 'Consideraciones sobre el artículo 155 de la CE como instrumento de coerción estatal' (2019) 18 *Cuadernos Manuel Giménez Abad* 42–66
Harguindeguy J-B, Rodríguez GS & Díazet JC 'Between justice and politics: The role of the Spanish Constitutional Court in the State of Autonomies' (2018) 8 *Territory, Politics, Governance* 222–240
Helmich M 'Spain, Catalonia, and the supposed authority of the judiciary: On the self-constitutive moment in adjudication' (2020) 2 *Jus Cogens* 259–79
Jiménez F 'Building boom and political corruption in Spain' (2009) 14(3) *South European Society & Politics* 255–72
Jiménez F, Villoria M & Garcia Quesada M 'Badly designed institutions, informal rules and perverse incentives: Local government corruption in Spain' (2012) 10(4) *Lex localis: Journal of Local Self Government* 363–81
Lafuente Balle JM 'El artículo 155 de la Constitución española (El acuerdo del Senado)' (2018) 103 *Revista de Derecho Político* 79–85
López-Laborda J, Rodrigo F & Sanz-Arcega E 'Is the Spanish Constitutional Court of the central government against the autonomous communities?' (2018) 29 *Constitutional Political Economy* 317–37
Roig E 'The Catalan sovereignty process and the Spanish Constitutional Court: An analysis of reciprocal impacts' (2017) 54 *Revista Catalana de Dret Públic* 24–61
Sala G 'Federalism without adjectives in Spain' (2014) 44 *Publius* 109–34
Vírgala E 'La coacción estatal del artículo 155 de la Constitución' (2005) 73 *Revista Española de Derecho Constitucional* 55–109

Case Law

ECHR Decision *Costa i Rosselló and others v Spain* on the Admissibility of Application No. 29780/20, 27 February 2025
Constitutional Court of Spain Judgment 42/2014
Constitutional Court of Spain Judgment 154/2015
Constitutional Court of Spain Judgment 259/2015
Constitutional Court of Spain Judgment 89/2019
Constitutional Court of Spain Judgment 90/2019
Schenck v United States 249 US 47 (1919)

Legislation

Basic Law for the Federal Republic of Germany, 1949
Constitution, 1978
Law for the Guarantee of Democracy in Local Councils and the Security of Councillors (Ley Orgánica 1/2003)
Law on the Basis of the Local Government (Ley 7/1985)
Law on the Electoral Regime (Ley Orgánica 5/1985)
Law on Urban Planning of Andalusia, 2002
Standing Orders of the Parliament of Catalonia, 2005
Standing Orders of the Senate, 1994
Statute of Autonomy of the Basque Country, 1979
Statute of Autonomy of Catalonia, 1932
Statute of Autonomy of Catalonia, 1979
Statute of Autonomy of Catalonia, 2006

Reports/Internet Sources

'The independence conflict in Catalonia' (9 October 2019) Real Instituto Elcano available at https://www.realinstitutoelcano.org/en/work-document/the-independence-conflict-in-catalonia/
Centre d'Estudis d'Opinió (CEO) *Baròmetre d'Opinió Política 3/2024* Barcelona: Generalitat de Catalunya (2024) available at https://upceo.ceo.gencat.cat/wsceop/9528/Dossier%20de%20premsa_1112.pdf (accessed 1 March 2025)
Council of Europe European Committee on Local and Regional Democracy (CDLR) 'Interim dissolution of the local/regional councils: Results of RRS No 10 LR-IC (2009) 12 Bil.' (6 October 2009) available at https://open.overheid.nl/documenten/ronl-archief-bf973662-6eea-4011-a0cb-7ce85a49f940/pdf (accessed 1 March 2025)

12. The balance between autonomy and intervention: lessons from near and far

Nico Steytler

1. INTRODUCTION

The problematics of intervention have been a perennial interest of mine for over a quarter of a century. As an academic, I have observed and analysed the law and practice of intervention; as a consultant, I have dispensed advice at home and abroad in constitutional reform processes in various contexts. My 'intervention journey', usually part of a broader trip destined towards multilevel government, commenced in a small town in South Africa in 1999 and then took me abroad – first to Kenya, next across the Red Sea to Yemen, and, ultimately, to the other end of the world, the Solomon Islands in the South Pacific – before returning me home to the Western Cape, hopefully as a wiser person.

In what follows, I use the term 'intervention' to mean the process in which a superior level of government exercises the power to enter the domain of an inferior level, either by directing it to perform specified tasks which it had omitted to do, or by performing those tasks on its behalf. An extreme expression of intervention is the dismissal of a democratically elected legislature or executive.

While elements of hierarchy may be found in all federal constitutions, in mature federations intervention is in practice a rare occurrence, and then mostly at local level. In newly disaggregated federations, the quest for autonomy is loudly asserted but it is then that the need for intervention is the most acute, lest the federal project fail in practice. Particularly in post-conflict countries, granting autonomy to belligerent territorially based groups is key to peace, but the very novelty of the new subnational institutions renders them vulnerable to mismanagement and, ultimately, to failure. In all cases, the danger that intervention powers will be abused is ever-present.

This necessitates an effort to strike a balance between autonomy and intervention, and here two issues come to the fore. How and to what extent can a 'superior' government protect the residents from a subnational government's abuse of its governance power? At the same time, how can the 'superior' government be prevented from abusing its intervention powers? The underlying assumption is that, in a federal context, the federal government is equipped to prevent subnational state failure.

In reflecting on my experience of supervision in federal or quasi-federal systems (or envisaged federal systems), two interlinked questions arise. First, what have I learned about how these two issues above have been addressed in practice? Second, how has my own understanding of what an appropriate balance is developed over the past 25 years?[1] With regard to the latter question, the focus is not on whether my engagements have made any difference, but on how my approach and thoughts may have evolved over time.

2. SOUTH AFRICA

I enthusiastically supported the balance struck in South Africa's 1996 Constitution. The supervisory provisions were, after all, part and parcel of 'the best constitution' in our not-so-modest view in the 1990s. The justification for the intervention in the constitutional space of an 'inferior' order of government was twofold: protecting residents from provincial and local service delivery failures, and preventing these subnational governments from harming the key interests of other 'superior' orders of government.[2] However, interventions excluded any interventions that would touch the democratic basis of provincial and local governments: no dismissals of democratically elected bodies were permitted initially.

As a check and balance against overzealous provincial and national governments, political protection was afforded by the National Council of Provinces (NCOP), the second chamber of parliament – it was composed of provincial delegations that could veto a national or provincial intervention in a province or a municipality, respectively. The NCOP institutionalised a form of peer review: the collective of provinces would pronounce on whether the national government could intervene in one of them, and, in the case of municipalities,

[1] I stumbled upon the genre of 'autoethnography', the elements of which 'combine a narrative of the author's own personal experiences ("auto") with artefacts, such as published work, that encourage reflections on those experiences through "space, time and circumstance" in the context of "cultural norms and expectations" (the "ethno")'. The 'graphy' is then the account of the interaction between the 'auto' and the 'ethno'. See Dixon B 'Colonial confessions: An autoethnography of writing criminology in the New South Africa' (2024) 20 *The British Journal of Criminology* 1–17 at 2.

[2] Sections 100 and 139(1)(b), Constitution of South Africa, 1996.

on whether one of them acted appropriately in invading the constitutional space of a municipality.

It was not long before provincial interventions in municipalities began to occur. In 1999, Jaap de Visser[3] and I travelled along a lonely road between large tracts of maize crops to a town in the Free State Province called Tweeling. Our mission: to investigate the first intervention in a municipality in that province in terms of section 139 of the new 1996 Constitution.[4]

Tweeling, the Afrikaans word for 'twins', was a newly created municipality that joined the white town of Tweeling and the black township of Mafahlaneng. They were indeed twin towns, joined by social and economic bonds which apartheid had sought to keep asunder. In terms of transitional arrangements made during negotiations at Kempton Park (the same negotiations that produced the 1993 Interim Constitution), 40 per cent of councillors in newly established local councils were voted in from the old apartheid structures (mainly whites) and 60 per cent from the more numerous black communities which had been previously disenfranchised.

Tweeling's council could neither elect a mayor nor pass a budget, in both cases contrary to legislative mandates. The town clerk explained the situation as follows.[5] The first local election, held in 1995, returned six African National Congress (ANC) councillors, representing Mafahlaneng township, and four white councillors, representing the ratepayers of Tweeling. They had to form a government of local unity during the transitional period. When two of the ANC councillors crossed the line and voted with their white compatriots, they were expelled from their party and lost their seats. With the two

---

[3] Jaap de Visser more than merits a lengthy footnote. As a Master's student, he was, for his internship, posted to Parliament in 1997 to assist the Portfolio Committee on Local Government in drafting the new local government legislation. It so happened that 1997 also saw the first intervention in a municipality, which the NCOP then had to review. Jaap realised that something was in the offing, and wrote his Master's dissertation on supervision (under my supervision). The thesis was reworked into a manual on how to apply section 139, a manual eventually endorsed by the national Department of Provincial and Local Government (DPLG) as its official policy. Twenty-three years later, the Constitutional Court in 2023 referred with approval to this same policy document (*Premier, Gauteng and Others v Democratic Alliance and Others; All Tshwane Councillors who are Members of the Economic Freedom Fighters and Another v Democratic Alliance and Others; African National Congress v Democratic Alliance and Others* [2021] ZACC 34 para 99).

[4] See the report by Levy N & Tapscott C (eds) *Intergovernmental relations audit: Towards cooperative government* Department of Provincial and Local Government (2000) ('IGR Audit Report').

[5] Interview with Mr LB Mafokosi, the town clerk, Tweeling, 15 October 1999.

groups now having four councillors each, it was a stalemate. To quote from a letter by the town clerk: 'Every time when council is to hold a meeting, a quorum is not formed. Either the ANC councillors stage a walkout or the Rate Payers councillors will stage a walkout.'[6] For eight months there were no meetings. The consequences were as predictable as they were dire. No mayor could be appointed, no budget could be adopted. No decisions were taken, no staff appointments were made, no electricity or water invoices were issued. The result: no water, no refuse collection.

Why the stand-off? An ANC councillor replied: 'The core of the problem is political power – who wants to be mayor. [It's] not about issues of the budget or service delivery, but who is in the majority.'[7] Of the government of municipal unity, he said: 'If we remove the problem (who is mayor), we can function effectively.' The result was that the town operated without leadership until a by-election could resolve the question of a majority.[8] The Free State Provincial Department responsible for local government could not provide much support before or after the intervention, impeded as it was by its own capacity and financial constraints.[9] At the root of the problem: a clear case of abuse of political power at the expense of residents.

According to the ruling party in the national parliament (to wit, the ANC), Tweeling's problem was temporary, given that the government of municipal unity was only a transitional measure. Come the first fully democratic local election in 2000, democracy would prevail:

> After the next [local government] election, the municipalities that were created as result of Kempton Park [negotiations] will fall away. After democratisation the burden will be less. Interventions is not about the failure of municipalities, but all about the failure of provinces.[10]

So it was hoped, at least. After the first democratic local government elections were duly held in December 2000, municipalities were established wall-to-wall

6 Letter from Mafokosi to Mr MS Msibi, the Head of Local Government, Free State Provincial Administration, 28 March 1999.

7 Interview with Tweeling councillor HS Ntombela (ANC), 15 October 1999 (transcribed 3 December 2023).

8 The impasse was resolved when the by-elections gave the ANC a majority in the council.

9 Department of Provincial and Local Government (DPLG) (2000) The intergovernmental relations audit: Towards a culture of cooperative government. Pretoria: Government Printer.

10 Interview with Naledi Pandor, chairperson of the NCOP, and Mohamed Bhabha, chair of the NCOP Standing Committee on Constitutional Affairs, Parliament, Cape Town, 18 August 1999.

across South Africa and equipped with a brand-new set of framework laws – but even these could not solve the problem of dysfunctional councils. Intervention powers were restricted to executive obligations, not legislative obligations; the sanctity of the democratically elected was preserved. Only councils could pass the budget, as this was the primary legislative power of a council, and there was no way out in the event of a dysfunctional council.

Thus, in 2003 the 'undemocratic' step was taken: the Constitution was amended to provide for the discretionary dismissal of a council 'if exceptional circumstances warrant such a step'.[11] Under the pressure of the National Treasury, dismissals were mandated when a council did not adopt a budget or was in a serious financial crisis.[12] The dismissal of a council had to be followed by an election within three months. Although the intervention provisions of national interventions in provinces and provincial interventions in municipalities were initially almost identical, provincial legislatures remained immune from dismissals.

What did I learn from the Tweeling intervention, as well as subsequent interventions?

First, politics – the contestation for power – underpinned many, if not most, dysfunctional municipalities. The misuse of provincial interventions for political ends did occur on occasion. More prevalent, though, was the *non-use* of interventions powers when the same party governed at national, provincial and local levels.

Second, while I did not question the balance that was struck in the original 1996 Constitution – protecting democratic institutions – in the light of failures of municipal politics, I did demur when the dismissal of a local council in 'exceptional circumstances', or for failure to adopt a budget or rectify a financial crisis, was introduced in the Constitution.[13] But Jaap and I consistently gave a restrictive interpretation to the new intervention powers.[14]

Third, time taught me that political control of provincial interventions via the NCOP was a deep design flaw. Even policing the constitutional time limits for a valid intervention does not happen when members of the NCOP review their own provincial comrades' intervention efforts.[15] Moreover, where an

---

11 Constitution of South Africa Eleventh Amendment Act of 2003, adding section 139(1)(c).

12 Constitution of South Africa Eleventh Amendment Act of 2003, adding section 139(4) and (5).

13 Constitution Eleventh Amendment Act of 2003.

14 Steytler N & De Visser J *Local government law of South Africa* LexisNexis (2007 and subsequent yearly issues) chapter 15 'Supervision'.

15 De Visser J & November J 'Overseeing the overseers: Assessing the compliance with municipal intervention rules in South Africa' (2017) 9 *Hague Journal of*

intervention is politically driven, the political supervision by the NCOP is meaningless at the very moment it is needed the most.

A prominent example came 20 years after Tweeling's political crisis, this time in the Tshwane Metropolitan Council. No longer a dusty rural town, in other words, but a highly cherished political prize: the executive capital of the country and the fourth-largest metropolitan council in South Africa.

Here, the ANC-led Gauteng provincial executive dismissed Tshwane Metropolitan Council, controlled by the Democratic Alliance (DA), due to 'dysfunctionality': the council could not take decisions because councillors of the ANC and Economic Freedom Fighters (EFF) walked out of meetings, devoiding the council of a quorum to elect a mayor – the same strategy followed in Tweeling. The Constitutional Court held that the Gauteng Government's action did not meet the requirements for a dismissal of the council and thus set it aside.[16] The point to make, however, is that an ANC-dominated NCOP (eight of the nine provincial delegations were ANC) would hardly have censured one of its provinces when the prize of a new election may have produced an ANC majority. As in its other activities, the National Council of Provinces should be more aptly termed the National Council of Political Parties.

These rather sceptical lessons came only after years of experience. My engagement with constitutional reform processes elsewhere, mainly on devolution, was then informed by a strong belief in the value of South Africa's model of supervision.

3. KENYA: THE TWINNING OF CONSTITUTIONS

Since the early 2000s, a central component of Kenya's constitutional law reform process was devolution. It was seen as the bulwark against an imperial presidency and key to equitable development. While South Africa's Constitution was a major influence on Kenya's Constitution of 2010, it was in the field of devolution that real twinning took place. Many aspects of South Africa's model of decentralisation were followed, and with certain issues it was virtually a case of just copy-pasting the provisions of the one to the other. The end product was hence more or less a non-identical twin.[17] One of the

the Rule of Law 109.

[16] *Premier, Gauteng and Others v Democratic Alliance and Others; All Tshwane Councillors who are Members of the Economic Freedom Fighters and Another v Democratic Alliance and Others; African National Congress v Democratic Alliance and Others* [2021] ZACC 34.

[17] Cottrell J & Ghai Y 'The contribution of the South African Constitution to Kenya's Constitution' in Dixon R & Roux T (eds) *Constitutional triumphs, constitutional disappointments: A critical assessment of the 1996 South African*

features of devolution that did not enjoy much attention during the reform process, however, was supervision.[18]

The first draft constitution, that of the Constitution of Kenya Review Commission, appeared in 2002 and provided only that the national government could suspend district governments in an emergency, in a war, for gross inefficiency, for corrupt practices or for failures to comply with the Code of Conduct applicable to district authorities. Again, the twofold concerns: citizens' interests and those of the nation. The corrective measure envisaged at the time was to recalibrate the democratically elected district council.

The next iteration, the so-called Bomas Draft of 2004, strengthened checks and balances after a suspension by adding a presidential and Senate veto (the Senate being the second chamber of parliament) and an election within 90 days.[19] Parliament (or, specifically, Attorney-General Amos Wako) gave the draft a more centralised slant, but this draft (the Wako draft), which emerged in 2005, was defeated in a referendum in that same year. The draft did, however, contain an independent procedural safeguard: a district council could be suspended only after a commission of inquiry recommended such a suspension to the President, who was bound by the recommendation.[20]

After yet another stolen election and the subsequent ethnic clashes of 2007, the task fell to a Committee of Experts (CoE) to harmonise the Bomas draft with the Wako one. The Harmonised Draft's provisions on intervention swung the pendulum back to a political check and balance. A suspension was permissible only after the President agreed with the commission's findings and the Senate, the second chamber of parliament representing districts, authorised the suspension (the latter could also terminate a suspension).[21] The underlying thinking was that the core of democratic government should be maintained; only the useless or corrupt politicians should be replaced democratically by better ones.

Before this harmonised draft was submitted to Parliament for final tinkering and approval, Yash Ghai, who chaired the initial Constitution of Kenya Review Commission, hosted a workshop with the CoE in December 2009,

---

Constitution's local and international influence Cambridge: Cambridge University Press (2018) 252–93. See also Kangu JM *Constitutional law of Kenya on devolution* Nairobi: Strathclyde University Press (2015) at Chapter 2.

18 The research work of Melissa Ziswa, a doctoral student at the University of the Western Cape, on the influence of the South African Constitution's devolution provisions on Kenya, is acknowledged and appreciated.

19 Clause 210B, Draft Constitution of Kenya (Bomas Draft, 15 March 2004).

20 Clause 204(2) and (3), Wako draft constitution.

21 Clause 235(1)(b), Harmonised Draft Constitution of Kenya, 17 November 2008.

where he invited a number of foreign experts to comment on the harmonised Draft. I made a few comments on the supervision provisions, drawing on my South African experience. My first point was that intervention is a necessity in a newly devolved system:

> The careful supervision [intervention] of county governments is an important element for the successful devolution of power. The implementation of devolution policies in Africa has been confronted with two perennial problems. First, devolved governments often lack the necessary skills and capacity to perform their functions and comply with statutory requirements. Second, devolved governments are also subject to the corrosive effect of corruption and maladministration. Local autonomy tends to insulate local fiefdoms and patronage networks from external scrutiny. In the end, residents who do not receive the services they are entitled to, decry devolution and call for national intervention.[22]

Second, interventions are necessary, but they should be nuanced. The draft referred only to the suspension of a county assembly (the renamed district councils) and a re-election within 90 days. My very South African critique was as follows:

> It is my view that the supervisory provisions in the draft Constitution do not provide sufficient and nuanced intervention measures that are able to assist and guide counties to realise self-governance … Because the dissolution of an assembly is such a drastic measure, it will come late in the decay of a county government. Exceptional circumstances will mean that the country's government has collapsed. The election of a new assembly will then have the enormous task of rebuilding a collapsed government.[23]

My third recommendation, however, moved beyond the South African framework:

> It is recommended that the more appropriate response is to monitor, support and through selected intervention measures (with the necessary safeguards) prevent the collapse of county government. These measures should fall short of the dissolution of the assembly. Such measures could include: the establishment of an independent inspectorate of counties, giving the auditor-general teeth to invalidate corrupt

---

22 Author's commentary prepared after a workshop with the Committee of Experts on the Draft Harmonious Constitution, Nairobi, 11–14 December 2009, at para 25.

23 Author's commentary prepared after a workshop with the Committee of Experts on the Draft Harmonious Constitution, Nairobi, 11–14 December 2009, at paras 26 and 29.

contracts, the partial assumption of responsibility by the national government of specified functions (with the necessary safeguards against abuse).[24]

The CoE Revised Harmonised Draft, produced at the beginning of 2010, brought the intervention powers closer to those of their South African counterpart.[25] In a new clause, under the heading 'Support for County Government', national legislation may provide for the national government to give directions and, if necessary, assume responsibility when a county

(a) … is unable or unwilling to carry out its functions; or
(b) has failed to satisfactorily operate a system of financial management that complies with the regulations.[26]

In addition, such legislation 'may provide for a process by which the Senate may bring the intervention to an end'.[27]

When Parliament finally approved the draft and a referendum endorsed it, the newly adopted 2010 Constitution of Kenya contained national intervention powers supporting both counties and their suspension.[28] The Senate continued to play its peer review role. Where the directly elected governor is impeached by a two-thirds majority in a county assembly, a majority in the Senate must sanction his or her removal.[29] Where the President suspends a 'county government' in case of an emergency arising out of an internal conflict or war, or 'in exceptional circumstances', he or she may do so only at the recommendation of an independent commission of inquiry and with the Senate's authorisation.[30] The Senate may also end a suspension at any time. Included in the term 'county government' is a county assembly; the members' tenure ends upon the election that must be held within 90 days.[31] The overall thrust of the provisions is a balance in favour of the centre. What started off on a strong devolutionary

---

24 Author's commentary prepared after a workshop with the Committee of Experts on the Draft Harmonious Constitution, Nairobi, 11–14 December 2009, at para 30.

25 Section 139(1) and (5), Constitution of South Africa.

26 Clause 162(2), Revised Harmonised Draft Constitution of Kenya (29 January 2010).

27 Clause 162(4)(d), Revised Harmonised Draft Constitution of Kenya (29 January 2010).

28 Articles 190 and 192, Constitution of Kenya of 2010.

29 Article 18, Constitution of Kenya, 2010, read with section 33 of the County Governments Act of 2012.

30 Article 192, Constitution of Kenya, 2010.

31 Section 129, Constitution of Kenya Country Governments Act 12 of 2012.

note thus became attenuated over time. The fear of secession and internal conflict, as well as a prevailing centrist ethos, influenced that shift in balance.

Looking back at my advice, the following assumptions and policy choices are evident:

- First, to preserve democratic governance, lesser intervention measures must precede the dismissal of a democratically elected body.
- Second, distrust of the political process was already creeping in: independent institutions should assist in determining when an intervention should take place.
- Third, for the sanctioning and policing of interventions, I maintained my trust in the political process of peer review, in this case the Senate representing the 47 counties. It would protect residents against, on the one hand, abuse of power by county governments, and on the other, abuse of intervention powers by the central government. The assumption was that the Senate, as a body representing counties, has the interests of all counties at heart; the Senate, as a form of collegiate review, would protect one of its own.

That assumption has been as far from the truth in Kenya as in South Africa. Party interests in the Senate come first. So far, of the 17 impeachment notices the Senate received from county assemblies, only 3 suspensions of governors have been approved, suggesting that other governors may have been let off the hook for reasons of party loyalty and national politics.[32] Likewise, so far no suspension by the President of county governments has occurred, not for a want of cause but due to a lack of capacity, structures and even a proper understanding of the application of the constitutional and statutory provisions.[33] In hindsight, then, political control of interventions proved to be ineffective.

4. YEMEN: THE CASE OF THE MISSING SIBLING

Federal arrangements lay at the core of the political settlement in Yemen between the North and the secessionist South. After the upheaval of the Arab Spring revolt, the National Dialogue Conference (NDC), representing most political players, adopted a set of broad principles in 2013 which a Constitutional Drafting Committee (CDC), composed of nominated Yemeni

---

[32] Information and opinion provided by Dr Conrad Bosire, an expert on Kenyan devolution. Private communication 13 March 2024.

[33] Information and opinion provided by Dr Conrad Bosire, an expert on Kenyan devolution. Private communication 13 March 2024.

members, had to concretise in a draft constitution. After approval by a political body (the National Oversight Agency), the draft would be subjected to a referendum. The envisaged federal arrangements were a true case of 'holding-together' federalism, emphasising as they did strong subnational autonomy with limited intervention. The Southern Working Group of the NDC, on a quest to find 'a Just Solution to the Southern Question', had this to say on the subject of intervention:

> The central authority shall not interfere with the exercise of authority of the executive, legislative, judicial and administrative bodies of the other levels of government [of which there were two] in their area of exclusive responsibility, except in exceptional circumstances as regulated by the constitution and law, and only for purposes of ensuring collective security, essential common standards or to protect one regional authority from interference by another.[34]

As a United Nations (UN) adviser to the Constitutional Drafting Committee (CDC), I started off, very modestly, with a brief structure of the federal arrangements, including the following on intervention:

> The federal government should have the power to intervene in a regional government when the latter fails to perform its functions. Such an intervention may take place only in accordance with clear conditions and safeguards defined in the Constitution.[35]

The devolution model that emerged was multilevel; two levels of government below the regions were to be established – governates and local governments. For regional interventions into these levels of government, my advice was, again, very South African:

> Where a wilayas [governate] or a local government is unable to perform one of its functions or becomes dysfunctional, the regional government may intervene to ensure that the function is performed. Such an intervention may take place only in accordance with clear conditions and safeguards set in the Constitution.[36]

---

34 Outcome of the Subcommittee of the Southern Working Group, Agreement on a Just Solution to the Southern Question, Sana'a, 23 December 2013.

35 Memorandum on 'Levels of government and their powers and functions', prepared for the UN team assisting the CDC, 16 July 2014. ('CDC Memorandum').

36 CDC Memorandum.

When the CDC completed its work at the end of 2014,[37] the intervention provisions were similar to the original NDC Outcomes, in addition to which they sported a further federal tail. Article 346 read:

> The Federal Government may not intervene in the powers and authorities of the regions and wilayas, unless necessary and in the following exceptional circumstances:
>
> 1. To protect the security of society.
> 2. To ensure basic common standards of the State.
> 3. To protect a region from intervention by another region.

The twofold objects of intervention were thus to protect citizens by guaranteeing 'essential common standards' and to preserve the nation and the federal set-up against the backdrop of civil war between the North and the South. As a check and balance against the abuse of this power, the following federal veto was added:

> The intervention by the Federal Government in the circumstances prescribed in article 346 requires the approval of the Federal Council following consultation with the legislative and executive authorities in the respective regions and that shall be regulated by federal law.[38]

The Federal Council was a typical federal second chamber: it comprised 12 members, with one from each of the six regions and a further six members from the two cities, Sana'a and Aden.[39] Faith was again placed in the idea that, through the Federal Council, subnational entities would protect the interests of their members, notwithstanding that Yemen is a deeply divided and territorially fractured society.

The depth of one of the several cleavages became evident when the emissary of the CDC took the draft constitution to the President on 7 January 2017: the draft never reached the President and the government because the Houthis, a political group from the North East, staged a coup d'etat. They were not part of the constitution-making process and did not like its federal elements, particularly the way in which Yemen was carved up into six regions. A civil war ensued, one which continues to the time of this writing in 2025.

---

[37] For discussion of the tension between homogeneity and distinctiveness, see Steytler N 'Concurrency of powers in deeply divided countries: The case of Yemen's draft constitution' in Steytler N (ed) *Concurrent powers in federal systems: Meaning, making, managing* Leiden: Brill Nijhoff (2017) 279.

[38] Article 347, ibid (emphasis added).

[39] Article 141, ibid.

What were the lessons, if any? What does the Yemen experience tell us about intervention in general, and, in particular, my own approach to supervision?

First, intervention was not an issue of contention – in the CDC debates, it was hardly discussed. The focus was on self-rule and its institutions: the regions, the governorates (*wilayas*), the cities (Sana'a and Aden) and the local authorities. The dominant question was: Would the federal elements be attractive enough to the South to get its buy-in? Detailed attention to national intervention was thus avoided. This was a context in which the South wanted to secede and the North had a history of invading the South, having brought the former federation of 1991 to an end in 1994; there was hence little appetite for extensive intervention powers. The NDC's basic principles regarding interventions were more or less carried through to the draft Constitution. Giving effect to the NDC requirement that intervention should be 'regulated by the constitution and law', only one check and balance was inserted in the draft.

Second, to control for abuse by the federal government, political oversight was entrusted to the second house of parliament, the Federal Council, which could veto an intervention. Moreover, during the transitional period, a matter that affected the 'vital interests of the south' required the approval of two-thirds of the representatives of the South (the regions of Aden and Hadramount).[40] The 'southern' fear of a 'northern' intervention thus resulted in a de facto southern veto because an intervention arguably could have affected 'the vital interests of the south'. After the transitional period, the Federal Council would, like most second chambers in federations, move towards political-party alignments rather than be protective of subnational interests.

Third, the idea of a second chamber in the national legislature, one representing regions and acting as a bulwark against federal hubris, was probably advanced by the various UN and other international advisers. My surmise is that there was a common conventional understanding of how federations ought to work. In the case of the original structure of the United States and its replicas, including South Africa on this point, the assumption is that the second chamber – representing and protecting the interests of the subnational governments – is a core element, if not the most important feature, of 'shared rule' or co-government between the federal government and the subnational units. This is more of a reflexive than a reflective understanding of the centrality and utility of this element, given that evidence as to how well it works in practice is inconsistent.

40 Article 143, ibid.

5. SOLOMON ISLANDS: THE WAYWARD KID

At the same time, halfway across the world – in the Solomon Islands in the South Pacific – a constitutional reform process was under way with the aim of embracing federalism. The population of more than 700,000 islanders was scattered among six archipelagos; the latter comprise nine provinces, which are the constituent units of a rudimentary decentralised system. Provincial populations ranged from 150,000 to 4,000 residents. Ever since communal violence broke out in 2001 between the two most populous islands, Guadalcanal and Malaita, solutions had been sought to the 'communal tensions', with federalism chief among them.[41] After the Federal Constitution of Solomon Islands Bill of 2004 found no support in Parliament,[42] a slow process of constitutional reform commenced in 2007. To this end, a Constitutional Reform Unit was established in the Prime Minister's Office, which in turn assembled a constitutional review body, called the Constitutional Review Congress. The latter consisted mainly of representatives from the nine provinces, along with an Eminent Persons Group appointed by the Prime Minister and counting among its members a former governor-general. The body worked in fits and starts for ten years and produced a Draft Federal Constitution in June 2018.

The federal project of the draft constitution was animated by the goal of securing significant autonomy for the provinces (termed 'states'). I came aboard in 2017 as one of the constitutional advisers to the body, finding myself worried about the possible failure of small units in the proposed highly decentralised federal system, given that most of these units had no history of governance. Unsurprisingly, I raised the issue of federal intervention powers, but the delegates had little appetite for it. As the end of the body's mandate approached, the matter was raised once more. I quote from field notes I took at the time after a decisive meeting, and do so at length because these remarks capture the nub of the issue:

> No interim state constitution is ready by 9.30, when the meeting congeals into a quorum. Another idea (and text) is floated: the federal government should have intervention powers where a state fails in its governance task, which is likely to happen in a new system, with the proviso that the federal government may not dismiss the elected state Parliament. And I trot out ample South African examples in support. Some initial support for the new text; but then the hardliners hit back: we don't want the feds to take over. The man from Malaita: 'This smacks

---

[41] Nanau G 'Unifying the fragments: Solomon Islands constitutional reforms' (2002) 60 *Development Bulletin – Australian Development Studies Network* 15; Corrin J 'Breaking the mould: Constitutional review in Solomon Islands' (2007) 13 *Revue Juridique Polynésienne* 143 at 167.

[42] For a discussion of the Bill, see Corrin (2007).

> of a master-servant relationship. We need to protect our leaders from failing the people, but I don't want my leaders being subjected.' Others concur: we had bad experiences of how the central government dismissed provincial governments. It is always politics. 'An intervention must only take place when a state requests an intervention (!), otherwise all my ambitions will be lost.' A moderate voice: 'As we move into the ocean of uncertainty, we need some objectivity in an intervention.' There must be strong evidence for the intervention; the ombudsman or the auditor-general should give some report. And so the idea develops slowly that the envisaged Independent Commissions and Offices (Ombudsman, Auditor-General, Human Rights Commission, and so on) must be the key players. The end result is, as Phil, the drafter, formulates provision after provision on the overhead projector, that when the ombudsman (or other independent commission or office) on receipt of a complaint (or on own initiative) finds non-compliance with a statutory obligation, it may issue directives to the state government to take corrective action. If the latter fails to do so, the ombudsman may use any of its powers, including to refer the matter to the Director of Public Prosecutions, or go to court. And now for the innovation: it may also, in the case of a systemic failure, ask the federal government to intervene to the extent of its findings and recommendations. What an amazing morning: I started with an idea based on the South Africa Constitution, and in time for lunch, the standard way of addressing subnational state failure is turned on its head by the delegates; an entirely new system – unique in the world – is developed which may effectively cleanse intervention from political interference. Truly home-grown and a new model for the world. Wow![43]

Rereading the notes, I say again: Wow! Unfortunately, the text never saw the light of day. It still had to clear the hurdle of passing with a two-thirds majority vote in Parliament, as was required for a constitutional amendment to be valid. However, given that Members of Parliament (MPs) had had no say in drafting the constitution and that many provisions ran against their interests (for instance, it abolished the Constituency Development Fund that each MP otherwise receives in order to dish it out at will), the requisite approval was most unlikely. The drafters then wanted to start a revolution themselves to get their constitution adopted, and cast about in search of ways to circumvent Parliament's constitutional amendment procedure.

The process of constitutional reform has again been ignited. In December 2023, the Solomon Islands Parliament adopted a constitutional reform act[44] establishing a Constitutional Assembly mandated to review the 2018 Draft Constitution and propose its adoption (or not) to the Parliament, where it would, once more, face the two-thirds-majority hurdle. The Constitutional Assembly was given a deadline of 31 December 2024. This deadline was not

43 Private field notes, Honoraria, 27 April 2017.

44 Constitution (Amendment) (Constituent Assembly) Act 18 of 2023.

met, however, and a legislative attempt to extend it by two years was defeated in Parliament.[45]

What lessons are on offer?

First, the supervision regime did away with post hoc review within the political system of the national executive decision. In any event, the draft constitution did not provide for a second chamber in the national legislature representing the states, and this did not detract from its federal nature.[46] Placing such a veto power in the hands of a parliament operating on Westminster principles was not an option; instead, the controls were placed in the hands of the independent institutions that would act *ex ante* any intervention decision.

Second, the highly decentralised tenor of the draft, including the intervention provisions, was a product of the provincial or local interests of the drafting body. They were intent on securing a decentralised federal system,[47] and their aversion to political interference from on high was palpable. The balance they sought was one that excluded political decision-making.

Third, I was enthusiastic about the innovative ideas the meeting generated, ideas that elicited a 'wow!' I approached interventions on the basis of past experience, which was useful up to the point of knowing intervention is an important issue. Not so useful was the lack of ideas of how a balance could be struck. I was operating within a path-dependency frame of mind that followed – rather uncritically, if not even arrogantly – the orthodox framework of federalism, including notions of shared rule.

---

45 Osifelo E, 'Constituent Assembly Amendment Bill defeated' (22 December 2024) *Solomon Star* available at https://perma.cc/T7HC-BDUM (accessed 20 January 2025).

46 It is important to note that the draft constitution illustrates the point made later by Alan Fenna and Johanna Schnebel that bicameralism is not practically or theoretically an essential feature of federalism. They argue that '*the one essential feature of federalism is entrenched autonomy*, manifest in the existence of two orders of government with constitutional status, each enjoying a direct relationship to the people with meaningful powers, and whose status and powers are constitutionally protected. Entrenched autonomy embodies the fundamental principle of federalism that allows a meaningful degree of self-government to different communities within one overarching political system' (emphasis in original). See Fenna A & Schnabel J 'What is federalism? Some definitional clarification' (2023) 54(2) *Publius: The Journal of Federalism* 13.

47 See generally Steytler N 'Equality and advantage in emerging federations and the dilemma of non-renewable natural resources: The cases of Solomon Islands and Trinidad and Tobago' in Belser EM, Bächler T, Egli S, et al. (eds) *The principle of equality in diverse states: Reconciling autonomy with equal rights and opportunities* Leiden: Brill (2021) 197.

6. WESTERN CAPE: BORROWING FROM ABROAD

In 2018, the Dullah Omar Institute was approached by the Western Cape Provincial Department of Local Government to conduct an assessment of the past experience of interventions in the province and 'develop a framework which could guide the Province Government in executing its constitutional mandate as the primary supervisor of municipalities, and lead to a common understanding among the Province and municipalities'.[48] My colleagues Jaap de Visser and Tinashe Chigwata and I worked through all the past incidences of interventions, analysed the jurisprudence on the topic and came up with what in our eyes was a coherent approach to addressing the pathologies of interventions in the province.

Some municipalities in the Western Cape shared the same dysfunctionality as many others in the rest of the country. Politics stood at the heart of most problems, in exactly the same way as it had before in the Tweeling Municipality. Political contestation for power – that is, for control of municipalities – was intense, leading often to political instability that undermined service delivery. Provincial intervention measures were also complicated by the fact that the Western Cape was governed by the DA and that 'troublesome' municipalities were in opposition hands. We found, inter alia, that

> [t]here is clear evidence that intervention powers have on occasion been used for political purposes where political gain can be achieved. This is also prompted by the political games played at local level. A political party (or alliance) would cling to power despite a change in the balance of power, and provincial intervention should then be required.

The core of our recommendations was to make interventions in terms of section 139 more apolitical and predictable and thus more effective. Although the ideal would be to make interventions fully apolitical, we knew that it was unrealistic, given that politicians were empowered to make the relevant decisions at municipal and provincial levels. Nevertheless, we sought to make the process of provincial decision-making apolitical. Key to this strategy was identifying a set of 'objectively verifiable indicators' that could show when a municipality was in trouble and when an intervention should be triggered. Furthermore, the information that was fed into the indicators had to be reliable and, where possible, also routine. We wrote:

---

48 De Visser J, Steytler N & Chigwata T *An assessment framework for provincial interventions undertaken in municipalities in the Western Cape* (2018) for the Western Cape Province Department of Local Government (unpublished).

> The evidence must be reliable and thus beyond contestation so that the consideration of intervention measures does not get bogged down in factual disputes between the Province, a municipality, and the national government. The reliable information should, where possible, also become available on a routinised basis in order to facilitate the early warning system. Such information should emanate primarily from the institutions which collect or possess critical information independently from the municipality and the Province, including: independent constitutional institutions of the Auditor-General, the Public Protector, and the Human Rights Commission; the South African Revenue Services; and bulk services providers of electricity and water.

The proposal was, of course, a double-edged sword: inasmuch as objective indicators would support an intervention in opposition-held municipalities, they would also trigger interventions in ruling party-controlled municipalities. Implementation of the recommendations did not ensue: the report is probably gathering dust in an administrator's drawer, while the conflictual relationship between the province and opposition municipalities continues unabated.

What lessons are there to be learnt, other than that advice remains just that – advice? The circumstances must be propitious for the journey from advice to practice to happen.

First, political contestation leading to political instability (resulting in service delivery failures) remains a central cause of municipal dysfunctionality and hence the trigger for interventions. Such interventions are inevitably mired in politics, which fundamentally undermines their effectiveness. The approach called for is thus one of making the process as apolitical as far as possible within the confines of a system that embeds politicians as key decision-makers.

Secondly, as to my own thinking, the debt that I owe to the Solomon Islanders is obvious. Having begun as an exporter of the South African model and ended as an importer of a new approach – using independent institutions as key players in the process of supervision – I had completed a full circle. Experience takes one only so far: an open mind can go further.

7. CONCLUSION

What are the overall lessons I have learnt from the various contexts of supervision in the Global South in countries where federalism or multilevel government has recently been established or envisaged to deal with deep cleavages in society? Only in South Africa and Kenya can we observe intervention models in operation, whereas in Yemen and the Solomon Islands the engagement is limited to a theoretical modelling of suitable intervention regimes.

First, underlying the intervention rationale common to all the countries is the twofold purpose: protecting residents from subnational governments abusing their governance power, and protecting subnational governments from the national governments' abuse of their intervention powers. In each country the balance between autonomy and intervention was struck differently.

Second, where we could observe the practice of intervention – in South Africa and Kenya – the abuse of power lay largely in politics, that is, in competition for power, and not necessarily for better governance. Although the abusive democratically elected subnational government could be dismissed (only municipal councils in South Africa), faith was still placed in democratic institutions, thus requiring the holding of replacement elections.

Third, as a check and balance against abuse by the 'superior' government of its intervention power, trust was placed in a second chamber of the national parliament, one representing the interests of the subnational governments. The effectiveness of such a body – the NCOP in South Africa and the Senate in Kenya – in performing a 'peer review' function proved to be doubtful. Instead of their being houses of subnational governments, political-party interests eclipsed that goal. The draft constitution in the Solomon Islands showed, however, that bicameralism is not a central or defining feature of federalism. Furthermore, in the absence of such a body 'protecting' subnational autonomy, other methods of restraining the federal government interventions are possible.

Fourth, because an intervention is imbued with politics and hence with contestation, the idea emerged of inserting independent apolitical players into the process. In Kenya, a commission of inquiry became a requirement, although its findings are not binding. It was only in the Solomon Islands that the process was entrusted entirely to independent constitutional bodies.

What did I learn personally along the supervision journey?

First, expertise based on past experience is useful, but it can easily lead to path-dependency of thought. Past experience primes one to anticipate problems; it does not necessarily prime one to see solutions. The model that was most familiar to me got rehashed in one country after another. In other words, the theory and practice of supervision in South Africa became my *vade mecum*. This may well be based on the arrogant notion that the 'leading light' of South Africa – the country with 'the best constitution' – illuminates the path for other countries that are emerging from conflict and searching for a federal solution.

Second, it is never too late to learn. The experience of listening to the ordinary folk of the Solomon Islands brought new insights not only on supervision but also on federalism as a mode of governance in divided societies. Let that be my *vade mecum*.

BIBLIOGRAPHY

Books

Kangu JM *Constitutional law of Kenya on devolution* Nairobi: Strathclyde University Press (2015)

Levy N & Tapscott C (eds) *Intergovernmental relations audit: Towards cooperative government* Pretoria: Department of Provincial and Local Government (2000)

Steytler N & De Visser J *Local government law of South Africa* LexisNexis (2007)

Chapters in Books

Cottrell J & Ghai Y 'The contribution of the South African Constitution to Kenya's Constitution' in Dixon R & Roux T (eds) *Constitutional triumphs, constitutional disappointments: A critical assessment of the 1996 South African Constitution's local and international influence* Cambridge: Cambridge University Press (2018)

Steytler N 'Concurrency of powers in deeply divided countries: The case of Yemen's draft constitution' in Steytler N (ed) *Concurrent powers in federal systems: Meaning, making, managing* Leiden: Brill Nijhoff (2017) 279–99

Steytler N 'Equality and advantage in emerging federations and the dilemma of non-renewable natural resources: The cases of Solomon Islands and Trinidad and Tobago' in Belser EM, Bächler T, Egli S. et al. (eds) *The principle of equality in diverse states: Reconciling autonomy with equal rights and opportunities* Leiden: Brill (2021) 197–223

Journal Articles

Corrin J 'Breaking the mould: Constitutional review in Solomon Islands' (2007) 13 *Revue Juridique Polynésienne* 143–68

De Visser J & November J 'Overseeing the overseers: Assessing the compliance with municipal intervention rules in South Africa' (2017) 9 *Hague Journal of the Rule of Law* 109–33

Dixon B 'Colonial confessions: An autoethnography of writing criminology in the New South Africa' (2024) 20 *The British Journal of Criminology* 1–17

Fenna A & Schnabel J 'What is federalism? Some definitional clarification' (2023) 54(2) *Publius: The Journal of Federalism* 13

Nanau G 'Unifying the fragments: Solomon Islands constitutional reforms' (2002) 60 *Development Bulletin – Australian Development Studies Network* 15

Case Law

Premier, Gauteng and Others v Democratic Alliance and Others; All Tshwane Councillors who are Members of the Economic Freedom Fighters and Another v Democratic Alliance and Others; African National Congress v Democratic Alliance and Others [2021] ZACC 34 para 99 (4 October 2021)

Legislation

Kenya

Constitution (Amendment) (Constituent Assembly Sitting) Bill of 2024
Constitution of Kenya, 2010
County Governments Act 17 of 2012
Draft Constitution of Kenya (Bomas Draft, 15 March 2004)
Harmonised Draft Constitution of Kenya (17 November 2009)
Revised Harmonised Draft Constitution of Kenya (29 January 2010)
Wako Draft Constitution

South Africa

Constitution of South Africa, 1996
Eleventh Amendment Act of 2003

Reports

De Visser J, Steytler N & Chigwata T *An assessment framework for provincial interventions undertaken in municipalities in the Western Cape* (2018) for the Western Cape Province Department of Local Government (unpublished)

Internet Sources

Osifelo E 'Constituent Assembly Amendment Bill defeated' (22 December 2024) *Solomon Star* available at https://perma.cc/T7HC-BDUM (accessed 20 January 2025)

Other Sources

Author's commentary prepared after a workshop with the Committee of Experts on the Draft Harmonious Constitution, Nairobi, 11–14 December 2009

Interview with Naledi Pandor, chairperson of the NCOP, and Mohamed Bhabha, chair of the NCOP Standing Committee on Constitutional Affairs, Parliament, Cape Town, 18 August 1999

Interview with Tweeling councillor HS Ntombela (ANC) 15 October 1999 (transcribed 3 December 2023)

Letter from Mafokosi to Mr MS Msibi, the Head of Local Government, Free State Provincial Administration, 28 March 1999

13. Intervention in federal systems: underlying rationales, legal bases, procedures and politics

Karl Kössler and Yonatan T. Fessha

1. INTRODUCTION

The tension between intervention, on the one hand, and the autonomy of subnational and local governments, on the other, is a key paradox in federal countries. This raises important questions about how much intervention can and should be allowed, as well as the conditions that justify and regulate these interventions. In this context, the corrective and coercive purposes of federal intervention have not yet been the subject of a major study; the balance between intervention powers and autonomy has thus not received the attention it deserves. This book changes that by bringing together contributions from three continents and ten jurisdictions.

A set of overarching research questions guided the contributions to this book, with the questions focused on understanding the dynamics of federal intervention in each of the case-study countries. First, contributors were required to trace the rationale for the introduction of intervention powers. Second, they were asked to examine the constitutional and legal frameworks that govern interventions in these countries. This question seeks to identify the grounds that enable higher levels of government to intervene in subnational or local governance, including the specific circumstances under which such interventions may be justified. Third, they were requested to reflect on procedures for intervention, particularly the safeguards which ensure that interventions are not applied arbitrarily or excessively. This exploration encompasses mechanisms such as legislative oversight and judicial review that mitigate intervention measures. Last, they were instructed to produce a synthesis of the ways in which political dynamics influence the use, abuse and frequency of federal interventions. This point emphasises the often overlooked but crucial role of political considerations in determining whether and how intervention powers are enacted and utilised.

2. UNDERLYING RATIONALES

The case studies in this book have demonstrated that the incisiveness of intervention powers and how they are designed is intrinsically linked to the circumstances of the times in which they were introduced. Political, social or cultural context is therefore key for understanding them. The cases of India, Brazil and Argentina, for instance, demonstrate clearly that powers of central government intervention are intertwined with infighting between various factions about their influence in nascent federal countries – not least of all their influence on the shape of a federal system still very much in the process of formation.

In the Brazilian case, both the introduction of intervention powers with the first federal constitution in 1891 and their subsequent expansion can be understood only against the background of such struggles between central and peripheral actors and within the peripheries, that is, the states. Naturally, these played out with even greater intensity during the early phase of Brazilian federalism when the system was still malleable and political actors attempted to assert – often by violent means – their place within it. For the central government, intervention was therefore a welcome and readily available tool for defending the unity of the country (and its own interests) against challenges by state opposition parties and also for having a say in political disputes *within* the states. After the 1926 constitutional reform expanded the grounds for intervention, it became even easier for the country's military and executive to leverage intervention powers as a tool for maintaining national unity.

Similar processes could be observed in Argentina and its provinces after the first federal constitution in 1853 had entrenched powers of intervention. A characteristic that probably stands out in this case is the enormous asymmetry that resulted from the wealth and power of the Province of Buenos Aires. In fact, many disputes revolved around control of the resources generated by its port, so much so that this province perceived central government interventions as illegitimate attempts to usurp these resources and its autonomy. Eventually, Buenos Aires managed to maintain both, given that early federal intervention focused on other provinces.

Whereas in the Argentine case the conflict over the status of the capital province provided the key context for powers of central government intervention, in India the central factor was the status of what would later become Pakistan. Indeed, the country's constitutional arrangement would have looked quite different without the partition of the subcontinent. Nehru's Objectives Resolution of 1946, adopted less than a year before this watershed moment, had envisaged a highly decentralised system. It was only with partition that decentralisation was abandoned, since constitution-makers did not have to cater to the Muslim League any longer and began to feel that the need to quench the communal violence that the division entailed would require a strong central government, one that also had powers of intervention. Thus, it was in this context that India introduced article 356 as an emergency provision: this allows the central government to declare President's Rule in the event that the (centrally appointed!) governor at the state level reports failure in the state's constitutional machinery. The explicit reasons for the introduction of this clause were essentially threefold: to suppress communal violence in the nascent federation; to prevent the rise of communism; and to safeguard democracy in a country with a strongly hierarchical society and several regions lacking experience in parliamentary government.

In other cases surveyed in this book, intervention powers did not result from early federal infighting between factions but came rather as an explicit counterweight – one demanded by the central government – to the concession of decentralisation in an until-then purely unitary (and sometimes even autocratic) country. This is obvious from the territorial reorganisation that took place in Spain after the fall of General Franco's dictatorship. The drafters of the 1978 Constitution clearly perceived the possibility that central government intervention under the new article 155 would serve to 'balance' the self-government of the regions, even more so in view of the country's experience in the interwar period during which Catalonia's autonomous government declared 'a Catalan State within a Spanish Federal Republic'. The introduction of an intervention clause placated the political forces concerned about the new level of autonomy, and thus contributed decisively to the compromise of 1978. The link between intervention powers and decentralisation is evident also in the Italian case, although here the process was a more incremental one. While the Constitution of 1947 lacked such powers, it was – tellingly – only with the decentralisation of powers to the regions in the 1970s that intervention was introduced. In line with this logic, a further decentralisation push with the 'Bassanini' laws of the 1990s went hand in hand with an extension of central government powers to intervene in the regions.

The desire of central governments to avoid losing control in the face of a decentralisation process is not limited, of course, to the European continent. Indeed, the South African Constitution of 1996 states clearly in its Section 40 that the national, provincial and local governments are not only 'distinctive' but also 'interdependent and interrelated', which arguably demonstrates that autonomy does not mean complete freedom from any central government interference. Article 6(2) of the Kenyan Constitution, modelled on South Africa's, uses similar language to similar effect by characterising government levels as both 'distinct' and 'interdependent'.

Autonomy, however limited, would also have been inconceivable without concomitant powers of intervention when the Nigerian federation was established under the aegis of British colonialism in 1954 and during the creation of Ethiopia's federal system four decades later, especially given fears that ethno-nationalist politicians in the states could exploit subnational and local autonomy to undermine the federal system. Article 50(8) of the Ethiopian Constitution therefore obliges the federal government and the states to respect each other's autonomy, but not without allowing the former to intervene in the latter by way of exception.

Thus, it is true that the specific rationales for the entrenchment of intervention powers have been shaped in these countries by various individual factors, such as concerns about subnational and local government capacities to fulfil their constitutional mandates in South Africa, the legacy of highly centralised post-colonial governance with an imperial presidency in Kenya and the enforcement of fiscal-responsibility laws in both cases. But what the two countries do have in common with each other (as with Spain and Italy) is the perception that intervention powers are a vital complement for unitary states embarking on a journey towards decentralisation – a journey during which the central government seeks to maintain a firm grip on autonomy.

It is therefore curious that such powers did not figure prominently during Malaysia's transition to federalism. Indeed, the Reid Commission which drafted the 1957 Constitution of the Federation of Malaya did not even discuss the introduction of a provision that would allow for interference in the affairs of the states. Apparently, it believed that a distribution of competences tilted in favour of a strong central government and combined with the general emergency power of article 150 (which was twice applied with regard to only one state) was a sufficient means to ensure that the – at any rate very limited – decentralisation of authority to the states would not get out of hand.

Another striking insight concerns the difference between rationales for intervention in subnational entities (provinces, regions, states and the like), on the one hand, and municipalities, on the other. The role of the former as constituent parts of the federation entailed that in many cases, as explained above, intervention powers were introduced mainly in two contexts: where there was infighting between subnational governments and the centre for influence in a still consolidating system, and where decentralisation processes within formerly unitary states created subnational entities with autonomous powers. By contrast, interference in the affairs of local governments typically follows different rationales.

First, intervention, whether by the central or subnational government, appears to be something that has always been considered essential or inherent to local government, as if befitting its more hierarchical relationship with its 'superior' levels of government. As the South African case study shows, the right to interfere in the affairs of local authorities predates democracy and has been seen as even more justifiable under the new constitutional dispensation that grants municipalities substantial autonomy. Second, intervention at the local level is clearly focused on concerns about political mismanagement, especially in financial terms, and about the capacity of local authorities to fulfil their duties to provide public services. In this regard, a broad range of clauses exist in a number of countries in different parts of the world (for example, South Africa, Brazil, India and Italy). In the South African case, the financial woes of local governments took on such proportions that a 2003 reform saw the need for intervention to become even more stringent so as to appease potential lenders to municipalities and thus ensure the latter's liquidity.

Irrespective of the concrete rationale for intervention powers in the countries examined in this book, several of our case studies reveal interesting patterns of migration of constitutional ideas. Indeed, the provisions in Argentina and Brazil's early federal constitutions that enable the central government to intervene with the purpose of guaranteeing the republican form of government are clearly reminiscent of article 4(4) of the US Constitution (the so-called Guarantee Clause). After all, what distinguished these three countries from their former colonial rulers was this form of government, which thus deserved to be emphasised not only for practical reasons but also as a symbol of anti-monarchism and anti-colonialism. To cite another example, Spain's article 155 is – like other parts of the Constitution of 1978 – inspired by the German Basic Law. Interestingly, such dynamics of emulation are sometimes not confined to models from other countries, as intervention in regions under article 155 served as a model for the regulation of local intervention only several years later in 1985. Parts of South Africa's legal framework for intervention are based on the German example, while Kenya's is, in turn, inspired by the South African experience.

A final observation about the rationale for interference relates to the expectations that constitution-makers have as to how intervention powers would be used. It is remarkable that in most cases these powers are conceptualised and introduced as instruments that are meant to be used only in exceptional circumstances. In short, conflict resolution by political or judicial means is supposed to be the rule and the use of these powers the exception. This is very clear, for instance, from the wording of article 155(1) of the Spanish Constitution, which permits intervention only '[i]f an Autonomous Community does not fulfil the obligations imposed upon it by the Constitution or other laws, or acts in a way seriously prejudicing the general interests of Spain'. The Indian case study demonstrates that article 356 was similarly envisaged for highly exceptional scenarios. BR Ambedkar, one of the chief constitutional architects, brushed away fears of the provision's abuse by maintaining 'that such articles will never be called into operation and that they would remain a dead letter';[1] it was his hope that the President would start by issuing a warning, then call a fresh election in the state to allow conflict resolution by the people themselves, and only as a last resort invoke article 356. As we shall see below,[2] in reality matters played out quite differently in the Spanish and Indian cases. Whereas in Spain the actual use of central intervention powers was consistent with their being envisaged as an instrument for exceptional circumstances, India became notorious for its excessive use of such powers.

3. LEGAL BASES FOR INTERVENTION

Intervention in subnational governments is both a legally and a politically sensitive issue. While intervention is often justified as a corrective mechanism, its implementation can also be coercive when it is used as a tool of political suppression. The countries examined in this volume demonstrate distinct approaches. However, despite their differences, several common grounds, forms and procedures of intervention can be identified. Some of them are discussed below.

3.1 Grounds for Intervention

Federations vary in the number of grounds they provide for intervention. Some have only a few grounds, while others have many. However, the length of the list alone does not determine whether the scope of intervention is broad or narrow. The scope of an intervention regime – particularly the extent of its intrusiveness – depends partly on how the grounds for intervention are formulated. Specifically, the question is whether the grounds for intervention are expressed in general terms or in more precise terms. Equally important in determining the scope of intervention is whether intervention is limited to selected executive functions or extended to all executive functions.

3.1.1 National interests

One common, and amorphous, ground for intervention is the protection of national interests. In Italy, for example, intervention is authorised, in the words of its Constitutional Court, to deal with threats to 'essential, general, and unitary interests'.[3] In Kenya, the County Governments Act states that a county's

[1] BR Ambedkar's remarks to the Constituent Assembly, cited in Sarkaria RS & Ramasubramaniam KA (for the Government of India) *Commission on centre–state relations* New Delhi: Government of India Press (1988) section 6(2)(13).

[2] See section 5.

[3] Judgments 236/2004 and 388/2004.

actions can be deemed grounds for suspension of county government if these are contrary to the common needs and interests of its citizens. In Spain, article 155 of the constitution allows the central government to intervene when an autonomous community acts in a way that 'seriously prejudices the general interest of Spain'. These vague formulations of national interests seem to lend themselves not to precisely limited grounds of intervention but rather to granting national governments significant discretionary authority. However, according to the law and practice of the jurisdictions covered in this book, there are certain indications that are used to define national interests.

Obviously, the reference to national interests is about protecting needs and interests that extend beyond subnational boundaries and involve the entire national community. More specifically, this could be about maintaining national security. In some of the jurisdictions covered in this book, threats related to national security are explicitly mentioned by the constitutions as grounds for intervention, including in Argentina, Brazil and Italy. Some of the other constitutions do not mention national security as an explicit ground. This holds true, for example, for the constitutions of India, South Africa, Kenya and Spain. Yet in some of these constitutions, the existing grounds of intervention are interpreted to include threats to national security. Article 356 of the Constitution of India, which permits intervention – commonly referred to as the President's Rule – does not specifically mention national security as a ground for intervention. However, of the four categories that the Sarkaria Commission identified in its 1983 reports as conditions deemed to constitute a constitutional failure that warrants intervention, several of them relate to national security. Similarly, in Spain, acts that prejudice the general interests of Spain, and which form the basis for intervention by the national government in autonomous communities, are interpreted to include threats to national security.

In some jurisdictions, specifically those where domestic security matters are devolved to the subnational level, even where national security is explicitly cited as a reason for intervention, a request from the subnational or local authority is still necessary. This is the case, for example, in Argentina and Ethiopia. While requiring consent from a subnational or local authority signifies respect for its autonomy, it is not always feasible, it is submitted, to make consent a prerequisite for intervention. Certain situations warrant intervention even without the consent of the affected subnational unit or local government. For example, if there is a security breakdown where the subnational unit is involved or indifferent, or where it engages in actions that threaten the territorial integrity of the federation or another constituent unit, then intervention should proceed without requiring consent from the subnational government. Arguably, a federal government should also be allowed to intervene when a domestic disturbance goes beyond the capacity of the authorities of the subnational unit, even if the latter has not requested or agreed to the intervention. This is because a domestic disturbance that exceeds the capacity of a subnational government has the potential to become a threat to national security and thus justifies federal intervention. However, as we move away from concerns related to security, it becomes increasingly challenging to determine whether interventions should require the consent of the subnational unit. Ultimately, it depends on the context of each situation.

In addition to national security, national governments intervene in subnational units in the name of the national interest to protect territorial integrity. As the chapter on Spain shows, acts that prejudice the general interests of Spain include those that threaten the territorial integrity of the country. A notable example is the 2017 national government intervention in Catalonia, which occurred following the latter's unilateral declaration of independence from the rest of Spain. In a country whose constitution does not explicitly allow secession, it is not surprising that a unilateral act of secession is viewed as a threat to territorial integrity.

Finally, the reference to national interests could also relate to protecting economic unity. This could involve achieving a minimum level of regulatory uniformity across the country. In Italy, the national government is authorised to intervene in subnational units that 'fail to comply with international or EU law', which suggests that intervention is a tool to harmonise regulatory frameworks. Reference to national interests could also be about ensuring equal access to essential services for all citizens. Indeed, the national executive in Italy is provided with a general power to intervene in subnational units, as Valdesalici points out in Chapter 6, 'whenever action is necessary to preserve legal and economic unity (and guarantee a basic level of civil and social rights)'.[4] The appropriateness of the use of intervention powers to achieve some form of economic unity depends, of course, on the degree of uniformity and integration that each federation considers desirable. Some federations might not have a commitment to the provision of equal or equitable levels of services, making intervention unnecessary. Even when there is a constitutional commitment to one degree or another of uniformity and integration within a federation, it is not clear if intervention is the appropriate tool for achieving these objectives. Some countries use the less intrusive measure of fiscal equalisation to achieve the same objectives. Conditional grants, used by some federations, albeit in

---

[4] On a related note, in 2015 the national government of Kenya attempted to suspend Makueni county, citing a violent power struggle between the governor and county assembly. This suggests that engaging in action that leads to governance paralysis and in turn to the failure to provide basic public services can justifiably be deemed as action contrary to the 'common needs and interests of citizens'.

different context, might also be a less intrusive method of achieving these federation-wide objectives.

3.1.2 Failure to fulfil (performance) obligations

Interventions may, in one way or another, have to do with the obligations of subnational or local authorities. An intervention can be triggered in, broadly, one of two ways. On the one hand, it can be prompted when these authorities violate an obligation outlined in the constitution or legislation, either through action (commission) or inaction (omission). In this context, the intervention arises from the failure of the subnational unit to uphold its constitutional or legal responsibilities. According to article 155 of the Constitution of Spain, the national government may intervene in an autonomous community if it fails to meet its constitutional or legal obligations. Article 120 of the Constitution of Italy also allows national government intervention in a region if the latter 'acts against the Constitution or engages in serious violations of the law'. In India, according to the Sarkaria Commission, 'non-compliance with constitutional directions of the Union Government, when a state government fails to comply with directions issued under the executive power of the Union Government or during a national emergency' constitutes a legitimate basis for intervention by the national government.

On the other hand, intervention may also be triggered when a subnational or local government has not violated any law but is de facto dysfunctional or unable to fulfil its functions. In this situation, the failure, which is typically due to omission rather than commission, is not attributed to any breach of obligations under the constitution or legislation but stems from a lack of capacity or other related factors. Several constitutions allow for national government interventions when a subnational government is dysfunctional or unable to fulfil its responsibilities. In South Africa, for example, the main purpose of intervention is to enable higher levels of government to address poor performance and dysfunctionality at lower levels. Senior government officials may intervene when their immediate local government fails to carry out an executive obligation. In Kenya, national government intervention is also triggered by a county government's inability to perform its functions. The constitution requires that national legislation be enacted to empower the national government to help restore the county's capacity to fulfil these functions. In Nigeria, when a state government is unable to perform its duties, this may lead to intervention by the federal legislature. Section 11(4) of the 1999 Constitution grants the National Assembly the authority to enact laws 'for the peace, order, and good government' of any state when the House of Assembly of that state 'is unable to perform its functions'. Similarly, in Italy, the national government is permitted to intervene in regional administrations for reasons related to poor performance.

The use of intervention powers to address malfunction or poor performance is more common in countries that permit subnational governments to intervene at the local level. In Spain, local governments can be intervened upon for breaches of obligations that might not even be constitutionally significant. The authors of the chapter on Spain note that local intervention can be triggered by less significant issues, such as the 'ungovernability' of a municipality or serious corruption. The aim of intervention at the local level is to ensure the provision of essential public services and the normal functioning of local government.

The same is true in Italy, where a 'failure or delay by municipalities or provinces to fulfil acts required by law' serves as a valid reason for regional government intervention. For example, a local government may face intervention if general urban planning tools are not approved. Additionally, non-compliance with municipal waste management obligations can result in intervention that may lead to the removal of a mayor. A similar situation obtains in India, where state governments have enacted laws allowing them to intervene in local government matters. Tillin in Chapter 5 argues that state legislation regulating municipal governance often enables state governments to dissolve municipal corporations if they are deemed to be incompetent or are failing to comply with state directives. In such cases, the state government can appoint officers to perform the functions of the municipal corporation. Additionally, municipal laws in many states grant the state government the authority to direct the municipal corporation to fulfil certain duties if it believes they are not being carried out satisfactorily.

In most jurisdictions, the failure to fulfil an obligation must be severe in order to warrant intervention, something that has been clarified by constitutional courts rather than constitutional texts. According to the Constitutional Court of Italy, 'simple inertia or inadequate compliance is an insufficient ground for intervention'.[5] The failures must be severe, and exceptional circumstances must also be present.[6] Although there is nothing in the South African Constitution which states that the failure to fulfil an executive obligation has to be so severe that a municipality (or provincial department) has to have collapsed to trigger intervention, the constitution's emphasis on co-operative governance demands that not every failure of an executive obligation should result in intervention. The Court has made it clear that failures, albeit numerous, cannot justifiably warrant intervention if they are not serious and could have been resolved in

---

5 Judgment 165/2011.

6 Although the high rate of municipal dysfunction has led to an increasing number of interventions, the effectiveness of the interventions is often questionable. It seems that interventions have allowed for encroachment in subnational or local autonomy yet without delivering the desired result of improving the functionality of subnational governance.

another manner.[7] Similarly, in Spain, it is a failure to comply with 'all types of laws' that might form the basis for intervention, but the Constitutional Court has made it clear that not all legal breaches can form the legitimate basis for intervention. The legal breach, according to the Constitutional Court, must be 'flagrant, manifest and contumacious'.[8] The breach must have also been committed by 'the higher bodies of the autonomous community (its parliament or government)' and not by those in 'the administrative levels'.

3.1.3 Financial mismanagement

Some countries make financial mismanagement the primary trigger for intervention. Two of the four circumstances that warrant national government intervention in the counties of Kenya relate to financial management. Article 190 allows for intervention when a county does not maintain a financial management system that meets the expenditure control measures set by national legislation. As Gichana has pointed out in Chapter 7, national legislation has not provided much clarification on what constitutes a failure to operate a compliant financial management system, or on how such an intervention should be carried out. The fact that the national government has also been reluctant to invoke financial grounds, even in cases where counties have failed to address severe financial irregularities, has not helped in identifying financial mismanagements that justify national government intervention.

The good thing is that the Constitution of Kenya is not the only one that triggers national government intervention due to financial-related problems. In fact, the Kenyan Constitution is likely modelled after the Constitution of South Africa, which permits intervention if the financial functionality of local governments is questioned. The Constitutions of Brazil and Italy also provide financial mismanagement as a ground for intervention.

Unlike the Kenyan Constitution, the constitutions of South Africa, Brazil and Italy provide for relatively detailed financial grounds for intervention, thus shedding light on specific finance-related circumstances that can trigger intervention in subnational and local authorities. The first is when a subnational or local authority fails to approve a budget or impose revenue-raising measures. The second relates to financial emergencies, which often serve as a basis for intervention in municipalities. This is the case when a subnational or local authority experiences a financial crisis that results in a severe or persistent

---

7 *Mnquma Local Municipality and Another v Premier of the Eastern Cape and Others* [2009] ZAECBHC 14 (5 August 2009). The failure to fulfil an executive obligation is the most commonly invoked ground for intervention. On many occasions, however, the list of alleged failures does not in fact reveal a failure to fulfil executive obligations but points rather to finance-related concerns.

8 Judgment 89/2019.

material breach of its obligations to provide basic services or forces it to suspend debt payments and other financial commitments. The failure to implement financial rebalancing measures may also form the basis for intervention.

It is worth noting that financially related dysfunction does not serve as an explicit ground for intervention in Ethiopia and India. Even in the case of South Africa, financial mismanagement at the provincial level is not a valid reason for national government intervention in the provinces. It is only municipalities that are subjected to interventions on the basis of financial grounds.

3.1.4 The use of emergency powers in lieu of intervention measures

In some of the countries examined in this book, there are no explicit rules regarding federal intervention in state governments. National authorities in those countries rely on more general powers available to address circumstances broadly regarded as emergencies, including natural disasters and pandemics, allowing them to engage in intervention with little or no parliamentary scrutiny. For example, the Malaysian Constitution does not explicitly provide for federal intervention in state affairs. Instead, such interventions occur primarily through the declaration of emergencies under article 150, which grants the federal government broad powers to manage state matters. An emergency can be proclaimed when a 'grave emergency' threatens the security, economic stability or public order of the federation or any part of it. Importantly, the act perceived to threaten security, economic stability or public order does not need to occur before an emergency is declared; the mere imminent threat of such an event is sufficient.

Similarly, successive Nigerian governments, in the absence of a specific constitutional provision mandating intervention, have relied on the emergency powers provided in Section 305 of the 1999 Constitution, which empowers the President to declare a state of emergency in the federation or any part of it under specific circumstances. This is the case, for example, when the federation is at war, is in imminent danger of invasion or is involved in a state of war, or if there is an actual breakdown of public order or public safety in the Federation or any part thereof requiring 'extraordinary measures to restore peace and security'. There does not however have to be an actual breakdown of public order and public safety in the federation or any part thereof. The fact that there is 'clear and present danger of an actual breakdown of public order and public safety' is sufficient. The occurrence or imminent danger of any disaster or natural calamity also constitutes a legitimate basis for declaring a state of emergency. The Constitution keeps the door of intervention ajar by stating that 'any other public danger which constitutes a threat to the existence of the federation' can form the basis for declaring a state of emergency. The declaration of the state of emergency need not always be unilateral: the Constitution envisages the declaration of a state of emergency based on a request the President receives from the governor of a state when there is imminent danger or actual breakdown of public order or safety within the boundaries of the state. A resolution of two-thirds of members in the state legislature must support the request.

In Ethiopia, there are specific provisions for declaring a state of emergency and for federal intervention. However, emergency powers have been used several times to address matters that should have been addressed through federal intervention. This misuse of emergency powers has undermined the autonomy of subnational regions. When subnational units are placed under a state of emergency, they do not receive the same level of protection and safeguards that they would if they were subjected to federal intervention. Using emergency powers to intervene in subnational units can diminish transparency, allowing federal governments to bypass the constitutional protections granted to these entities. Although the 1999 Constitution of Nigeria, when compared to the 1962 Constitution of Nigeria, includes 'a more rigorous stipulation of the conditions for emergency rule', legal scholars, as Suberu points out in Chapter 9, have criticised the more extensive provisions of the 1999 Constitution as verbose, vacuous and ultimately ineffective in preventing the misuse of emergency rule in the Fourth Republic. For example, section 305(f) of the 1999 Constitution refers to 'any other public danger' as a constitutional basis for declaring emergency rule – this is a vague clause which is susceptible to misuse.[9]

3.2 Forms of Intervention

The appropriate measures for intervention vary among federations depending on the specific grounds and the severity of the issues at hand. These measures can include the soft measure of issuing directives that require subnational governments to take certain actions or refrain from particular activities. For example, in South Africa the Constitution allows an intervening national or provincial government to issue a directive that outlines the extent of a lower government's failure to fulfil its obligations and specifies the steps necessary to address these failures. The same is true in Ethiopia, where the national parliament, after being convinced that there is a large-scale human rights violation in the state that authorities are unwilling or unable to control, can issue a directive to the state authorities detailing the measures they must take to resolve the

[9] Based on a brief review of conditions that may warrant federal government intervention, it seems that it typically occurs in situations involving violence, widespread human rights abuses or a breakdown of law and order. In these cases, federal intervention is generally not considered necessary if the situation is peaceful. This is especially true in Ethiopia, where federal intervention is not explicitly associated with the failures or poor performance of the subnational government.

issue. Although there is no explicit provision for this, the national executive in Italy, before resorting to more intrusive forms of intervention, has on several occasions sent notes to a subnational authority directing it to take a specific administrative or legislative action. In Kenya, too, a county government which is unable to perform its functions is first provided with a recovery plan by the minister responsible for finance, with this plan being prepared in consultation with the county government. The latter is expected to implement the plan, the aim of which is to boost the county's ability to resume its functions.[10]

In situations where the intervening measures are limited to issuing directives, the intervening government does not take over the execution of functions within the subnational unit. Instead, it allows the lower level of government to carry out the instructions. The national government retains the power and responsibility to regularly monitor and ensure the implementation of the measures outlined in the directives. In some instances, the subnational government is required to report to the intervening government on the progress it is making in addressing its failures to meet its constitutional obligations to the citizens within its jurisdiction. Underlying this circumscribed form of intervention are the principles of loyalty and cooperation that are at the heart of some of these constitutions. In Italy, for example, Valdesalici makes it clear that 'the demand for loyal cooperation, in the eyes of the Court, necessitates "participatory" procedures, wherein the entity under scrutiny is empowered to fulfil its obligations and thereby prevent the need for substitution'.

Issuing a directive might not be effective or even the first step in intervention taken by an intervening government. In most jurisdictions, an intervention could take the form of assuming responsibility. This is the case in Kenya, where, according to the Constitution, intervention can extend to taking over the powers of a county government. When a county government fails to perform a function, and the recovery plan does not resolve the issue, the national government may assume the powers and functions of the subnational government, either wholly or partially. Article 120 of the Italian Constitution also provides for the national executive to act in substitution for regions, provinces and municipalities, which entails a temporary take-over of legislative and administrative powers. The same is true in South Africa and Brazil, where the national executive can issue a general or sector-specific intervention decree that involves assuming subnational responsibility. In India, the President of the Union can take any or all functions of the state government, as well as any powers held by the governor or any other authority within the state, except

[10] Another, if slightly different, mode of limited intervention comes from Kenya. Here, the minister responsible for finance stops the transfer of funds to a county government which is in serious or persistent material breach of legislative measures aimed at ensuring transparency and control of expenditure.

those held by the state legislature. Moreover, the President has the authority to declare that the powers of the state legislature shall be exercised by or under the authority of Parliament.

The most intrusive form of intervention involves the dissolution of the legislature and/or executive at the subnational and local level. In India, the national executive can dissolve the state legislature. In the case of Italy, the national executive is allowed to dissolve the regional council and dismiss the region's president for reasons of national security, or in cases of serious violations of the law or where a 'truly exceptional situation' arises from acts contrary to the Constitution. The President of Kenya, with the approval of the Senate and the apex intergovernmental forum, the National and County Government Co-ordinating Summit, can suspend a county government 'where it is found to engage in actions that are deemed to be against the common needs and interests of the citizens of the county'. In South Africa, the Constitution does not permit the dissolution of a democratically elected provincial government. By contrast, a provincial executive is allowed to dissolve a municipal council, although only in 'exceptional circumstances'. The Constitution does not define 'exceptional circumstances'; however, national government guidelines deem exceptional circumstances to exist when there is 'failure of the intervention … due to the Council's unwillingness to resolve the problems'. Section 34(3) of the Municipal Structures Act of 1998 allows a provincial minister of local government to dissolve a council if an assumption of responsibility under Section 139 has not led to the council's being able to fulfil its functions. Local government in Ethiopia is perhaps the sole level of government which is subject only to this most intrusive form of intervention. Current state laws regarding state intervention in local government allow only for the suspension or dissolution of a *woreda* or city council as methods of intervention: there are no provisions for less intrusive forms of intervention, regardless of the reasons behind the intervention.

A key question about the most intrusive form of intervention concerns the matter of how and when normal governance is restored. In some countries, these interventions have clear time limits, while in others, there is a risk of their being prolonged. For example, in Kenya, county suspensions last for 90 days, after which elections must be held to restore governance. In Argentina, the law limits the duration of the intervention to 180 days, with the option to renew it once for an additional 180 days. In Spain, an intervention in Catalonia lasted seven months and concluded with regional elections. However, the Constitutional Court has emphasised that article 155 should never be used indefinitely. In India, President's Rule under article 356 of the Constitution expires after six months unless renewed by Parliament, a stipulation that ensures that interventions are reviewed regularly. In Brazil and South Africa, interventions are not typically completely open-ended, but the structure of the countries' intervention mechanisms often raises concerns about prolonged national control of state and municipal governments.

The existence of various forms of intervention – ranging from the soft measure of issuing directives to the most intrusive measure of dissolving a democratically elected subnational government – raises the question of whether progressive application of the measures is a requirement. Does an intervening government have to apply the less intrusive form of intervention before it deploys the most intrusive ones? The idea that intervention is acceptable only in exceptional circumstances might suggest that states should first attempt to achieve the objectives of intervention using less intrusive measures, an approach that calls to mind the principle of proportionality (often used to adjudicate rights). Logically, too, this approach entails a progressive application of intervention measures; it also implies that responses to breaches or failures to meet obligations should be proportionate to the severity of the issue. For serious violations, more stringent measures may be necessary; conversely, for minor breaches or failures, less intrusive ones should be implemented.

The counterargument to this is that although the intervening authority must always consider the possibility of achieving its objectives through less intrusive measures, it should not be a requirement that the measures have to be successive. According to this view, the use of less restrictive means before resorting to other measures is not mandatory. This is the position adopted by the courts in South Africa concerning provincial intervention in local government, where a constitutional amendment has made it clear that the steps are not necessarily successive. The Constitutional Court has confirmed that 'the appropriateness of an intervention does not automatically hinge on the sequence of the steps adopted under section 139(1); rather, the focus is on what is a "suitable" form of intervention, that is, one which is an appropriate fit'.[11]

4. PROCEDURES OF INTERVENTION

The process by which federal or national governments intervene in subnational entities or local governments is a crucial determinant of whether such interventions are legitimate, transparent and corrective, or whether they simply serve as instruments of political coercion. As such, the different countries considered in this volume have established varying procedural safeguards to prevent the abuse of intervention powers.

---

[11] *Premier, Gauteng and Others v Democratic Alliance and Others; All Tshwane Councillors who are Members of the Economic Freedom Fighters and Another v Democratic Alliance and Others; African National Congress*, paras 81–84.

In some jurisdictions, and particularly under certain circumstances, intervention must be requested by the affected subnational government itself, as is the case in Ethiopia with respect to interventions in case of a breakdown of law and order. In Brazil, the federal government can intervene at the request of a state government. In fact, in some cases it is obliged to heed the request for intervention. However, in all of the jurisdictions covered in this book, there are specific circumstances under which the national government can choose to intervene unilaterally, meaning that it does not require a request from, or the approval of, the subnational government.[12]

Most of the countries in this book require parliamentary approval for interventions, which is intended to ensure democratic legitimacy and prevent overreach by the central government. Usually it is the second chamber of the national parliament that plays a crucial role in approving, monitoring and reviewing interventions.

In Ethiopia, for example, an intervention triggered due to the alleged existence of acts endangering the constitutional order must be initiated by the House of Federation, the second chamber of the federal parliament. Before a decision is made to order federal intervention, an investigation must take place to gather concrete evidence substantiating the alleged acts and to present various options for addressing the situation. The House of Federation presumably plays a vital role before and after ordering a federal intervention, as it has the responsibility of preventing the federal executive from intervening in a state in the absence of a ground warranting an intervention; it also has the authority to receive periodic reports from the Prime Minister on the process and the effect of the federal intervention. Furthermore, the House of Federation can order the federal government to cease its intervention if the grounds for the intervention are no longer extant. To defend its autonomy, a state can request the termination of a federal intervention that the House of Federation has initiated. The important role that the House can play in mitigating the effects of federal intervention is undermined, however, by the fact that the same party dominates both levels of government, the result of which is that the House has become a body that rubber-stamps the decisions of the executive.

Similarly, in Spain the Senate plays an exclusive role in approving federal interventions under article 155. The process includes a parliamentary debate, with opportunities being available for the regional government to present its case. In Kenya, the Senate must approve both financial interventions and

---

[12] In countries such as Ethiopia, Nigeria and Brazil, a federal intervention emanating from a security crisis is usually followed by a declaration of a state of emergency. In Spain, India, Kenya, South Africa, Argentina and Italy, federal intervention follows a structured legal processes without the necessity of an emergency declaration.

county suspensions. The Public Finance Management Act also requires quarterly reviews by an Intergovernmental Technical Committee to assess the effectiveness of an intervention. Likewise, in South Africa the National Council of Provinces, the second chamber of the bicameral national parliament, must approve interventions in both municipalities and provinces, thereby ensuring a multilevel oversight framework.

In some of the countries, and with respect to specific grounds of intervention, both houses of parliament might be involved. In the case of India, for example, approval by both houses of parliament within two months is mandatory for interventions under article 356. In Argentina, the power to declare intervention rests with the legislature. The executive can decree intervention in a province or the city of Buenos Aires only if Congress is in recess. Even then, it must immediately convene the Congress, which then has to approve the intervention. The emphasis on authorisation by Congress reflects, as Goyburu notes in Chapter 2, a departure from past practice in which the national executive frequently resorted to intervention unilaterally without consulting Congress. This also aligns with the Supreme Court's decision, which assigned the power of federal intervention to the legislative branch of the federal government. In Brazil, similar rules apply: no intervention can occur without the approval of the legislative branch.[13] Only those interventions that the federal government makes because of legal obligations (requests for interventions that cannot be ignored) do not require the approval of the legislature. In Ethiopia, in the case of intervention grounds related to human rights violations, the act of intervention must be initiated by the House of Peoples' Representatives, the lower house of the federal parliament, and subsequently sanctioned by both houses of the federal parliament. The national executive, particularly the Prime Minister, is tasked only to oversee and ensure the implementation of the measures adopted by the House of Peoples' Representatives – something which represents a departure from the usual roles in which executives adopt intervention measures and parliaments oversee their implementation.

The involvement of the second chamber in regulating the intervention process is underscored by the fact that, in most countries, it is a house where subnational units are represented. The idea is that a second chamber prevents the national government from overreaching and using intervention as a tool of centralisation. The importance of parliamentary involvement in the intervention process becomes more evident when one observes the situation in Nigeria and Malaysia, where emergency powers are used to intervene in subnational

[13] The President is also required beforehand to consult with, and solicit the views of, the Council of the Republic and the National Defense Council (articles 90 and 91).

units. In those cases, intervention is allowed without substantial, or indeed any, parliamentary scrutiny. At the same time, there is no guarantee that the second chamber will be effective in its role of protecting the interests of subnational units in the intervention process. It is often argued, for example, that the political composition of Spain's Senate limits genuine checks and balances, as the Senate usually favours the central government. Weak enforcement often undermines parliamentary control. Although intervention in Ethiopia, Argentina and Brazil requires (as mentioned earlier) the approval of national parliaments, thus ensuring a degree of institutional oversight, military and authoritarian governments, both in the past and today, have often bypassed legislative controls and hence centralised intervention powers.

Aside from parliamentary oversight, another essential element for preventing the misuse of intervention powers is judicial review. Courts in some countries, such as India, Italy, South Africa and Spain, have played an active role in limiting political interventions. In India, in the *SR Bommai* case, the Supreme Court ruled that President's Rule is subject to judicial review and emphasised that state governments cannot be dismissed on vague or politically motivated grounds. The ruling marked a turning-point in limiting central government overreach, as it led to the courts scrutinising President's Rule far more closely than before. Similarly, Spain's Constitutional Court has established significant jurisprudence on intervention, as seen in the case involving Catalonia, where it clarified the nature, scope and limits of intervention measures. In its 2019 rulings involving Catalonia, the court emphasised that although the 2017 application of article 155 to Catalonia was constitutional, intervention has to remain temporary and proportionate to the crisis at hand. Similarly, the Constitutional Court in Italy has adjudicated several cases that required balancing the need for intervention with the protection of subnational autonomy.

In South Africa, courts have gone beyond adjudicating interventions to safeguard the autonomy of lower levels of governments from unwarranted interventions in that they have compelled reluctant national and provincial governments to intervene. While using litigation to force interventions may have some advantages, the chapter on South Africa points out that it 'does not guarantee effective government intervention'. Court-ordered provincial interventions face challenges, such as an unmotivated provincial executive or one that may be experiencing its own financial difficulties; additionally, the provincial government may lack the necessary resources to carry out a successful intervention.[14] As a result, winning a court case is unlikely to lead to sustained improvements in service delivery in the long term.

---

[14] Wright J, Dube F & Du Plessis A 'Judicial enforcement of mandatory provincial interventions in municipalities in South Africa' (2022) 55 *Verfassung und*

In contrast, while Nigerian courts have a role to play in judicially overseeing federal interventions, that role is a limited one. In Ethiopia judicial oversight has been non-existent, as courts have rarely intervened in emergency or intervention declarations, hence allowing broad executive discretion. In both countries, the lack of consistent judicial review has enabled politically motivated interventions. In cases where courts were involved, they largely adopted the policy of judicial avoidance. In regard to Nigeria, Suberu argues that parliamentary oversight has been more effective than judicial review in constraining the overzealous federal government, except in a few instances where the court invalidated the impeachment of state governors.

There are also jurisdictions where the power of intervention is not subject to judicial review. In Argentina, the Supreme Court has determined that decisions regarding federal intervention in provinces are political acts that fall solely under the authority of the legislative and executive branches; as a result, these decisions are not subject to judicial review. The Supreme Court in Brazil might only be involved in intervention to compel the national government to intervene under limited circumstances, either on its initiative (when the intervention has to do with enforcing a court order) or when a case is brought before it by the Attorney General seeking federal government intervention in a state on the ground of a violation of constitutional principles. Article 150(8) of the Constitution of Malaysia precludes courts from revising the proclamation of emergency provisions that the national government of Malaysia had used in the past to intervene in state governments.

5. POLITICS OF INTERVENTION

A first question that authors were asked to answer about the politics of intervention concerned the frequency of central government intrusion. The picture that emerges reveals marked differences between the countries under review. To begin with, there are some countries where intervention has occurred only very rarely: Spain, Argentina, Kenya and Malaysia. In the Spanish case, local intervention has been limited to only a single case with rather extreme circumstances, namely the dissolution in 2006 of Marbella's local council due to egregious corruption. As for interventions in regions, there were only two abortive attempts in this regard prior to the central government's first ever use, in 2017–2018, of the country's article 155 procedure, this in response to Catalonia's declaration of independence. The near-consensus in Spanish politics is that interference that goes as far dissolving democratically elected bodies must be limited to extremely serious circumstances. In the aftermath of the

---

Recht in Übersee 105 at 123.

Catalonia case, however, the use of the power to intervene has twice been suggested by left-wing parties as a tool against regional governments that included the right-wing party Vox, but it has never been actually implemented.

Similarly, in Argentina, the period since the country's return to democracy in 1983 has seen only six instances of interference in the provinces. As the case-study chapter points out, intervention in this period – in contrast to its earlier misuse against opposition parties or intra-party competitors – has been used for what the author calls 'political normalisation' in the face of extraordinary situations such as armed conflict, serious economic crises, or cases of high-profile corruption and other crimes.

As for Kenya, its counties have even been completely unaffected by interference, although, as the chapter in this book argues, there would have been justifiable grounds for the central government to use the respective powers in response to financial troubles at the subnational level. However, it did not use them for political reasons or out of ignorance of and/or indifference to its legal obligations. Tellingly, the only case in which the intervention procedure was initiated (but not completed) was that of Makueni county in 2015, where the intervention unfolded on entirely different grounds, namely the existence of a conflict between the county's governor and its legislature. Similar inter-institutional conflicts in Malaysia led to the only (and long past) instances of intervention, namely in the state of Sarawak in 1966 and Kelantan in 1977. In both cases, entirely normal constitutional issues to do with democratic majorities in Parliament were exploited by the central government to secure a state government to its liking.

The four countries above stand in contrast to those where the use of intervention powers is widespread: Nigeria, Ethiopia, Italy and India. In the Nigerian case, interference is commonplace at the local level but so too in the states. In fact, interventions have been rampant throughout the country's federal history. The tone was set by the state of emergency declared in 1962 in the Western Region, an intervention which triggered a chain of events that resulted in the military coup of 1966. Since then, the central government has declared states of emergency in response to a number of circumstances, including political infighting in states, outbreaks of communal violence and the impeachments of state governors. Interestingly, the Nigerian case study points out that the fact that emergency rule has not been imposed for more than a decade is not reassuring but rather a sign that the centralisation of government power is by now so routine that formal declarations of emergency rule are redundant.

The case study of Ethiopia also reveals a high frequency of interventions, albeit that they have occurred in the course of a much shorter federal history. While state intervention in local government through the issuance of instructions or the removal of officials is, according to the authors, extremely frequent, the five states of emergency that have been declared under the

1995 Constitution are only part of the story. This is because the central government has often intruded in state affairs, even by military means, either without declaring an emergency or intervention or by doing so only retroactively. It is striking that federal security forces have been sent to each of Ethiopia's nine original states at least once over the past three decades.

Widespread intervention is by no means limited to African countries. In Italy, regional non-compliance with health-care recovery plans is a major and widespread issue. As the chapter in this book points out, 39 hospitals or other health-care structures located in eight different regions are currently under commissioner status. While this situation is temporary in some cases, the Calabria region's entire health-care sector has been entrusted to a central-government-appointed commissioner for some 15 years already. While such commissioning is also widespread among local governments (for example, for waste and water management), the latter are frequently targets of even more far-reaching intervention, namely the dissolution or removal of elected municipal bodies for both political and non-political reasons, such as financial mismanagement and criminal infiltration (there have been some 360 cases of municipalities with mafia links over the past three decades).

India is another case of high-frequency interventionism. Contrary to the constitutional architects' hope that article 356 would be a last resort, President's Rule has been used 134 times so far; only 3 out of the 28 states have never been subjected to it, with 2 of these states having been created only as recently as the year 2000. The latter point is important because the period since the mid-1990s witnessed a general drop in the frequency of intervention in comparison to the preceding period since the late 1960s, an era in which President's Rule was widely used to remove opposition-ruled state governments. However, this overall tendency did not prevent the central government from using President's Rule in 2019 to annul the special autonomy arrangements for the states of Jammu and Kashmir. Intervention is equally widespread in relations between the states and their municipalities, and to such an extent that efforts are under way in some cases to limit interference through instruments such as state-appointed administrators.

A third category of cases shows significantly more instances of intervention at the municipal level than at the subnational level (South Africa and Brazil). Although the South African case study reveals a dramatic increase in interventions in municipalities over the past decade, only a few provincial governments have undergone formal intervention. A similar divergence can be observed in Brazil, where action against financial mismanagement by local authorities is frequent; as for the states, by contrast, only three central interventions have occurred under the Constitution of 1988. While it is striking that all of these interventions concerned public security and were carried out since 2018, the author of the Brazilian chapter does not anticipate increased interventionism but rather attributes these three instances to very specific crises and circumstances, most notably the involvement of the governor of the Federal District in a coup attempt carried out by supporters of former President Bolsonaro.

In view of the differences in the prevalence of central government intervention as a political instrument, it may be asked: What accounts for these differences which have been identified both between the countries surveyed and within them over time? Broadly speaking, the factors determining the relevance of an intervention may be classified as either political or legal. As for the latter, some of the case studies demonstrate that reform of the laws regulating intervention powers can have a significant impact. Indeed, the chapter on Argentina cites the constitutional amendment of 1994 as one central reason for the far more limited use of these powers over the past decades. This reform better regulated the process and criteria for interventions, thus making them instruments of last resort and enhancing the autonomy of the provinces. India provides a similar example of an impactful legal change, albeit through case law rather than constitutional reform. The above-mentioned *Bommai* judgment of 1994 regarding President's Rule under article 356 of the Constitution dramatically curbed the misuse of this clause. To be sure, BJP governments came to power a little more than a decade ago, but when they tested the limits of the *Bommai* safeguards, two crucial intervention attempts were overturned by the courts in 2016. It is striking that, in the light of the Argentine and Indian examples, the chapters in this book also identify countries where repeated reform initiatives have not had any tangible effect, with Nigeria being the most obvious case in point.

When it comes to concrete legal provisions that influence the prevalence of intervention, the authors in our volume refer to a broad variety of clauses. In Italy, for instance, the fact that both the central government and the respective regional government may intervene in municipalities appears to have increased the frequency of such interference. The same seems to hold true for South Africa, where a 2003 reform introduced the possibility for the central government to 'leapfrog' over the provincial authority and intervene directly in a municipality. As for countries where intervention is a rare phenomenon, this state of affairs is at least partially attributed in the case of Kenya to the oversight role that the Senate plays in regard to the counties – the Senate lacks enforcement powers but at least provides an appearance of central government action.

Interestingly, in Brazil, the main legal barrier to more frequent use of intervention powers seems to be a rule which is not strictly linked to the legal regime of these powers themselves. As the case study shows, it is a constitutional clause disallowing constitutional amendments while interventions are under way – this prompts central governments to shy away from using these extraordinary powers. The author acknowledges that there are other reasons for the low frequency of interventions, such as strict procedural requirements, the availability of alternative judicial and administrative mechanisms and intergovernmental dynamics that prioritise dialogue over coercive measures. Yet evidence for the significant impact of this legal provision is seen in the high frequency of interventions *before* its enactment in 1988 and the fact that constitutional amendments occur often in Brazil, as they are common in presidential campaign promises.

In terms of the political factors that have a bearing on whether interventions are prevalent or not, a country's demographic make-up seems to play a role. The Nigerian chapter in particular highlights the adverse impact of the country's deep ethnic and religious fault lines. Arguably, they serve as a convenient rationale for the central government to invoke intervention powers and at the same time prevent the formation of a cohesive, unified opposition of civic actors against intrusion. Another political factor is the party system. In India, it is easy to see why the frequency of interventions increased in the late 1960s of all times. This was the period when the Indian National Congress (INC) lost several state elections to opposition parties, with the result that President's Rule came to be used as a tool to prevent the latter from forming state governments. The situation worsened when the Janata Party coalition government took power at the national level in 1977 and swiftly dismissed – long before the *Bommai* safeguards – as many as nine INC state governments, only for the INC to retaliate by removing the same number of Janata-led state governments upon its return to national power three years later.

The regionalisation of the party system from the late 1980s onwards affected interventions in myriad ways. The emergence of regional parties certainly fragmented parliamentary coalitions. While in some instances such parties then helped to frustrate attempts to invoke President's Rule, they successfully pushed in other cases for its invocation against regional opponents. As for Kenya, one factor accounting for the reluctance to intervene is arguably the central government's uncertainty about the political consequences of intervention (especially in counties affiliated with the ruling party) in a new post-devolution context of multilevel party politics.

The party system can also influence the prevalence of intervention powers insofar as the hegemony of one party may offer alternative – and perhaps preferable – means of bringing other government levels into line. This is what arguably occurred in South Africa: such powers were largely unused during the first 15 years after apartheid, a period when – in a young democracy with new provincial and municipal governments – one would have anticipated more, rather than fewer, interventions. In this early period, however, when the dominance of the African National Congress (ANC) was still much stronger at all government levels, the party preferred resorting to (often intra-party) informal intervention so as to avoid the embarrassment of inflating problems through the use of drastic formal action.

In the Kenyan case, the central government has similarly circumvented formal financial interventions over the years. The alternative means that were used were directives to the counties to settle outstanding payments under the threat of initiating a procedure to halt financial transfers, something which is both easy to do and causes little political inconvenience. Interestingly, in the Indian case, the reduction in the use of President's Rule since the mid-1990s was accompanied a simultaneous increase of informal interference in state affairs, such as politically biased investigations into sitting chief ministers in states ruled by non-BJP parties.

The above comparison of the factors determining the relevance of intervention powers in a given country at a given point in time already indicates that a high frequency of interference is often associated with these powers being misused rather than used for their intended purpose.

As for the misuse of powers of intervention, there are arguably two main dimensions. These powers can be abused either by not being used in situations in which they should be invoked, or by being used in situations when they should not be. This distinction is best illustrated by the South African case. As the chapter in our book argues, a lack of justifiable, and indeed necessary, intervention, which has been due to the same party governing at different levels of government, has been the bigger problem. By contrast, abusive and overtly politically motivated invocation of intervention powers has been rarer (for example, a 2005 dissolution of a municipal council in KwaZulu-Natal) and, when it occurs, difficult to prove.

In other countries, clearly unjustified interventions seem to be more prevalent and/or politically more impactful. This certainly holds true for Malaysia. The above-mentioned interventions in Sarawak and Kelantan can be characterised as abusive for two reasons. First, they both helped the central government to exploit the purely constitutional issue of forming a state government to impose its party-political will and install a well-disposed chief minister. Second, the central government resorted to clearly illegal methods in the run-up to the Sarawak intervention, such as capturing state assembly members and compelling them to sign a letter of no-confidence against the chief minister. While Malaysia has witnessed only two interventions, they were politically impactful because they made it clear that interference could always be used (or threatened) even in cases of a merely alleged 'constitutional breakdown' in a state that does not endanger security, that could be resolved on the basis of the state constitution and that was created by the political machinations of the central government itself.

India's 'constitutional breakdown' clause has been invoked much more often than Malaysia's, with many of these instances being clear misuses, particularly during the nadir of partisan use of President's Rule from the late 1960s to the mid-1990s. This is best illustrated by the report of the Sarkaria Commission, which reviewed all such interventions until 1988 and found that only slightly less than half of them were 'inevitable' and thus justifiable instances of emergency rule. In the other cases, the central government had misused President's Rule, so the report claims, in order to prevent other parties from testing their majority in the legislative assembly, or to tackle intra-party problems or alleged maladministration by an elected state government typically led by the opposition. It is striking to see, then, that the chapters on the two Latin American federal systems ascribe very much the same reasons to the misuse of intervention powers. In Argentina's early federal history in the 19th century, the central government instrumentalised such powers to target opposition leaders in the provinces, a stratagem which was aided by fact that the respective constitutional provisions of 1860 left ample room for interpretation and manipulation. After the Second World War, the misuse of intervention became particularly widespread, oscillating between moves against the provincial opposition and moves against rivals in President Perón's Justicialist Party. The chapter on Brazil draws similar conclusions. In this case, too, the wording of the intervention clauses, especially those regarding public security, facilitated their misuse in resolving political disputes in the central government's favour.

As in the Argentine and Brazilian cases, the practice of intervention in Nigeria and Ethiopia has been plagued by the exploitation of vague legal frameworks, but it also offers additional insights. Nigeria is characterised by a dynamic which we might call the abuse–counterabuse conundrum. This refers to cases in which the government subject to intervention has indeed acted in a way that justifies, or even necessitates, intervention, but where the intervention is then carried out in an abusive manner. As the Nigerian chapter shows, such dynamics have played out at two levels. While many targeted state governors were indeed guilty of serious financial mismanagement, in several cases they were removed under the mantle of emergency rule rather than through impeachment. Thus, the central government capitalised on misconduct to get rid of political opponents, and did so by choosing to misuse intervention powers rather than follow the more cumbersome procedures prescribed by the Constitution.

Similarly, the chapter on Ethiopia highlights that interventions in many states (for example, the Somali state and Oromia) have failed to follow the required constitutional procedure. In the curious case of the clashes between the Fanno militia group and the security forces of the Amhara state, the central government had already sent its troops into the state before the subnational government requested the declaration of a state of emergency or the federal parliament had given its legally prescribed approval. The declaration thus served merely to rubber-stamp what had already begun to take place on the ground. According to the chapter, misuses of intervention powers include interference which is either not based on legally justified grounds or is indeed based on justified grounds but follows a constitutionally skewed procedure. At any rate, a particular concern is that the central government routinely chooses to declare emergencies to intervene in states, arguably in order to enjoy the broad authority to restrict individual freedoms. In fact, six of the seven states of emergency declared under the 1995 Constitution have involved interventions in states that were carried out in disregard of legal procedures such as the mandatory involvement of the House of the Federation.

It seems self-evident that a misuse of intervention powers will lead to their being ineffective. Thus, the chapter on Nigeria points out that the political instrumentalisation of emergency rule often prevented it from achieving its declared purpose of restoring public order and security (such as in the case in 2013–2014 of emergency rule in Borno, Adamawa, and Yobe in northeastern Nigeria). Such intervention is indeed counterproductive given that the unlawful way in which it is carried out further alienates the local population. Yet even when powers of intervention are not misused but applied correctly and in line with the purposes they were designed for, there remains the question of whether they are ultimately truly effective. As we argued in the introduction to this book, interference – notwithstanding its rationale as a legitimate remedy in exceptional situations – may end up as a cure which is worse than the disease. Are interventions thus sometimes unproductive or even counterproductive?

The evidence from our case studies suggests that this holds true to different degrees. The authors of the chapter on Spain emphasise that the intervention in Catalonia in 2017–2018 was effective insofar as it prevented the secession of the region. However, in contrast to this short-term impact, the central government intervention did not, of course, solve the underlying issue, that is, the accommodation of demands for increased self-government, which would be too much to expect of it. In the case of Marbella, intervention in itself was not sufficient to get rid of corruption, but it certainly did spark a change in the local political elite and contribute to the avoidance of major scandals in the future. Italy's experience of interventions concerning health-care recovery plans can be described as partially effective, given that some of the regions quickly improved their financial situation and service quality while others did not and have remained under the intervention regime with few noticeable positive effects. However, the most clear-cut case of interference frequently resulting in an even greater deterioration of the situation seems to be South Africa. The case study here highlights that municipalities often emerge from an intervention in a worse condition than they were in the first place, with, for instance, their dysfunctionality having been aggravated, or their debts having doubled.

Several factors appear to cause ineffectiveness. First, both the South African and Italian case studies refer to the problem of capacity constraints on the intervening authority in terms of budget, expertise and staff resources. Second, intervention efforts can be actively sabotaged, or at least hindered, by non-cooperation on the part of the staff being targeted by such interference. Third, administrators tasked with improving the functionality of a South African province or municipality depend on unwavering political support, but this tends to fade away when they begin taking unpopular decisions. Fourth, interventions seem to have a better chance of being effective if there is external pressure. It is no coincidence that, in Italy, interventions relating to wastewater treatment and the cleanup of illegal landfills were more successful than others – these interventions came in response to Italy's condemnation for its failure to comply with European Union law.

Finally, contributors were asked whether intervention powers have an impact in countries even when they are not invoked. As the reasoning goes, such powers might have a 'chilling effect' in that the prospect of intervention hangs like a sword of Damocles over the heads of its potential targets – and thus these powers make an impact even if they remain unused. In the Spanish case, the one case of intervention in a local government, that of Marbella, did not have the effect of curbing corruption in other municipalities (given that it remains a problem). As for Malaysia, by contrast, there is no doubt, according to the case study in this book, that intervention in the state of Sarawak in 1966 had a chilling effect. While the most blatant misuses of President's Rule in India have been reined in by judicial fiat, threats to invoke these intervention powers against partisan opponents at the state level have become normalised as a political tool. As the chapter on India notes, such threats go hand in hand with the politicisation of the office of the governor, upon whose report President's Rule is initiated.

6. CONCLUSION

Intervention models, as discussed in the various chapters, differ significantly, as is evident from the diversity in terms of their underlying rationales and the grounds used for intervention, which range from national security to ensuring financial stability and avoiding subnational governance failure. It is submitted that constitutional frameworks should permit intervention powers vis-à-vis subnational and local governments to prevent governance failures, financial crises, or violations of constitutional principles. Without such powers, federal systems risk fragmentation since subnational entities may weaken the broader national governance framework while claiming to protect their autonomy.[15]

Yet federal intervention carries the risk of overreach. While intervention can be important, it may lead to excessive centralisation and undermine the self-governance of subnational and local governments. There are numerous instances where intervention powers have been misused for political purposes. For example, in India, article 356 has been invoked more than 130 times since 1950, often leading to the dismissal of opposition-led state governments. Similarly, in Nigeria, emergency rule has been declared in states with political contestation, which undermines the electoral process. In Ethiopia, federal intervention has been used to discipline subnational units that do not align themselves with the political demands of the federal government. These examples illustrate how federal intervention can become a coercive tool for central control rather than serving as a genuinely corrective mechanism.

The ultimate challenge in federal or federal-like systems of governance is therefore the ever-present tension between intervention and autonomy. On the one hand, for instance, South Africa's municipal interventions demonstrate that excessive intervention can weaken the capacity of local governments, leading municipalities to rely increasingly on national support rather than proactively seek ways to improve service delivery on their own. On the other hand, the experience of Kenya shows that a reluctance to intervene can be equally harmful, as counties that are failing continue to struggle in the absence of necessary corrective measures. As Ronald Watts argues, effective federalism requires a careful balance: it must be strong enough to provide federal intervention as a tool to achieve federation-wide objectives, yet not so powerful that it undermines self-governance.[16]

BIBLIOGRAPHY

Books

Elazar D *Exploring federalism* Alabama: University of Alabama Press (1987)
Watts R *Comparing federal systems* Montreal: McGill-Queen's Press (2008)

15 Elazar D *Exploring federalism* Alabama: University of Alabama Press (1987) 31.

16 Watts R *Comparing federal systems* Montreal: McGill-Queen's Press (2008) 31–2.

Journal Articles

Wright J, Dube F & Du Plessis A 'Judicial enforcement of mandatory provincial interventions in municipalities in South Africa' (2022) 55 *Verfassung und Recht in Übersee* 105–25

Case Law

Mnquma Local Municipality and Another v Premier of the Eastern Cape and Others [2009] ZAECBHC 14 (5 August 2009)

Premier, Gauteng and Others v Democratic Alliance and Others; All Tshwane Councillors who are Members of the Economic Freedom Fighters and Another v Democratic Alliance and Others; African National Congress

Report

Sarkaria RS & Ramasubramaniam KA (for the Government of India) *Commission on centre–state relations* New Delhi: Government of India Press (1988)

Index